A BOY CALLED H

A BOY CALLED H

A Childhood in Wartime Japan

KAPPA SENOH

Translated by John Bester

KODANSHA INTERNATIONAL
Tokyo • New York • London

THE KAN YAMAGUCHI SERIES

Publication of this book was assisted by a generous grant provided by Ms. Kan Yamaguchi of Tsuchiura City, Japan. A select number of interesting works in English on Japan have been given such assistance.

Originally published in 1997 by Kodansha Ltd. under the title *Shonen H.*

Permission to reproduce lines from "*Ringo no uta*" (Song of the Apple) was given by JASRAC. License no. 9912288-901. Copyright © Hachiro Sato 1946.

ISBN 4-7700-2325-1
First edition, 1999
99 00 01 02 03   10 9 8 7 6 5 4 3 2 1

Translator's Preface

This "autobiographical novel" follows the fortunes of a boy, the "H" of the title, and of a nation, Japan, from the fateful prewar 1930s to the early postwar period.

When it begins, Japan has embarked on its adventures in China and is flirting with the Axis powers in Europe, while at home militarism, with the concomitant Emperor-worship, is steadily strengthening its grip over the whole of society.

When it ends, the nation lies in ruins, with a leadership utterly discredited and a bewildered populace about to make a new start under the banner of "democracy" raised by the occupying powers.

The external events are a matter of history, but the characters who appear in the novel are also based largely in reality; in fact the author told me he contacted many of those who are still alive in order to confirm facts and conversations.

The immediate setting is H's family home in the port city of Kobe. The father, Morio Senoh, is a hardworking tailor, a decent, normally taciturn but not unimaginative man whose sturdy common sense provides a good foil to the personality of the mother, Toshiko, who is emotional, impulsive and frequently obsessive. They have two children, H himself and his young sister, Yoshiko.

They live in a perfectly ordinary, quintessentially Japanese district of the city, and are surrounded by human types still recognizable, *mutatis mutandis*, even today. It would be interesting, in fact, to try matching the basic behavior patterns of the characters who appear in the book with their counterparts in the undoubtedly different—freer, for one thing—society of today. Either way, nothing about any of them, whether pleasant or otherwise, rings untrue when tested, for example, against my own experience of Japan over the years.

There are two things, even so, that distinguish the Senohs from their neighbors. First, they are members—thanks originally to a whim of Toshiko's—of the congregation of a small Christian church (though their Christianity is of a peculiarly Japanese variety, while H himself can hardly be counted as a believer). Secondly, Morio's work as a tailor brings him into frequent contact with the non-Japanese of many different nationalities who were such a prominent feature of prewar Kobe.

The son, H, is in some ways a typical, neither over-virtuous nor over-studious schoolboy with many of the usual schoolboy preoccupations; he is self-centered, yet basically compassionate. At the same time he possesses the acutely observant eye and precociously skeptical turn of mind that mark him out both as a future artist and as something of a loner in an essentially conformist society. (The author, incidentally, is quite aware of what must, one feels, have been H's rather irritating precociousness—"Just look at the brat's expression in that photo!" he said to me.)

It is H's powers of observation, together with the march of history itself, that provide the driving force behind the narrative. His skepticism—increasingly intense as public events and his own personal development progress—is directed not just at the people he sees about him every day but at the leaders who take the country into an ill-conceived, basically hopeless war; at the relatively few individuals who cooperate with them most positively; and at the mild, ill-informed, misled masses who stumble—however eager they seemed in the event—in their wake.

All this is presented with a light touch. Fifty short chapters yield a series of episodes that are constantly varied in mood, setting and scale. Humorous, dramatic, ironic, horrifying, intensely moving in turn, they are often, taken individually, so interesting and self-contained that the work may seem, literally, "episodic" until one notices how carefully everything is organized. A small detail in one chapter will be recalled, to varying effect, many chapters later; a brief, again seemingly insignificant episode will be seen to play its part in building up a picture of a national mentality.

The picture is not, it should be noted, always flattering; some of the most unpleasant as well as the more attractive aspects of the national character can all be deduced from the miniatures presented here. And it should be remembered that Japanese society of this period was largely a closed one—closed not merely by a passively accepted censorship, but also by the fact that, until the raids began, the battlefields were far away and home leave for the forces rare.

The prose itself is simple (though not necessarily to translate!) and without obvious literary pretensions; the author wanted, he said, to make the work available to young people as well as adults. The literary value lies, rather, in the skill in handling each short episode, and above all in the careful building up of a kind of mosaic—except that here two different pictures emerge in the end: of a boy growing up surrounded by family and schoolmates, and of a whole nation moving inexorably toward a predetermined fate.

Abstractions apart, however, the total effect is of a richly varied and very readable novel that may well alter some of the non-Japanese reader's preconceptions and help make a sometimes distant-seeming nation more immediate and understandable. It may even have played a similar role for Japanese reading about their own comparatively recent past. It is significant, and somehow heartening, that the work should have had such an outstanding success in Japan itself.

John Bester

1

Red Label

"So—you're Master Senoh, eh?"

The question, coming from a stranger in the street, was a shock to the boy.

"How did you know my name?" he asked, puzzled.

"Because you've got it written on your chest," said the man with a smile. "You might just as well be walking around with a label on you."

Ever since first grade at primary school, the boy had been dressed in a sweater with the name "H. Senoh" knitted on the chest.

His mother, Toshiko, had got the idea from a letter that had come from America, with their address written in English on the envelope, and a photo inside. The photo showed a woman wearing a sweater with letters on its chest.

The person in the photo was a Mrs. Staples who'd once lived in Kobe as a Christian missionary and who was much admired by Toshiko for, among other things, her dress sense.

The sight of her standing there smiling, in her lettered sweater, had brought back pleasant memories of this lady she'd known so well.

Back then in 1937, nobody had had anything like that sweater, even in Kobe, with its many foreign residents. Toshiko, who was the kind of woman who threw herself enthusiastically into any new idea, decided she'd knit a similar one for her son, emblazoned with "H. Senoh" in large Roman letters.

Done in white on a dark brown background, the name stood out even at a distance. But the boy, far from sharing his mother's pride and pleasure, found the idea of wearing something so different from other boys' clothes a major embarrassment.

Worse still was knowing it was his own name that was written there so large.

"I'm fed up," he complained, "walking around in something with my name on it like this. Just make it H for Hajime, couldn't you? Nobody'd know with just the one letter."

So from third grade on it was agreed that it should be just the letter H.

Since pencils often had "H" engraved on them, it was one letter of the alphabet that everyone could read, and in no time "H" became his nickname.

H's father was a tailor. If you'd said to anyone living in Kobe, "The tailors at 6 Honjo-cho on the road down to the sea from Takatori Station," they could have got there without a map.

Partly, of course, that was thanks to a big vertical signboard saying "Senoh, High-Class Men's Tailors" that hung from the eaves over the second floor, but actually there were no other tailors in the district.

The self-proclaimed "high-class men's tailors" was in fact a small business in an ordinary house in which the family also lived, and which faced the road the buses went along.

They were not far from the residential area of Suma, but unlike that quiet, affluent district this one, on the east side of the Myohoji River, was typically working class, with a market and a small rubber factory, shops, drinking and eating establishments, public baths, an ironworks and suchlike, all mixed up with the dwellings.

But though the atmosphere of the area was utterly different from that of neighboring Suma, the two were equally lucky in their setting, which was close to both the hills and the sea.

Although H's parents were keen on education, they believed that homework should be done after the evening meal, and that those daylight hours when the children were not at school were a time for them to play. Thanks to that, once H got back from school every day he was free to amuse himself in the hills or on the beach without interference. All in all, H's days were a busy round of fun.

The hilly area that was one of H's playgrounds was quite close to his home. A particular favorite was Mount Takatori, whose summit was only a four-kilometer trek to the north, and which the children were almost convinced was their own private territory.

There was a sandy beach, too, just three hundred meters south of the house, which was virtually their own exclusive stretch of shore.

So during the summer holiday H's mornings were spent climbing in the hills and his afternoons swimming in the sea.

H was particularly fond of the sea. Rushing out of the house wearing nothing but a loincloth, he would race down the street and plunge straight into the water.

So he was proud of the district where they lived, and he felt still more smug at the thought that these were things the rich kids of Suma could never do....

There were lots of other hunting grounds besides, all calculated to make the children of the well-off districts envious. The marshaling yards to the north of Takatori Station were full of all kinds of locomotives belching smoke and steam as they went about their business, and the stretch of open land where the branch line ran to the Rising Sun oil tanks made an ideal baseball ground.

Rising Sun was an oil company originally financed by American capital, and the railway tracks were used to convey oil, brought by sea, from the tanks where it was stored. The freight trains would come through twice a day, in the early morning and around noon, so the children playing on the open ground had only to be careful at those times. But even those trains had become steadily more infrequent; in fact they were now quite a rarity, which made it a still more convenient place for H and his friends to play in.

"Not many freight trains go through nowadays," he told the man at the charcoal store. "The rails are beginning to get rusty."

"That's because the war with China's still dragging on," the man said in a low voice. "It's a sign they're running short of oil. But you mustn't tell people that—it's a military secret." And he nodded with a rather stern look.

H didn't take the military secret bit too seriously: the charcoal man was known for telling tall stories.

His store sold *okonomiyaki*, too, a kind of pancake with various vegetables, meat and so on mixed in it. In summer it turned into a store selling cold drinks and the like, and a banner saying "Ices" fluttered in front of it. In the season for ices—which meant plain shaved ice with flavored syrup poured over it—the place attracted a lively crowd of children on their way home from the public bath. With his fund of information and his gift of the gab, the shopkeeper was a favorite among the local kids. But they didn't set much store by his tales: too many of them were too good to be true.

There were plenty of other unusual people in the neighborhood besides the charcoal man. There was the "young man who might be a man or a woman"; the young man from the noodle shop who went around on his bike singing at the top of his voice; the "old soldier" who said that everything was done "for the sake of His Imperial Majesty"; the man at the Yumiya toy store who yelled "Out of my sight!" and brandished a bamboo sword whenever he saw a child....

H's own favorite was the young man at the noodle shop farther along from them on the other side of the main street. The grownups living thereabouts couldn't quite place him. "Seems he's from Tokyo," they'd say. "He looks too smart for a delivery boy."

The young man himself said he was a relative of the family, but the proprietor's wife always insisted he wasn't a relative but the son of an acquaintance. The lively way he delivered things was popular among their customers, she explained, so they kept him there on a live-in basis.

The way he spoke was certainly a bit odd. He did his best to talk like Kobe people, but sometimes he'd lapse into Tokyo speech, and H would poke fun at him.

He did his rounds on a bicycle, singing loudly as he pedaled along. That was what attracted H: whenever he heard the delivery boy singing he'd jump on his own bike and pedal off after him.

The way H rode his bike, unfortunately, was not exactly graceful. They'd bought him, secondhand, an adult's bike, and his feet wouldn't reach the pedals if he sat on the saddle, so he had to put his foot through from the side. Even so, he got up quite a good speed and would tail the delivery boy closely, singing along with him as he went.

In H's home there was a ban on singing anything apart from hymns and the officially approved songs taught at school, so he was careful not to start up until he was quite a way from the house. It was fun, bellowing "Woman is fi-hi-ckle...."

Then one day Noodles said to him, "If you're so keen on singing, why don't you come up to my room one evening after supper? I'll play some records for you. But don't tell anyone. Sneak out when you come so they don't see you."

H left home saying he was going to the bathhouse. After walking quite a way along the main road in that direction, he dived off into a sidestreet, then went around so as to get into the noodle shop from the rear entrance. As he went in, he looked back to make sure nobody was watching.

The kitchen was deserted, work done, the big, empty room visible in the dim light of a bulb hanging from the ceiling. H, who'd never been behind the scenes like this before, moved about rather timidly, poking his nose into things here and there.

The two cauldrons used for cooking the noodles stood side by side, still warm around the outside. There was a big pot that gave off the smell of the stock used for the noodles. H lifted the lid and stuck a finger in to taste; perhaps it had still to be seasoned, because it didn't taste too good.

"Hey—what are you up to?" His friend was coming down the stairs, so H hastily turned on the water tap and wetted the cotton towel he had with him.

"I told them I was going for a bath, so it'd look funny if it wasn't wet, wouldn't it?"

Noodles slapped playfully at H's head. "I can see you're the intellectual type of criminal."

H didn't know what an intellectual type of criminal was, but took it as a compliment. "Not *really*," he said with an embarrassed little smile.

The young man's room was a poky place only three tatami mats in size on the left at the top of the stairs, but there was a bookshelf lined with lots of books and a large number of records.

"Here—stop gawking at everything," Noodles said. "Would you like some coffee? It's a bit bitter, but if you don't mind that …"

H, sensing that he was being treated as an adult, felt pleased and said, "That doesn't bother me. Yes, please." They always drank black tea at H's home. He'd never once had coffee.

With a smile, the other took a box down from a shelf, put some dark-colored beans in it, and ground them with a loud rasping sound. There was a smell rather like tobacco, which H found a bit disturbing, but he did his best not to show it.

The first mouthful of coffee was incredibly bitter.

"How is it? Do you like it?" asked Noodles.

"I think I'll like it when I've had it a few times and get used to the bitterness," said H.

"Hey—you don't have to force yourself to like it! I don't want you drinking *all* my coffee." Busily turning the handle of a phonograph, he placed a record with loving care on the turntable. "This is a record by Yoshie Fujiwara that includes the song I'm always singing."

He lowered the needle gently onto the record. There was a scratchy noise for a moment, then suddenly the sound of a male voice singing.

"What!" H exclaimed in surprise. "Is Yoshie a man?" Yoshie was more common as a woman's name.

"You thought he was a woman, did you? He's a famous tenor. Of course he's a man. 'Like a feather in the wind' is a famous aria."

"What's an aria?"

"A song in an opera that makes you feel particularly good."

It really did make you feel good, thought H. He got him to play it again, and then again. The third or fourth time, his friend got fed up and said—in Tokyo dialect—"Come on, that's enough. You'll wear the damn thing out."

H didn't want to go home yet, so he pressed him to play something else instead.

"This Fujiwara record is a 'red label' one made in America and it's a lot more expensive than ordinary records. He's the only red-label Japanese singer there is. Okay, then, shall I play 'Leaving the Harbor' for you?" he said, winding up the gramophone as he spoke.

"Is that an old song?" asked H.

"What year were you born in?"

"1930."

"This went on sale in 1928, so it's before you were born."

"I know it!" H burst out. "It's a nice aria, isn't it," he added self-consciously.

The young man laughed. "This isn't an *aria*!"

He played other songs for H, too, things like "Moon O'er the Ruined Castle" and "Pretty, Pretty Plover."

H still couldn't tell the difference between them and an aria. Even so, he ventured an opinion: "This Yoshie Fujiwara is good, isn't he! He can sing all kinds of different pieces."

"Right," said Noodles looking pleased. "If you can tell that, then I'll play some for you again another day. That is, if you don't tell anyone you came here and listened to records."

"No, I won't tell anybody," said H. "Here—let's swear on it." He crooked a finger and held it out.

"If you don't keep your word, I'll boil you alive," his friend said, smiling as he crooked his little finger around H's.

Almost every evening after that, H went to the young man's room.

After three days in a row without going to the bathhouse, he was afraid his mother was going to find out, but just in time his father, who seemed to have some inkling of what H was up to, saved him by remarking, "You ought to wash a bit more thoroughly."

After a number of visits to his room, H found himself liking the delivery boy more and more and decided that as a mark of respect he'd give him the nickname "Red Label."

The next time he went to visit, he told him about it.

To his surprise, the smile was wiped off his face in a flash. "No, thank you!" he said in a loud voice. "You stick to 'Noodles'—I don't want any 'Red Label.'"

H was startled; he'd never been shouted at like that by him before.

"All right," he said, though he didn't know what he'd done wrong. Either way, he didn't want to put him out.

A few days later, the young man told him not to come that day. "I've got a friend coming tonight, so it's off today," he said, peering hard into H's face. "You're not to come under any circumstances. Okay?"

He sounded so firm about it that H said in a knowing voice, "All right, I won't. I expect you've got something private to talk about."

The fellow looked taken aback for a moment, then said, "It's a friend I haven't seen for a long time."

The noodle shop, being not far up the road on the other side, was plainly visible from the upstairs window of H's home, so he looked across at his friend's room after it got dark. The curtain was drawn, so he couldn't tell who was there, but the light was on in the room. There seemed to be someone there. H felt a bit left out, but tried to accept it.

Late that night there came several shrill blasts on a whistle and a clamor of voices: "There—up on the roof!"

H was asleep but awoke, startled.

"What was that whistle?" he asked his father, who was in bed next to him and had woken up too.

"The police are after someone. But you're not to go outside, okay?"

H raced upstairs and furtively peered across the road through a crack in the curtains. He could just make out human shapes scrambling away on all fours over the rooftop. There were two of them; one of them he recognized at once, with a thumping of his heart, as his friend.

Three men in black who'd got onto the roof from the drying platform leapt on him from in front and behind and pinned him down. There was a short struggle with loud cries of "Hey! Stop!" before someone called out "Got him!" and the young man disappeared with them over the roof to the other side.

The blasts on the whistle ceased, and a sudden silence fell.

The commotion seemed to have woken up other people in the neighborhood, for lights went on in windows here and there, only to go out again almost immediately. No one opened a window. Probably they were all, like H, peering through windows from inside darkened rooms. He sensed at once that something really scary had happened.

At the idea of his friend in the hands of the police, he suddenly began to tremble.

"Back to bed, now," said his father from behind, tapping him on the shoulder.

"Just a bit more," said H, still staring down at the road in front of the noodle shop. As he did so, men in dark clothes appeared out of nowhere and gathered in the main street. A fair number of policemen must have been in wait there. H strained his eyes to see if his friend was in one of the groups as they went off, but it was too dark to see properly.

The next morning, H heard a knot of neighbors talking to each other in hushed voices:

"It gave me a turn. I mean, half past one in the morning! Four of them caught, they say."

"He really *was* a Red, then."

"It's Dangerous Thoughts, so the secret police will really put him through it."

"What're Dangerous Thoughts? Who're the secret police?" H asked them anxiously, but the grownups suddenly clammed up.

"Keep your voice down," he was told with a look of fierce disapproval.

So, thought H, it *was* something private his friend had been discussing, something he didn't want the police to get wind of....

"Anything about the noodle shop?" he asked his father that morning, thinking it might be in the newspaper. But there wasn't a single line about it. Nor was it in the next day's paper either.

In the winter of the previous year, when an actress called Okada and a stage director called Sugimoto had fled across the border into the Soviet Union, the papers had reported it and there'd been a great fuss, but not a word appeared about the delivery boy from the noodle shop. It must be because he wasn't famous, H concluded. Even so, it puzzled him how the police had got to know about him.

"One of his pals must have informed on him," his father said. "They've begun clamping down recently, so you can't be too careful even with your friends."

H, who knew what "informing" meant, felt his heart begin to thump suffocatingly.

He remembered various things now: how his friend had looked almost angry when he'd called him "Red Label," and forbidden him to use the nickname; the large number of records and books that he'd had; and the awkward look on his face when H had said "something private to talk about." No, he hadn't been an ordinary delivery boy.

"Red," they told him, meant a communist.

"I kept my promise!" he declared silently. "I didn't tell anyone. It wasn't me who informed on you." And every day, even at school, he worried in case the police came and took him away too. He decided that if they did question him he'd say nothing about how the young man had played a red-label record for him: even that aria might be something they'd forbidden.

Possibly the proprietor of the noodle shop had been taken in by the police as well, since the shop didn't open again for about a week after that. And from then on, the neighbors took care never to mention Noodles again. When H plucked up courage and asked the proprietor's wife, "Where's your delivery boy now?" the woman looked annoyed.

"Seems he's been put in the army. I don't suppose he'll be back again. Don't go asking me about him anymore—we've had enough trouble on his account as it is!"

2

Tambourine

H hated the sound of the tambourine. He'd been used to hearing it ever since he was three, but had taken a sudden dislike to it.

It was after he entered primary school that he'd suddenly developed this aversion to it. By third grade the feeling had grown still stronger, till he could detect the sound even when it was too distant and faint for other people to hear.

When he heard the sound of the tambourine coming, he would flee into a back alley and keep out of his friends' sight. The sound as it gradually approached was always mingled with the thumping of a drum. It meant that a group of Christian street preachers were on their way. The man beating the big drum was Mr. Yamaoka from the Maruya drugstore, while the woman banging the tambourine and singing a hymn twice as loudly as anybody else was H's mother, Toshiko.

The route they took included all the streets round about the Nagara Primary School, which H attended, so that his classmates were all familiar with the sight of H's mother going past beating her tambourine.

The next day H would invariably find himself surrounded by a bunch of children chanting "Amen ... Amen!"

Since H always went to church on Sundays, he was used to being poked fun at as the "Amen" boy, but the morning after a bout of tambourine-beating the teasing got on his nerves even more than usual. He'd already appealed to his mother several times:

"I'm not asking you not to go to church. And I'll go on attending Sunday school. But I just wish you wouldn't go around singing and banging that thing."

But it was no use. Every time, she'd say with a puzzled look, "Why? We're bringing God to poor people who don't know about Him, so whatever is there to be embarrassed about?"

It was after she'd left her home in Hiroshima and come to Kobe that Toshiko had become a Christian. Her family were farmers in a village called Miyuki, over the hills from Fukuyama City.

Her mother had been the daughter of a priest of the Nishi-Honganji branch of the Shin sect. The whole family were Buddhists, so no one had dreamed for a moment that she might become a Christian, and it caused quite a stir in the village.

Her parents, siblings and other relatives were all scandalized. "Why ever should a priest's granddaughter go over to Christianity?" they demanded indignantly. "Anyone who gives up Buddhism should be thrown out of the family." "We're not having anything to do with a Jesus freak!" "She ought to've been on her guard against it," said others resentfully, "what with all those foreigners in Kobe." And they wrote trying to persuade her to give it up.

Her parents, though, felt a bit bad about it. They felt guilty because they suspected that the trouble in the first place had been their forcing Toshiko to marry and go off to live in Kobe.

She'd been only eighteen when she'd been obliged to agree, against her will, to the marriage arranged for her by her parents.

She was the fourth daughter in a family of six children. At that point, she herself had never yet given a thought to marriage, and the shock was all the greater in that her elder sister Mineko had gone as a bride only a short while before.

"We've still got to find somebody for Minoru and Masao"—her younger sister and brother—"so it would be a good idea for you to marry Morio," her father told her.

Toshiko had objected fiercely—particularly to the idea of marrying Morio, of all people.

The Morio in question was Morio Senoh, second son of the main Senoh family. Born in 1902, he was three years older than Toshiko, who belonged to a branch of the same family. The main and branch families lived next door to each other, so the two of them had been brought up like brother and sister ever since they could remember.

Toshiko, who'd never for a moment dreamed of becoming the wife of this childhood playmate, was implacable.

"You may not like it," her father said, "but the other family has already agreed to the match and there's not a single relative who's against it."

Faced with such family collusion and the loud approval of all their relatives, Toshiko had little choice but to resign herself to her fate. Even so, the idea of leaving her parents and siblings and going off to live in a distant, unfamiliar town filled her with dread.

The man she was to marry had left home eight years before and gone to Kobe to become a tailor.

In 1918, when Morio first made up his mind to leave home, almost all Japanese people, even in the towns and cities, still went around in kimonos and wooden clogs.

The thing that had made the fifteen-year-old boy decide to go to Kobe and become a tailor's apprentice was a conviction that before long everybody in Japan would be wearing Western dress. With the help of a relative who had gone to live in Kobe, he got himself accepted as a live-in apprentice at a rather superior tailor's in Motomachi known as "Torakichi Shimazaki, High-Class Gentlemen's Tailoring."

When he first presented himself at the Shimazaki shop bearing a cloth bundle containing his belongings and a letter of introduction, he'd been a short, slightly built boy. The first time they met, his future employer had looked worried.

"You're a small lad," he'd said. "Is your health all right? You know, it takes ten years to learn the job properly—d'you think you're tough enough to make it?"

The reason why Morio had decided to leave home and learn a trade as soon as he left higher primary school was that the spendthrift ways of his father and elder brother had brought the main branch of the family to the verge of bankruptcy. They still lived in a spacious residence, but it was only a matter of time before this too, in the same way as the fields and the wooded hills at the back, would be mortgaged and pass into some stranger's hands.

Their haste in arranging the marriage between Morio and Toshiko might well have been aimed at getting it done while the family residence was still there.

When Morio, with leave of absence from Kobe, arrived home in Western dress, his appearance was the source of some amazement.

"Quite the young gentleman!" exclaimed relatives and villagers. "Trust Kobe to be in the fashion!" they said.

Morio and Toshiko's wedding ceremony was due to be held in the big best room of the main house; but on the morning of the great day, disaster struck. Morio's younger brother Shiro, who'd come home with tuberculosis from the textile wholesaler's in Osaka where he was apprenticed, and who'd been laid up in the guest room in the annex, died.

Finding themselves about to attend both a wake and a wedding on the same day, the assembled guests were in quite a state.

Toshiko would have preferred to postpone the ceremony for at least a day, but her wishes were overruled. It would be too much of a bother for the relatives to get together on a different occasion, and the specially ordered food had already been delivered, so it was decided to hold the funeral and the wedding ceremony on the same day but at different times.

A quick change of plan was made, with the funeral service to be held in the best room, where Shiro's body was laid out, and the reception later in the same room. A priest, hastily summoned from the Shozenji Temple, arrived and started reciting the sutras.

One of the relatives, a middle-aged woman, suggested that it would be better to shift the reception to the house next door in case the food got to smell of incense, so the younger members of the family were hurriedly mobilized to transport the food that had been delivered to the kitchen of the main house over to the branch family's house.

To the sound of feet thudding along the corridors, Toshiko retired alone to the small, dimly lit room where the family ancestral tablets were enshrined and, stifling her sobs, wept.

Along with her depression at the marriage she was being forced into, she bitterly resented her bad luck in having the wedding coincide with a funeral. The contrast with her elder sister Mineko's wedding, when the splendid bridal procession had stretched right along the embankment, was too great. She felt crushed by the unfairness of it all, by a sense of being a victim cast out of her own home and packed off alone to an unknown city.

Once that bizarre day, with its hectic succession of funeral, wedding

ceremony and reception, was over, Morio preceded his new bride back
to Kobe.

Two months later, when he came back again to fetch her, she still
didn't want to go. Having waved till her parents, who'd come to the
station to see her off, were no longer in sight, she still went on crying
in the train. Morio felt wretched seeing his new bride still weeping
openly. He'd known for some time that she wasn't happy about marrying him, but this made him feel almost like a slave trader.

Their new home, a four-and-a-half tatami rented room on the second
floor of a house in Kano-cho, near Sannomiya, lacked almost any of the
feminine appurtenances that a bride would normally have brought with
her. Toshiko sat in it all day, simply waiting for her husband's return,
unbearably lonely.

"Why don't you go out sometimes," Morio said, "instead of staying in
the house all day? You could get on the train and go as far as Suma.
There you've got the sea in front of you and the hills behind—nice
scenery that would take you out of yourself."

In the end, Toshiko stirred herself and did as he suggested.

Back home the only trips to the sea she'd taken had been to Tomo-
noura, to reach which you had to cross the hills to a place called Fukuyama, then take quite a long bus ride. So she was astonished to find
the shore so close at hand.

She'd been on the Suma beach for quite a long time, amusing herself picking up shells and the like, when with a blast of its whistle a
passenger train, drawn by a steam locomotive, went past on the main
Sanyo line that ran along the coast. This she knew would pass through
Hiroshima, where her home was, and as she watched it disappear into
the distance, the tears spilled over and ran down her cheeks.

The fact was she was always crying in those days. She thought she
should make an effort to go into the town as much as possible, but
even shopping made her shaky and uncertain, since on one occasion
she'd been laughed at openly for the way she spoke.

Discovering that the best way to stop herself relapsing into her home
dialect was to talk as they did in the school readers, she practiced every
day as if learning a foreign language, modeling her pronunciation on
that of the radio announcers.

One day when the woman who ran the local market asked her whether she was from Tokyo, she was delighted. "Oh, *no*," she replied in her best enunciation, "I am from *Hi-ro-shi-ma*." Her intonation was probably still wrong, but the fact that her speech sounded at least something like the standard gave her confidence.

From that time on, she began going to all kinds of places of her own accord. She spent whole days looking around a department store or drifting around areas—such as the "American Pier," where ships sailing foreign routes lay alongside—that afforded glimpses of unfamiliar worlds.

Morio viewed this astonishing change with wry amusement: it was better, at least, than having her spend all her days crying.

The change in her was enough to surprise her brothers and sisters back home, too. "Our Toshiko was always such a crybaby," they said to each other in their country accents. "Who'd have thought she'd turn into such a lively girl? But then, there's no telling what'll happen once a person starts to change.…"

It may well have been that, once she was away from her immediate family and free from outside interference, the lid came off, releasing a natural curiosity.

In the fifth year of their marriage a boy was born. It was a difficult birth feet first. When he eventually emerged, he showed no signs of life, finally giving his first cry only after much slapping of his bottom by the midwife.

As befitted a first child, the boy they'd so long wanted, he was named Hajime—"Beginning." Morio, though, waited six days before registering the birth, faithfully following the advice of the midwife, who told him that boys were naturally weaker than girls and that it was best to make sure they were going to live before reporting the birth. If the child died a few days after the official notification was made you had to register the death as well, so it was usual to wait and see before doing anything official.

As a result, Hajime's birthday was listed in the register as June 23, 1930, later than the actual date. Morio, however, kept this delay a secret from his wife, telling her that he'd been to report the birth the day after it occurred, in case she thought it meant that a baby who'd failed to give his first cry wasn't expected to survive.

Babies always cried, but Hajime cried much more than ordinary ones.

"They say a crying baby is a healthy baby, but this one cries *too* much," said Morio with a smile as he rocked it in his arms. "He takes after his mother."

Two years after Hajime, a girl was born. To the parents' relief, this one gave a lusty yell as soon as she appeared. She was called Yoshiko, meaning literally "a popular girl."

Morio's apprenticeship ended, to be followed by the customary period of service in the same establishment. Then he worked for a while in another shop till, finally, the time came for him to set up his own business. It was decided that the family should take the opportunity to move from Sannomiya to a place near Suma, at the western edge of the city. To be so far from central locations such as Motomachi and Sannomiya was a business handicap, but the much greater proximity to the sea and hills pleased Toshiko. It was a good environment to bring children up in, she declared, possibly because she personally had found some peace of mind there in her early days in Kobe.

Toshiko's first encounter with Christianity occurred around that time.

One day she heard the beating of a drum and tambourine, and a party of people singing hymns went past the house. She'd been wondering who they were for some time past, so she went after them, pushing the three-year-old boy and seven-month-old baby in a baby carriage, as though led on by the sound of the music. They were a party of Christian street preachers, and their destination proved to be a kind of marquee set up temporarily in the park nearby.

The pastor and congregation who were already inside the tent accepted Toshiko, as she came in pushing her baby carriage, with no sign of surprise. The interior of the tent was dim, lit only by acetylene lamps, but there was none of the forbidding air of a Buddhist temple, so she didn't feel nervous.

The gist of the sermon the minister gave on that occasion was that all human beings were sinners, but anyone could be saved and go to Heaven if only he or she repented of their sins and sought forgiveness of God.

To Toshiko, the idea came like an electric shock.

"You mean, if you've sinned you can avoid going to Hell by praying to God?" she asked the minister.

"You can. Christianity is the religion of salvation. The church is a place for healing those in trouble."

Again, a thrill of emotion ran through her.

Ever since she was a little child she'd felt daunted by the altars in Buddhist temples and the sutra-chanting of the priests. Her parents had told her that people who did bad things went down to Hell, where their sufferings continued even after death. She was scared too by the old picture scrolls portraying the torments of Hell that they showed her. These early impressions must have taken deep root, for even as a grownup she couldn't get rid of the idea that death meant Hell, and shrank from it as a child fears the dark.

On Sunday, three days later, she again put the two children in the baby carriage and went to the church.

The church was an ordinary wooden house. As she slid open the rattling lattice door at the entrance, the minister's wife came out to greet her. The church inside was floored with tatami, on which some thirty men and women of all ages were sitting on cushions, singing a hymn.

When the hymn was over, the minister, Tokutaro Ueda, introduced her to the others. Then he read aloud a short passage from the Bible, and the congregation offered up a prayer.

Trembling, Toshiko began: "I hated the marriage my parents arranged for me, and rebelled against them.... I've always felt I had bad luck.... Can God forgive and save even somebody like me?"

"Your sins are forgiven," the minister told her. "You have been given eternal life, and your name has been recorded in Heaven as a child of God."

When Toshiko got home, she immediately told Morio what had happened at the church.

"Why don't you come along with me next Sunday?" she said. "You'd understand still better then."

"Yes, why don't I?..." he answered vaguely, knowing that to contradict Toshiko, who acted impulsively whenever she got some idea into her head, would set her talking for an hour at least.

"They say there are many different kinds of Christianity," she told him. "The place I went to is 'Protestant,' apparently. You know that fine stone-built church in Yamate-dori? Well, that's 'Catholic.' *Their* headquarters is in Rome, it seems. Our preacher said that although our church doesn't have a beautiful altar or stained glass or anything, you don't need a fancy building to pray to God in. 'It's as if the individual is his own church; God is inside your own heart,' he said." Everything the minister had said she passed on in enormous detail, even imitating his way of speaking.

The idea that a church as such was not the one, true abode of religion seemed to arouse Morio's interest rather. The customers for whom he made suits included a number of foreigners, and to him the differences between Buddhism and Christianity tended to mean, if anything, purely "cultural" differences.

Unlike Toshiko, whose conversion to Christianity took place almost overnight, Morio came to the faith gradually. Before long, however, both of them were sufficiently ardent believers to have themselves baptized.

From then on, the motto of the Senoh household was: "Rejoice evermore. Pray without ceasing. In every thing give thanks" (I Thessalonians 5:16). And a good part of Toshiko's days thereafter was spent marching spiritedly in the forefront of a band of street preachers, beating a tambourine which measured about thirty centimeters across.

Apparently determined that her two children should grow up as "spotless angels," she had them undergo a ceremony at the church corresponding to the baptism of infants in the Catholic Church. Having thus formally dedicated her children to God, she was content that the whole family was now Christian.

It followed as a matter of course that H, and Yoshiko too, should be sent to the church for Sunday school every week.

Toshiko's education of her children was aimed, first and last, at producing "children of God." Even before he went to primary school H was made to read from a Bible in Japanese, with the pronunciation of the difficult characters written alongside them. Thanks to this he was early in learning to read, and picked up quite a rich vocabulary. In this way, at least, Toshiko's approach to education was a success.

Once he'd learned to read, H wanted to read things other than the Bible, but this was strictly forbidden.

"You are not to read anything else," Toshiko announced to the children. "It'll only teach you wickedness."

The one book that was an exception was an illustrated volume called *Pilgrim's Progress* that had been bought for them at the church.

This work, the story of a dangerous journey undertaken by a man carrying a large bundle on his back, was interesting enough but heavily religious in tone. Tired of reading the same book over and over again, H would have liked to read *Boys' Club* and comics, but that was out of the question.

Another thing that annoyed H was the way his mother would tell him almost every day: "You've been given up to God, so you mustn't do anything wicked. Try to be a good boy, always."

On one thing, though, he made up his mind: he'd never go against his mother until he was in a position to express himself properly, as an adult. But that meant holding out until his fifteenth birthday, when a boy traditionally ceased being a child. He'd go to church, too, but his real self wouldn't be the boy his mother pictured to herself. He would play the good boy for her sake, since being found out was more trouble than it was worth.

So from the time he was in third grade, he was a "good boy" in a way that would have horrified Toshiko if she'd known the awful truth. Playing at being "good," though, meant putting up with all kinds of things, of which the sound of the tambourine was one.

3

Girly Boy

In a narrow street, the second back from the main road, a young man known to the children of the neighborhood as "Girly Boy" lived with his elderly mother.

He'd acquired the nickname not just because of the mild way in which he always spoke, but because of something unmanly about his general build and his gestures. Late in 1937 there'd been a neighborhood parade to celebrate the fall of Nanking, followed by an amateur theatrical show put on by local residents. On that occasion, the young man had performed a dance wearing a woman's kimono, for which he'd won great applause. His face when made up was prettier than that of any of the local girls.

It was on that evening that he'd been dubbed "Girly Boy." H himself, in fact, was the first to use it.

There was no hint of malice in this, for Girly Boy had always been nice to H; it was just that H felt the name somehow fitted. Nor did it seem to annoy the person concerned, who just smiled when he heard it. He may actually have liked it.

About a kilometer away from H's home there was an entertainment area centered around a street called Taisho-suji and, crossing it at right angles, a bustling shopping street called Rokken-michi.

H was very fond of both. With its movie theaters—Shochiku-kan, Goraku-kan, Mikuni-kan—dotted about on both sides, the area was infinitely livelier than Honjo-cho, the neighborhood of small houses and shops where he himself lived. Girly Boy worked in one of the movie theaters in Taisho-suji.

"You're not to go to Rokken-michi or Taisho-suji," his mother had told him. "If you spend your time in places like that, you'll go to the dogs in no time." But the area had a fascination for H just the same. "Going to the dogs," of course, meant becoming a delinquent, and the area, with its strong gangster element, was in fact a bit scary. Even so, from the time he'd been in first grade at primary school, H—already, perhaps, a promising candidate for delinquency—would happily make the long trip to Taisho-suji and Rokken-michi just so that he could hang about the streets there.

But though he might lurk in the vicinity of the movie theaters, H, who didn't get a single sen in pocket money from his parents, couldn't go in but had to content himself with gazing at the posters and photos outside, which were quite enough anyway to set his imagination racing.

Those were the days when movies were known as "motion pictures," and a few silent films still lingered on, shown with the assistance of live narrators who commented on the action taking place on the screen. Even though almost every film by then came with a soundtrack of the actors' own voices, the posters still went out of their way to say it was a "talkie."

One day, outside the Shochiku-kan movie theater, H bumped into the man who ran the local tofu store.

"Hey! Children by themselves aren't allowed in to see this kind of film."

His heart gave a lurch, but he tried not to show it, saying as casually as he could, "I'm just looking at the posters."

"But if you're as keen on movies as that, why don't I take you in?"

"Would you? Really?" H was delighted, but still hung back for fear of being betrayed to his parents.

"Don't worry—I won't tell anyone," said the man, who may have guessed the reason for his hesitation. "And I'm not going to pay your share, either. Small children are free, so if you hold on to my hand … but you'll have to keep well down when we go past the woman who clips the tickets."

H took admiring note of this trick, which promised to be useful.

He was rather nervous as they went past the lady clipping the tickets, but she just gave him a glance and let them through without a word.

A black cloth hung at the entrance to shut out the light from outside. It had a kind of dirty sheen to it, and H felt rather put off.

Parting the curtain, they went in. In the sudden darkness he collided with the iron railing marking off the aisle and nearly fell over. Peering around in search of a seat, he saw two empty ones in the corner at the back, placed rather higher than the rest, where they'd have a good view.

"I'm going there," said H.

"No—those are the inspection seats," the tofu man whispered.

"What does that mean?"

"They're where the police sit when they come to make sure they're not showing bad movies and that there's no suspicious-looking characters around. They're empty now, but they sometimes drop in on their rounds."

H gave a start at the mention of the police, even as he reflected wistfully that *they* could see movies for free....

The tofu shop man must have wanted to avoid more questions, because he said, "You can watch nearer the front if you like. Just go home any time you want to," and went off to find a seat in the middle of the house.

H moved down to the very front row. The film showing was *Entwining Passions*, and he knew the names of the actors because he'd seen them on the notice boards.

The actor and actress on the screen at the moment were Ken Uehara and Kinuyo Tanaka, but their faces were so big that looking up at them H soon began to feel queasy. Personally, he didn't find the movie as interesting as he'd heard grownups at the bathhouse saying it was. Perhaps, having come in halfway, he didn't understand the plot properly. Even so, he had a pleasantly excited kind of feeling, just sitting there.

He went on watching for a while, but the film hadn't finished before he felt like leaving. The theater stank of urine, and besides he was afraid he'd get told off if he was too late home. There was one place, though, that he wanted to have a look at before he left—the room with the small window through which the all-important flickering beam of light emerged. That, he figured, must be the place that housed the machine projecting the film.

The room was near the entrance. Someone who'd just arrived on a bike bringing a canister of film had gone inside, and the door was open. The person in charge was complaining as he took the film:

"You're late! If you don't bring the last reel soon, the movie'll break off before the end."

To H's great astonishment, the person speaking was Girly Boy, but a different Girly Boy from usual; even his voice wasn't the same, more like an ordinary man's.

"So *this* is the kind of work you do," H said to him, "here in the theater."

"That's right—I'm the projectionist," he replied with an almost comically abrupt switch to his usual soft voice.

"Maybe that's why you can do all kinds of voices, like an actor," said H, "because you're watching movies all the time?"

"Could be," he said with a diffident smile, setting about mounting the film on the projector. His movements were brisk, and it occurred to H that though he liked Girly Boy when he was behaving like a girl, the projectionist role suited him too.

He didn't know this at the time, but his friend had originally been an actor taking female roles in a traveling troupe of kabuki players, and his friend's mother too had apparently worked with the same company. When she fell sick, they'd left the troupe and come to live near H's home. Girly Boy had been born in Amagasaki, it seemed, and an uncle who still lived there would sometimes come to see them, bringing his young mistress with him. Girly Boy, who presumably disliked this uncle, would promptly slip out of the house.

H often went to pass the time at Girly Boy's home, the chief attraction being the snippets of old film that he was given there. As he handed them over, Girly Boy would hold them up to the light, give an imitation of the actors' voices, and explain each scene to him.

H on his side showed his gratitude by giving him movie leaflets that he'd colored himself with crayons.

For all his fondness for Girly Boy, when H was with his friends he'd take the lead in teasing him, just for the fun of it. The little brats were curious about his sexual endowment, and were fond of greeting him with chants of "Let's see your willy! Let's see your willy!"

24

Even in the bathhouse, though, Girly Boy always kept his small cotton towel clasped to his crotch, so that absolutely nothing was visible. The charcoal storekeeper's second son, who claimed to have seen it, said it was very small, like a kid's.

The barber's son denied this emphatically—*he* had got a look, he said, and there was no willy at all. So they decided to have a bet on it. The stake would be a water ice, and the showdown would take place on Thursday evening at the bathhouse. Since Girly Boy always went for a bath after finishing work, this was usually close to midnight, but on Mondays and Thursdays, when he was on the early shift, he arrived at the bathhouse around seven o'clock.

Five of the young conspirators gathered there to wait for him. H himself volunteered to be the one who pulled away the towel. The role had the advantage that whichever side won he would be treated to a water ice too, and he yielded to the flattering suggestion that only he would be capable of carrying out the maneuver swiftly enough.

Once Girly Boy had stripped off, H kept close to him without seeming to do so, then, just as the other was getting out of the bath, snatched away the protective towel. Desperately, Girly Boy pressed his hands down between his thighs; but the boys' beady eyes had seized the moment and there was an immediate chorus of "E-*norm*-ous!" With a look of distress on his face, he sank to his haunches on the tiled washplace.

At that moment, without warning, Iwao from the tatami store, who was there washing himself, gave H a great slap across the face. H fell over backward and slid along the tiles till he collided with Girly Boy and came to a halt.

Girly Boy helped him up. "All right?" he said.

Suddenly H felt thoroughly ashamed of what he'd done. "I'm sorry," he said in a small voice.

Yet even after this outrageous prank, Girly Boy continued to spend time with H just as he'd always done. He would let him see, for free, films that weren't supposed to be shown to children, becoming a secret friend whom H could under no circumstances mention to his parents.

In spring, when H had just entered fourth grade, Girly Boy's call-up papers came.

H was worried for him, feeling sure he would never make a soldier, and went to his house to see him.

The papers he was shown weren't a "red form," as such papers were usually known, but a slip of thin, pale pink paper. Girly Boy's mother, who was sick, was sitting up in her futon, crying.

While they were there, the chairman of the neighborhood association and Mr. Omori, a former army officer, came in.

"Congratulations on joining up!" they shouted.

"We'll look after your mother while you're gone, so you don't have to worry," bellowed Omori. "So off you go, now, and do your job fighting for His Majesty!"

This made Girly Boy's mother burst into tears again.

"Don't cry, it's all right," her son said, rubbing her back soothingly.

On the day he left, the local neighborhood association saw Girly Boy off as far as Takatori Station, where his train pulled out to the cries of "Banzai!" that followed any new conscript going off to war.

Mr. Omori was in high spirits, possibly because he'd had some of the special ration of saké doled out to all enlisting soldiers. In fact, he gave the impression of enjoying doing his "I've been there before" bit every time anybody went off to join the fighting.

Three days later, members of the secret military police and ordinary police arrived at Girly Boy's house and disappeared inside. They heard his mother saying "My son's joined the forces—he's not here," and an MP bawling, "He hasn't joined his unit—that's why we've come to look for him, you fool!"

The policemen suddenly emerged from the house again, so H and the others fled.

The news soon spread among the neighbors that Girly Boy hadn't joined his unit but had run off somewhere, absent without leave.

A circular from the neighborhood association came around to each house in turn: "... any sighting of him is to be reported forthwith. Note that to sight a deserter and not report the matter is a more serious offense than giving refuge to a thief."

H asked his friends at school whether they'd seen the circular. Some of them knew that Girly Boy had gone absent, but the circular seemed not to have gone around other districts.

Before long, people stopped talking about Girly Boy altogether. They hadn't forgotten, but were scared to mention his name.

One day about two months later, H went into the hills to gather fire-wood together with Kiyoshi Hirai, a fifth-grader who lived next door, and Ikuo, the second son from the charcoal store.

"Even the kid from the charcoal shop has to collect firewood these days," said Ikuo with a grin.

"Collecting firewood" simply meant picking up dead branches and carrying them home on their backs, and they went into the hills for that purpose roughly once a week.

The task also served as a chance to let the boys play in the woods. Because of the fuel shortage, every household was obliged to gather its own firewood by now, and each time they went they had to go a bit deeper into the woods to find branches.

The outing this time took H and his friends up Mount Takao, on a piece of land belonging to the Suma Imperial Villa. If you went down the steep slope on the west of the hill, there was a stretch of virgin forest that people were forbidden to enter. The slope was so steep, though, that even if you managed to get down it, to get back up again carrying dead branches on your back was quite an effort.

In silence, the three of them rustled around in the undergrowth look-ing for fallen branches. H was just thinking to himself that this was the kind of place that Girly Boy could hide in without being found when Ikuo suddenly said, with a serious expression:

"I've got something to tell you. You mustn't let on to anyone, though."

"Okay, I won't."

"It's a promise, then. What d'you think—I saw Girly Boy in the alley at the back!"

"You did? *Really*? I mean, you're like your father, the way you tell stories...."

"This isn't a story! I saw Girly Boy in the alley last night. I called, but he ran away." Ikuo hadn't told his father yet, he said, though he felt scared about keeping quiet.

"I'll bet he came back because he was worried about his mother."

"They say she's in a bad way. The pain in her inside isn't getting any better."

"Someone said the neighborhood association would look after her, but that's bullshit, isn't it?"

"I wonder where he's holed up. I bet he's hungry."

While they tied the dead branches into bundles with rope, they promised each other not to tell anyone else about the matter.

H was in a hurry to get home. Maybe he'd strained his belly climbing up the bank—anyway, he'd soiled his pants. He'd been needing a crap for some time, and he regretted having held out so long.

For some time lately, his bowels had been loose. He knew the cause—he'd got into the bad habit of putting anything that looked edible into his mouth to see what it was like. The trouble this time must have been some shellfish he'd roasted and eaten on the beach the day before. The grownups had told him that the clams under the wharf belonging to the Rising Sun refinery upset your stomach because of the oil they'd absorbed, and they'd been right.

H's pants felt unpleasantly sticky inside, but he didn't tell the other two. Once previously, when he'd been squatting in a thicket in the woods having a crap, he'd noticed a whole undigested bean in his stool. He'd been poking at it with a twig, wondering whether it would put out a shoot and grow, when he'd heard a rustling behind him. Turning, he felt a sudden panic on seeing the faces of three of his friends watching him.

"We saw you!" they chorused. "We saw you, eating your own shit!" He still remembered the trouble he'd had stopping the shameful story from going the rounds....

They followed the Tenjo River down its course, and had just passed under the railway bridge near Takatori Station when his belly began to hurt again.

He didn't think he could hold out as far as his home, but reckoned he could make it as far as the filthy toilet at a gas station on the way.

Leaving his two friends, he walked on slowly, clutching his belly.

The "gas station" was in reality a deserted ruin. Since the only vehicles to be seen in the town by then used substitute fuel, running not on gasoline but by burning charcoal, it had long since gone out of business.

Until quite recently it had been an ideal haunt for H and the other boys, who played war games there, going under cover in various spots in and around the abandoned site. Their interest was heightened by the fact that the windowpanes were already broken, which meant they could throw stones at them with impunity.

Lately, however, they'd stopped using it much, because the bits of glass scattered all around made it difficult to move about freely, and the waste overflowing from the toilet made a terrible stink.

Arriving at the place for the first time in months, H recoiled from the idea of squatting over the filthy hole in some boards that passed for a toilet. He hesitated for a moment, then, unable to hold out any longer, grabbed the door handle. The rusty metal door opened with a creaking sound and H saw, right in front of his eyes, a pair of boots and legs. A human figure was dangling there.

With a start of horror, he looked up: it was Girly Boy.

Girly Boy had hanged himself. His eyes were open, and flies were buzzing loudly about his face. His trousers were wet with urine.

H himself wet his pants with the shock. On top of that, his bowels started dribbling again, so that he felt a sticky wetness spreading down his lower parts.

He went home and told his father what he'd found.

"I'll go and tell them at the police station," said his father, setting off in a hurry.

H dashed into the family toilet, then washed himself all over with a hose in the backyard. That done, he put on some clean pants and ran off to the gas station again. It was wrong, he felt, to leave Girly Boy alone there.

Girly Boy was still hanging there, but H no longer felt afraid. His friend hadn't wanted to be a soldier, he thought to himself: suicide was the only alternative. He wondered if hanging himself had seemed better than being killed by a bullet on the battlefield....

A policeman rode up on a bicycle and a middle-aged man came from the fire station pulling a cart.

They cut the rope encircling his neck, and Girly Boy came tumbling down with a thud.

Turning their faces away and trying not to dirty their hands, the grownups loaded the body onto the cart and roughly flung a straw mat over it.

"Where are you taking him?" asked H, but the policeman said in an angry-sounding voice:

"That's no business of yours. You're not to come after us."

As he watched the cart receding into the distance, H finally burst into tears.

He felt sorry, terribly sorry, for Girly Boy. He wiped his eyes, but the tears kept spilling over.

A week later Girly Boy's mother died. The neighbors got together to give her a funeral. A policeman arrived and went around asking everybody if there was any relative present.

"Not even one!" said H.

"I'm not asking *you!*" the policeman shouted, turning on him.

"There's an uncle from Amagasaki, but I know him by sight and he's not here," called H as he fled. "That's all I meant."

It wasn't just relatives—there wasn't a single person from the movie theater where Girly Boy had worked, nor any other friend at all.

4

Knives and Forks

H had used a knife and fork to eat his meals ever since second grade at primary school.

The silver cutlery was big and heavy, difficult for a child to handle.

His younger sister Yoshiko, who was still only five, struggled along bravely in clumsy imitation of him.

If they got used to a knife and fork now, their mother insisted, they'd feel the benefits one day. Her idea, it seemed, was to familiarize them with the Western style, so that when they grew up they'd be able to eat out anywhere without feeling awkward. So there was no help for it, and the two children suffered together at mealtimes.

The problem was that the things they ate along with their rice at home were the kind of dishes you'd find in any ordinary Japanese household, and very different from Western food.

With something like potato cakes it wasn't so bad, but on days when they had boiled fish or stewed vegetables *à la japonaise*, they found it pretty hard going.

When she first made the children use knives and forks, Toshiko also put their bean-paste soup in Western-style soup plates instead of bowls, then tried to get them to eat it with a spoon and without making any noise. But the miso soup, with its floating cubes of tofu, just didn't taste right eaten with a spoon.

"That's going too far," said their father. "I think you should teach them to eat it from an ordinary bowl. I mean, children have got to learn to use chopsticks properly, too."

Thanks to his intervening in this way, they were at least spared the ordeal of spooning soup from plates, which was a relief.

But although H might be willing to put up with eating with a knife and fork, he was absolutely opposed to the idea of his friends witnessing the spectacle. The sight of the four of them, parents and children, sitting on cushions placed on the tatami around a low, circular table—a typically Japanese domestic scene—but with the children eating with knives and forks, was bound to look peculiar.

The silver cutlery—far too grand for H's home—was a parting gift from that American missionary, Mrs. Staples, when she left for America.

Along with the knives and forks, she'd also given them two sets of six large plates bordered with a flower design. H was rather fond of them, as they were pretty things, but it was still quite an effort to eat rice off them with a fork.

Toshiko had first got the idea of introducing knives and forks at home when she'd been invited to Mrs. Staples' place and had a meal served in that fashion. Seeing Toshiko in difficulties with her knife and fork, Mrs. Staples had said, in good Japanese, "Shall I fetch some chopsticks?" but Toshiko had refused and struggled on through the meal, doing her best to copy what her host was doing.

It was this that had convinced her of the need to instill Western-style table manners in her children.

Mrs. Staples owed her fluency in Japanese to the fact that she'd been in the country for six years, since 1928, working to spread Christianity here. The American sect she belonged to had connections with the church that Toshiko attended, and a Mr. Aycoll, another missionary, who had been in Japan even longer and had traveled all over the place, also dropped in frequently at the Kobe church.

Since the family was friendly with both of them, they all had ample opportunity to see at first hand how people with different customs behaved. Toshiko was impressed, among other things, by the effort these expatriates put into learning to speak good, accurate Japanese. This resulted in her promptly deciding that besides getting her children used to using a knife and fork, she'd also improve the way they talked, making them use standard speech as far as possible at home instead of the local dialect.

That way, the children wouldn't have any handicap in future where

the way they talked was concerned, even if they went to live somewhere other than Kobe.

"I don't care so much when you're outside," she told H, "but I want
you to use standard speech at home."

"*Standard* speech? Oh, come off it! I'm no *good* at it! Is Yoshiko supposed to speak it, too?"

"I'd prefer that she did, but she's younger than you. You should set
her an example. Standard Japanese is what the announcers speak on
the radio. I want you to copy the way they talk. I practiced in the same
way when I first came to Kobe, so I'm sure you can manage it too."

H smiled in amusement as he listened, because his mother had herself suddenly changed her way of speaking halfway through.

"Do I always have to talk like that?"

"You should try to as much as possible."

H could never go against his mother when she looked so serious
about something, so he grudgingly gave in.

"I'll try … but … I mean, it's Japanese all right, but it's a lot different
from the way we talk in Kobe. Either way, I absolutely don't want my
friends to catch me talking 'standard Japanese.' You'll just have to
understand when they're around."

"*Why?*"

"They'll poke fun at me again because my family's so peculiar."

"*I* don't see what's peculiar about it…. Think how people admired
those Americans for the nice way they spoke Japanese. People *admire*
you if you talk the standard language."

"I don't want to be admired," said H irritably, but his mother utterly
failed to see what made him so embarrassed.

H couldn't really remember if Mrs. Staples' Japanese had been so good,
having been only four at the time. He did remember quite clearly,
though, seeing off a big ship alongside the "American Pier" on the day
she went back to the United States. A gong had sounded, and as the
ship slowly drew away from the wharf, the colored tape he'd held in
his hand had gone round and round, gradually unrolling. A siren had
wailed mournfully; the five-colored tapes connecting the wellwishers
with the ship had broken and, fluttering in the breeze, dropped to the
water where they floated, rocking on the surface. Then, gradually, the

ship had receded into the distance. Things like that were imprinted indelibly on his memory.

It had been H's first conscious experience of parting from someone quite close to him, a fact that must have deepened the impression.

That same memory was at the back of his mind whenever he used a knife and fork, thanks to which he'd never felt that America was such a terribly distant country.

After that, occasional postcards would come from Mrs. Staples. Looking at these, or at her Christmas cards, H would tell himself, "I'm going to America too when I grow up!"

The postcard she sent to congratulate him on starting primary school had a photograph of a towering skyscraper in New York.

"How do you think they build them as high as this?" he asked his father in astonishment.

"Well, America's a remarkable country, you know. Their technology's the best in the world. I'm going to see Mr. James next week, so I'll ask him about the building on the card for you."

Mr. James was the American owner of a trading company called James and Co. in the Yokohama concession. His taste in clothes, according to Morio, was flashier than that of English people, even though he spoke the same language. He was a cheerful, loud-voiced, generous man who always gave Morio a tip in addition to the tailoring charge. The fact of the matter was, though, he always beat him down on the original price of his suits.

"Foreigners ask you straight out for a discount," Morio had once told H with a smile, "but they give you a tip, so it comes to the same thing in the end. It's funny, the way customs are different."

Once, Mr. James had given H a terrific toy for Christmas. A model of an American fire engine, it had a long collapsible ladder that extended in several stages—probably because American buildings were so much taller than Japan's—and was an object of great envy among H's friends.

"Well," his father said on arriving home one day from a fitting with Mr. James, "I asked him. The tall building in the photo is called the Empire State Building, and it seems it was built in 1931—that's a year after you were born."

H was delighted at the idea that such a tall building was one year junior to himself.

"It's awfully tall for a younger brother, though, isn't it?" he chuckled.

His father went on to tell him about the subway, too. "They say the New York subway started operating twenty-seven years before Tokyo —in 1903, the year after I was born—which makes the American subway *my* younger brother."

Together they gazed at the photograph on the postcard. With younger brothers like these, the elder ones would have to look to their laurels…. H decided he'd better try to improve his knife and fork technique.

"Do French people use knives and forks the same way when they eat?"

"Of course. I've got a fitting with the chef at a restaurant in Sannomiya soon. Shall I take you along?"

"Yes please!—even if I have to take a day off from school."

In taking H to the French restaurant, Morio was motivated by a desire to please his son in another way, too, but he kept quiet about it.

One afternoon some two weeks later, when H got back from school, his father said, "Come on, let's go!" It seemed he'd adjusted the time of that day's fitting and had been waiting for his return.

To get to Sannomiya, one could go either by the municipal streetcar, which took forty minutes, or the electric railway, which took fifteen. H, wanting to have as long a ride as possible, plumped for the former.

The restaurant in question stood on the street with the streetcars, on the opposite corner from the Daimaru department store in Motomachi.

The dining room was on the second floor. The first floor was a bar, with rows of bottles of various drinks.

The handrail of the stairs leading to the second floor curved upward, with entwined leaves and flowers carved in gold.

Opening out directly at the top of the stairs, the dining room had deep red velvet curtains. Candles, unlit as yet, stood on the tables. A chandelier hung from the ceiling, but this wasn't lit either, so the room was in semidarkness.

"It's like being somewhere outside Japan!" said H excitedly, walking around among the chairs and tables. "I saw a room in a picture once that was just like this. We could be abroad!"

Morio pushed open a swing door beside a large mirror that led into the kitchens, and H hurried to follow him. Beyond the door lay a spacious kitchen with rows of pots and gas rings. The man who came up smiling to shake hands with H's father was tall and blonde. This was Pierre, the French chef, and Morio introduced H to him saying "This is my son."

In his tall white hat, Pierre looked as though he might bump into the ceiling. Since H's father was small, the sight of them side by side was almost comical, like something out of a cartoon.

"If you go down the stairs and out the back way, you'll find something you like," said Morio to H with a smile.

H did as he was told, opening the back door to the bar and going outside. He found himself in a narrow passageway with another door on the other side. He opened it, and was startled to find that it led into a movie theater.

H worked it out: the restaurant and theater were adjoining buildings looking out onto a shared passageway, which you couldn't get into from outside. It seemed likely that when his father came for a fitting he sometimes saw a film while he was about it.

The movie being shown right then was a foreign one, and a man with a moustache and a funny, knock-kneed way of walking was being pursued around the inside of a factory. Before long he got caught up in the cogs of a huge machine, trying desperately to escape. It was hilarious.

It was only a film, not reality, H thought to himself. If the man had really been caught up in the cogs, he'd have been killed. H wondered how they'd managed to film it, but couldn't work it out.

It was a foreign film, with no dialogue, but H had no trouble following what was going on. In fact, he thoroughly enjoyed it: it was more fun than *Entwining Passions*.

Much to his disappointment, though, his father soon came to fetch him.

"I'll bring you with me when I come with the finished clothes next week, so you can watch again then," said Morio. "Oh—and Pierre says he's got something he wants to give you." This restored H's good humor immediately.

Pierre's present turned out to be a cake, a soft kind that H had never had before.

He was wondering how he was going to get it home without squashing it when Pierre brought a plate and a little fork, put them on the table, and told him to eat it then and there.

He must have said it in French, but H understood what he meant at once, which he found strange. Come to think of it, Pierre always spoke to his father in French too, while Morio replied in Japanese. Both of them seemed to treat this as a perfectly ordinary way of talking.

Suddenly H thought he knew why. The customers who ordered clothes from his father were of many different nationalities—French, American, German, Italian, Chinese—but his father didn't seem to care: he treated them as individuals—as Pierre, or Friedrich, or whatever— and where clothes at least were concerned he seemed to understand roughly what they were saying. H had often wondered how many languages his father was able to speak. In fact, he just talked away quite happily in Japanese.

One afternoon the following week, they paid another visit to Pierre's restaurant.

H went into the cinema again with high expectations, but was disappointed to find they were doing the same scene as before. If only they'd come a bit later, he thought ruefully, he could have seen the next part....

He complained when his father came to fetch him.

"It isn't good for Pierre," he was told, "if I come too late in the afternoon, just when he's getting busy with the cooking for the evening. I expect it'll be a different film next week, so you can watch a bit longer today if you like. You stay here while I go and buy some lining and buttons."

His dad was okay, thought H to himself.

About an hour later, when his father came to get him, H learned that the film was called *Modern Times* and that the man with the moustache was called Chaplin.

Pierre told him that he had a son the same age as H himself. He showed him a photograph and invited him to his house the following Sunday. His wife, apparently, was Japanese. All this was "interpreted" for H by his father.

The present he got that day wasn't a cake but a piece of cheese, strange-smelling but good.

Back home, H was bothered by the fact that, compared with the gleaming knives and forks at the restaurant, their own were rather dull.

"Why don't you try polishing them with tooth powder?" his mother said.

He tried it on one, and it came up bright and shining just as she'd said. Delighted, H set about polishing the whole lot. He was busy at it when he discovered a fork with one of its four prongs slightly bent.

He tried pressing it back with his finger, but it was too stiff. The only way to put it right, he realized, was to hit it with a hammer, so, not wanting to mark it, he wrapped it in a cotton towel first. After a few blows, the prong bent too far in the other direction. Dismayed, he was desperately trying to bend it back again when this time it snapped off completely.

H thought he was really for it now, but, to his surprise, his mother didn't get angry. Then, just as he was thinking "You never can tell," she said:

"Keep it for yourself from now on. It'll be easy to tell which is whose."

This, along with his relief, made him feel a bit put out, but he was making up his mind not to complain when his little sister said:

"No—*I'll* use it. Hajime shouldn't have to use a fork with a prong missing."

Most of the time, H felt that the way Yoshiko, two years younger than himself, clung to her big brother was a nuisance, but now he felt ashamed. It wasn't fair to treat her always as if she was in the way.

"Don't worry, Yoshiko," he told her awkwardly, "I won't let you get lost again."

This was a reference to something that had happened when Yoshiko was four. H and his cronies, annoyed because she always wanted to join in their games, had got her to be "it" in a game of hide-and-seek, then instead of hiding had gone off somewhere else to play by themselves. Some while later, H realized he'd left his sister there covering her eyes, and hurried back, only to find her gone.

Yoshiko, searching in vain for the boys, must have got lost somewhere.

Feeling alarmed, H got his friends to help look for her, but search as they might they still hadn't found her by dusk, and a great fuss ensued.

It was beginning to get dark when they saw her coming home on the back of a stranger, a middle-aged housewife. H almost collapsed in the road with relief.

Surrounded by her mother and the neighbors, all uttering delighted exclamations, Yoshiko had looked quite unconcerned, as though she'd no idea what all the fuss was about.

According to the lady who'd brought her back, she'd found Yoshiko quite far away, walking alone by the sea. This seemed a bit odd to her, so she'd spoken to the girl.

"I asked her where she lived, but all she said was 'This way' or 'That way,' and I had a job making it out. We went all over the place, I can tell you! Even so, she didn't cry. She just kept telling me that her big brother had let her play with them. She may be small, but she's a good little girl, she really is!"

Hearing this, H had put his arms around his little sister and said, "I'm sorry, Yoshiko! Really sorry!"

Later, of course, H had been given a thorough telling off.

But though he'd repented at the time, he still found it annoying to have her hanging around, and cut her out of his activities whenever he could without his mother knowing.

The affair of the fork, though, changed his feelings toward her.

Whenever he tried putting the fork with the missing prong next to his own plate, Yoshiko would quietly change their forks over when he wasn't looking. It had a chastening effect on him.

It made him feel that this little sister was nicer than he was.

5

Two-Sen Paste

A couple of kilometers from H's home, up the Myohoji River in the direction of the hills, stood the Gongen Shrine, familiarly known to the local children as Gongen-san. At its annual festival, all kinds of stalls would be set up in the shrine grounds, and H, who was fond of anything out-of-the-way, went regularly every year.

"I'm in fourth grade," he declared as he left the house that year, "I can go by myself now."

Beside the path just inside the shrine gateway, he spotted an odd boxlike structure fitted with lenses. It hadn't been there last year; this must be the first time it had featured at Gongen-san, and he wondered where it came from. It looked interesting, so he went up and stood for a while gazing at it.

The box, which was mounted on a trolley, was rectangular, about the size of a standard sliding door turned on its side, and painted with black lacquer. In various places it had gilt studs, which gave it a distinguished air.

In one of the two bigger sides were fitted some ten lenses about five centimeters in diameter. They were in two rows, one above the other, the higher row apparently intended for adults and the lower for children. On top of the box, a middle-aged man and woman were seated facing each other on thick cushions, beating loudly on the roof with pieces of bamboo like wooden rulers split at the end, and chanting a kind of prologue to the show. After a spell of chanting, the man tugged at a cord hanging by him, whereupon there was a clattering noise as though something had fallen down inside the box.

H wanted to look through one of the lenses to see what was happening inside, but unfortunately had no money with him.

Racking his brains as to how he could get a look, he had a good idea. Sidling up to a grownup who was looking through a lens, he murmured, "Ah—so this is the kind of thing that spreads trachoma. No, not for me."

Trachoma, of course, was an infectious eye disease. Lots of people at the time had got it and were going around with bright red eyes. It was a leading cause of blindness, and the students at H's school had all had their eyes washed in the infirmary.

H had been hoping that if he muttered something in someone's ear about catching the disease they'd get worried and move away from the lens. As it turned out, though, it wasn't that easy. Three grownups just ignored him, but he went patiently from one person to the next, murmuring his message by the side of each in turn.

The fourth person, a middle-aged man, took his eye from the lens and glared at H. "What a nasty little brat!" he declared and walked away.

H darted to the vacant lens to peer into the box, but just as he did so he was given a mighty thwack on the head, enough to make him see stars. He looked up in time to see the man on the box raising his bamboo rod ready for another blow.

Jumping nimbly out of range, he said, "The gentleman before me said it was all right for me to see the rest."

It wasn't clear whether the man had swallowed this ploy of his or not, but he was already going on with his chant as though nothing had happened. Probably he'd decided not to bother, unwilling to let this odd little boy interfere with his work.

Keeping an eye open for another sally with the man's rod, H peered in through the lens. The box inside was brightly illuminated by two electric bulbs hanging from above so that a picture like a kabuki poster leapt to the eye. The clothes of the people shown in it had real material in bright colors stuck on them, padded to make them look three-dimensional. Gazing at them in rapture, his heart beating fast, H wondered if this was what real kabuki was like.

The picture showed a great fire, with the streets a mass of crimson flames. A woman with disheveled hair had climbed to the top of a lookout tower as though to view the conflagration. The next picture, which came down from above to cover the first, showed the same woman arrested and bound by the authorities. Finally, the woman was shown being put to death by being hung on a cross and stuck with spears. After about five successive changes of picture, the show ended and the lights went out, leaving the box pitch dark inside.

"Thank you," said H with a deep bow as he moved away. "I enjoyed it. The pictures were really lovely!"

To his relief, the man and woman were both smiling. Their annoyance had disappeared.

Encouraged by this, H resolved to come for another look the following day.

The next day Yoshiko wanted to go to the festival too, and asked H to take her, but he refused.

"No, you'd almost certainly get lost," he said, and went off to the shrine alone.

Without approaching the box immediately, H looked around from a distance for gullible-looking grownups. He kept himself half hidden behind a pillar of the shrine gateway, but the keen-eyed man on the box spotted him and without stopping his chant stretched out the hand holding the bamboo toward H, who shrank back.

To his surprise, however, the man was beckoning to him, signaling that it was all right for him to have a look. H made a gesture indicating that he had no money, but the man nodded as though to say, "Come on—it's okay."

Somewhat reassured, H, who'd never for a moment expected to get a free look just like that, decided he liked the man. Rather naively, he tended to feel well disposed toward anyone who did what he was hoping they'd do.

So, to his great satisfaction, he was able to see the whole show right from the beginning, which he hadn't done the day before. He'd have preferred, also, to see it not once but several times, but suppressed the wish, feeling guilty about asking.

Instead, he stood with his eyes fixed on the mouths of the couple up on the box as they chanted, imitating the words and inflections as they went along, all the while remembering the scenes he'd witnessed in the box and matching them with the words they were singing.

He ended up listening to the same thing five times through, till the man, exasperated, said to him in a Tokyo accent: "What grade are you in, son? If you're so fond of this stuff, why don't we take you back with us as an apprentice?"

This scared H a bit, and he slipped away from the box when they weren't looking. He'd just remembered one of the local housewives saying that people operating this sort of booth sometimes ran off with children.

Back home, he checked to make sure his mother was out at church, then privately told his father—who wouldn't, he judged, get angry—about the man with a Tokyo accent and the wonderful box he'd looked inside.

"That's what they call a 'puppet peepshow,'" his father explained. "They have the same thing in these parts, too, but if the man had a Tokyo accent, I suppose he came from there. I read something in the paper quite a while ago saying that all sideshows are being banned from the grounds of the Yasukuni Shrine in Tokyo as inappropriate at 'a time of crisis' like this, so I imagine they've been shut out of shrines in Tokyo and are traveling around the country giving local performances instead, and came to Kobe on the way. What sort of play were they doing?"

H, who hadn't understood the story properly, said, "There was a big fire and a woman in a kimono on top of a lookout tower. Then she got arrested and was hung up on a cross and killed." He accompanied his explanation with an imitation of the showman's voice as he remembered it, beating time as he sang by rapping the table with the wooden measure his father used. Though he could only do the very first part, it was enough to give the feeling of the "puppet peepshow."

Before long his father, who had been watching his son singing away, broke in with a scandalized expression: "That's from the play *Oshichi the Greengrocer's Daughter*, but do you know what the words mean? They're about indecent things—you'd better not sing it in front of other people."

"What's indecent?" asked H. "What's it about—tell me!" He pressed so hard that his father was obliged to tell him the meaning of each phrase as he sang.

H was astonished to find that the story was about something that actually happened long ago, in the days when Tokyo was called Edo. At the time of a great fire in the city, Oshichi, daughter of a greengrocer, had taken refuge in a nearby temple, where she had fallen in love with a handsome young priest. When she finally returned home and the two were separated, she was so frustrated that she conceived the idea of setting a fire deliberately so that she could meet her lover again. There was a great conflagration, but unfortunately her part in it was exposed and she was put to death.

H went on with his recitation until he got to a part that said, "Long eggplants she liked, and corncobs hairy from base to tip—let's burn down the greengrocer's again, then," whereupon his father stopped him.

"That's enough!" he said, but H asked cheerfully:

"So this greengrocer's daughter—she was fond of eggplants and sweet corn, was she?"

His father hesitated for a moment, looking embarrassed, then said:

"It's got another meaning—one that's indecent. That's why I said you shouldn't sing it. Particularly in front of your mother. And you mustn't sing it at school, either. Peepshows are for adults."

H couldn't see what was "indecent" about eggplants and corncobs, but the unusually stern look on his father's face stopped him from pressing the point. Even so, he permitted himself to say, with as much reproach as possible:

"There were lenses for *children* to look through in the peepshow box."

"Those are for children with their parents."

It wasn't like his father to give such a lame explanation; he must be off form today, thought H, changing the subject. "Mum says that even the *kamishibai*, which all the other kids watch, isn't good for me, and she won't give me the money. It's awkward for me. She won't give me any pocket money to buy *oyatsu* with, either."

Every day when the time came for the children's *oyatsu*—the afternoon snack supposed to keep them going until suppertime—Toshiko gave each of them an aluminum plate with a few sweets on it. Her attitude was that since the children had everything necessary bought for them by their parents, there was no need to give them pocket money, and that it was through using pocket money as they pleased that children "went to the dogs."

"There's no need for you to go buying unhygienic things at the sweetshop," she said. "If there's some special kind you want, tell me and I'll get it for you."

Quite unconvinced, H would slam the aluminum plate down on the table in a fit of peevish exasperation, so that by now it was dented all over. Yoshiko's plate, however, had no dents on it at all—you could easily tell which was which. His mother was aware that H wasn't happy with her policy, but stuck to it all the same.

So H, swearing his sister to secrecy, would furtively slip the sweets from his plate into his trouser pocket, then trade them later with his friends. The method he used was to go with the others to the sweetshop, get them to buy the things he wanted, then swap his own for them.

These transactions were of mutual benefit. His friends liked the sweets they got from H because, though the quantities might be small —a piece of chocolate in silver paper, three fruit drops, a few peanuts, a couple of biscuits—they were different from the kind of things they sold at the sweetshop. And H, on his side, was free to choose from any of the shop's array of goods, whether the peppermint-flavored sweets known as "bombs," or sugar cigarettes, or the rice-and-millet cakes covered with brown sugar.

Much to his annoyance, though, he just couldn't get to see the *kamishibai*.

The sound of the wooden clappers announcing the arrival of the *kamishibai* man, with the miniature "theater" whose scenes he changed as he recited his stories, always came at about four o'clock and immediately put him on edge. As the click-clacking noise went on its round of the neighborhood, the local children would dash out of their homes and assemble on the vacant lot in the alley. H ran out after them, but never managed to get close to the bicycle on which the *kamishibai* was mounted.

The elderly man would unlock the drawer of the box on the luggage rack and sell candy from it to the children. Having no money to buy anything, H would conceal himself behind a stack of shelves lined with pots of flowers that stood in front of a nearby house, and wait for the show to begin. Usually, though, the man noticed him and drove him away as if he were a dog.

"Oy," he'd shout, with exaggerated gestures, "buzz off! There's no

45

watching for free. If you want to watch, go and get some money from your mother." But H would refuse to give up, and managed to watch from a distance by dint of stretching himself to his full height.

After all, how could he enjoy a proper conversation with his friends unless he knew the plots of "Golden Kite," "Wonderman White Hood," and so on?...

Pocket money—that was what he really needed. Once in the past he'd tried fiddling the change when he'd been sent shopping, but had been found out and given a dressing-down by his mother, who forced him to say a prayer asking God's forgiveness.

Toshiko, who kept an ever-vigilant eye on the cash, knew immediately if so much as a sen was missing. To complicate matters, the drawer in which she kept her purse was made so as to give a loud *ping* whenever it was opened or shut, so theft was out of the question.

"I need some pocket money," complained H one day. "I want to pay for the *kamishibai* so I can watch it from the *front*."

This seemed to remind his father of something suddenly, because he said, "Would you go and buy me a couple of packets of starch?" and handed him eight sen.

Puzzled as to what should have set his father off on this line, and what connection there was between starch and pocket money, H set out nevertheless with a small bucket dangling at his side.

Starch was used in tailoring—for example, when sewing the lining of a suit—and they always bought commercial starch for the purpose at a shop run by a Mr. Odawara at Futaba-cho 5-chome, eight blocks away. It was H's regular task to go and get it.

The starch shop, a small establishment with a street front only three meters or so wide, made and sold nothing but starch—or "paste," according to the use to which it was put. There were various kinds, some runny, some stiff, depending on the trade: the starch used in fulling kimonos, the starch used in dry cleaning, the paste used by makers of paper lanterns, and so on. What H bought was a rather stiff kind, and there were lumps of it floating like tofu in a tub of water standing in front of the glass doors of the shop. It differed from tofu, though, in the semi-spherical shape imposed on it by the rice bowl they used as a mold.

The reason why H had to go to the starch shop almost every week

46

was that the paste there didn't contain preservative, and went moldy if you bought too much at a time.

When H got back, his father surprised him by saying: "You got two pieces, right? Then I'll lend you one of them till next week. I want it back, mind you. One of these pieces costs four sen, but a small bottle of the paste they use in handicrafts classes at school costs eight, doesn't it? How many bottlesful d'you think you'd get from one piece of this starch?"

"Four," answered H, catching on at once. He himself, in fact, always put some of the starch from his father's workplace in an empty gum bottle to take to school.

H was hugely impressed by this clever idea.

"This is strictly between ourselves, mind," his father said with a smile.

The next day, in the classroom, H told his friends: "I can give you a good bargain in paste tomorrow. The bottled stuff costs eight sen, but you can buy it from me for *two*."

"How's that?"

"I'm letting you have some of the commercial stuff specially. If you get eight sen from your father and spend two sen from it, that's six sen left. You can use that as pocket money. But I warn you, there's only enough two-sen paste for four of you, so it's first come first served."

This immediately prompted six boys to ask him to keep some for them, and he had to get them to do "paper-scissors-stone" for it.

"It's cheap, but that means you mustn't tell your parents or the teachers about it. If they found out, that'd be the end of it."

Next day in the handicrafts class, the boys who'd bought starch from H showed it proudly to their other friends, boasting about how cheap it was.

H's paste was a popular success. He gave his father back the money for the first piece and bought some more for the next batch of orders out of the remaining money.

"What d'you expect?" he told one boy who complained that his paste had gone moldy. "It's not the same as the expensive bottled paste that never goes bad. But if you take the lid off the bottle and put it in water, it'll last for a couple of weeks. What's wrong, anyway—you made six sen, didn't you? You don't *have* to buy it if you don't want to!"

For all his tough stance, though, the amount of paste they used in a

47

handicrafts class wasn't all that large and the less experienced of the boys had a job stopping their leftover paste from going bad. So H gave them a piece of rather unscrupulous advice:

"You'll have to tell them you used it all up in class, and get them to give you the money for some more."

The boys who bought from him made six sen clear every time, so it was a good deal on both sides. H's two-sen paste business expanded at an unexpectedly steady rate. At first he had divided one piece of starch into four, but the following week he bought three pieces, which gave him twelve batches to sell. The week after that, it doubled again. Accepting orders the day before a handicrafts class was due, he had quite a job going to buy the stuff without being seen by his mother, but he persevered.

In another way, too, it was hard work earning his pocket money. Since the trading took place in the classroom, he had to be careful not to get caught by the teacher, and to distribute fruit drops, filched from the cupboard at home, as a way of persuading his classmates who didn't buy any paste not to give him away. It was all worth the trouble, though, for in one month, much to H's satisfaction, his income came to over two yen fifty sen.

His father hadn't given him a single sen in pocket money, but he'd taught him a way of making an independent income, and cooperated in various other ways as well, such as keeping the bucket with which he'd gone to buy starch the day before hidden beneath the veranda.

Armed for the first time with his own money, H bought the *kamishibai* man's candy and watched in state from the very front.

In the same way, to be able to drop in on the way home from the bathhouse and buy a water ice or the kind of filled pancake known as *nikuten* gave him a delicious sense of extravagance.

Privately he resolved that next year his activities would include watching the peepshow as a paying customer.

One day, though, Ikuo, the kid from the charcoal store, who was a year older than H, startled him by saying in a grownup kind of voice, "We'll keep quiet about it for you, but if talk gets around and your mother gets to hear of it, you'll be in for it! You know, they always say that it's when people notice he's getting too free with his money that a thief gets caught."

It shocked H to hear himself being compared to a thief, but he saw the danger. From then on, he decided to be careful not to spend money in too conspicuous a way.

To start with, he changed the place he hid his money from a drawer in his desk to a spot in the back alleyway where no one would ever find it. This was a hole behind a removable brick in the wall behind a shop selling sticky rice-cakes two houses up the street, near the trap-door where the men with the honey-buckets came to haul up the waste from the household toilet, and he'd used it in the past to hide marbles and other things in. Being close to somewhere smelly and dirty, it made the ideal safe, and no one else had ever noticed its existence.

Although H had at last found a way of providing his own pocket money, he was still a little uneasy, since something told him that the trade in two-sen paste wasn't going to last forever.

In handicrafts classes for fourth-grade pupils, they used cardboard to make pencil boxes, postcard boxes and the like, but in fifth grade they would be shifting to woodwork, sawing up and planing boards to make things such as bookstands.

If that happened, H wouldn't be able to rely indefinitely on two-sen paste as a source of income.

"Business isn't all smooth sailing," he told himself. "It has its downs as well as its ups."

6

Maps and Eggs

H was running, his school bag on his back, fighting the desire to pee. Grimly holding on, he ran at top speed, faster than he'd ever run at a school sports meeting, so that the contents of his pencil case rattled fiercely. He really should have gone at school, he told himself regretfully.

He *had* gone into the toilet, actually, only to find it full for once. Confronted with the backs of a row of figures facing the urinals, he'd given up and hurried out of the school gates thinking he could bear it till he got home.

On the way, he passed a classmate peeing against a utility pole. It must be nice just to let go like that, he thought enviously; but he held out, because he'd been strictly forbidden by his mother to urinate by the roadside.

Finally arriving home, he flung down his satchel and would have dashed straight into the toilet if the door hadn't been firmly shut. He rapped on it smartly.

"Hold on," came his sister's voice. "I'll be out in a moment."

He waited, but she didn't emerge.

"*That's not a moment!*" he shouted, unable to hold out any longer.

He would have to pee into the yard from the veranda.

Feeling a bit guilty about this, since the yard was covered in concrete, he was in such a hurry that he couldn't get his willy out at once. Then, when the flow finally began, it somehow lacked power and didn't reach far.

And at that point, he woke with a start.

He'd done it again. His underpants were wet. If only he'd woken a bit earlier he'd have been in time, he thought ruefully.

Although he was in fourth grade by now, he still wet his bed regularly once or even twice a night.

His little sister Yoshiko, on the other hand, had never wet the bed even when she was small. The contrast between them was a source of guilt and despondency for H.

The family always slept in two beds, H between the same quilts as his father and Yoshiko with her mother, but the two pairs lay with their heads on opposite sides of the room, away from the center. This was sensible, because when winter came, they could all sleep with their feet in the *kotatsu* in the middle.

H's head was on the side of the corridor. It was a bit chilly there in the cold season, so he would stand a small folding screen by his head to keep out the draft.

Ironically enough, this chilly spot was ideal for H, since it was the nearest place in the house to the toilet.

Even so, there was no point in being close to the toilet unless he felt the urge and got up. In most cases when he woke up in the night, the damage would already be done. When H realized this and started fidgeting about, it usually woke his father who was sleeping next to him.

To put out a set of fresh futons would mean making a noise which might wake up his mother and little sister, so emergency measures were applied instead. These involved a thin, square pad about half the size of a tatami which they referred to as "the map-hider" and which was placed over the wet patch. The pad had been specially made by Toshiko by folding an old blanket into several layers and sewing them together.

Not that it made H any happier about making a toilet of his futon. If things went on like this, he told himself, he wouldn't even be able to go to middle school in three years' time.

He always did his best to wake up somehow or other of his own accord so that he could relieve himself in a fully conscious state, but this was easier said than done.

One night, he felt the urge, woke up with a start, then with a glance at his father sleeping next to him, got up and made his way to the toilet. On his way in he met Yoshiko coming out.

"Oh—you woke up?" she exclaimed, and he told her, "Yup, it's okay." Then, having made sure that he was in fact wide awake, he let go—triumphantly, for once—and found to his dismay that he was still inside the futon.

What had depressed him most at the time was his own inability to tell how far he was dreaming and how far awake. The idea worried him that if he went on being unable to trust himself he might end up going funny in the head.

His little sister's frequent appearance in his dreams was probably an effect of his inferiority complex. Not that she had ever made fun of him; on the contrary, her brother's bed-wetting seemed, if anything, to distress her.

The one bright spot for H was that his parents didn't complain or give him lectures about his bed-wetting. The family didn't pretend it didn't happen, but they were careful at the same time not to make it a subject of conversation. One sign of this was that they didn't use the word "bed-wetting" but referred instead to "map-making."

It was Yoshiko who'd first used the expression. She'd been of kindergarten age when she'd seen the wet patch on H's futon and said "It's like a map!"

"Right—I've been map-making while I was asleep," H said with a smile of relief.

From that time on, "map-making" took the place of "bed-wetting" in the family, but the change did little to alleviate his sense of shame.

He tried not drinking anything before going to bed and getting his father to shake him awake from time to time, but nothing seemed to help much.

In summer when he was in third grade, when he went to stay with Aunt Minoru—his mother's younger sister who'd married a man in the village of Kumano in Hiroshima prefecture—he wet his bed just the same.

There were five children, the eldest called Noriyuki, in his aunt's family, and he'd been so afraid of disgracing himself that, when they went to bed, he repeated to himself over and over again like an incantation: "You're not at home now, this is your cousins' place. If you feel you want to pee, you've got to get up straight away. You're not at home now!"

But when he woke up the next morning, the futon was wet. The discovery gave him a bad fright. Hastily, he folded up his bedding and thrust it into the closet, hoping to pass it off somehow. Just then his aunt came into the room. He gave a guilty start, but she exclaimed "Now, there's a good boy for you—puts his own futon away!" She turned to the other children. "You should follow his example," she said.

H broke out in a cold sweat.

He'd originally been going to stay for two nights, but decided on the spur of the moment to change his plans and take the afternoon bus that day back to his grandmother's.

His aunt tried to make him stay longer. "But I thought you were going to stay another day and have someone come to fetch you," she said.

"I got here by myself, so I can get back as well," said H. "Fukuyama's the terminus, so all I have to do is stay on the bus."

Even now, he still remembered how sorry and ashamed he'd felt as he looked back at his aunt and cousins who'd come with him to the bus stop and stood waving until the bus was out of sight.

Even though he had plenty of troubles in his own young way, H always assumed an unconcerned expression, as though he hadn't a care in the world. So even when confronted with the latest stain on his futon he'd pretend to take it lightly, saying something like "Today's map looks like America." In fact, though, he felt utterly miserable.

On mornings after he'd disgraced himself, he would wash the map part of the futon as best he could, then fold it up, put it on his head, and carry it upstairs to the drying platform. Before spreading it out to dry on the wooden railing, he'd make a very careful survey of his surroundings in case he should be seen hanging stained bedding out to dry by Mitchan, daughter of the family in the house at the back.

Being rather fond of Michiko Sugai—which was "Mitchan's" full name—H was most unwilling that she should discover his secret.

Her home, on the other side of the alley behind theirs, was a single-story house, so you looked down on it from the drying platform of H's place. However, since it wasn't directly behind but one house to the side, you couldn't see the whole of their back garden, only the part of it close to the toilet.

The effect of this was that, if the "map" was not to be visible from Mitchan's house, you had to keep it away from the center of the platform and close up against the pillar on the north side. That way, it was possible to keep it out of sight of anyone in Mitchan's home.

H's mother, though, objected to this way of drying the futon, since it got the sun and the breeze better in the center.

Before he left for school, H would surreptitiously go upstairs again to make sure the futon hadn't changed position; sometimes, if he didn't keep his eyes open, his mother would have switched the futon to the center.

One day, he found it had again moved to the center from the place where he'd so carefully put it. Muttering with annoyance at his mother's stubbornness, he hauled up the futon prior to shifting it back again, but as he did so, it slipped out of his hands and flopped down into the back garden. As it fell it must have taken with it a washbasin hung on the wall outside, for there was a startling clatter, perfectly audible to all the neighbors.

"What are you up to?" his mother called in a loud voice from downstairs.

H was appalled: Mitchan, who had just come out of the toilet and was washing her hands, had looked up, startled at the sudden crash. To make matters worse, their eyes met. It was most unlikely that she'd seen the futon with the map on it falling, but for some reason the fact that their eyes met threw H into a panic of shame.

Every morning recently he'd been accompanying Mitchan on her way to school, pretending that their paths had crossed by chance, but from that day on he couldn't bring himself to walk beside her.

After the incident, Mitchan had almost certainly looked up at the drying platform across the alley and discovered H's secret. The idea was agony to him.

And in this rather peculiar way H's first love affair came to an end....

H was ready to do anything to cure his bed-wetting.

One day his mother, who must have been talking about it to somebody, said to him, "They say there's a doctor in Kakogawa who's a specialist at curing bed-wetting and diarrhea with moxibustion. Shall we give him a try?"

She'd been expecting H to object, and his uncomplicated "Okay, let's," came as a surprise.

"It burns," she added, to make sure. "Do you think you can put up with it?"

"I'm fed up with map-making. I can put up with it if it'll really cure it." H meant what he said. As for his diarrhea, he didn't see how moxibustion could do any good, since it was caused by the odd things he ate from time to time, but about that he said nothing.

It was a long way to Kakogawa; it took the best part of an hour, even by train, so they decided to get all the visits over in the summer holidays, when he'd plenty of time.

H didn't like the talk of moxibustion, but he was happy at the prospect of riding on a train drawn by a steam locomotive rather than an electric train. The electric cars went as far as Akashi, but for Kakogawa, three stations further on, the only way, fortunately, was to take a proper train.

Getting off at Kakogawa Station, Toshiko and H left by the south exit and began walking. Following the road on the map they'd been given, they walked a little way along the main highway, then, turning off to the south, found themselves suddenly in a lonely lane between paddy fields.

H felt worried. "Do you really think a famous moxibustion doctor would live in a place like this?" he asked his mother.

"I wonder, too. Shall we have another look at the map?" Closing her parasol and handing it to H, Toshiko took the map out of the front of her kimono and, smoothing it out, had another look. "It looks all right to me," she said. "Yes—this is the right way." Putting her parasol up again, she started walking.

White cumulonimbus clouds were billowing up in the sky, and as they made their way along the path between the paddy fields under the blazing summer sun, the air was heavy with an almost stifling smell of vegetation.

After twenty minutes of walking, wiping the sweat away as they went, they finally reached their destination, which proved to be a straw-thatched farmhouse.

Chickens were running about in the front yard and moos were coming from a cowshed at the side of the house.

H was taken aback. Could this really be the place that was famous for moxibustion? To him, it smelled suspicious.

Stepping up into the house from the earthen-floored entrance, they were shown into a large room where a dozen or so people were sitting waiting their turn. There were old women and children among them, and they all looked as though they'd traveled a considerable distance to get there.

The comparative coolness inside the house was a relief, but it looked as though they'd have to wait some time before their turn came.

To pass the time, H picked up a magazine he found lying in the big room that served as a waiting room, glancing at his mother as he did so. Quietly, he turned the pages, but much to his delight she still said nothing.

He'd been afraid that even here she would enforce the usual ban on reading anything apart from the Bible, but he'd got away with it. He stretched out comfortably on the tatami to read. He could hardly believe that he was reading a magazine openly in front of her.

"The moxa may hurt, but I'm sure it'll cure you," Toshiko told him—and began to pray, right there in the waiting room. This wouldn't have mattered if she'd done it in silence, but she mumbled audibly, going on and on till H was thoroughly embarrassed.

The people around them watched Toshiko with astonished expressions, but as soon as she finished praying and opened her eyes they all hastily looked the other way.

After a wait of around an hour and a half, H's turn finally came. Toshiko and H were shown into a room at the back and seated themselves in front of an elderly gentleman with a beard who was referred to as "Doctor" and who demanded without any preliminaries:

"Bed-wetting?"

H felt offended. "Can you really cure it?" he asked.

"That depends on you how regularly you come and see me," the man replied pompously, and with a jerk of his bearded chin signaled to H to lie down on a split-bamboo mat spread on the tatami.

H was worried they might apply the moxa to the tip of his willy. Resigning himself, though, he was starting to take his underpants down when the "doctor," to his relief, said, "Hey—you don't have to take your pants off!"

They put little mounds of moxa in various places on his belly and legs and set fire to them. H tried to be brave, but it hurt so much that he wailed in pain.

"I'll treat you to an *oyako-don* for putting up with it so well," said his mother as they left.

They went into a noodle restaurant. Toshiko rarely gave the children a meal out, so going to a restaurant was a thrill in itself. Besides, this time it wasn't *tamago-don*, a bowl of rice topped with egg and trimmings, but *oyako-don*, which was more expensive—both egg *and* pieces of chicken on top of the rice—a reward of the first rank.

What was more, he didn't have to use a knife and fork here, but could shovel the rice into his mouth with chopsticks; his face was already beaming just at the thought of it.

When the *oyako-don* came, with the egg bright yellow on top of the white rice, they both exclaimed at the sight. Eggs were already getting scarce in those days. The rice was of good quality too, and eggs and chicken were both fresh, so they thoroughly enjoyed it.

Even so, H told himself, it was a pity they'd wasted such good eggs by cooking them till they were hard; it would have been much nicer if they'd put the bits of chicken in a fluffier and softer bed of egg.

Sometimes at home H would wield the frying pan himself and make an omelette that was still soft inside, just as he'd seen the cook in the kitchen of the French restaurant do it. The result always won praise; this had gone to his head and made him rather conceited where cooking was concerned.

"Can we buy some eggs when we leave? Let's," he pleaded. "I'm sure eggs like these would make a good omelette." Hearing them praised like this the woman, who apparently kept chickens at the back of her own house, was only too glad to fetch half a dozen eggs from the coop. Wrapping them in newspaper, she handed them over. The eggs were new-laid and still slightly warm.

"I'll hold them against me to keep them warm on the way home. Maybe we'll get some chicks," H said playfully.

"Be careful," his mother said, "—they'll break if you hold them too tight. And mind you don't fall over!"

But no sooner had she said it than H fell over on the station stairs, missing his footing because of the package he was busy holding in front of him.

57

To his dismay, a quick check revealed that the newspaper was already wet and two of the eggs were actually broken.

"Quick—suck it up before it's too late!" his mother cried. Hurriedly H took out one of the broken eggs and sucked at it. Toshiko herself pursed her lips and pressed them to the other, but the white dripped down from the egg and made the front of her kimono sticky. The other people waiting for the train smiled as they watched mother and son frantically sucking eggs; it was most embarrassing.

The following week, H wailed loudly again with the pain of the burning moxa and again followed his mother into the restaurant by the station.

"Hello—here we are again!" he said as they sat down at the table. "*Oyako-don*, the same as before, please." This time, though, since it looked as if they were going to have *oyako-don* here regularly from now on, he'd decided to come out with what he thought and, getting up, he barged his way into the kitchen at the back. The proprietress was surprised enough to see a child come in without a by-your-leave, but even more startled when the brat said:

"D'you think you could do the eggs a bit more light and soft, without letting them get hard? And it'd be nice if you could slice the leeks on the slope instead of just chopping them into long pieces."

"Well, now," the woman said with a smile, "*here's* a customer who's hard to please!" But she did the food as H had asked, and the result really was far better than before.

The next time, too, he duly cried during the treatment and was taken to have *oyako-don* at the usual place.

"Well, my lad," the woman told him as she came out from the back, "I made it as you said, and everybody praised it to the skies. I'm quite grateful to you—really I am."

"I know what I'll do," said H, getting a bit above himself: "I'll do a picture of *oyako-don* for you and bring it next time. Why don't you put it up in the shop?"

When he got home he did a picture of a bowl of *oyako-don* in crayon on drawing paper. He couldn't help feeling proud of the yolk of the egg, which looked quite appetizing.

The next time they went to Kakogawa, he dropped in at the restaurant as soon as they left the station and gave them the picture. "We'll come in again on the way back," he said.

On their return journey they called in at the shop as usual and ordered *oyako-don*.

"I must say, the picture's well done," the woman said. "I'm sure I'll get more orders for *oyako-don* when I put it up in the shop. So today it's on me. You don't have to pay."

"Oh, but I couldn't let you do *that*," Toshiko protested noisily, "not just for a picture by a child!" She continued to resist quite strongly, but the woman won out in the end and gave them their meal for free, as she'd promised.

So a single picture had turned itself into two bowls of *oyako-don*, which was an improvement on selling two-sen paste. And suddenly an idea occurred to H—*this* was what he'd do from now on. If only he could sell his pictures, then he'd do as many as people wanted!

The summer holidays came to an end, but every Saturday for another month they made the trip to the moxibustion clinic in Kakogawa. Every time H wailed his head off, and every time they had *oyako-don* at the same restaurant.

H put up with the pain seven times within two months, but the claims for this particular treatment in stopping bed-wetting proved, in the end, to be pure invention. For long after that, poor H went on "making maps" on his futon.

7

Love

It was a week since the notice, written with a brush in black ink on a largish sheet of paper, had been pasted up on the glass window of the shop front: "Wanted—Apprentice in the Tailoring Trade."

Toshiko had written it. H's father never wrote anything himself—his handwriting was too awful, he said—so all letters, forms to be submitted to the local ward office and so on, were done by her.

Toshiko was far more fluent than Morio where the spoken word was concerned, too. The neighbors and members of the congregation at their church would all have described Morio as a mild man of few words. In H's view, though, the right phrase wasn't "few" words but "just the right number"; his mother got on his nerves she talked so much.

"About the apprentice-wanted notice," Toshiko had said: "Don't you think it would be better to say, 'Wanted: cheerful young man, in good mental and physical health …'?"

"No, I don't," Morio had replied. "So long as he wants to be a tailor, that's good enough for me." With which H heartily agreed.

The reason for this sudden posting of a "situation vacant" notice was that the previous live-in apprentice, Junji Miyamoto, was leaving to start a business of his own. "Jun," as the family had called him, had been conscripted into the army during his apprenticeship, then sent home again on account of poor health. Because he was already past thirty, Morio felt, apparently, that he should be allowed to go independent. Toshiko was rather disgruntled at the idea of letting him quit a year and a half before his term was up, but Morio insisted they should do as Jun himself wanted.

H had been sorry to lose Jun, but by now he was more interested in who was going to apply for the job next. So the first thing he did when he got home from school was ask whether anybody had applied that day. On the third day after they put up the notice, a man turned up who said he had some experience in tailoring, but he just glanced around the shop, asked something about the salary, and promptly left again. The impression was of someone already in a job who was on the lookout for a new and better-paying one. "He's not the sort of person we're looking for," said Morio.

H was there when a young man turned up late the following afternoon, so he saw him for himself.

He was tall, built like a baseball player. H's father was slight and unusually short, barely over 150 centimeters. tall, which made the young man look enormous.

These were the only two who came in the first week. It suggested to H that there couldn't be many people who wanted to be tailors, but Morio said that on the contrary he hadn't expected so many.

H took this opportunity to tell his father: "I don't want to be a tailor myself, I'm afraid. I'd hate to work sitting in the house all day." What he wanted to be was a waiter at Pierre's place in Sannomiya, or a cook at Mr. Chin's Heiwaro restaurant. The reason was extremely simple: that way, he thought, he'd be able to eat all kinds of nice food.

"If you think waiters get to eat everything served in their restaurants, you're wrong," said his father when he heard this.

"But they know all about the food, don't they? I don't think they'd know so much if they hadn't had it themselves."

"They've had it, perhaps, but only a bit of each kind—as part of the job, not for pleasure. If you want to eat things properly, you'll have to wait till you're grown up and can go to these places as a customer."

That wasn't quite what H had had in mind, but he didn't pursue the subject further; he wasn't sure any longer.

"You don't have to make up your mind now, do you?" his father went on. "You'd better give it some proper thought around the time you leave middle school. And another thing—you'd better not tell your mother now that you don't want to be a tailor."

H thought about it, and decided to keep it to himself.

One day about ten days after they'd started looking for an apprentice,

H came home from school to find his parents discussing whether to take the notice down or not.

Toshiko agreed to the idea, and had just started to pull it down when a young man shot by outside the window on a bicycle, peering into the house as he went.

"The same man was looking at the notice as he went past yesterday," said H. "I remember him." At that moment the man came coasting back again and this time stopped in front of the house and got off.

"I think somebody's come about the job," H called to his father, and stood waiting for the glass door at the entrance to open.

The young man who opened it and came into the entrance hall had a bad leg, and his body tilted sharply to one side at every step.

"I've been past several times and seen the notice," he began shyly.

Toshiko came out from the room at the back and greeted him. As she did so, she noticed that he couldn't straighten one leg, and looked momentarily dismayed.

Morio, though, proceeded to question him quite unconcernedly. "Sit down and try moving your good leg as if you were at the machine," he said straightforwardly. "How do you sit when you're sitting on tatami?"

In the end, they got him to write down his address and sent him away saying they'd let him know by postcard the day after next.

After supper that night H's mother and father had a dispute over which of the two applicants to take, the tall boy or the one with the bad leg. It was the first time H had seen them so at odds.

"Being a tailor isn't just sewing," Toshiko said. "He has to go to people's houses for fittings and to go around visiting customers. Surely a bad leg would be a handicap?"

Privately, H thoroughly agreed with her. Jun, the young man who was leaving them, was a good swimmer. He'd often played at "Urashima Taro" with H, diving into the sea with him on his back just like the turtle in the fairy tale who'd carried the hero down to the sea king's palace. Sometimes he'd play catchball with him too. So H personally was hoping they'd take the second fellow, who was even bigger than Jun.

"I think we should take the tall one," Toshiko said. For once, H thought, his mother was right. But his father had different ideas.

"With a healthy fellow, there are any number of different jobs he can do. Besides, you never know when a young man who's physically fit is going to be called up. Anybody who really wants to can be a tailor, even if he's not fit enough to be a soldier. It was because I was so small that I got the idea of being one myself. And what kept me at it was the feeling that even somebody like me could earn a living making clothes. I think we should have the boy with the bad leg. It won't stop him from becoming a tailor. I'll see that he makes a good one."

H was a bit disappointed, but resigned himself to defeat. He could appreciate what his father said.

He'd never heard him speak his own mind so clearly before, either. Yoshiko too, small though she still was, must have felt the same way as her father, for she chimed in, "I think so too!"

In the end, Toshiko was prevailed upon and they decided to take on the lame young man.

"It's 'love' that's behind it, isn't it?" she told her husband. "I can tell!"

"Come off it!" said Morio with a sheepish grin.

The apprentice, who was due to start in four days' time, was called Shigeo Yoshimoto, and it was decided they should call him Shige-san.

Shige-san's home was in Noda-cho 8-chome, only three blocks or so away. He could come by bike in less than five minutes, so he was to live out, going back home for his meals.

When Shige left that day, H followed him on his bike until they reached his place, where a middle-aged woman who must have been Shige's mother came out and bowing politely to H said, "Thank you—I hope you'll make something of him." Startled, H fled back home.

He was going to tell his parents about it at suppertime, but kept quiet; his mother, he was sure, would only want to know why the woman hadn't come to pay her respects properly to *them*.

The thought reminded him that perhaps he himself ought to go and see Mr. Chin at the Heiwaro restaurant and tell him politely that he wouldn't be coming to his place after all. He remembered that Mr. Chin had said to him, "You come work at Heiwaro, eh? Me teach you cook, very nice job." But H had only grunted noncommittally.

By now he'd begun to feel that to be a waiter in a Western-style restaurant might be rather better than being a cook in a Chinese place, but he was reluctant to tell Mr. Chin outright because he was sometimes given little parcels of unusual Chinese snacks to take home.

H decided that the next time his father went to Heiwaro for a fitting, he'd go with him and say that he'd make up his mind later, when he grew up, and that Mr. Chin wasn't to count on him. He really ought to do this, he told himself, even if it meant no more little parcels.

A couple of weeks later, when he went with his father to call on Mr. Chin, he plucked up courage and told him.

Chin laughed and slapped him on the shoulder. "That all? Don't worry—I can wait you grow up to make up mind. But I wonder I still be in Kobe. I mean, Kobe my home, but …"

H got the point immediately. Japan was at war with China, and there were people who called them "Chinks" to their faces or told them, "You're an enemy—go home, go back to China!" It occurred to him that Mr. Chin himself must have been called a Chink sometimes, and probably had to deal with lots of other unpleasant things too.

"There were Chinese people living in the foreign quarter and the Motomachi area a long, long time before we ever came to Kobe," he remembered his father telling him. And in H's home at least, they never said "Chinks."

"*I* don't think you're a Chink, Mr. Chin," he told him outright. "It makes me mad, the way the veterans association man and the rest of them keep talking about Chinks. I *respect* you, I think you're *much* better than them."

Mr. Chin looked taken aback for a moment, then said "Thank you." His voice was quieter than usual, and H wondered uneasily if he'd said something he shouldn't have.

Out in the street again, he asked his father if he'd said something wrong. "I'm sure Chin was surprised," Morio said, "but I don't think it matters: you just said what you really felt. Still, I expect most people would think it was a bit strange of you. You'd better keep that in mind."

Hearing this confirmed something he'd already heard about his family—that they were "a queer lot." "They're a queer lot at the tailor's," he knew people had been saying, "they've let a room to a *Chosen*!"

For a while, about six months earlier, they had in fact rented out a room to someone from Korea. It was someone Toshiko had got to know through an acquaintance, and they'd let him have the eight-mat room upstairs.

He worked in the market, and his real name was Kim, but he always called himself Kaneda. At that time, all Koreans in Japan were obliged to use Japanese-style names.

"Koreans never used to change their surnames," his father said, "not even women when they got married, so they must hate it now they have to call themselves by Japanese names."

It was no wonder people thought they were "queer," to take in a lodger who belonged to a social group that was generally despised and discriminated against in various ways.

Kaneda hadn't been with them for three days before word got around the neighborhood. Their immediate neighbors seemed to be fairly tolerant of "those Senohs," but a group of wives in nearby 7-chome were whispering among themselves. H had heard them himself: "There are districts for Koreans in Karumo-dori and Higashi-Shiriike—why do they have to rent a room to one of them *here?*"

"Yes, they're a queer lot, those Amens."

Thanks to things like this, H had realized for quite a while now that his family wasn't an ordinary one.

In letting a room to a Korean, Toshiko had been influenced by the missionary, Mrs. Staples. Mrs. Staples had once told them in church, "Human beings should never discriminate against one another. It says so in the American Constitution, for example, but white people still discriminate against black people. It's a very sad thing. The effort to eliminate such behavior is the first step toward true 'love.'"

H had been a child of four at the time, and all he remembered of Mrs. Staples was being picked up and held in her arms, nothing else. But time and again he'd heard his mother say reminiscently, "'Discrimination is wrong,' Mrs. Staples used to say. 'Love knows no boundaries or race.'"

Kaneda-san, he thought, must have a hard time keeping quiet and controlling his temper when he was always being discriminated against as a *Chosen*. He was a man of few words, who on returning home from work in the evening would immediately disappear upstairs, coming down again only for a visit to the toilet before going to bed.

One day, H caught him as he came down and asked him why he didn't object to being called a *Chosen*. Kaneda gave a slight smile. "Well, I *am* a Korean, so it can't be helped. If every little thing annoyed

65

me, there'd be nowhere for me to live anywhere in Japan."

When H told his mother this, she said, "Kaneda-san is a fine man. He behaves like a good Christian, the way he 'turns the other cheek' and forgives those who mistreat him. That kind of person goes straight to Heaven.... I must talk to him more about the love of Christ." And she went upstairs with a Bible.

"It bothers me," said Morio as though to himself, "the way she talks about Christianity to anyone and everyone." Hearing him, H wished he hadn't spoken out.

But although the members of his own family felt no prejudice at all where Kaneda was concerned, there was just one thing that H found hard to take. This was the way Kaneda would come downstairs at breakfast holding a one-liter saké bottle with the urine he'd produced during the night slopping about noisily inside.

"You should tell him we don't like seeing that bottle at breakfast time," H complained.

"There's no toilet upstairs, so it can't really be helped," his mother countered. "He doesn't like to come downstairs in the night when we're all asleep. It just happens at breakfast because he has to go to work and there's no other time, so we'd better put up with it."

But three months later Kaneda left.

There'd been a rather embarrassing episode.

H had come back from school and was taking off his school bag when he heard his mother upstairs saying loudly, "Why? You shouldn't do that kind of thing!"

His father was out, having gone to Sannomiya on business, and Jun was pedaling the sewing machine.

Startled, H ran upstairs to find Kaneda and his mother sitting staring at each other angrily.

"What happened? What's Kaneda-san done?" H asked.

"I haven't done anything!" Kaneda said. "Look," he said to Toshiko, "now even the boy thinks I did something wrong. I admit I may have got the wrong idea for a moment, and I apologize. Even so, you know, *anybody* would get the wrong idea with you going on about love the whole time every day."

"Of course I do!" snapped Toshiko. "God tells us to 'love one another,' doesn't He? 'Love' is what the Bible 'goes on about' all the time. Chapter sixteen, verse fourteen of the First Epistle to the Corinthians, for example: "Let all things be done with love."

H understood the situation at once, having himself got into trouble once on account of the word "love."

When he was in second grade a girl called Kimi-chan had given him a rice-cracker, so in return the next day he'd given her, wrapped in paper, a pretty, purplish-colored shell he'd picked up on the beach.

"Are you sweet on Kimi-chan then?" asked his friends, who'd seen this.

"Yes, I love her," he replied. There was an immediate burst of laughter, and little Kimi-chan had started crying. It was then that he'd first realized vaguely that the word "love" as used in church and in his home was different from what other people meant by it.

The Bible might say "love thine enemy," but you had to explain it quite carefully or people misunderstood. This was something he'd realized at the movies, when a man and a woman who'd fallen for each other had said, not "I like you," but "I love you." In the same way, something had clicked again in his mind now: poor Kaneda had mixed up biblical love and the kind you got in the movies.

Anyway, it must have embarrassed their lodger, because he left them not long after that.

H was relieved at not having to hear the saké bottle go slip-slop any longer; but he didn't say so to his mother, in case he was told it showed a "lack of love" on his part.

It wasn't that he felt she was wrong to talk about "loving one another," but he did think she ought to be more careful.

For him, "love" was mixed up in his memory with a bad shock he'd had soon after entering primary school. One day, just when he'd been feeling particularly happy at finding himself a first-grader, he'd been surrounded by a group of other boys who said to him, "Your family are Amens, aren't they? You people are supposed to love your enemies, right? So you love Chinks, do you?"

Frightened, H was so keen to get away that he blurted out tearfully, "I'm not a Chink-lover. I don't love them. I *hate* Chinks!"

The incident continued to bother his conscience long after that, to the extent that when he went out of his way to tell Mr. Chin that he didn't think of him as a Chink, he'd almost added "because I love you."

He'd suppressed the impulse, though; it would only have startled him.

H had therefore decided to be careful about that word "love": it would be much safer just to assume that it wouldn't get across to anyone other than the members of their church.

"I wonder why he left? He was in an awful hurry," H's father said in a troubled voice after Kaneda had gone. "Do you think the neighbors said something to upset him?"

But H kept quiet about the real reason for his departure. Somehow, he felt that was wiser.

After the Kaneda episode H sometimes told his mother, "It's all right to love people as long as you're careful how you go about it. If you talk about love to anyone and everyone, they may get you wrong."

But Toshiko's enthusiasm for passing on the "love of Christ" remained undiminished, and continued from time to time to cause trouble.

8

A Boy and the Sea

The seashore was H's playground. The beach, the sea itself—everything belonged to him and his friends. If he just wanted to swim, he had only to walk westward from his home and through the grounds of the Rising Sun refinery to the coast at Suma.

The children were particularly keen on the Suma beach because it was spacious and the sand was clean.

Occasionally they couldn't take the path through the oil company's grounds because the gates were shut, but most of the time they were open. Even so, you couldn't get near the oil tanks themselves, since the area where they stood in rows was sealed off behind a wire-netting fence.

H and his friends would gaze up at the huge tanks as they walked through the densely overgrown, tall summer grasses of the path beside the fence. This shortcut to Suma was more or less their own private route, seldom used by grownups.

At times when the gates were closed, H bathed on the beach near his home. The Honjo-machi beach, only three hundred meters from his house, was literally his "own" sea.

On the local beaches there were all kinds of things to do besides swimming. On one occasion they'd made some salt. Once when H was in third grade, he'd got off at Akoo, on the way to Hiroshima where his parents' homes were, and had seen salt being made at the salt beds, so afterward he'd suggested to his friends that they should try making it themselves. It took a lot of time and firewood to boil down seawater in an iron pot, but they finally succeeded in producing a strongly salty liquid.

"This is what's known as *kansui*," explained H in a self-consciously didactic tone. "All you have to do now is dry it in the sun."

So they put the solution to dry in the sun.

The substance that resulted was quite different from the salt they were familiar with—sticky and a funny pinkish color. They tasted it: it was salty, sure enough, but horribly bitter too, and no one would believe it was the real thing.

The pinkish color, H learned later, was due to rust from the iron pot, and the bitterness was because they hadn't removed the bittern. H was all for repeating the experiment, but his friends deserted him so he gave up the idea.

By the water's edge there stood a concrete kelp-processing shed. On the beach around the building were lots of drying racks, made with horizontal bamboo poles, on which the seaweed was put to dry. It had already been flavored for use in sushi, and on fine days gave off a sweetish smell as it streamed out in the breeze.

H and his friends would crawl up to the racks out of sight of the man in the shed, pull down pieces of kelp, brush off the sand and eat them. The thrill of having stolen them somehow enhanced the flavor, so that they seemed like a real delicacy. If the boys got caught, though, they risked a crack on the skull, hard enough to make them see stars, with a bamboo pole.

H particularly enjoyed the summer evenings. During the holidays they were allowed to stay up until quite late without being told off, so after supper the boys would leave home on the pretext of fishing for conger eels and gather on the beach. There, after going through the motions of casting their lines out to sea for a while, they'd sprawl on the sand on their backs, looking up at the stars and roaring with laughter at private jokes about things their parents knew nothing about.

Although H's parents didn't forbid him to play on the beach, he had to get their permission every time or he was in for a sharp scolding. There was a particularly strict ban on going straight there on his way home from school. He'd been made to promise always to go home first and deposit his school bag before going out to play, announcing his destination as he went.

H found this rule hard to observe, feeling embarrassed at having to go home by himself, then follow on later, when the others went off in a group to play after leaving school. So sometimes he'd spend some time with them on the way home without telling his mother.

But even when he thought he'd given himself a clever alibi, he was more often than not found out. Nor was an unwilling confession in the face of incontrovertible evidence enough.

"Now say a prayer, as penance!" he'd be told, and be obliged to confess his transgression to God.

Yasuo Suzuki, who was a fisherman's son, teased him about it one day: "Your ma's like a detective, isn't she!"

Seated on a dinghy drawn up on the beach, H was carefully fishing sand out of his navel with a finger moistened with spittle. "Right!" he said. "Only the other day she suddenly made me take my pants off and found I'd got sand in my belly button. You can't be too careful!"

Even so, he'd persisted in sin. The friends he made playing games mattered more to him than anything.

Jumping down onto the sand from the boat, he dashed into the sea and thoroughly rinsed himself off. Then, having checked that not a single grain of sand still clung to him, he went home.

As he opened the front door with the usual call of "I'm back," his mother appeared in the entrance hall and, grabbing his shaven head suddenly, gave it a lick.

"You've been to the beach, haven't you! I can tell at once—you're all salty!"

This completely floored H, who'd never dreamed he might have his head licked.

Resigned though Toshiko was to the children playing in the sea, she still thought it was dangerous. Invariably as H was going off to the beach, there came the parting warning: "Be careful, now, don't get carried out. And don't swim too far out by yourself."

In bad weather the sea *was* undoubtedly rough and dangerous. H and his friends, though, had an interesting game that was only possible when the waves were high. This involved plunging into the water in the direction of a great wave just as it drove in and was about to break on the beach.

If you dived into a wave much higher than yourself, you were spun around in its crest then flung down onto the sand. At this point you had to get up quickly and dash off up the beach; any hesitation and you were carried off by the wave as it drew away again. It was quite a dangerous business, and the game of course had to be kept an absolute secret from their parents.

Of the friends who played with H on the beach, it was Yasuo, the fisherman's son, whom Toshiko trusted most. This was partly because she knew his father, who she bought fish from directly, and partly because both father and son were good swimmers who, she felt, would rescue H in an emergency.

"If you find my boy doing anything risky on the beach, just go ahead and give him a good telling-off—really!" she'd said to the father. Little did she know that, far from being rescued by him, her boy had actually been put in danger of his life.

When he'd been in second grade, H had been deliberately thrown into the sea from Yasuo's father's boat and made to swallow an unpleasant amount of seawater.

It had been a scary experience. Looking up as he sank, he could see the bubbles of air streaming upward from his own mouth. From the boat, Yasuo's dad watched in silence, then, just when H thought he was done for, came diving down and hauled him back onto the boat by the scruff of his neck.

The fisherman rubbed his back helpfully as he retched violently, spewing up seawater. But then, just when H thought the worst was over, he suddenly picked him up and threw him into the sea again.

H flapped his arms desperately. Again he swallowed large quantities of water—then suddenly found, to his surprise, that he was swimming by himself.

He'd never thought a grownup could ever do something so violent to him, but thanks to the experience he finally learned to swim, which he'd never managed before.

"Someone who's learned to swim when he thought he was going to drown is safe ever after," the fisherman said.

For a while after that, H was afraid even to go near him, but eventually began to feel that what he'd said had been true.

Yet H and his friends knew that even fishermen, who were supposed to be good swimmers, sometimes got drowned. When the sea was rough, fishing vessels occasionally capsized offshore and the men who'd been on board were washed up onto the beach. This occurred at least once every year, and a group of people would go pounding past H's home from the direction of the beach carrying a wooden door on their shoulders. Lying face down on the door would be the limp figure of a drowned man.

The group was heading for the public bathhouse, and the children of the neighborhood would race after them crying "A wreck! A wreck!" Then, when they reached the bathhouse, they set the body down on the tiles where people usually washed themselves, and poured hot water over it while artificial respiration was applied.

The children too would strip off and help fetch hot water from the bath in wooden tubs. Two men in particular were known to be good at pumping the victim's chest and blowing air into his mouth; one had a little shop selling kelp near the beach, the other ran the local ironworks. Normally they weren't on very good terms, but on these occasions the two of them made an impressive team.

Sometimes, as they watched, things would go well and the fisherman would start breathing and come back to life. But there were other times, too, when their efforts were in vain and his eyes remained closed.

Through scenes like these, H and his friends learned how to make someone expel the water in his lungs, and other lifesaving techniques.

In fourth grade at primary school, they all had to take a test of their swimming ability. H was put in the third category, which wasn't specially good, but from then on he wore the black ring showing his grade on his bathing cap.

One day, after they'd done their exercises before going into the sea, the teacher in charge of swimming classes told them: "There's no point in trying to swim fast. The best thing is to be able to swim slowly and keep going indefinitely. And when you swim you should never kick up a spray. Swim gently, with just your head above water. If you make a great splashing, the enemy will see you and open fire."

The two strokes that they concentrated on were sidestroke, with one arm stretched out in front and one behind, and the breaststroke, which they called the "frog stroke."

They were also told to practice swimming upright in the water so that they could hold something in their hands. Either way, it was drummed into them that they weren't to swim fast, which, coming not long after the Tokyo Olympic Games had been canceled, suggested that swimming races—at least officially—were a thing of the past.

Just before the summer holidays, there was a day devoted to long-distance swimming. Going into the sea in single file, with sixth-graders at the head and the others down to third-graders following in order, they swam out doing the breaststroke. The instructor kept an eye on them from a boat, banging a drum to whose steady beat they had to move their arms and legs "quietly and slowly, for as long as possible, without splashing about." That was the aim of long-distance swimming.

"If your ship sinks," they were told, "whether you survive or not will depend on this. It might seem difficult now, but it should become second nature to you. This is the navy's way of swimming."

H didn't care whether it was navy-style or not, but he did feel that learning to tread water was worthwhile, since it came in handy when spearing octopuses or gathering oysters.

Children who went diving all had their own homemade spears. Called *yasu*, they were really a kind of harpoon; they could be bought cheaply at a fishing tackle store, but the boys took pride in making their own.

You got a thick piece of wire, heated it, beat it into the right shape with a blunt chisel, then plunged it with a hiss into cold water to temper it, sharpened the point of the spear, and bound it to the tip of a slender piece of bamboo. The resulting weapon was primitive, but to a boy it was a source of great pride.

H had borrowed a grinder from the ironworks on the corner diagonally opposite his home and used it to make a professional-looking spear, with which he fancied he cut quite a dash as he dived underwater, pointed it at his prey, and let fly.

The currents were fierce off Suma, and swimmers were sometimes carried away while diving beneath the surface. You had to be constantly on your guard, but so long as you kept your wits about you, you could often catch octopuses of quite a size.

When you'd caught one, you called out to the others, "Hey!—I got a big one!" and proudly showed it off. Then, slamming it against the concrete breakwater to kill it, you beat it with a stick to soften it up, cut the tentacles off with a sharp knife, and roasted it over a bonfire ready for eating.

Oysters were often eaten raw, but they were also good cooked in the shell and eaten piping hot.

Yasuo, who was an expert diver, was also a dab hand, as you'd expect of a fisherman's son, at rowing a dinghy.

"You should get my dad to show you how," Yasuo said, when H insisted on being taught to row himself. "Mind you, though, he's a strict teacher." H hardly needed reminding of that, but he was still willing. And in the end it was decided that the four of them would learn together.

When H got into the boat and tried to grasp the oar, he found it was too high for him to reach. Seeing this, Yasuo swiftly made a pile of three fish boxes. "I can't reach either," he said, with a flash of his prominent white teeth. "This is what *I* always do."

The first thing Yasuo's father taught them was to move the oar in a figure of eight, but though H did as he was told, the boat turned aimlessly in circles without going forward at all. It took three days of practice before it finally began to move in the direction he wanted.

Usually they would wait for Yasuo's father to get back from a fishing trip, then ask him to let them row the boat before he pulled it up on the beach. One day, though, when Mr. Suzuki was taking a day off to attend to some business in town, they asked if they could use it on their own, promising to leave it drawn up on the beach again as they'd found it. Permission granted, H and the other four lost no time in piling aboard and putting out to sea in fine style.

They were all quite good rowers by now, and the boat moved swiftly away from the shore. The weather was fine, with a few small clouds in a blue sky and a calm, smooth sea. They could clearly see Awaji Island directly ahead of them on the other side of the straits.

"The tide's running west at the moment and the weather's fine, so we might be able to make it to Awaji," said H.

Startled, Yasuo objected fiercely: "Not Awaji—it's too far! My father would give us hell."

H himself didn't seriously think they could reach the island, but he said, "We don't have to go all the way—let's take turns rowing and see just how far we can get."

75

Yasuo started whimpering, worried sick in case something happened to his father's precious boat, but the other three were all for rowing a bit further out.

"Let's see what the four of us can do together," they said. "Yasuo—if you don't want to, you can just sit there and watch."

After they'd been rowing for a while, though, H and his friends began to get a bit worried. The boat, they realized, was obstinately refusing to head west and was being driven eastward instead.

It must already be past the time when the tide changed.

"Let's pack it in and head back. Any beach'll do." And they began to take turns rowing with all their strength against the tide, any idea of making for Awaji Island now forgotten.

Row as they might, they seemed to be getting no nearer to the shore. They began to feel panicky. The flow of the tide out at sea was far stronger than H and his friends had thought, not at all like the water they were used to near the shore. The Komagabayashi beach from which they'd put out was rapidly receding to one side of their field of vision.

They were still rowing desperately when on the beach, which they could still see out of the corner of their eyes, they saw Mr. Suzuki, who had got back and was waving at them, shouting something.

His voice was totally inaudible but with his arms he seemed to be telling them he was going east. Then he jumped on his bike and started pedaling.

He soon disappeared behind the houses of the village, but his plan seemed to be to go around and get ahead of them.

They battled on, taking turns rowing, but soon the places on the palms of their hands where blisters had formed and broken were unbearably painful. In the end, touched off by Yasuo, who was crying loudly, they were all crying together. But they went on rowing even as they cried.

The breakwater at the mouth of the Shin-Minato river loomed larger and larger, and the boat finally drew closer to the shore.

Mr. Suzuki was there. He flung his bike down on the sand, stripped and, dashing into the sea, began swimming.

"Saved!" thought H.

The others must have stopped worrying too, as they suddenly started blaming it all on him.

"He'll be mad. It was your fault, H!"

"It's you who got us into this!"

H, who couldn't help agreeing with them, had half a mind to jump overboard and swim out of reach, but resigned himself instead to waiting for Yasuo's father to arrive.

Mr. Suzuki's hand came over the gunwale, so H stretched out an arm and helped him into the boat.

He shut his eyes tight, waiting for the expected blow. But instead he felt a wet arm drawing him closer and, opening his eyes in surprise, found that the fisherman was hugging the whole bunch of them toward him.

H was too startled by this turn of events to do anything.

"You're all safe, so it's all right," Mr. Suzuki was saying. "I won't say anything more. Just don't let this make you afraid of the sea. Remember the song 'I'm a son of the sea.' Okay? Tell me it's okay!"

"Okay," they replied, blubbering.

It was less than a month later that Yasuo's father got his call-up papers.

Other men of various ages living round about were getting their papers these days, so they'd been half expecting it, but this was sooner even than they'd thought.

Yasuo's mother had died of some illness many years ago, and he'd been brought up by his grandmother. Now that his father was going into the army, there'd be just the two of them, Yasuo and the old lady.

When H told his mother about it, he asked her anxiously, "D'you think Dad will get his papers too?"

"I don't expect so," she said. "He's so small, and he got a C in his physical. You see, Yasuo's dad got an A grade because he's tough and well-built.... Poor them," she sighed to herself. "Poor them," she repeated, then added, "Tell them I'll come and help in the kitchen on the day he goes, will you? There's no wife in their family to do the preparations...."

H rounded up his fellow survivors from that abortive voyage and they went to Yasuo's place, where they found his father talking to the fishermen who were to look after his boat for him.

The boys persuaded Yasuo to come down to the beach with them.

Just as on that earlier day, the sky was a clear, deep blue with white clouds floating in it, the sea calm and smooth.

They climbed onto the dinghy drawn up on the beach and sat in a circle around Yasuo.

His mother's family in Mita were going to take him in, he told them. "Mita—that's way inland from Kobe," he said, "in the hills, where you can't see the sea at all...." He'd been holding back the tears, but as he said this his shoulders shook with sobs, followed by a violent fit of weeping. They all wept with him.

"Come and see us sometimes," said H. "We'll be expecting you. We can have fun by the sea as we've always done."

But as he said it, he suddenly wondered whether they'd ever really see Yasuo again.

9

Flood

H came home from school to find his father waiting for him.

"I have to go to Sannomiya on Sunday next week to deliver a suit. Shall we go and have a look at the Ikuta River while we're about it?" he said.

"Oh yes, let's!" H was delighted that his father had remembered the promise he'd made a good two years ago.

In 1938 a great flood had swept over Kobe, swallowing up almost the whole city, and his father, who'd taken him to see the damage, had said, "Remember what it looks like now. I'll bring you to see it again when it's been put to rights."

That had been only three weeks from the time of the disaster, and the scars of the flood were still visible in many parts of the city.

Not long afterward, the newspapers had carried a report that work had begun on a "new river" that would help prevent flood damage. When his father told him about it, H asked, to make sure, "You really meant it, didn't you, when you said we could go and see the river once repairs were finished?"

"Yes—I expect you'll be in fourth grade by then," he'd said.

H had been rather dismayed at the thought he'd have to wait two years, but now the time was up. Along with his pleasure at finding that his father's offer hadn't been mere talk, he found himself remembering the event in some detail.

The great flood that descended on Kobe had occurred when H was in second grade at primary school—on July 5, 1938, though it had first started raining around midday on the third. So vivid had the whole thing been that he even remembered the dates.

July 3 was a Sunday, and the whole family had gone to church.

It wasn't raining yet when they got back around noon. H had promised his friends to go climbing with them on Mount Takatori that afternoon, and had planned to leave directly after lunch, but his father had said, "You're not to go into the hills today." This was odd: he hardly ever placed any restraint on his activities like this. "They say it'll start raining heavily in the afternoon," he went on. "The forecasts are often wrong, but today they'll be right—the air's heavy, it's going to rain all right. You keep clear of the hills—it's too risky."

Thanks to this repeated order, H couldn't go with his friends when they came to fetch him, but it wasn't long before he realized that his father's advice had been sound. The rain started, then turned into a downpour.

The friends who'd left intending to go up into the hills came running back, drenched to the skin. "We'd only got as far as Itayado when the rain started, so we turned back. Lucky you listened to what your dad said and didn't come!"

After that, it had gone on pouring all night. On the second day the rain showed no sign of letting up, but it was Monday, so H went to school. Lessons for the lower grades, though, were cut nearly an hour short, perhaps because a flood alert had been issued, and pupils were told to go home as soon as possible.

Mr. Hayashi, the teacher in charge of H's grade, came out to the entrance hall where the racks for their shoes were and told each of them individually to make sure they went straight home without wasting time on the way. Outside the school gates, H found the road between the houses running with water like a shallow river.

The woman in the stationery shop was calling out to children as they went by, "Don't walk by the edge of the road. It's dangerous—there's a ditch!"

Arriving home, he found the water had already got into the lower part of the entrance hall which was on a level with the road.

"The water may rise in the afternoon," his father said. "Let's get the tatami up while there's time."

They put two tea chests on top of his work table so that they could pile the tatami on top of them. The mats were surprisingly heavy—too heavy for H to carry one by himself—but he worked as hard as he could, glad to feel he was doing his bit.

Even Yoshiko, who'd just had her sixth birthday, went around pretending to help.

It occurred to H that this was the first time the whole family had ever worked together on one undertaking.

Taking up the tatami revealed the old newspapers spread underneath, which they'd laid down at the time of last year's spring-cleaning. Taking these up in turn instantly transformed the room into an unfamiliar board-floored space. It was that unfamiliarity, perhaps, that suddenly made it feel disturbingly like someone else's house.

"I don't suppose the water'll come up as high as this," his father said, gazing at the pile of tatami. His mother was busy filling buckets and pans with clean water from the tap while it was still available. After that, she put the clay stove and charcoal in the corridor next to the living room so they wouldn't get wet, and put some water on to boil in the kettle.

Once things were more or less done, they set out some straw-woven cushions on the bare boards and sat drinking a cup of black tea as they gazed at the downpour outside.

There weren't many people walking in the rain, but an occasional bicycle or bus still went by, sending up a spray of water.

Watching through the window as a bus drove past, H thought it looked more like a boat, and was wondering whether it was all right to drive an internal-combustion engine through water when, right before his eyes, the bus stopped.

The timing was so perfect that it made him laugh, which earned him a rap on the head with his father's ruler. The thing he found funny, though, wasn't other people's misfortune but the timing—the way the bus, instead of going straight past as usual, had drawn up in front of their house as if it were a stop; it was like something out of a comic strip.

The people in the bus, he suspected, felt embarrassed about being watched through the window of the house right in front of them; they seemed to be pretending not to be concerned, avoiding looking in their direction.

The bus stayed put, with absolutely no sign of movement.

A child on the bus appeared to be staring at them through the window and saying something. Noticing this, Toshiko beckoned.

Then, taking the child's place, they saw a middle-aged woman, who was probably her mother, pointing at their house and saying something to the driver. He listened for a while, then nodded and opened the door. Alighting, the woman and child came stepping through the flowing water, slid open the door of the house, and came into the entrance hall. As they did so, a muddy, foaming tide flowed in with them.

"I wonder …," the woman began hesitantly, "I wonder if we could use your toilet. My little girl here says her tummy hurts.…"

"Yes, come on in," said Toshiko immediately. "Come right in, just as you are."

Mother's doing her "God is love" bit again, thought H, but said nothing. The child, who must have needed a crap badly, was almost in tears as she trotted after her mother in the direction of the toilet. The two of them were soaked from the knees down and left a trail of damp marks on the bare boards.

With a shudder of disgust, H pictured the little girl's turds swirling round and round on the floodwater. Almost certainly the muddy water outside was coming into the toilet through the outlet at the back of the house, swirling around the cess tank, then flowing outside again. The water running through the streets, he realized, must be filthy, all mixed up with piss and shit. He was still thinking about this when the woman and the little girl came back from the toilet.

Waiting till they'd washed their hands, Toshiko gave them each a cup of tea.

After a while, another four people who must have been watching through the windows of the bus got off and came over.

Since getting off meant having to splash through the water, H thought they must be a bit stupid, until it occurred to him that, since the whole town was now under water, they were probably past worrying about getting a bit wet. The middle-aged men and women who came in now were drenched from the knees down, and the boards were soon so wet from the water dribbling from their trousers and shoes that there was hardly a dry place left.

H's mother had in fact said, "The boards aren't particularly clean to begin with, so don't bother to take your shoes off," but even so H was rather shocked that they'd come into the house in their shoes.

With a "Me too, if you don't mind," each of the newcomers in turn used the toilet. Even after they came out, though, they were in no hurry to leave and stood around indecisively, so Toshiko started providing tea. "Which would you prefer," she asked each of them, "black tea or ordinary?"

H, sitting on his cushion, was obliged to look up at them from below. Probably they didn't want to sit down in their wet trousers, but even so he found the way they stood there drinking their tea without saying anything a bit unnatural and offensive.

"Terrible rain, isn't it?" one woman said as though to break the awkward silence. But only one of the others, an elderly woman, said "Yes, isn't it?" The rest stayed silent. They almost seemed to be waiting for something, though their expressions showed they didn't know what it was.

I wonder why they don't go back to the bus? fretted H. Surely they aren't going to stay the night, are they? We don't have all that many futons.

After a while the answer occurred to him: it was simply that they felt rather more secure inside than sitting, wet through, in a stalled bus.

Until then he'd found the way his mother fussed around attending to them rather annoying, but now he decided there might be something in her "God is love" after all.

About half an hour later the driver came in. "The water's got into the engine and it won't budge," he said. "I've phoned to ask for a relief bus, but I don't know when it'll come.... What d'you all want to do?" This seemed suddenly to make them recall where they were and, in a flurry of murmured thank-yous, they trooped out.

When H looked out the window after supper, the bus was no longer in front of the house. They must have brought another vehicle and hauled it away; he wished he'd seen it.

On the third day, July 5, the deluge showed no sign of ceasing; in fact, what followed was still worse.

They heard the announcer on the radio talking as though Kobe were being wiped out, but then there was a power cut, so they never knew what came after that.

All around H's home, the muddy waters were flowing like a river toward the sea.

In the late afternoon, H's "Uncle" Hadano reached the house, wet through and carrying his bike on his shoulders. He'd once rented a room in their house for three years, during which time H was born. Although he was married now, with a son of four and another in first grade at primary school, he'd kept up with them ever since that time almost as though he were a relative. He was a civil engineering expert with the city hall, working at the Tenjogawa office not far from H's home.

"The bridge over the Tenjo was under water and looked as though it might collapse. I only just got across. Another thirty minutes and it might have gone altogether. I can't get home today—do you mind putting me up?"

H was delighted. "*You* can stay as long as you like," he said.

Uncle Hadano, who unlike H's father was sturdily built, used to give him piggybacks when he was small. H had an early childhood memory of seeing, from some high place, a great pillar of fire shooting up. The scene, apparently, had been the ceremonial burning of New Year's decorations at a Shinto shrine, which he'd witnessed sitting astride Uncle Hadano's shoulders. "When you were three," his mother had explained, "he took you to see the bonfire at the Hachiman Shrine at Komagabayashi. I expect that's what you remember."

To H, Uncle Hadano was like another father. He listened, all ears, as Hadano told them about the flood damage.

"Some houses along the Shin-Minato River and the Myohoji River have been washed away, and the damage in other places too is really bad. A lot of people have been killed or injured. I was talking on the phone with the city hall about the damage, and everywhere it was the same—sandbagging the breaches just didn't help any longer. The next thing I knew, my own desk at the office was starting to float and the phone went dead, so I got out while I could."

It seemed he'd escaped with his bike on his back only minutes before the wooden office building went under.

"Under the railway bridge on the west side of Takatori Station the water came up to my chest and I was afraid I was going to be washed away, bike and all. It was a close thing."

He'd brought his bike with him because he foresaw that even after the flood had subsided transportation would be paralyzed for some time. Late that night, the rain was still falling. Here and there flash floods gushed out of the hills, gouging away the slopes and falling on the built-up areas in a torrent of mud, rocks and water. The damage was particularly bad, they said, in the district east of Sannomiya.

H was worried about Uncle Hadano's house, which stood by the Myohoji River, but was told, "It's all right—the river runs deep there, and there's quite a long flight of steps from the road up to the house."

On the fourth day, the rain finally stopped. As soon as they got up that morning, Uncle Hadano got H to help bail out the muddy water and silt that had got into the entrance hall and under the raised floor of the house. Then, after he'd had breakfast, he left on his bike for the city hall, promising to come again.

That afternoon the water on the roads finally began to recede, but there was no question of any buses or streetcars running yet.

"We were lucky," said H, gazing at the damp stains on the boards left by dripping bus passengers two days before. "Our only damage was from the water that came under the floor, the floating turds in the toilet, and the people that came in from the bus."

A few days later his father, after ascertaining that the streetcars were running on certain routes, put on a pair of rubber boots and set out for Sannomiya, first to deliver a suit ordered by Mr. Chin, which was now ready, and then to call on various customers to inquire how they'd fared in the flood.

It was dark before he got home.

"I didn't manage to see anyone in the end," he said. "I didn't get to hand over the suit either, naturally enough. Everything's buried in mud. Damage in the eastern part of town is much worse than I'd expected, quite different from around here. There's no telling when things'll get back to normal."

According to Morio, the streets in the Sannomiya area were clogged with houses that had collapsed, furniture and belongings carried down by the water, and mud and rocks, with mud-covered streetcars stranded where they'd been derailed. It was no place for people to go, he declared; as things were you just couldn't get around.

"This is what you call an 'act of God,' isn't it?" said H, feeling sure that floods caused by torrential rains were not the kind of disaster that human beings could do anything about....

"No, it isn't!" his father snapped. "It wasn't an act of God!" he went on when H, puzzled, questioned him further. "The rivers were angry because human beings had meddled with them to suit their own purposes. The worst thing was, they covered them over, shutting them in underground. It's *our* fault, not God's."

"What do you mean, underground?" H asked.

With a piece of tailor's chalk, his father drew a picture for him on the wooden table. "You bury a river below ground level by putting a lid on it, like this. That way you can build roads, parks and so on over the top. In some places they changed the courses that rivers had always followed. And nothing bad happened for ages, so people felt pleased with what they'd done. But just now, six hundred millimeters of rain fell in only three days—half the amount that usually falls in Kobe in a whole year. Even the experts didn't foresee anything like that, apparently."

A lot of the built-up areas of Kobe consisted of residential districts made by leveling the slopes stretching up to Mount Rokko and Mount Maya, which had involved cutting down the trees.

"A mountain without trees can't hold the water, so whatever rain falls runs away immediately. When prolonged rainfall makes the earth on the mountain soft, landslides of soil and stones loosened by the water rush into the underground tunnels, which get choked up. A river that's choked up can't do its usual work, and quite naturally the water overflows onto the roads. The reason why somewhere like Sannomiya, which is far from any river, got wrecked is that long before your time the big road from Kano-cho to Sannomiya was the course along which a river flowed. The underground waterway encased in concrete that was built instead couldn't cope with all the water, and it gushed out into the streets. The water still remembered where the river had been in the old days."

This, besides being interesting in itself, was the first time H had ever heard his father talk for so long and so coherently. It renewed his admiration for him, and made him think wistfully that if only teachers talked like that at school, even a second-grader would understand....

Three weeks later, when the situation was beginning to get back to normal, his father took him to the eastern part of the city, which still showed the effects of the flood in various places.

They had to go straight by train to Ashiya without stopping, then come back in stages to the west.

The first place they saw, the area along the Ashiya River, was littered with piles of rocks, astonishingly large to have been brought down by running water, among them huge boulders still lying on the houses they had crushed.

The area around Okamoto, the next station on from Ashiya, had been wiped out all the way from the hills down to the sea.

The Sumiyoshi River seemed to have caused relatively little damage. "They were lucky here," said H's father. "This river's wide and straight, so it went on flowing as it should."

Then, on to the west of the Sumiyoshi River, everything was a shambles again.

In Kobe City, his father told him, more than 159,000 houses had been washed away or damaged and more than 690,000 people suffered the effects of the flood in some way or other. He'd seen the figures in the paper.

The damage was particularly bad in the areas bordering the Aotani, Oishi, and Ikuta rivers, which had been covered over. Up to then, it seemed, the rivers had been placidly putting up with things, but now, their patience finally exhausted, they'd gone on the rampage.

H had never heard of some of these rivers, and he wrote their names down with a pencil in his notebook in case he forgot them.

Two years had passed since then. He was in fourth grade by this time, and, as promised, his father had brought him for another look at the rivers now that repair work was completed.

Just as they'd done when they'd gone around viewing the flood damage before, they went by train in gradual stages from east to west. But the scars of those days were nowhere to be seen.

The "lids" on the rivers which had been a major factor in aggravating the damage had been done away with. The Ikuta River had been refashioned into a fine, broad stream running straight from just below the Nunobiki Falls to the sea.

"Well," said H, "now I expect the rivers will just flow without getting angry."

"Yes," said his father, "but they say disaster strikes when you've stopped expecting it. You can never be sure: people may think everything's taken care of, but there's always something else. Forget that, and you're going to suffer again."

At home, H asked for the map they had of Kobe City and used a red pencil to color in the districts where he remembered the flood damage had been worst.

10

The Three Treasures

One of H's classmates, Haruo Ota, was known to the others as "Blackpatch."

The nickname was a reference to a blackish birthmark he had on his head. Since, like all the other boys, his hair had been close-cropped, using clippers, the birthmark was visible through the stubble, a sure mark for friends looking to give him a nickname.

When H's mother heard him using it, she told him off. "What did you give him a name like that for? I'm sure he hates it."

"*I* didn't give it him," said H. "They've always called him that, and I don't think he minds." But his mother shook her head.

"You shouldn't call him Blackpatch," she insisted. "I'm sure he *does* mind and is just putting up with it. Yoshiko's the same: she doesn't like being called Squinty, either. Don't you remember?—you got angry and started a fight because the others were teasing her."

His sister's left eye turned inward. Not long after she'd entered primary school, H had found her being teased by some of her classmates. "Squinty, Squinty!" they were chanting. "Which way are you looking? Can't you look straight?…"

This had made him see red, and he rushed at them. The offenders, though, were a notorious trio of young thugs, and they'd thoroughly beaten him up. But it still infuriated him to hear people call his sister Squinty.

Now, reminded by his mother, he could see the similarity between the two cases, and it put him on the spot. "Okay," he said, "I won't call him that anymore. I'll just call him 'Don-chan.'"

She still didn't seem completely satisfied: "Actually, you shouldn't call him Don-chan either. Why don't you just call him Ota-kun?"

But H didn't reply. He was sure his friend would only be puzzled if he suddenly started using "Ota-kun" instead of "Don-chan." H didn't know where the latter nickname came from. *Don* did in fact occur in a lot of words—like *gudon*, "stupid"—that had an uncomplimentary meaning, but he was quite sure that wasn't it. After all, Don-chan was head boy of the class, and his grades were good, too.

H was on particularly good terms with this Don-chan, who was always generous in lending him books. In fact, dropping in at his place on the way home from school to have a read in what he called "the Don-chan library" had become one of his greatest pleasures. It was thanks to Don-chan that he was able to discuss popular comic strips of the day like *Norakuro* and *The Adventures of Dankichi*, or stories like Kenji Miyazawa's *Matasaburo the Wind Imp*, with his friends in the classroom.

But he knew he'd be in trouble if his mother found out, so he kept the existence of the Don-chan library strictly secret from her. Although her son was in fourth grade at primary school by now, Toshiko still insisted he shouldn't read anything apart from the Bible and school textbooks.

"They don't put cartoons and made-up stories in your textbooks, do they?" she demanded.

Though H was always terrified in case she found out about the "library," for some reason she approved of the friendship between the two boys. Whenever he announced that he was calling in at Don-chan's place on the way back from school, it seemed to set her mind at rest.

Perhaps it was because Don-chan's father was something high up in the city hall and they lived in an impressive house, but Toshiko seemed convinced that as long as H played with the son of such a family he'd never become a delinquent. Likewise, H was smart enough to keep quiet about other connections she was likely to disapprove of and to report only the names that were likely to please.

Don-chan's house was in Noda-cho 7-chome, straight ahead as you went out of the main gate of the school. The grounds were enclosed by an impressive wall built of rounded stones, and the entrance to the house itself stood well back from the gate. To the left of the entrance hall there was a Western-style living room, with the Japanese-style reception room of the main house on the right. The extensive garden which this best room overlooked was well kept, with carp swimming in a pool and large frogs waddling casually about.

In spring the children would catch tadpoles in the pond at Don-chan's place, and in summer they were treated to watermelon which had been cooled in the well.

H had never met Don-chan's father, but knew his mother well because it was she who always brought them tea and cakes when they went calling. She, on her side, seemed to trust H because he was fond of reading and could speak politely; the little devil in him seemed to remain unsuspected....

When H said that Don-chan was lucky to have such a big garden and so many books, his friend had generously offered to lend him some. "Why don't you take some home?" he said. "I can't lend you my father's books, but if you want you can read them on the couch in the living room when he's not around."

The leather-covered couch was well stuffed and comfortable, and there were rows and rows of books on the shelves, so you felt you were in a real library.

One day H found in the bookcase there a book of children's stories called *The Three Treasures*, written by a man called Ryunosuke Akuta-gawa. It was bound in orange cloth and the edges of the pages were a shiny gold. It was a surprisingly big book, nearly fifty centimeters wide when opened out flat. There were six stories, and the pages were interspersed with a number of colored illustrations—not ordinary children's-book ones but attractive, grownup pictures.

What impressed H, however, wasn't so much the luxurious appearance of the book as its content. For H, who disliked the smarmy tone of the average children's storybook, this was something quite different from anything he'd come across until now.

"Shiro," for example, was a strange tale about a dog of that name. Shiro is walking along the road when he happens to see a neighbor, a stern, middle-aged man, catch Kuro, the black dog that lives next door, in a trap. He hears Kuro howling piteously, and his own fur turns jet black, perhaps from fear, without his realizing it. He flees in fright, but when he gets home his owner not only refuses to recognize him as his own dog because of the black fur, but drives the "strange dog" away in disgust. Shiro is dismayed when he becomes aware of the change that has overtaken him. From then on he wanders disconsolately about the streets, avoiding looking at his own reflection in mirrors and puddles. And so the story leads to a surprising ending.

H read the other stories in the book with the same keen absorption. He enjoyed "The Spider's Thread" and "Toshi-shun," but the one he liked best was "The Three Treasures."

This relates how a prince, while on a journey, meets three bandits in a forest and buys from them three objects with wondrous powers: a cloak that confers invisibility on the wearer, a pair of boots that enables the owner to fly, and a sword that will cut anything. In actual fact, the talk of magical powers is pure fabrication, but at this point the prince doesn't realize that he has been deceived.

At the inn where he stays when he gets to town, he hears that a wedding is shortly to be held between a black king and a princess. Rumor has it that the princess detests the black king and is being forced into the marriage.

Hearing this, the prince determines to save the princess and rides alone into the castle intending to challenge the villain to a fight using the three "treasures" to bring him to his knees.

In reality, though, the cloak, boots and sword the prince has been sold are fakes and of no use whatsoever.

On the other hand, the black king himself has a real magic cloak, boots and sword, and in no time the prince is in danger of his life. But he continues to defy the black king, until the latter eventually confesses sadly: "I used to think that if only I had the three magic treasures I could win the princess, but I was wrong."

It transpires that the black king, the "villain," is in fact a good man, while the prince, so sure that he himself was the champion of justice, has been under an illusion.

This reversal of roles appealed to H. "What a great writer!" he declared ecstatically, much as though he'd discovered Ryunosuke Akutagawa himself. "Would you lend me this one?" he asked Don-chan. "I'd like to take it home and read it again without hurrying."

"No, not that one!" exclaimed Don-chan, looking shocked. "My father's very attached to that book, so I can't."

H was surprised. He'd never heard Don-chan speak so emphatically before, quite unlike the easygoing Don-chan he was used to.

But this refusal only made H, contrary by nature, more eager to borrow the book than ever.

"Just for one day! I'll give it straight back to you, and I swear I won't get it dirty. Go on … please."

H's hectoring tone must have got to Don-chan, for he suddenly made an outrageous proposal.

"Okay, then," he said. "I'll lend it to you if you can do a double somersault. *Double*, I mean—single won't do."

He and the other classmates who were present all gazed intently at H.

Although H could do a single somersault by now, he'd never even considered a double. Their PE teacher had told them, "If you can do a double somersault you're set for the Olympics." Even so, H had a feeling that if only his takeoff were powerful enough he might just about be able to manage it.

"Right," he declared, getting up. "Here I go!"

Chattering noisily, he and his friends shifted from Don-chan's house to the school sandpit. The takeoff board they'd used in PE class still stood where it had been left.

When he realized that H had every intention of trying a double somersault, Don-chan, who hadn't taken him seriously at first, shouted at him almost tearfully, "You mustn't! Don't do it!"

But H was already running.

He hit the board and took off.

His body was through the first somersault and halfway into the second when he fell and plunged headfirst into the sand.

He heard a cracking sound and simultaneously felt an intense pain in his right shoulder.

"I very nearly did it," he declared, reluctant to admit defeat and bitterly disappointed at the thought of how close he'd come to being able to borrow *The Three Treasures*.

"Whatever you do," he warned his friends, who were looking a bit nervous, "don't tell my mother I got hurt because I wanted to borrow a book."

Shocked when her son came home in tears, Toshiko hauled him

straight off to the Honda surgery at Ohashi 9-chome. His right shoulder was swollen and bright red from internal bleeding. He'd broken his collarbone.

"I fell over in the sandpit," he said in the consulting room when asked how he'd done it. But the doctor stared at him suspiciously.

"Could you *really* do this just by falling over?" he demanded.

The bandage they wound around his chest and upper arm prevented him from using either chopsticks or a pencil with his right hand. But H wasn't too depressed: Don-chan had smuggled *The Three Treasures* out of his house and brought it over to lend him.

"You can keep it till you're better, but don't let anybody else see it." He repeated this several times as if to make sure.

"Don't worry, I'll hide it where no one will ever find it. And I won't get it dirty, either."

As H said this, he clutched the book to him with his left hand in a way that made Don-chan look a bit anxious. Possibly the disturbing thought had struck him that he might never get the book back.

H decided to hide the book upstairs behind the framed calligraphy hanging over his desk. It meant he could only get the book by standing on a chair and reaching up, which was inconvenient but worth it, and he went about as chirpy as a cricket—almost as though *The Three Treasures* was his own now.

His mother, worried about the slow progress he was making, was given some advice by Mrs. Igarashi, wife of the owner of the rice store on a corner of the crossroads:

"If the bone's broken you should go to a bone-setter," she said. "If you leave it as it is he'll never be able to move his right arm properly again. I'll tell you a good place—Akakabe, the judo bone-setters in Shinkaichi."

"I want to go *now*," said H, scared by the talk of losing the use of his right arm.

Shinkaichi, incidentally, was Kobe's main entertainment district, its streets lined with movie theaters. If they let him start attending the clinic by himself he could take the opportunity to pop into the Shuraku-kan and Shochiku-za, which were two of the best-known places.

When they went to Shinkaichi, his mother took Yoshiko along for

the ride. This was a special treat for the little girl, who had been wanting to go on a streetcar. They found Akakabe with no trouble at all,
since the name meant "Red Walls," and it actually was painted a bright
red. A judo training center stood next door, with a sign saying "Red
Wall Dojo" and, coming from inside, the fierce cries of judoists in training accompanied by heavy thumps.

H began to feel a little uneasy; he hoped "judo bone-setting" didn't
mean he was going to be slammed on the floor in the process.

About ten people were already sitting on the tatami in the waiting
room. By now H was more than a little nervous, remembering the moxibustion clinic he'd attended at Kakogawa.

From the next room came a cry of "No, no!" and almost simultaneously a howl of pain. H wanted to go home, but Toshiko glared at him
and said in a threatening tone, "Do you want to have a useless right
arm for the rest of your life?"

"I'll be good if you'll take me for a curry on the way home," said H,
hoping to strike a bargain. On their way to the clinic he'd noticed a
good smell and seen a restaurant with a short white curtain over the
entrance, fluttering in the breeze and bearing, in big letters, the legend
"Curry Rice."

"So it's curry this time," said his mother, smiling. "You always have to
be bribed with something to eat, don't you!"

When H's turn came, he was shown into a back room where they
took the bandage off his shoulder.

"Why on earth didn't you come sooner?" said the doctor, who was in
judo uniform, in an angry tone. "Your collarbone's setting with the two
halves overlapping. What's that?—you went to an ordinary surgery? That's
like taking a bellyache to an eye doctor. It won't heal properly unless I
separate the two bits of bone and rejoin them. It'll hurt, so you'll have
to be brave."

Without further ado, he grabbed H's arm and shoulder and with a
sharp exclamation tugged hard.

H let out a shriek of pain and passed out on the spot.

When he came to he was lying on the floor of the waiting room,
with Yoshiko sobbing by his side.

"You're lucky. The doctor says the bone's come together," his mother
said. "You'll have to come back a few more times, though."

H was quite subdued by the pain. It was a throbbing pain, worse than when he'd first broken the bone at the sandpit, so, just to reassure himself, he said, "I *can* have a curry rice every time I come, can't I?"

The curry didn't have much meat in it, but he enjoyed the flavor, which was different from what he was used to at home.

"*I* shan't come again," said little Yoshiko. "The curry's too hot for me, and I feel so bad when they hurt you."

By the time he'd been attending the clinic for a month or so it began to stop hurting, and H actually started to look forward to going to the Red Wall bone-setters, since he got a plate of curry and rice every time. Those were happy days. Although his right arm was in a sling, the inconvenience was outweighed by the pleasure derived from his friends' admiration for his ability to draw and write with his left hand. And he was always aware of *The Three Treasures* waiting for him at home.

This happiness was rudely interrupted, however, when he came home from school one day to find his mother standing with *The Three Treasures* in her hand and a stern expression on her face. The weight of the book he'd hidden behind the calligraphy had made it fall down, thus revealing its existence.

"What does this mean?" demanded his mother. "Have you been reading Ryunosuke Akutagawa's stuff? He's the novelist who killed himself."

H was doubly shocked, both by the discovery of the book and by the information that Akutagawa had committed suicide. According to Christian beliefs, one should never, under any circumstances, kill oneself. His mother, too, seemed just as upset by the discovery that the book was written by a man who'd actually killed himself as by the shock of finding that her son was secretly reading fiction.

"Did the teacher at school say you could read books like this?"

"Mr. Matsuoka said it was a good book and we should try it, so ..."

The lie came out almost without his thinking about it, but his mother promptly tucked the book under her arm and slipped on a pair of wooden clogs.

"Then I'm going to the school to talk to Mr. Matsuoka himself," she said, and hurried off.

H hadn't for a moment thought his mother would rush straight off to see his teacher, and it threw him into a panic. Almost certainly Mr. Matsuoka, if challenged by his mother, would be shocked and would indignantly deny the charge. What would happen if they found out it was Don-chan who'd lent him the book, and Don-chan's father got to know about it? How could he ever apologize? He felt almost faint with the thoughts swirling around in his head.

An hour or so later his mother came back. Her expression was unexpectedly mild, and he immediately felt a bit relieved.

"Mr. Matsuoka said that yes, he *had* advised you to read Akutagawa's *The Three Treasures*. He said reading books like that would stop children from going astray, but not letting them read anything apart from the Bible wasn't likely to do them much good. So from now on you can read books, but not in secret: you must show them to me first."

H's mind boggled at this astonishing change in his mother. At the same time he was surprised at the way Mr. Matsuoka had overlooked the lie and skillfully saved the day for him—not to mention his telling Toshiko that H should be allowed to read more books. Until now H hadn't cared much for Mr. Matsuoka. He was always yelling at them, and his PE classes were so strict that they'd earned him the nickname of "Puncher." But now the same teacher had actually covered up for him, and H, who was nothing if not pragmatic, suddenly found he quite liked him after all.

It was like the story of the black king who seemed to be wicked but turned out to be good, he reflected.

The bandages were still on his shoulder, but he decided to give Don-chan back *The Three Treasures*. On the day before he did so, he read, for the first time, the bits in small print—a piece by a man called Haruo Sato headed "In Place of a Preface," and an afterword by the Ryuichi Oana who'd done the illustrations. Reading them, he learned how the book had come to be written. It seemed that Ryunosuke Akutagawa had had the idea of making a large, beautiful book that several children could lay open on the table and sit around and read together, but in fact he'd killed himself a year before the book was ready.

So in the end Akutagawa never saw what a fine book *The Three Treasures* had made. Somehow, the thought gave H a funny feeling. He was flipping through the pages one last time when he suddenly found himself crying.

The illustrator had written: "The author, Ryunosuke Akutagawa, fell ill and died before the book was completed." The note, dated October 24, 1927, must have attributed the death to sickness in order to conceal the fact of the author's suicide from children reading it.

The next day, on the way home from school, he dropped in at Don-chan's place to return the book. Taking out the cardboard case that still stood empty on his father's bookshelf, Don-chan carefully replaced *The Three Treasures*. He must have been on tenterhooks every day in case his father discovered that the case was empty, and H felt very guilty for what he'd done.

The last page of *The Three Treasures* showed the price of the book, which H hadn't known until then: five yen. Again, he was astonished. For an adult, the price of admission to a movie theater was fifty sen, and a plate of curry and rice cost fifteen sen; so five yen was an enormous amount to pay for a single book. You could have more than thirty plates of curry for the price of this one volume alone! Now he could understand why Don-chan's father had forbidden him so firmly to let the book out of the house.

So *The Three Treasures* was itself a treasure even for an adult like Don-chan's father.

When he grew up, H resolved, he'd buy a copy of *The Three Treasures* for himself, without fail.

11

The Living God

On the right, just inside the main gate of the Nagara Primary School which H attended, was the sandpit, and on the left a raised sumo ring, next to which was a building known as the Hoanden.

The Hoanden, a concrete structure looking a little like a large safe, housed the "Imperial Likenesses," together with a copy of the Emperor Meiji's celebrated "Imperial Rescript on Education."

The "Imperial Likenesses" were official portrait photographs of Their Majesties the Emperor and Empress.

It was decreed that every day, as they arrived at school in the morning and left it again in the afternoon, students must make a profound obeisance, without fail, in the direction of the Hoanden.

When ceremonies were held to mark national holidays, the Imperial Likenesses were moved to the school assembly hall where they were hung at the back of the dais in the center, but since they were screened by curtains it was impossible for the boys ever to catch so much as a glimpse of them. None of them had ever witnessed the Imperial Likenesses being carried from the Hoanden to the hall, much less seen what kind of photos they were.

But H wanted to see them, and while he was about it he wanted to find out what the inside of the Hoanden looked like.

He also wanted his friends to join him in sneaking a look, but none of them showed any interest.

That being the case, on the day of Tenchosetsu, the Emperor's birthday, H went to school alone an hour and a half before the ceremony was due to begin and waited patiently near the Hoanden.

About thirty minutes later the principal and vice-principal appeared almost simultaneously in formal morning dress, and rapidly mounted the steps to the main entrance of the school. After a while they appeared again in the entrance and came walking toward the Hoanden, where H was waiting. Now they were carrying black-lacquered trays, and each wore the same unapproachable expression.

H was afraid he was going to be told off. Relieved when they said nothing, he said politely "Good morning, sirs," but found himself ignored, exactly as though his voice had been inaudible.

As the vice-principal used the key in his hand to open the lock, H went closer and tried to get a look inside. At this the principal suddenly said in a loud voice, "Profound obeisance!" so H hastily bowed his head.

He stayed in this position for a few moments, but then, hearing the sound of a key being turned, surreptitiously raised his head—only to find the door already closed. He'd seen nothing after all.

The next thing he knew, the principal was raising a large, square box, wrapped in a purple cloth, up to the level of his eyes and, keeping it there, was starting to walk back in the direction of the school building.

Watching him from the rear, H told himself he'd better give up any hope of seeing the Imperial portraits.

"How did it go?" his friends inquired when they arrived at the school; then, when he confessed he'd seen nothing, "What'd you expect? You want to know everything, that's the trouble," they said scornfully.

"But I want to know what I'm bowing to," he retorted.

H disliked these ceremonies in the assembly hall which always began with everybody bowing deeply to the Imperial Likenesses. He found them a strain. There were fourteen national holidays or commemorative days a year, but few of them were full-day holidays for the school. For example, on Kigensetsu (February 11), Shunki Koreisai (the day of the spring equinox in March), Tenchosetsu (April 29) and Meijisetsu (November 11), the "Imperial Rescript on Education" was read aloud at the school in a rite throughout which everybody was required to remain standing stock still. It wasn't only H who detested such days; all the other boys too found the ceremonies a pain in the neck.

While the principal was reading in reverent tones from the scroll bearing the text, everyone present was supposed to stay for three minutes with head bowed and not to move for any reason whatsoever. This was the most trying thing of all.

During this period the curtain covering the Imperial Likenesses was, in fact, drawn back briefly, then closed again once the ritual was over.

H was still determined to get a good look at the portraits.

Once the reading of the Imperial Rescript began, he made sure that everybody had his head dutifully bowed, then furtively raised his own.

To his surprise he found that the Imperial Likenesses displayed on the altar-like arrangement in the center were nothing more nor less than the familiar portrait photographs of Their Majesties that everybody had hanging in their homes.

"Well," thought H in disgust, "it's the same old photo! Nobody bows deeply to the Imperial portraits at home, so why do we have to at school? And why mustn't we look at them?"

Another reason why not only H but all the other students too found it a trial to listen to the Imperial Rescript with their heads bowed was the danger of their noses dripping. Since it was forbidden under any circumstances to make the slightest sound during the reading of the Rescript, they had to screw their noses up tight, repressing the urge to sniff.

H knew the whole of the 315-character Imperial Rescript by heart, but this was nothing special—by the time they were in fourth grade, quite a number of the other boys did too.

> Know ye, Our Subjects:
>
> Our Imperial Ancestors have founded Our Empire on a basis broad and everlasting, and have deeply and firmly implanted virtue; Our subjects ever united in loyalty and filial piety have from generation to generation illustrated the beauty thereof. This is the glory of the fundamental character of Our Empire, and herein also lies the source of Our education....

And so it went on, seemingly forever, while they stood with eyes downcast, waiting for the principal to finish, wondering how much longer it would be before he finally wound up with "The Imperial Name and the Imperial Seal."

As soon as the recitation was over, the hall would erupt in a chorus of sniffs and snuffles, the sound of a whole school clearing its collective nose.

H had simply memorized the Rescript automatically, without understanding the meaning of individual words and phrases. But there was one thing he did know: that the difficult, rarely encountered Chinese character with which his own name, Hajime, was written occurred near the beginning.

"It means 'beginning,'" his father had told him, "but it doesn't mean the beginning of any old thing; it's only used in talking about the beginning—the *founding*—of a nation."

"Why did you give me a name like that?" he'd asked resentfully. "I'll never found a country, so what connection is there? Besides, it's so complicated—it's a nuisance to write, and I don't like it."

His father had looked rather disappointed and said in a small voice, "I think it suits you. I mean, it's not just any run-of-the-mill Hajime."

There were lots of things about both the Imperial Rescript and the Imperial Likenesses that H didn't understand. The photographs, for example, both looked the same as those at home, so where was the difference? Probably the vice-principal could make it clear to him, he thought.

"I know His Majesty the Emperor is a very important person," H ventured, "but why aren't we allowed to look at the Imperial photograph at school? Why do we pay our respects to it as if we were worshiping a god?"

"Well, you see," the vice-principal explained, "when the principal reads the Imperial Rescript, it's the same as if His Majesty had graciously honored the Nagara Primary School with his presence and we were hearing him read it in person. You know, don't you, that whenever His Majesty visits anywhere, the people along the route have to keep their heads deeply bowed and mustn't look directly at the Imperial Countenance? Well, it's the same as that. His Majesty the Emperor may *look* like an ordinary person, but actually he's a living god, a 'god-in-this-world,' as they say."

The expression "living god" puzzled H. In what way was it different from the gods in Shinto shrines, he wondered, or the god of Christianity? Could a living human being really be a god?

He asked his mother when he got home.

"His Majesty the Emperor *isn't* a god," she said firmly. "The only god is Our-Father-Which-Art-In-Heaven—surely you know that? It says as much in the Bible, doesn't it?"

She was so definite about it that H regretted not having asked his father when his mother wasn't there.

"What do you think, Dad?" he asked.

"For a Christian, I suppose, Jesus Christ *is* the only god, but other religions have different ones. You know the Muslim mosque over in Yamate, don't you? That belongs to what they call Islam, and the people who go to worship there believe there's only one god, whose name is Allah, and no others. It's not so much a question of which is the true god; it's just that different people believe in different ones. That doesn't matter, does it?"

"Then is it 'religion' when you say that His Imperial Majesty is a god?"

"I suppose you could say that. There are lots of other gods in Japan, but you could see him as one of them, I suppose."

"Do you, a Christian, really *believe* that?" put in H's mother immediately. "You mean you recognize the gods of the heathen?"

"Well, you know," said his father, "if you're going to call religions that other people believe in 'heathen,' you can't complain if other people refer to Christianity as heathen. And most Japanese go to shrines to pay their respects to their favorite gods—you have to recognize that, too."

Maybe his father was right, thought H.

He was quite relieved, because he had a particular favorite among the Japanese gods whose name was Susanowo. He was the younger brother of Amaterasu Omikami, a goddess who appears in the *Kojiki*, a book of ancient Japanese myths.

This Amaterasu Omikami, the greatest of all the many gods, was worshiped at the Ise Shrines as the ancestress of the Emperor, but her brother Susanowo was a very unruly god, which was what had endeared him particularly to H.

It had started with something he'd read in a textbook: "Amaterasu Omikami had a younger brother called Susanowo, who often behaved violently. Even so, the goddess was always very kind to her brother and never scolded him until one day when he dirtied the room where she did her weaving. At this, the goddess finally went and hid herself in the Cave of Heaven, closing the entrance behind her with a big rock...."

An illustration showed a maiden called Amenouzume-no-mikoto dancing in front of the cave in order to persuade Amaterasu Omikami to come out.

This time H didn't ask the vice-principal about it, but went to see Mr.

Yamazaki after class; the vice-principal would only have said difficult, abstract things that he couldn't understand, just as he'd done on the previous occasion.

Mr. Yamazaki, who wore dark-rimmed glasses, wasn't H's home-room teacher, but you could ask him about anything and he always explained things clearly.

"What were the 'violent' things the textbook says Susanowo-no-mikoto did?" asked H.

"Hold on a moment," Mr. Yamazaki said, and went to fetch the *Kojiki* out of the bookcase.

"Here it is—this is where it tells about Susanowo-no-mikoto," he said, flipping through the pages as H watched. There were long rows of Chinese characters, nothing that H himself could ever even hope to read.

"Here's what it says," said Mr. Yamazaki, reading aloud and explaining the meaning in ordinary language as he went. "Susanowo-no-mikoto was breaking down the raised paths that human beings had taken so much trouble to build between the paddy fields, and generally rampaging about the place. What was worse, he flung turds about inside the palace and flayed the skin of a horse and threw it into the room where the women were weaving cloth. At first the goddess had taken her younger brother's side, but this finally made her really angry, and she shut herself up in a cave."

H was delighted to hear that even the gods sometimes did outrageous things.

Another thing he found out was that although Susanowo-no-mikoto was a grown man with a big, bushy beard, he was still capable of crying his heart out because he wanted to see his mother, who had died. H was beginning to feel better and better about this "god."

"Why don't the school textbooks tell you about such things in a way you can understand?" he asked.

"It wouldn't do for a textbook to put exactly what it says in the *Kojiki*," said Mr. Yamazaki, smiling. "Actually, in the original it says that when Amenouzume-no-mikoto danced in front of the cave, she was stark naked. This naked dance was so entertaining that all those watching burst out laughing. Amaterasu wondered what was going on and made an opening so that she could peek out. That gave a powerful god called

Tajikarao-no-mikoto the chance to force open the door of the cave and drag her outside."

But the illustration in H's textbook showed Amenouzume wearing a kimono.

"She's got clothes on in the textbook picture, hasn't she?" he insisted. "It's a lie, isn't it? Why? And why don't they tell you that Susanowo-no-mikoto was the kind of god who threw turds about the place? Because they don't want people to know that one of the Emperor's ancestors was a peculiar kind of god? They cover up anything that's awkward for the Emperor, do they?—even if it's in the *Kojiki*...."

"You'll understand when you're a bit bigger," Mr. Yamazaki said, overwhelmed by so many whys. "And," he added in a warning tone, "it might be a good idea, too, not to talk about His Majesty and Susanowo-no-mikoto in the same breath."

So there are some things I mustn't say even to a teacher, thought H, a bit disappointed, and wondered if he'd be arrested by the police for *lèse-majesté*.

Even children who could never have written the difficult word "*lèse-majesté*" knew it stood for something terrible.

And it really did, too: you could be hauled off to the police station for "*lèse-majesté*" just because you'd said something facetious about the Emperor.

H knew for a fact that the man who lived behind the drugstore in Taisho-dori had been arrested for it. Rumor had it that he'd told some local kids that the Emperor ate and shit just the same as them, so he was a man like anybody else—and the police had got to hear of it.

H was sure that no *real* god would ever shit, and was inclined to believe what the man had said. But he decided not to tell anyone what he thought, and firmly resolved to beware of "His Majesty the Emperor" as a topic of conversation. There was no telling who mightn't give you away.

At school, for example, they started instilling the idea that the Emperor was divine right from first grade. If you so much as heard the phrase "His Majesty the Emperor," you had to come to attention on the spot, wherever you were, and remain motionless. You'd never get away with saying "I was just joking."

The ex-army officer, Mr. Omori, who took every opportunity to use the phrase, was fond of getting the children together and telling them, "When you grow up, you too will go into the army and fight and die for the Emperor. To do so is a duty, an honor for all men who serve their country."

According to the same former officer, all official orders in Japan were the Emperor's personal orders, to be obeyed under any circumstances. Going into the army, and attacking the enemy's positions in your capacity as a soldier, were part and parcel of the same principle.

H found this a bit strange. How could the Emperor himself personally give an order to attack? But he was told that in this case the unit commander was giving orders on the Emperor's behalf, and that all orders from superior officers were to be taken as orders from the Emperor himself.

"*Children* aren't soldiers, though, so does that mean they don't get any orders from the Emperor?" H asked. At this the veteran lost his temper.

"Japanese children are all children of His Majesty. You're all his offspring, d'you hear?" he shouted. "And would you disobey your own parent?"

This was the first time H had heard the word "offspring"; but even when it was explained to him, he hadn't the faintest idea what it meant in this context.

Whether it was "offspring" he was talking about or something else, the retired officer would use the phrase "His Majesty the Emperor" again and again, and every time it occurred H and his friends would have to stand to attention.

It wasn't just him, either; other adults were fond of saying "everything is His Majesty's will" too, and H found that just as odd. After all, how could everything be an Imperial order when the Emperor himself had no idea what kind of orders all those unit commanders and others were giving?

Though he'd kept it to himself, H had never much cared for the Emperor, seeing him as a somehow stiff and forbidding figure, until he found out what the *Kojiki* said about Susanowo-no-mikoto. But now he knew that the Emperor was a descendant of that same unruly deity, he suspected that he wasn't such a perfect "living god" after all.

Morio, who was worried by his son's habit of saying the first thing that came into his head, warned him in much the same terms as Mr. Yamazaki had: "You'd better not talk about Susanowo too lightly!"

Mr. Yamazaki, in fact, had stopped talking to him about Susanowo altogether. H had privately dubbed him "Kojiki-sensei," and would pester the hapless teacher to tell him more about Susanowo whenever they met, but Mr. Yamazaki would pretend not to have heard.

Just when everyone else seemed so careful about the slightest mention of the Emperor, there was one woman who had no such qualms, but went about town chanting in a loud voice: "Gladly we give our lives for the Emperor! Three cheers for His Majesty! Hip, hip, hurrah!"

H couldn't tell how old she was, but she had red circles painted on her cheeks, lots of ribbons in her hair, and was dressed in a grubby kimono, with battered clogs on her feet.

According to one of the local housewives the woman lived at Taino-hata, a long way upstream on the Tenjo River. "She seems to have gone a bit funny in the head after her husband and son were killed in the war," she said, though it wasn't clear whether this story was true or not.

It seemed the woman went on her rambles every day. Sometimes she would come to the district where H lived and go past the house calling, "Three cheers for His Majesty." But somehow the words didn't ring true to H.

"She'll get taken in for *lèse-majesté*, won't she?" he asked his father anxiously.

"She'll be okay," his father replied. "She isn't actually saying anything disrespectful."

With her shouting as loud as that, there was no need for anybody to inform on her—everybody knew already—and H was sure she'd get arrested sooner or later, but she didn't.

"If she were in her right mind, you could give her a warning," said Mr. Omori, the ex-army officer. "But with *her*, you just can't...."

Gladly we give our lives for the Emperor! The cry came again and again in the twilight, winding its way about the streets. *Three cheers for His Majesty! Hip, hip, hurrah!* Somehow, H found it scary.

12

Tripartite Alliance

"There's something here about the Takarazuka Girls' Opera," H's father said to him, looking up from his newspaper. He probably thought H would be interested because he'd once taken him to see them. "Seems there was a great fuss because the Takarazuka Opera School didn't take part in the 'Citizens' anti-British Rally.' The director was summoned by the military police and given a thorough dressing down."

"What does 'anti-British rally' mean?" H asked anxiously, being something of a Takarazuka fan himself.

"People got together to make clear their disapproval of Britain and its actions, but the girls at Takarazuka wouldn't join in. They went on a friendship mission to America last year, visiting the International Exposition in New York and so on, so I expect they found out all kinds of things about other countries that you never get to know as long as you stay in Japan."

As for what was happening in other countries, H didn't know much about that, but he didn't approve of "anti-British" because quite a lot of his father's customers were British. Mr Howard, Mr. Campbell and others at Strong and Co., in the foreign quarter, were all valuable customers of Senoh Tailors.

"Mr. Campbell was saying only the other day that it looked as though trade with Japan was going to get more and more difficult, and he'd be going home to England before long," Morio said. "We may not be able to carry on with tailoring the way we have up to now. There aren't many Japanese people ordering new suits nowadays, either."

In fact, his father did seem to be doing nothing but alterations these days; very seldom did he unfurl a new roll of cloth on the table in his workshop and start snipping away at it with his scissors anymore. H liked the sound of cloth being cut, and he missed it now that there were so few orders for new suits.

"It's not just a matter of new suits, either," his father added. "I'm worried that if Japan, Germany and Italy sign a tripartite alliance, things will get even worse."

Most of the neighbors were saying that for Germany and Japan to form an alliance would greatly strengthen Japan's position as a nation, so H was puzzled to hear his father say just the opposite. He knew it wasn't just a question of personal preference, since their customers included both Germans and Italians, and he was curious to know what his concern was.

"You're not to tell anyone else under any circumstances," Morio said. "If anyone hears what I say we'll be labeled as 'un-Japanese.'"

"Not even Mother?"

"Not even her. She might talk about it to someone, and then we'd all be in trouble."

H was pleased his father would confide in him when he didn't trust even his own wife.

"Signing a tripartite alliance," his father went on, "would mean a tie-up with Germany, which hates England, so Japan would have to regard England as an enemy too. America's wary of any such alliance. It seems Roosevelt—that's the American president—said that if Japan joined a tripartite alliance, America would give England military aid and increase its support for China at the same time. But if, for example, Japan ever went to war with America, the triple alliance it'd be supposed to rely on wouldn't be any use at all. Germany and Italy are much too distant from Japan for them to come to its aid."

"How do you know all these things, Dad?" asked H. "Did you read them in the paper or something?"

"No, Mr. James told me the other day."

H knew Mr. James well. He was an American who ran another trading company close to Strong and Co., the English firm, and he was always nice to H.

"It seems America's really annoyed," Morio went on. "It's not just bluffing when it says it'll take steps to counter any tripartite alliance.

Only the other day it banned the export of scrap iron to Japan. Japan's already at war with China, but if things go on like this it'll fall out with America and make enemies in other countries besides. That's why it's so stupid to carry out anti-British campaigns and the like just to please Germany."

Recently, H had begun to feel he didn't like German people, though for no better reason than an unpleasant experience he'd had at the home of a German naval officer called Klaussen. He'd been playing a game called Corinthian with Klaussen's eldest son, who was a year older than himself, while waiting for his father to finish a fitting. The other boy must have been annoyed because H had won three times running, for he suddenly flew into a temper, shouted in Japanese, "Japanese and Jews are all stupid!" and overturned the board they'd been playing on.

Later, when he and his father had left and were walking down the slope in Kitano-dori, he'd said to Morio, "Do you like Lieutenant Klaussen, Dad? He seems rather stuck-up to me, as though he thinks tailors aren't really worth bothering about. I'm not sure I like Germans very much."

"But you shouldn't assume all Germans are like him, you know," said his father. "There are all kinds. Lieutenant Klaussen is a Nazi officer, so he's something of a special case."

H understood. In fact he knew quite well that some Germans were different from others. For instance he'd found the Oppenheimers, a German-Jewish family, very nice indeed. He said so to his father, who laughed so much that H had to put in hastily: "And it's not just because Mrs. Oppenheimer cooked some sausages for me either!"

Accustomed as they were to having foreigners living in their midst, the people of Kobe got on perfectly well with nationals of any country, although recently—probably because subtle international tensions had begun to filter through to them—they'd begun to distinguish between, say, British, Americans, French and Germans. For one thing, there'd been a sudden increase in the number who favored Nazi Germany.

This was apparently the result of a visit to Japan the summer before by a party of Hitler Youth consisting of thirty youngsters between fifteen and eighteen years of age. Much to everyone's astonishment, they'd all been between 170 and 190 centimeters tall, and not one of them had been wearing glasses. What was more, they'd all been in smart, military-style uniforms and had behaved with impeccable military discipline, thanks to which they were greeted with frantic enthusiasm wherever they went. During their three-month stay they'd visited various cities throughout Japan before finally leaving by sea from Kobe Harbor.

"The Hitler Youth presented a model for all young people," wrote the newspapers admiringly after their departure. "Japan has much to learn from the virtues they displayed."

No wonder, thought H: they'd been an attractive-looking crowd. Their visit to Japan had been very influential, and had helped foster overwhelming public support for a tripartite alliance.

H had heard that Italy, too, had a leader, Mussolini, who was a lot like Hitler, as well as a young people's organization similar to the Hitler Youth. The Italians living in Kobe were a cheerful crowd for the most part and more easygoing than the Germans, if not so "correct." Even so, once talk of the pending alliance got around they started to become popular, and the ordinary man-in-the-street was soon treating Italians like brothers.

"Sooner or later, I suppose, we'll have a triple treaty," said H's father gloomily, "and then there'll be no stopping things. And the war with China's still on, too.…"

"But there are other people who think the same way as you, aren't there?" H said impatiently. "And if so, why don't they say something?"

"If they did they'd get hauled off to jail by the military police. The other day a man called Takao Saito made a speech about it. He's a member of a place called the House of Representatives, in the Imperial Diet, and he said that though people say the war in China is for the sake of 'Greater East Asian Coprosperity,' and call it a 'holy war' to protect world peace and order, the fact is that war is a power struggle between countries, and to call it 'holy' is all lies and deception. He was right, and a lot of the other members applauded him. But the war minister was angry, and in the end Mr. Saito had to resign. The Diet is supposed to be a place where you can talk about national affairs, but nobody can say anything nowadays. Anybody who opposes the army's policy is got rid of. Politics is such a mess, there's nothing can be done about it."

"I see. You mean it's 'complex and bizarre'…?" "Complex and bizarre" was a phrase in vogue at the time. H had heard that it meant "too much for me to understand," and had taken to using it himself in all kinds of contexts.

Actually the phrase had first been used a year previously by the prime minister, Hiranuma. Listening to his father, H realized that it had all kinds of tricky political connotations

It had, in fact, been used in connection with Germany. Just when Japanese forces were fighting the Soviet army across the border with China at a place called Nomonhan in Manchuria, Germany had signed a treaty of non-aggression with the Soviet Union, promising that the two countries wouldn't quarrel with each other. Japan was at a loss, because the Japanese forces at the time were in danger of defeat by the Russians. Germany had betrayed Japan at a moment when the latter was assuming that Germany was sympathetic to its awkward position. The result was that the Hiranuma government had resigned, the prime minister's parting remark being that "the situation in Europe is complex and bizarre."

Hearing this from his father, H made up his mind that Germany was a wily nation and not to be trusted.

Nine days after Germany signed the treaty of non-aggression with the Soviet Union, it launched a violent attack, without warning, on its neighbor Poland, throwing in such enormous numbers of tanks and planes that Poland soon looked in danger of collapsing, whereupon the Soviet Union promptly attacked it from the rear. Helpless in the face of these twin attacks, Poland surrendered. It had all happened within a matter of a couple of weeks. Like two wild beasts falling on a lamb, Germany and the Soviet Union divided their prey between them, each taking half its territory. It seemed as if they'd already had a secret agreement to divide up Poland when they signed the treaty.

The previous year Germany had already annexed Austria and sent its forces into Czechoslovakia. Britain and France had issued a joint declaration saying they could no longer tolerate Nazi Germany's territorial expansionism. Thus the "Second Great European War" had finally begun.

H now understood only too well why signing a tripartite alliance meant making enemies of England and France. He began to wonder anxiously whether grownups in Japan really knew what kind of country Germany was. Japan was already short of iron; now America was refusing to sell it scrap iron, and imports of oil had become impossible.

"Not only does Japan not have supplies of iron and oil—it's running short of the money to trade with other countries, too," said H's father.

"What, no money either?"

"A country's money doesn't mean paper notes; it means how much actual gold it's got. Actually, paper notes are supposed to be just substitutes for gold coins, but now that's no longer so. About ten years ago every note had printed on it that it was exchangeable for gold if you took it to a bank, but the new notes don't say that."

H hadn't realized till then that notes were used instead of gold coinage. "Do we have any of the old notes in the house?" he asked. "If so, I'd like to see one."

"Yes, we do. Both kinds have the same design, and the amounts are the same, so ten yen is ten yen in either case."

The two notes his father got out of his billfold for H to see had exactly the same design, but the new one was missing the "promise to pay the bearer ten yen in gold coinage in exchange for this note."

"If you took the note saying 'exchangeable' to a bank, would they change it for a gold coin even now?" H asked.

"No, they wouldn't."

"You mean it's a fraud?"

"What they'd say nowadays is 'We can't exchange it for gold, but the value of the money's the same, so you must trust the state.' It's not just that they won't change it for gold, either; nowadays they want *you* to tell *them* how much precious metal and gold you have in the house. Last summer every household got a form headed 'National Census of Gold Holdings.' It was a compulsory thing—you were supposed to put down everything except your gold teeth and gold pens—so you couldn't tell any lies. Sooner or later, I'm sure, we'll have to hand over to the government anything we have that's made of gold."

"What, even gold wristwatches?" H demanded angrily. "Did you tell them about Mother's wristwatch? That's *my* watch! How come you reported it without telling me?"

There was a story behind his claim. At the age of five H had been on a swing in Triangle Park, near their house, when he'd found a watch lying on the ground.

"Let's take it to the police station together," his mother had said. But H, alarmed, had burst into tears.

"I didn't steal it," he bawled, "I *found* it! I'm not a thief, I don't want to go to the police."

"The person who dropped it will be missing it. If you keep it without saying anything it's the same as stealing. One thing, though: if nobody claims it within a year the watch goes to the person who found it and handed it in."

This made H feel better, and he went to the police station with his mother.

Later, when H had already forgotten all about the watch, a postcard came one day saying, "The owner of the watch has not appeared, so please come and collect it, bringing your seal."

As they handed the watch over to his mother at the local police station, H, who was standing at her side, stretched out his hand and said, "It's mine!"

The policeman looked awkwardly at Toshiko and said to H soothingly, "Look, son, this is a woman's watch, a grownup's watch, and besides it's made of gold so it's very valuable. Why don't you give it to your mother and get her to promise to buy you a man's watch when you grow up?"

In the end they agreed that H was lending it to his mother. In short, the inappropriately expensive-looking watch his mother always wore was really *his*.

"Yes, I know it's yours," his father said placatingly, "but we can't hide it, because the neighbors all know that your mother wears a gold watch. And we can't pawn it, because the pawnshops are forbidden to buy things made of gold anymore."

So, thought H, it's another case of "can't be helped." The phrase was popular at the time, even among primary school students, who used it on any and every occasion. For adults, though, it had a more sinister meaning.

More and more the individual was finding himself at the disposal of the state, with little or no say in his own destiny. For instance, a National War Work Order had come into force, which stated that anyone who possessed some occupational skill was obliged to comply immediately if a war work notice came for him. This notice was called a "white slip," to distinguish it from the draft notice which was known as a "pink slip."

"Dad, if you get a white slip, do you *have* to go?"

"Seeing I have tailoring skills, I suppose I'd have to go to a factory making military uniforms."

"What if you said you didn't want to?"

"Then I'd get up to a year in prison or a fine of up to a thousand yen."

"Does Mother know that?"

"I think so, but she never talks about it. I can only guess that she doesn't want to talk about something that worries her. If I go on making suits I imagine I'll get a white slip, so I'm thinking of joining the wardens."

The wardens were local groups put together by adult male civilians to organize military and firefighting drills in the neighborhood.

Besides these wardens' groups, which were for men only, there'd been a government directive calling for the formation of organizations of local residents known as "neighborhood associations." Tokyo had them already, and now they were being formed in Kobe as well.

"In the old days, in the Edo period," Morio explained to H, "they had what they called 'groups of five,' and if one of the members committed some crime it was considered to be the responsibility of the whole group. The people in the group helped each other, but at the same time they were supposed to keep an eye on each other too. The neighborhood associations are much the same kind of thing."

The duties of the neighborhood associations included seeing off men who were going to join the army, giving support to families whose menfolk were away or had died in battle, encouraging each other to avoid extravagance, arranging the buying and allocation of national bonds, and organizing civilian air raid and firefighting drills. There had long been organizations called "district associations," but from now on the "neighborhood associations" were to take everything over from them. If you didn't join your neighborhood association, you might not get your rations. That was how it was at that time.

On June 14, 1940, the German forces invading France occupied Paris almost without bloodshed. Though there were ongoing reports of scattered partisan resistance, it seemed that Nazi Germany had won complete control over France.

Three months later Foreign Minister Matsuoka finally signed an agreement in Berlin under which Japan became a member of the Tripartite Alliance.

Shocked, Morio stopped talking much, even to H. It wasn't just the Tripartite Alliance as such; there was another serious problem that threatened to deal a decisive blow to the tailoring business.

A law called the National Dress Order had been passed. Although he'd been more or less prepared for it, Morio was horrified when a circular came from the Tailors' Union explaining the details. One section of the order declared:

> Clothing in our country has imitated that of the West to excess, showing almost no independent creativity. This must be remedied. The history of world civilizations shows that the development of a nation has always been accompanied by a forward-looking clothing culture. Japan too must create its own unique style of dress, one capable of outstripping the rest of the world and pointing the way for the peoples of East Asia. It is hoped, therefore, that all union members will put their individual skills to good use and cooperate in producing the newly established "national dress."

Patterns for this "national dress" were enclosed, together with a picture of the completed article.

The "national dress" was to be of the same khaki color as military uniforms; the material used was to be cotton or wool, and the headgear was a "national cap" resembling the service cap worn by the military.

When they were wearing national dress with the cap, even ordinary civilians were supposed to salute each other in military fashion.

"Will *everyone* have to wear this dress?" H asked. "Will they be arrested if they wear a suit?"

"They won't be arrested," his father said, "but I expect they'll have to wear puttees, even with a suit. The national dress is designed so it can be used at any time as a military uniform, and they've decreed that it's acceptable for formal occasions too, so I expect everybody will start wearing it from now on. The suit I'm making for Mr. Howard will probably be the last I'll make."

He looked sad.

The suit for Mr. Howard was a three-piece that Mr. Campbell, who was going home to England, had ordered for him as a parting gift. Morio must have been given plenty of time for the work, because he went at it slowly, almost regretfully, as though reluctant to complete it.

He probably had the feeling, as he'd said, that this would be the last suit he would make. Since the tightening of controls on civilian suits, material for menswear was predominantly khaki, and it was now difficult to get hold of ordinary cloth for suits.

Shige, the apprentice, was sitting by Morio intently watching the movement of his hands. Probably he too felt that this would be their last suit.

About three weeks later a new ordinance entitled "Order Prohibiting the Manufacture and Sale of Luxury Goods" was issued. Its provisions included one banning all made-to-order three-piece suits that cost one hundred thirty yen or more for a winter suit, or one hundred yen or more for a summer suit.

Since the suits Morio made cost from eighty-five to ninety yen for even the best-quality winter suit, they didn't qualify as "luxury goods," but even so the days of the Western-style tailors were obviously numbered.

The placards in the streets proclaiming that "Luxury Is the Enemy" were becoming more and more common....

13

Military Secrets

"From now on you have to say *toshu* in Japanese, instead of using the English 'pitcher,' and *hoshu* instead of 'catcher.'"

"*Toshu* and *hoshu* aren't too bad, but Japanese words like *yoshi* for 'strike' and *dame* for 'ball' are too soft; there's no punch to them."

H and his friends were laughing about such things as they played baseball.

A directive from the home ministry had put out the word that "the hitherto prevailing vogue for things foreign hinders the fostering of the Yamato spirit. The use of certain transliterated foreign words and expressions is forthwith prohibited. This shall apply, for example, to expressions considered as violating the spirit of the times, morally undesirable expressions, stage names imitating foreign names for the sake of cheap novelty, and the like."

The drive to get rid of English expressions had had repercussions in every field.

"Did you know that pitcher Stalkhin's name is out too?" said Kosaku Mita from next door. H hadn't known. "So what do you think they're going to call him from now on?" Kosaku went on. "'Suda'! He's had to change it to 'Hiroshi Suda' so it can be written in Chinese characters."

"Stalkhin to Suda—that's too much!" said H. And the boys reeled off for each other as many newly proscribed foreign words as they could remember.

"'Golden Bat,' the name of the cigarette, has been changed to 'Golden Kite.' The old bat's turned into a kite—you know, the one that perched on the Emperor Jimmu's bow in the legend. Some promotion, that!"

" 'Oyster fry' has become *kaki-yoten*—'Western-style oyster *tempura*.' I saw it on the board at the fried-food shop in the market."

"They say 'soda pop' has to be 'fountain water' from now on; I saw it myself in the paper the other day. 'Cases of bottled fountain water were dispatched as presents from home for the troops in the field.' "

" 'Fountain water' … I suppose it's not *so* strange. I mean, it does look all bubbly. It reminds me of a fountain I saw in a park somewhere."

"What about 'H', then? That's English too, isn't it?"

"Yes—they're already selling pencils with the 'H' and 'B' on them changed to the Chinese characters for 'hard' and 'soft.' Are you *sure* the 'H' in your name is okay?"

H's friends stared at him accusingly. He was disconcerted for a moment, but soon rallied.

"H isn't just English," he said, "they have it in German, too. You know 'Heil Hitler,' don't you? That starts with H's—so it's not *only* English."

This seemed to satisfy them. "Okay," they said. "Germany's on our side, so we can go on calling you H."

H himself, though, wasn't happy about this. "Heil Hitler," he knew, was a way of praising Hitler, of proclaiming loyalty to him, and he regretted having spoken as though he'd allied himself with Nazi Germany when in fact it had only been a way out of a momentary difficulty. Even so, there was a danger in future of his being ostracized because "H" was English, so he tried to think of some other way of getting out of it.

"You can stop calling me H and use 'Senoh-kun' instead, if you like," he suggested, but this was promptly turned down.

"Don't be silly. H is much shorter and easier to say."

If they wouldn't change the way they addressed him, he supposed he'd have to fob people off with the "Heil Hitler" bit. But he swore to himself that he'd never wear a sweater with "H" on the chest again.

English wasn't the only thing that was being steadily erased from his surroundings; even Japanese disappeared sometimes. He'd heard talk about postcards being delivered with some of the writing blacked out, but still he was startled when a postcard actually came for them with nearly half the writing obliterated. It was from a young man, a relative, who'd been conscripted into the navy. "So he's finally going to the front,"

H's father remarked, gazing at the official services postcard which had been liberally marked with black ink.

This form of censorship was said to be "for counterespionage purposes," which meant to prevent spying.

"They're gradually tightening up counterespionage," his father had told him, "so you'd better not go climbing on the main roof of the house anymore."

"What's spying got to do with climbing on the roof of your own house?" asked H, puzzled.

"Because they've decided people mustn't look down from anywhere that's over a certain height. From now on, if you start going up on the roof and drawing pictures you'll be hauled in as a spy."

H suspected that his father, who knew his son liked climbing around on the roof, was just using this to discourage him from doing something dangerous rather than telling him directly to quit, but he also knew that such things were, in fact, considered to be "spying."

In December the previous year, 1939, the rules for application of the military secrets law had been revised to make any "bird's-eye" photography or sketching from a high place forbidden.

Besides this, there were all kinds of other reminders in everyday life of the dread Military Secrets Protection Law.

When a naval vessel was visible offshore, it was forbidden even to sketch, much less photograph it. In fact you weren't even supposed to look at the scenery on the shore from a train window. As soon as a train heading west from Kobe left Suma Station, passengers were supposed to voluntarily lower the blinds of the windows on the side overlooking the shore; otherwise they were infringing the Military Secrets Protection Law.

This gave H pause for thought. Since he himself played within sight of the sea almost every day, the chances of his unwittingly violating the law were greater than he could ever have imagined.

Playing on the shore, he often watched ships sailing past out at sea, and would sometimes draw them in considerable detail.

"It's okay to draw them from photos or books," his father reminded him in all seriousness, "but you must give up sketching the real thing."

At first H was amused: whoever could have dreamed up such a thing? The next moment, though, he felt rather scared, and decided he'd give up sketching outdoor scenes. You couldn't tell any longer just what you were or weren't supposed to do.

"Right," he resolved, "from now on I'll stick to pictures of sumo wrestlers."

It had already occurred to him that if he did drawings of sumo wrestlers on paraffin wax paper, he could earn money selling them as "negatives" for the "daylight photos" then in fashion. Sold under the impressive label of "scientific toys," these were all the rage among children at that time. On a sheet of sensitized paper the size of a name card you placed a paraffin-paper negative, secured it in a case with a glass top, and left it in direct sunlight for three minutes, thus producing a picture printed by the sun's rays in the same way as you'd develop an ordinary photograph. The only difference was that you didn't use any fixative, so the picture faded away after a few days. Despite this drawback, the attraction of "developing your own photographs" made it extremely popular.

The basic necessities for making daylight photographs could be bought from a middle-aged man who sat on a piece of straw matting by the roadside near the school. The set came complete with twenty-five "negatives" printed on paraffin paper. In practice, many of the boys were tired of always using the same negatives, and the pictures of the "Forty-Eight Skills" of sumo that H drew sold just as well, if not better.

H racked his brains for some efficient way of mass-producing his pictures without having to draw each one separately. The idea he hit on was to do the pictures on the stencil sheets used for mimeograph printing and then print them on special paraffin paper, thereby making it possible to produce forty pictures from one original.

For this he got Mr. Yamazaki to let him use the mimeograph machine at school. In return he helped the teacher out whenever he needed small illustrations to go with something he was printing.

He borrowed the material on which he based his drawings of the "Forty-Eight Skills" from a boy called Iwao Hayashi, who was in the same grade and was the Nagara Primary School's champion wrestler. Nicknamed "Yokozuna"—grand champion—he was naturally well versed in sumo, being regarded as something of an authority on the sport; besides which he had lots of pictures and photos. It was Hayashi who first told H that the sumo ring had originally been square, not round, and that until 1931 it had been four meters in diameter, half a meter less than at present.

Apart from being well built, Hayashi was a bright student and was good at drawing. He and H regularly found themselves rival exhibitors at the Primary School Art Exhibition. He was a particular favorite with Toshiko, who was always urging H to be friendly with him: "He's such a *lively* boy, and clever as well." Whenever she took H with her to the department store where the exhibition was being held, she'd invite Iwao as well and treat them both to a meal in the store's restaurant. This effectively served as a return for the loan of the sumo materials. Morio was quite relieved to find his son preoccupied with sumo pictures, and Toshiko declared with satisfaction that she wouldn't have minded having another son, provided he were like "young Hayashi." All in all, Iwao was a most convenient talisman for warding off adult displeasure.

Thanks to the cooperation of "Yokozuna" Hayashi, sales of the daylight picture negatives went well and earned H quite a lot of pocket money. But before long he got tired of the business.

"What—fed up with it already?" said his father. "What are you going to draw next? Not military secrets, I hope!" He passed this off as a joke, but seemed a bit anxious, even so.

"I'm not doing pictures anymore," said H. "I've had a better idea. But don't worry—it's to do with sumo again, not with military secrets. Don't tell Mother about it, though. I have to get some pocket money, you see."

He proceeded to explain his latest business project, which was to act as the middle man in the exchange of photos of sumo idols. It would require a bit of time and effort, but it was an entirely new kind of business, with no need for capital.

"No capital ... that's a good thing. But you're not to go cheating people, d'you hear?"

"There's no cheating about it. I arrange for people to exchange photos they don't want anymore for photos of wrestlers they do want. If anything, I'm sure they'll be grateful to me. I'll be able to collect photos myself, too, without spending any money. Anyway, Dad, wait and see. Whatever happens, at least it'll be better than having you worry about military secrets!"

Morio still looked unconvinced, but H went ahead and bought a notebook in preparation for his new business venture.

Here again, of course, he needed to enlist the cooperation of "Yoko-zuna" Hayashi in furnishing the specialist knowledge. First H listed in his notebook, one to a page, the names of all the sumo wrestlers and put small circles by them to indicate their degree of popularity. This was to determine exchange values.

The regular tours of the provinces made by sumo wrestlers in the intervals between main tournaments rarely took in Kobe, but even so the sport was tremendously popular in the city. There were two annual national tournaments of fifteen days each, one in spring and one in summer, and whenever there were live broadcasts on the radio, adults and children alike would be glued to their sets. Futabayama, who'd been enjoying a long winning streak, was particularly popular, and the enthusiasm he aroused even rivaled the ecstatic response to a similar series of victories achieved by Japanese forces in the fighting in China. Even when finally beaten by Akinoumi, after a series of sixty-nine consecutive victories, he remained a national hero.

"Photos of Futabayama are hard to come by, so he'd better have six circles," said Hayashi, and H dutifully inscribed them in his notebook.

Photographs of sumo idols were on sale at Bunseido, the right-hand of the two stationery stores that stood opposite the school gates.

Each photo, mounted on cardboard, was enclosed in an envelope made of old newspaper, and for one sen the boys were allowed to take their pick. Most of them would be praying "Futabayama, Futabayama" to themselves as they drew, but only rarely did they hit on one of the more popular wrestlers. To secure a photo of a particular wrestler they'd have to invest in any number of draws, and photos they didn't want piled up correspondingly.

H went around canvassing his friends, listing in his notebook the photos they wanted to put on sale or buy, and collecting data as to who had how many photos of such-and-such a wrestler and who was after what.

On going into business his first customer was Ryoji, the elder son of the owner of the tofu store.

"If you'll really get me a Futabayama," Ryoji began, a bunch of photos in his hand, "I'll give you Haguroyama and Terukuni, and Nayoroiwa too if you like."

H flicked through his notebook and decided to try Matchan, who had two Futabayamas. Matchan was still at school, today being his turn to do the cleaning, so H called him out into the corridor and told him about Ryoji's offer.

"I don't need the Terukuni," he said, "but I could use a Saganohana or a Kamikaze. I don't mind giving you a Futabayama for either one of those." Ryoji was reluctant to give up his Kamikaze, but in the end desire for a Futabayama won the day, and the deal was clinched.

For his pains, H extracted from each of them one copy of a photo they could do without. Even though *they* didn't need them, H soon found someone in his notebook who was a fan of the wrestlers in question, so they weren't wasted. His private collection of photos obtained in this way expanded steadily, and after two and a half months he'd collected a more or less complete set of all the wrestlers. From time to time, when he gave Hayashi a share of the profits, they told each other gleefully that it wasn't at all a bad business.

As a business, in fact, it wasn't particularly labor-efficient, but to be arguing noisily about sumo all day helped you forget the unpleasant things in daily life.

For grownups too, it was almost certainly the same: to get excited about sumo helped people forget the distress of the war and the increasing lack of personal freedom.

Where the theater, movies and books were concerned, the authorities were steadily stepping up censorship, with all its attendant controls and prohibitions, but where sumo was concerned they were positively encouraging. The existence of a "national sport," as sumo was referred to, was helpful in dissipating the frustrations of the people and in raising wartime morale. A clear sign of this was the increase in the length of each tournament from thirteen to fifteen days in 1940.

H's enthusiasm for acting as a sumo photographic agent lasted for a while, until quite suddenly he announced that he was going out of business.

One reason was that, having himself acquired almost a complete set, his enthusiasm for collecting photos of sumo idols was waning. But there was something else that had made him feel guilty about occupying his time with such things any longer.

This was the news that the bronze statue of Ninomiya Kinjiro which stood in the yard of his school was shortly to disappear. Around that time, everything in the town that was made of iron or bronze was disappearing. Cast iron mailboxes and manhole covers were replaced almost overnight by concrete ones. The big bell in the belfry of the Mampukuji Temple, where H often played, had gone, and since temple bells couldn't be made from concrete the belfry stood empty, the breeze blowing unhindered between its pillars. Even so, he'd never imagined that they'd go so far as to take the school's statue.

The principal had given them the news one day in a little speech after morning assembly: "Our statue of Ninomiya Kinjiro will be going to the front soon. He's being turned into shells to fire at the enemy. Be sure to say goodbye to him today as you're leaving school."

H felt depressed. To melt down the school's statue was going too far. Japan must *really* be in a bad way....

The headmaster's speech had gone on for a while after that, but H didn't remember what he'd said; he was recalling his initial encounter with Ninomiya Kinjiro, shortly after he'd first joined the school.

The statue was of a boy in kimono, with his hair done up in an old-fashioned topknot and a bundle of firewood on his back, reading a book as he walked. Finding this odd, H had right away asked Miss Hayase, who'd just been made their homeroom teacher, who it was. Miss Hayase was a gentle person, and H liked her.

"Every school has a statue of Ninomiya Kinjiro in its front yard, as a model for the children there," she said, "and each statue is made to be just one meter tall. You'd better remember that."

So it must be a good thing to read like that even while you're walking, thought H.

A few days later he was stopped in the schoolyard by another teacher, Mr. Kanai: "You there—you mustn't walk and read at the same time!"

"Why?" asked H. "Miss Hayase said we should model ourselves on the statue of Ninomiya Kinjiro."

"If you read while you're walking you may bump into something, and it's bad for your eyes too. 'Modeling yourself on him' means you should study hard, not that you should read as you walk."

"Then why do they put up a statue like that?"

"Kinjiro came from a poor family. He had to work even when he was a child, and he didn't have proper time to study. In spite of this he still managed to study while he worked, and grew up to be famous. That's why there's a statue of him."

This didn't satisfy H, and it still seemed a peculiar statue to him, with its miserable-looking face. He'd never got over that first impression; even now, in fourth grade, he couldn't help thinking of it as "that miserable statue."

He was still dwelling on such things when the headmaster's speech came to an end and he was replaced on the dais by the vice-principal, who said: "As you have just heard, our Ninomiya Kinjiro is going to the war like everybody else. Being schoolchildren you can't go to war yourselves, but what you *can* do is hunt out any iron or copper in your homes and bring it to school. Bring anything, however small it is, even rusty nails and bottle-tops you've picked up in the street. You may only be children, but you must do your best for the nation."

That afternoon after class, as H came out into the schoolyard, he went up to the statue to take a last look at it. It still looked depressed to him.

When his friend Hayashi came out of class, he suggested they should go to the park at Suma-ura. They hadn't been there for a long time, and H, feeling somehow irritable and resentful, wanted to go for a rather longer walk than usual.

Hayashi's home lay in the opposite direction from H's, so they decided to drop in at his place and leave their school bags there. They could get to the park either along the shore or along the main road where the streetcars ran, but decided finally to walk along the beach. The sky above was clear, with summer clouds piled high on the horizon.

"I'm to represent the school at the coming Kobe Schoolchildren's Sumo Tournament," Hayashi told H as they walked. "Mano Primary has a tough wrestler called Kurobuchi, and whatever happens I'm determined to beat him."

"You do that!" said H, with an admiring glance at Hayashi's sturdy frame. "If you win, you'll really be Yokozuna of Kobe!"

A train full of conscripts off to join their units was passing along the tracks that ran next to the beach. The windows on the side facing the water didn't have the shutters down, and every one of them framed faces gazing out at the sea. They must have seen the two boys walking along the shore, for they shouted something inaudible and waved furiously. H and Hayashi too waved back energetically.

"They're soldiers, so I suppose they can leave the blinds up without going against the law," said H. "There were eight cars, all full of them. Do you think they're going to join the regiment at Himeji?"

"Better stop that," warned Hayashi. "If you start counting the number of cars in a military transport train, you really will get had up under the military secrets law!"

When H went to school the next day the statue of Ninomiya Kinjiro had gone. He looked at the concrete pedestal standing empty in the schoolyard and felt sad.

He asked the school handyman, who told him that men had come with a handcart early that morning and taken it away. It had been heavy, he said, which probably meant that he'd helped them. Apparently there'd been another Ninomiya Kinjiro, from the neighboring Futaba National School, lying in the same cart with a sash around its chest. "Congratulations on Your Enlistment, Kinjiro!" it had said.

14

The Founding of the Nation

The owner of the noodle shop, who'd come to have a hole in his pants repaired, had settled down for a good grouse.

"They say the law against making luxury goods has put paid to the tailoring business, and it's the same with eating places too these days. There's a ban on using white rice now, so in a restaurant you can only use seventy percent hulled rice with a twenty percent mixture of wheat, otherwise they shut you down. I bet that before long they'll start rationing noodles, too, which will put *me* out of business."

This was an unusually long speech for the noodle man, who was for the most part a man of few words.

"Not to mention rationing sugar and matches," put in Morio sympathetically.

Matches had been restricted to five per person per day, much to the disgust of H, who liked playing with them and often got up to mischief. Now his mother had strictly forbidden him so much as to touch them.

On top of this general shortage of many basic commodities, the first of every month had been designated a day on which everybody was supposed to abstain from tobacco and alcohol, and drinking and eating establishments as well as theaters were obliged to close.

The owner of the tofu shop, the man who'd taken H in with him to see a movie for free, had complained about the latest coins, too.

"It's pitiful," he said. "The old copper ten-sen coins have been changed for shoddy little bits of aluminum. They float on water!"

The man claimed to have tried it himself, so H tried it too. The coin did indeed float.

Wherever you looked, things were getting more and more depressing; yet in spite of this, preparations were busily going ahead for some sort of festival to celebrate the "2,600th anniversary of the founding of the nation."

"The Western calendar's only got as far as 1940, but it seems it's two thousand six hundred years since Emperor Jimmu founded Japan," said H on arriving home from school one day. His father was treadling the sewing machine. "So Japan's senior to the West, with a longer history—is that right?"

Another of his son's "Is that rights?" Morio must have thought. But he ventured an "I think so," probably feeling it was better not to say too much at a time when the authorities were trying to raise national morale with a celebration of the nation's founding.

Wherever you went, the whole city's energies seemed to be focused on the coming November 10, when solemn rites were to be held to celebrate this 2,600th anniversary.

The first time H had really become aware of the planned celebration had been on the afternoon of New Year's Eve, more than ten months earlier.

Shogo, who was the son of a dried-fish merchant and lived by the beach, had come running to H's house.

"There's a fleet of warships offshore!" he panted. "Come on, quick!—let's go have a look"

H had hesitated briefly. "Is it really okay to go and look? I mean, isn't it a military secret?" But then he'd dashed off with Shogo anyway.

A great fleet of ships was indeed visible, though far out to sea. The children gathered on the beach were all talking excitedly.

"That's a cruiser on the right, and the one in front of it's a destroyer, isn't it?"

"The ones over there, one behind the other, are battleships, I think."

"I only hope some spy doesn't get a photo of this!"

Just then the elderly fisherman who owned the *Myojin-maru* came out of his house and told them something surprising.

"It's said they're going to fire their guns at nine tomorrow morning, New Year's Day," he explained, "to celebrate the beginning of the 2,600th year. You'd better come again tomorrow morning and watch. Then you can hear as well as see them."

Early the next morning, January 1, 1940, H and his friends met on the beach again.

An icy wind was blowing, so they gathered driftwood and made a bonfire. Some of the wood was damp and they had a job getting it going, but once it caught the wind soon fanned it into a crackling blaze. There was a heavy swell at sea, with white-crested waves, but the fleet rode the waters majestic and unruffled.

At nine o'clock, there was a great roar as the whole fleet fired a simultaneous salute, and the boys danced about the beach and yelled with glee at their first sight of real warships firing their guns.

"Say what you like, Japan's got a strong navy!" cried Shogo in a shrill voice.

"If it was a real war, though," said H, even though he was just as excited, "the enemy wouldn't just sit still, they'd fire back."

This prompted an immediate barrage of cries along the lines of "Whose side are *you* on anyway?" from the others, so H decided that from now on he'd better be careful about this habit of putting forward the other side of things....

1940, the year ushered in by that New Year's salute, had been nothing but "Founding of the Nation" celebrations all the way. Not just human beings but even animals, such as horses, were doing their bit.

One day, seeing a horse and cart with a load of granite going along the road near his house—the one with the streetcar tracks—H decided to follow to see where it was going. Perhaps because he'd been born in the Year of the Horse himself, he was very fond of horses.

The cart finally came to a halt at Suma-ura Park. The middle-aged driver, probably intrigued by this boy who'd followed them all the way on foot, informed him that the granite was for a monument to be set up in commemoration of the 2,600th anniversary.

"We've carried it all the way from Mikage, about fifteen kilometers away," he said. "Before you know it there'll be a great tower standing here."

The man's expression wasn't particularly forbidding, so H ventured to ask if he could have a ride on the horse, as he'd always wanted to try horseback riding just once.

"No, you can't," the man said. "This is the kind of horse used for drawing carts, not the kind people ride on."

H was a bit put out at this blunt refusal, but at least he'd learned something new: that some horses weren't meant for riding on.

The carrier told him a lot of other things he'd not known before, too. A couple of months earlier call-up papers had come for the man's horses, and one had gone off to the war. At the front, it seemed, there were places where vehicles couldn't get through, and it was better to rely on animals.

"This one I've still got is too old, so I don't expect he'll be called up. Most of the good, younger horses have been enlisted for military service. There's talk of making people provide horses for the Founding of the Nation parades—which'll mean that later on they'll be taken away too, you can be sure."

This was the first time H had heard of horses being enlisted.

"Which horses do they take?" he asked. "Are there 'first-grade conscript' horses, too?"

"That there are! First of all, they're divided up into three kinds depending on what they're useful for: riding horses, draft horses and pack horses. The riding horses, the first-grade conscripts, have to be able to carry sixty-two kilos, rider and pack together, over a six-kilometer course including hills and rivers, at an average of three hundred fifty meters a minute...."

H was wondering how the man came to know so much about horses when he found out that he himself had been in the army and had worked in ordnance, being responsible for carrying weapons, ammunition and foodstuffs on horseback or in vehicles. He'd dealt with horses all the time he was in the army, which was why he still worked as a driver now that he was a civilian again.

The reason he'd been released, he told H, was that he'd injured his left arm. A load had slipped and fallen on top of him, breaking the arm, and now he couldn't bend it anymore.

H was about to tell him that he'd once broken his own right collarbone but, reflecting that this had nothing to do with stories about the war or horses, gave up the idea.

"What about draft horses?" he asked instead.

"They're horses that can pull a cart carrying five hundred twenty kilos in baggage and men," came the answer.

"What can your horse do?"

"By now, I'd say, not much more than four hundred kilos. I don't like to overwork him nowadays—eh, old boy?" And he gave the horse a gentle pat on the neck.

Pack horses were the kind that could go six kilometers an hour carrying a load of one hundred sixty kilos.

"Good horses are in short supply these days, and even second-grade horses are getting their papers."

H drew a picture of a horse in his notebook, then tore out the page and gave it to the man to thank him for all the things he'd told him.

"I've got a kid in second grade at primary school myself," the man said, flashing his teeth in a smile. Much to H's amusement it made him look just like his horse.

Once the stones had been unloaded he put H on the cart instead and took him back to a spot near his house.

It was fun looking down at the familiar route from a horse-drawn cart; every time H spotted a boy he knew walking along the road he hailed him, and before long there were four of them on board.

H invited the man to come in for a cup of tea, but he refused. He didn't like to drop in at someone's place bringing a horse and cart with him, he said. H pressed him but he insisted that he "didn't like to," and, dropping the boys off at the Honjo-cho 4-chome bus stop, went off alone.

"Why would he be embarrassed about bringing his horse?" H asked his father when he went indoors.

"Men in ordnance aren't like other troops," Morio told him. "People hardly treat them as real 'soldiers.' They tend to despise them because they just carry things and don't actually go into battle at the front— 'non-combatant porters,' they call them. So I expect the man you met was ashamed to be seen in the streets of the town driving a horse."

H couldn't help wondering what the soldiers at the front would do without "porters" to bring them their ammunition and food supplies.

A month or so later he took Hayashi with him to Suma-ura Park in the hope of meeting the man with the horse again and getting another ride, but the monument was almost completed and there were no more stones needed for the former soldier to bring.

Gazing up at the lofty monument they saw, halfway up, the four Chinese characters reading "*Hakko ichiu*" carved in a vertical row in the stone.

"They mean 'bringing the world under one roof,'" a man working at the site told them. "In other words, Japan will take the lead in bringing the whole world together. You'd better remember how to write it."

Hayashi, standing by H's side, muttered to himself, "I could have told you that much myself," thus impressing H once more with his wisdom.

In the days that followed, the phrases "*Hakko ichiu*" and "2,600th anniversary" were to be seen and heard wherever one went in the town.

For at least the past six months, the radio had been broadcasting over and over again the song "2,600 Years Since the Foundation," officially designated the celebration's theme song. There was no one in Japan who didn't know it, or couldn't sing it:

> Praise ye now this happy morn,
> Bathing in the glorious light
> Shining from the Golden Bird
> That so long ago o'ersaw
> The founding of Japan.
> Ah, a hundred million breasts
> Pounding at the thought!

A kind of marching song, it was mandatory in schools. H himself sang it in a loud voice along with the rest of the school. The "Golden Bird" of course was the bird, a kite, that helped Emperor Jimmu, legendary founder of Japan, on his way, but H couldn't have said why people's "breasts pounded," nor what all the fuss was about.

The man at the charcoal store warned him not to tell anyone of his doubts. "There's a story behind it," he said. "Actually, they were hoping to stage the Olympics or a World Exposition to coincide with the anniversary, but that fell through because the war in China was still dragging on. So they looked around for something else to cheer the people up with, and decided to blow up the 2,600th anniversary ceremonies into all this great fuss. But that's a secret of course," he added, assuming a serious expression. "If it got about that I said such things, I'd be arrested!"

The old man had often told tall stories in the past, but H suspected this was the truth.

When he got home he couldn't keep quiet, but asked his father what he thought.

"I don't really know whether it's true or not," said Morio, "but you'd better not repeat to people what you're not sure about."

So it *is* true, H thought to himself. "Walls have ears and *shoji* eyes," he said with a knowing nod.

As the day of the commemorative rites approached, the posters on utility poles, walls and fences saying "Celebrate the nation's 2,600th anniversary—cheerfully and energetically!" multiplied.

"For the five days of the celebration, we're allowed to drink saké in the daytime," Mr. Omori, the retired army officer, announced to H and his friends, as though this could matter to a bunch of kids. "They say there'll be a special ration of saké, too!"

H and the other boys couldn't have cared less about the saké, but when he heard the rumor of a special ration of sugar too, H decided he approved of official celebrations.

The official, fixed price of sugar was twenty-seven sen for one *kin* (about six hundred grams), but it was almost impossible to get hold of, and the black market price was more than ten times as much, so rumors of a special ration were greeted with some skepticism.

"That's the first I've heard about it," declared H's mother. "And there's been no word of it in the neighborhood association circular either. I don't expect it's true."

H and Yoshiko too were both uneasy—and rightly so, for as the anniversary drew near there was still no special ration. The rumor had turned out to be just that after all.

H, who'd had visions of sweet bean-meal soup with rice-cake, was disgusted. "What's the good of telling people to celebrate energetically and cheerfully," he felt like shouting, "if they don't *have* any energy?"

On the great day, November 10, the sirens sounded just before noon. There was a ceremony at the school, but it was boring, as all such functions were, with its speeches, its obligatory singing of the anniversary song and three cheers for Emperor and Nation.

On their way home from school, four or five of the boys went down to the shore and sang the festival song in loud voices, standing on the concrete pier; the same song, but it felt better when they sang it alone and of their own accord.

At home his father, who had been listening to the radio, told him that the sirens had sounded at the same time all over the country, and described the ceremony that had been held on the plaza in front of the Imperial Palace in Tokyo.

The Emperor, in the uniform of a field marshal, had taken his seat on a throne, and the ambassadors of America, France, Germany and Italy had all been in attendance.

This bothered H. "I'll bet the foreigners were bored," he said. "I wonder how they felt, taking part in a ceremony telling them that Japanese history goes back further than their own?"

"It can't be helped," said his father. "*You* don't like ceremonies at school, but you attend them just the same, don't you? It's the same thing. They're supposed to attend to pay respects on behalf of their countries, so they can't very well not go, can they? If they didn't, it would mean that their country had deliberately missed the event, which would mess up relations and perhaps lead to a quarrel. A quarrel between countries—that means war, you see." H saw.

For the five days following the celebration the streets of the city were unusually bright and lively.

There were lantern processions and decorated streetcars. "Flower cars," which had been forbidden ever since they'd last appeared following the fall of Nanking, were specially permitted, and the streets were gay—"cheerful and energetic," as the slogans had trumpeted.

The "flower cars" were streetcars decorated all over with artificial flowers and small lamps. They made an attractive sight as they moved along the streets with their dazzling display of lights. H and his family had their supper early and went out onto the main street to watch.

Coming from the direction of Sannomiya in the east, the cars made for Suma at the western end of town, so there was quite a wait before they reached Honjo-cho where H lived. But the darkness of the surroundings made the lights seem to gleam all the more brightly, and as he watched them passing a second time after doubling back at Suma, it occurred to H that they'd make a good subject for a picture.

Back home he promptly got a piece of paper, did all the points of light on it with crayons, then did over the whole surface with a brush loaded with black Chinese ink. The crayon wax repelled the ink, so that the "flower cars" seemed to stand out in the midst of the darkness.

"It's lovely," said Yoshiko, who was watching over his shoulder. "Just like the real thing!"

"How much do you think I could sell it for?" asked H suddenly, encouraged. He'd just had yet another business idea—to do pictures of streetcars and exchange them for whatever he could.

"I'll give you a share," he told his little sister firmly, as a precaution, "so don't tell anybody, will you?" And that evening he did eight pictures in one sitting.

Artists' materials were precious and hard to come by at the time, but H had an ample stock of drawing paper, crayons and watercolors too, thanks to Masao Senoh, his mother's younger brother, who was an artist. Uncle Masao was seven years younger than Toshiko and lived at Onomichi in Hiroshima prefecture, where he taught art at a primary school. He was a member of the "Independent Art Association," and every time he went to Tokyo or Osaka for an exhibition he'd get off the train at Kobe and visit his sister and her family.

Whenever he heard that Masao was coming, H looked forward to it eagerly, since his uncle invariably brought him drawing materials. Masao was on good terms with a company in Osaka that made artists' materials, and could apparently get hold of such things as paints and drawing paper without much difficulty.

H enjoyed meeting Uncle Masao for another reason too: he knew his uncle would praise his pictures. H was someone who liked to be complimented.

What was particularly gratifying was that his uncle didn't just say, "That's well done," but would be more specific in his appreciation: "I like your use of color here, and the composition's not bad either."

"Sell them?" he said when asked, smiling, and in his typical Hiroshima accent. "Well, even full-time artists have a job doing that!" To H's relief, though, he didn't say, "You're only a kid—you mustn't think of trying to sell them."

Happening to be in Kobe at this time he saw H's pictures of the "flower cars," and praised his idea of brushing ink over the crayon.

"Your pictures aren't of the usual landscapes or flowers," he added; "they're what you might call 'topical' pictures. These pictures of 'flower cars,' for example, won't necessarily go on selling; it's the kind of stuff that does well only as long as the subject's in the front of people's minds."

He was right—astonishingly so. On the fifteenth, the day after the celebrations ended, all the posters saying "Celebrate—cheerfully and energetically!" which until the day before had been plastered all over the town had disappeared, to be replaced, in exactly the same spots, with other posters saying: "The celebrations are over—now to work! *Imperial Rule Assistance Association*."

The change had somehow been effected overnight. It was like magic. H felt uncomfortable, as though he'd been rudely awakened from a pleasant dream.

Seeing H going past, the man in the charcoal store beckoned to him from inside.

"Well," he said, "it was right, what I said, wasn't it? Five days' festival, then it's all over, just like that! The first lot of posters and now the second—they were both produced by the Imperial Rule Assistance Association. They had them all ready and waiting."

So it had been true after all. H felt let down. He gave away the pictures of the "flower cars" to those of his friends who wanted them. As for himself, though, he no longer felt like looking at, much less drawing, pictures of the wretched things.

His uncle had stayed for one night only and then gone back to Onomichi, so he wouldn't have known that the posters in the Kobe streets had been switched overnight. H would have liked to ask him whether similar posters had been put up and then swiftly changed by that association in Onomichi too.

The association had apparently been formed on October 12, only a month previously. The leading figure in it, he'd heard, was someone called Fumimaro Konoe, but what it was all about he'd no idea.

"I don't really know what kind of organization it is either," his father had said. "Some of the members are scholars, financiers and presidents of big companies, but on the other hand there are plenty of politicians with completely opposing views. You'd think they wouldn't care much for the military, but in the end I expect they'll just end up as an organization for carrying out 'national policy'—which means doing as the military say."

"It's all too difficult for me to understand," said H.

"I don't understand properly myself," said his father rather peevishly, "which is why I can't really explain it to you either."

H had seldom seen his father like this, so he decided to say nothing more.

One thing he did know, however, was that the number of matters one "didn't properly understand" was steadily increasing....

15

Treaty of Non-Aggression

In April of 1941 H entered the fifth grade at "national school," which was the new name for what had until recently been "primary schools."

"From today on," the head teacher told them in his speech to mark the beginning of the school term, "primary schools will become 'national schools.' And this applies not just to the name of the school, either, because from now on you students are all to be referred to as 'junior citizens.'

"Today, you see, even children are expected to grow up as citizens of the Japanese Empire who can take responsibility for the nation's future. From now on, your studies at school will involve learning more of the things that will help you grow into young men useful to the nation. The textbooks have changed, too. The first thing that children in first grade used to learn was 'It's bloomed, it's bloomed, the cherry blossom's bloomed,' but the new Japanese language textbook now reads 'It's red, it's red, the rising sun is red.' So I want you all to approach your studies in a new frame of mind. And I hope you'll all become strong, splendid junior citizens."

Back in the classroom there was a great uproar.

"Actually, 'It's bloomed, it's bloomed' was much better," said one boy.

"'National school'—what a funny name!" said another.

"I knew already; it was in the paper, and my dad told me about it."

"They've changed the 'do, re, mi, fa, so, la, ti, do' in music to *kana* letters instead—'*ha, ni, ho, he, to, i, ro, ha*.'"

"What! Really?"

"Didn't you know about it, H?"

"The nameplate at the school gates has been changed too. Now it's 'Nagara National School'—didn't you see it?"

H, who was usually pretty well informed, was put out to find there were so many things he didn't know.

As he was leaving the school he took a look at the sign by the gate to make sure. On a new, wooden board was written in black ink: "Kobe Municipal National School, Nagara." The old one had been a much finer affair, with the characters done in relief on a bronze plaque. No doubt the plate, like so many other things, had gone to make shells for guns....

The next morning, wanting to see the newly revised first-grade text-book for himself, H got hold of Yoshibo, the second son from the tofu store, on the way to school and had him get the book out of his school bag to show him.

It really did have the words "It's red, it's red, the rising sun ..." The picture on that page, which was in color, showed a rear view of four children with their arms raised toward the rising sun and a dog crouching nearby.

Gazing up at H, his school bag still open, Yoshibo suddenly began to whimper. Perhaps he was scared that this big fifth-grader was going to make off with his precious textbook.

"I'm sorry," H said, "I just wanted a look at it," and gave the book back. But to his dismay the little boy didn't stop crying.

Little sister Yoshiko must have seen him, because right at that moment she came running up from behind.

"Hajime!" she said furiously. "You shouldn't make a little boy in first grade cry!"

H's impulse was to make an excuse, but since he had in fact made the boy cry he redoubled his apologies instead. Somehow he always had to give in to his little sister....

Opening the front door on his return from school that day, H immediately saw there was something wrong with Shige. He was crying, and H's father was looking awkward.

"Dad, have you been making Shige cry? You shouldn't do that," H said, echoing the words Yoshiko had used to him only that morning.

"I didn't mean to make him cry," his father said. "All I said was that there was no telling what might happen to the tailoring business, so he should be prepared for the worst. I was hoping to make a proper tailor of him, but nowadays the opportunities for making suits are getting fewer and farther between, and to learn the business properly you have to have experience stitching all kinds of outfits. Even then it takes ten years at least. I worry because the only orders from now on are likely to be for *kokuminfuku*—'national dress'—or for turning and mending suits. I was just telling him about this kind of thing."

So that was what had upset Shige. On closer inspection, H noticed that his father's eyes also were a bit red.

"Let me stay a while longer," Shige said, rubbing his eyes with his fists. "I want you to teach me how to do repairs, too. Please!"

"That's all right so long as there are repairs to do," said H's father.

Listening to them, H had an inspiration.

"I've got a good idea," he said. "Why don't you stick a notice in the window saying 'Suits altered into *kokuminfuku*'?"

His father thought for a moment. "It might work," he said. "I couldn't actually alter a suit into a *kokuminfuku*, but I could do something like it. The only thing is that the color might be different from the 'national defense color' they prescribe. Perhaps I'll give it a go, though."

"Then I'll do a sign, with a picture. I won't charge anything since it's for you, Dad!"

The triumphant smile with which he said this made Shige's sad face brighten up as well.

The poster they put up in the window brought unexpectedly quick results. The first customer turned up the following evening. It was Mr. Shibata, who worked in a bank. Perhaps because he'd been to college and now got a good salary, he was a regular customer and had already ordered a number of suits.

Whenever he saw H he'd hail him with a "Well, my lad—studying hard?" and then give a loud guffaw even though it wasn't the least bit funny. So H didn't care much for him. Even so, he would always force a smile, since his mother had drummed it into him that Mr. Shibata was an important customer, and that it wouldn't do to look sour and walk out.

"I came because I saw the poster in the window," he explained. He looked somehow depressed, though, with not a trace of his usual liveliness. He did, it turned out, have something on his mind.

"They've decided that the bank I work at has to amalgamate with others," he told them. "Under the latest economic controls the small banks are being cut back and consolidated, which means that the next step will be personnel cuts. And the moment you're out of a job, a notice comes mobilizing you for factory work. You can't get away from that kind of notice, you know. I'm thinking it would be wisest for me to nip into an office job at an arms factory, say, before they set me to work as a machine operator or something else I don't know anything about. But that won't work unless I stop wearing a suit and get into a *kokuminfuku* as soon as possible."

"I see," said H's father. "Then I'll get the alterations done right away. And I'll do them for you at a special 'service' price."

Hearing his father use the English word "service," H spoke up.

"You shouldn't use English words, Dad," he said. "You should say, 'I'll give you a discount' or something; otherwise you'll get arrested."

The two adults laughed.

"You needn't worry about a little word like 'service,'" said Mr. Shibata once his loud laughter had subsided. "They won't arrest you for a trivial thing like that. Why, only the other day the paper had a piece about having a meatless 'day' once a week—'day' in English, you know."

But H was genuinely worried. He'd heard that a few days back a hairdresser in Rokken-michi had had his sign smashed just because it included the English word "barber." This had scared H and his friends. At the time, boys were supposed to keep their heads shaved, and this was usually done for them by their parents with a pair of clippers. It was a painful business, and to mitigate the discomfort they'd made a joke of it among themselves, referring to it as "the bah-bah punishment." They'd had no idea that this word "bah-bah" could lead to the smashing of signboards, and had begun to feel they should be wary even of a word they'd been using quite casually until now.

All the same, H thought with irritation, why should "day" be okay and "barber" not? Why should "soda pop" have to yield to "fountain water"?

In fact, the very existence of four "meatless *days*" every month was in itself a source of irritation. On the first, eighth, fifteenth and twenty-first of each month, butchers were forbidden to sell meat and had to shut up shop. This applied not only to beef and pork but to chicken too. Any infringement meant having one's store closed down on the spot.

"Why don't we buy it the day before," pressed H, "so we can eat meat on meatless days? Surely eating it isn't prohibited?"

But his mother dismissed the idea unceremoniously, saying only "We don't have to go out of our way to eat meat on a meatless day!"

H seemed rather unstable emotionally these days; one day he'd be in a good mood, the next unaccountably quarrelsome. Not just H but other boys in the same grade too were getting more and more "miffed," as they put it, partly because they no longer had any norms for what they were or weren't supposed to do, and partly because they never had a say in the things the grownups decided on so arbitrarily.

It was around this time that H's father, much to his surprise, gave him some pocket money—the first his parents had ever given him.

It wasn't an attempt to soothe his son's irritability, though. "Mr. Shibata's *kokuminfuku* turned out well," Morio told H as he handed him the money, "because the original material was good. Your idea of altering suits into *kokuminfuku* was a great success. So here's something for the poster you did—but whatever you do, don't tell your mother."

H decided he'd use his first pocket money to go and see a movie. He wanted to spend it on something that would stay in his memory.

He suggested to Shingo, who was also keen on movies, that they should go together to the Shinkaichi entertainment district. The film he had in mind was an American movie called *Destry Rides Again* that was showing at the Shochiku-za theater. He'd found an advertisement in the paper saying that the chief roles were played by Marlene Dietrich and James Stewart, and that it had plenty of gunfights and other exciting action.

After coming back from church on Sunday afternoon, he set off for Shingo's place. The latter was already waiting, sitting on the trash can outside the house. With a glance of recognition and a slight nod they set off walking. They'd told no one, of course, that they were going to Shinkaichi or that they were going to see a movie. Bubbling over with excitement at the prospect, they made so much noise on the municipal streetcar that they were roundly told off by a middle-aged woman passenger and by the conductor as well.

Unlike the Shochiku-kan in Taisho-suji, the Shochiku-za, the destination they were so eagerly headed for, was a fine building decorated with carved black lacquer. But when they arrived in front of the box office and tried to buy tickets, they were told by the young woman inside, "Children aren't allowed."

The brusqueness of the refusal and the chilliness of its tone annoyed them.

"It didn't say anything about that in the newspaper," protested H in disgust.

"Oh yes it did!—admittedly printed so small you'd hardly notice it. Look: it says the same here, doesn't it? Here, have a good look."

"Can't you let us in if we buy adult tickets?"

"No, I can't. It's against the law. And if you hang around places like this you'll get caught by the Guidance League."

Mention of the Guidance League stopped them in their tracks. Being caught by one of the vigilantes who worked to counter juvenile delinquency meant not just being hauled over the coals but having your school and parents informed as well.

Shingo wanted to call it a day and go home, but H felt it beneath his dignity to give up at this stage, so they set off south along Shinkaichi-dori. Gazing about them in wonder as they walked, they soon came to the Shuraku-kan.

The Shuraku-kan was a movie theater that was well known throughout Kobe; it was another place that H had always felt he'd like to see inside of at least once. They were showing a Japanese movie, *Furisode Goten*, and the boards outside proclaimed in large characters, "Everybody's Talking About It! The Long-Awaited Film—At Last!" It also said, "For General Viewing: Bring Your Whole Family!" This seemed to soothe Shingo's anxiety, so they bought tickets and went in.

The movie, though, was dreadfully dull. They came out so disappointed that they got straight on the streetcar and rode home, exchanging hardly a word on the way. H felt even more disappointed now at having missed seeing the American movie.

Back home he found his father had gone out. Shige, who was pedaling the sewing machine, pointed to a newspaper lying by his side.

"He said I was to show you this when you got home."

A headline in big characters said, "Japan-Soviet Treaty of Non-Aggression Signed in Moscow. Respect for Territorial Integrity." Right next to it there was a photograph of Foreign Minister Matsuoka with Stalin. On the way home from meeting Hitler in Germany, Mr. Matsuoka had made a stop in Moscow and reached an agreement with the Soviet Union that the two countries would not go to war with each other.

H had no idea at all of the reasons for this, but he was glad there wouldn't be any war.

Further headlines in the newspaper the following day said, "Japan-Soviet Neutrality Pact Shocks World"; and "Alarm and Disappointment Predominate in U.S.—Fears of Japanese Expansion to South."

"They've gone and put America's back up again," grumbled Morio. "Besides making an alliance with Germany, now they have to make a pact of non-aggression with the Soviet Union. I wonder, though, why the Soviet Union should get mixed up in a neutrality treaty when it knows how thick Matsuoka is getting with Germany...."

On the same day, the newspapers reported that German and Italian forces had invaded Egypt, and that British Prime Minister Churchill had said that Britain would defend Egypt come what may.

During the following month German forces made startling advances. They invaded Bulgaria, Yugoslavia and Greece in rapid succession, and sent massive numbers of planes to raid London, which they bombed for three successive days. Unlike most others, H's family could not be entirely objective about references in the papers to Britain and America.

Seating himself in front of a map of the world which hung on the workshop wall, H searched with the tip of his finger for the places mentioned in the papers. America was so far off across the Pacific ... he wondered if Mrs. Staples was well. And Mr. Campbell, who'd gone back to England ... had he arrived safely in London?

But he couldn't discuss that kind of thing either at school or with the neighbors. The only common, permissible topic was Japanese and German victories; if H had talked about America or England, even his closest friends would have accused him of being un-Japanese. The only person in whom he could safely confide was his father. The idea made him feel a bit forlorn.

One day his father, who had been out to Sannomiya and then on to the Yamate district, came home with a cloth-wrapped bundle under his arm. Even as he was taking his shoes off in the entrance hall, there was a strange smell from the parcel.

"What a stink!" H complained loudly. "What have you been doing?"

"Yes, everybody on the train was staring at me too. It was embarrassing," his father said. He'd been summoned by a postcard, in rudimentary Japanese, saying that Mr. Oppenheimer had a job he wanted done. Mr. Oppenheimer had taken him to the Jewish Association and introduced him to a large group of Jewish people, fifty-three in all, who had traveled from Poland to Vladivostok on the Trans-Siberian Railway, and were now stopping in Kobe.

"They're staying for three weeks before going on again, and I agreed to mend their clothes for them while they're here. That's what smells. They couldn't take a bath all the time they were on the train. Foreigners are different from Japanese, too; they have a stronger body odor, don't they? It got soaked into their clothes. Mr. Oppenheimer apologized but asked me to help them, so I couldn't refuse. I mean, it's about the only thing I *can* do to help them."

Even after this explanation, though, it was H's mother—who was always talking about "love for others"—who made the most fuss about the smell, so much so that H got annoyed and shouted at her: "Mother! What's happened to your 'love'?"

The smell was, no doubt about it, something like the smell of the animals' cages at the zoo. But H's father and Shige both got on with their work without complaining. Most of the clothes were torn in several places, and patching the holes looked as though it would take a lot of time and trouble.

As he sewed, H's father told him some of the things he'd heard: "In a couple of weeks they're due to sail on the Osaka Line's *SS Manila* for Cape Town, at the southern tip of Africa, a trip that takes forty days. From there they go by train, camel and on foot up through the central jungle and desert all the way to Egypt, and then on to Palestine. They say it'll take five months altogether."

Getting out the map, H pictured to himself the hardships of that great trek. Even if they reached the north of the African continent, would they get safely through the area of conflict in North Africa? He felt sorry for these people, obliged to set off again with no idea of what would happen in the next half year.

The party had at first intended to land somewhere on the American continent, but finding themselves shut out by all the nations of the Western Hemisphere they'd decided instead to make for the homeland of their dreams.

"It's just like the Exodus they talk about in the Old Testament," H's father said, "when the prophet Moses led them out of Egypt toward the Promised Land, several centuries B.C. The same thing's happening again. That first time, though, there was a miracle when Moses waved his staff and prayed and the waters of the Red Sea divided, allowing them to escape from their pursuers. I wonder whether any sort of miracle will happen this time?"

As soon as the clothes were repaired, Morio hurried to return them to the Jewish Association. Everybody there was really pleased, he reported; Mrs. Oppenheimer was in tears.

The smell permeating the house had dissipated to a considerable extent by the time June 23—a day that H had long been looking forward to—finally arrived. It was his eleventh birthday. In most Japanese homes at the time everybody's age went up by one year on New Year's Day, but in H's home it went up on the individual's own birthday.

This year H hadn't really expected the special meal and birthday cake that usually arrived on the table, but to his great surprise, there they were—a dish of meat and potatoes, and a cake.

They were a present from the Oppenheimers, he was told. It seemed they'd felt bad about not paying Morio for repairing the clothes, and when they'd insisted on showing their thanks in some form or other, Morio had finally told them of his son's upcoming birthday.

"Just fancy … when I'm sure the Oppenheimers themselves are short of food too," said H's mother. The grace she always said before a meal was particularly long that day.

On the same day there was another major incident that was to stay in H's memory for a long time after.

Germany launched an attack on the Soviet Union, and the German-Soviet war began. Reports said that some three million German troops had poured across the border over a wide area from the Baltic to the Black Sea. "Germany and Italy Declare War on the Soviet Union," proclaimed the headlines. "Several Thousand German Bombers Batter Soviet Territory."

"Hey, Dad," said H in astonishment, "Germany signed a non-aggression treaty with Russia, didn't it? Has it broken its promise again?"

"That was August 1939, so it's not two years ago yet, is it?" Morio, reflected.

"At that time they were friends—they invaded Poland together—but now they're fighting each other. A non-aggression treaty is something you can break any time it suits you, then?"

H wondered just how long the non-aggression pact between Japan and the Soviet Union would hold good.

Less than a month later the Konoe government resigned, the reason given being disagreement among its ministers. The cause of this was Foreign Minister Matsuoka's insistence that Japan should at once go to war with Russia, if only to aid Germany as a fellow member of the Tripartite Alliance.

"But wasn't it Matsuoka who signed something in Moscow saying that Japan and Russia wouldn't go to war with each other? Is he going to break his promise now and go to war?"

H began to feel angry at the whole way grownups were behaving.

Two days later, in yet another reshuffle, the third Konoe government was formed. Foreign Minister Matsuoka had been dropped, but on the other hand seven of the new cabinet ministers were army officers.

German campaigns seemed to be successful on every front, though there was a report that the *Bismarck*, the pride of the German fleet, had been sunk in a battle in the Straits of Denmark.

Mr. Oppenheimer had told them of a rumor that Lieutenant Klaussen, one of Senoh Tailors' regular patrons, had gone to sea on a German U-boat, leaving his family behind in Kobe. They were all surprised, having had no idea that a U-boat had even been in Kobe Harbor, much less set sail from it. It must have been an "official secret."

H, who had detested Lieutenant Klaussen, found himself praying that he would get safely back to Germany without being sunk on the way.

16

December 8

On October 16 the Konoe government resigned yet again.

"Not again!" H thought in disgust. "Don't they ever get tired of it? That's the third time they've quit!"

Once again, it seemed, the reason was differences of opinion within the government. The new prime minister, who was also apparently to fill the post of home minister, was General Hideki Tojo, who had been war minister in the previous government.

H and most of his friends, too, were familiar with the name Hideki Tojo. He was the man who had drawn up a tract called *Senjinkun* that had been published at the New Year. A set of rules for military personnel, its message generally speaking was that the pursuit of a soldier's duties were more important than personal survival, and that he should choose death rather than surrender and become a prisoner. It seemed to be aimed at instilling the same spirit not only in members of the forces but even in primary school boys, as future members of the forces.

At H's school, too, one teacher in the ethics course had quoted the *Senjinkun* on "not enduring the shame of being captured alive." The work had been recorded and put on sale, the voice being that of War Minister Tojo himself. Now the same man was the nation's new prime minister.

"So we've finally got a military man as prime minister," said Morio. "Konoe may have been vague and indecisive, but at least he seemed to be trying to find some way of not going to war with America."

The United States, he feared, would trust Japan even less now that it was headed by a military man.

A month later H's father looked up from the newspaper he was reading and said in a surprised tone, "From now on, it seems, even C-grade men are going to get their call-up papers."

"This referred to those who had been classified as "passed C" at the medical examination that every male had to undergo when he reached the age of twenty. "Passed" was in fact a misnomer, since they were all men found to have physical disabilities such as severe shortsightedness or difficulty in hearing, or were less than 155 centimeters in height. As such they were considered unfit for service, and no "pink slip" came for them.

Morio, who was only 153 centimeters tall, was in a sense a typical example. Far smaller than the men who passed as "A-grade," he quite obviously lacked the necessary stature to be a soldier.

In fact, however, even C-graders were to be called up from now on, so H, worried at the news, asked his father: "Do you think you'll get your papers?"

"I doubt it. The newspaper said it applied to 'men who were examined in or after 1931.'"

"When did you take yours?"

"1922," said Morio, grinning.

"With people like you in the army, Dad, we'd soon lose the war," said H, relieved. "You'd never manage long marches carrying a rifle and a heavy pack on your back like the A-grade men. But I wonder why they say they're going to take C-grade people—does it mean they've run out of men in decent shape and have to take what they can get?"

"I expect so. I was surprised only a while ago when they started sending B-graders their papers the same as A-graders, and now they've got down to C-grade...."

Reporting the change in the draft system, that day's newspaper presented a totally different picture: "Cheers for Our New C-Grade Conscripts," the headline said. "First-Rate Soldiers All!"

> For long we were dismissed as "C-grade," and felt inferior because of it, but from now on we can proudly call ourselves soldiers of the Imperial Army. The day has come when we too can shoulder rifles in the service of His Imperial Majesty. Nobody need feel inferior to the A-grade after all, so long as he has the Yamato spirit. No talk, either, about Japan now being obliged

"to draft even the C-grade"—Japan isn't as hard up as that!

"They talk as though everybody was only waiting for the chance to join up," H said sarcastically, "but it's not true. I've never seen a single man who was happy to get his papers."

"There may be some who really do look forward to joining up and going to the front," his father said, rather reprovingly. "Not that every single person looks forward to getting his papers, of course, but it takes all kinds to make a world."

Morio's words didn't succeed in changing how H felt, though.

He knew how it had been with Girly Boy, and with Yasuo Suzuki's father, the fisherman. It had been the same only the other day, too, when the young man at the wood-form maker's had got his draft notice. H often went to play there, so he'd seen everything that had happened.

The "wood-form maker's," which made the original forms used in producing molds for metal casting, was a favorite haunt of the neighborhood kids. H and his friends often got together there because they were given any leftover bits of wood that turned up while they were playing. For them, this "waste" was valuable material for making model planes.

They'd been amusing themselves there as usual when the postman arrived with the draft notice. As he handed the young man the "pink slip" and waited for him to put his seal on the receipt, the postman said "Congratulations," but his expression was if anything commiserating.

The young man's mother said something to him in a quiet voice as he stood staring at the slip in his hand, then went to the family's Buddhist shrine, joined her hands in prayer, struck the bell, and dashed upstairs without saying a word.

Her son stopped the machine he'd been working at and followed her up to the second floor, from where there soon came sounds of sobbing. Even so Katsuyoshi, the third boy in the family, who was playing with H, went on as though he'd heard nothing.

The woman from the tofu store next door, who must have heard about the draft notice from the postman, came rushing over. "So it came after all, did it?" she kept repeating, standing in the entrance hall. When the young man came down the stairs again, she intercepted him.

"If your notice has come it can't be helped," she said, "but don't go getting in the way of any bullets. You make sure you come back safe and sound, now. None of your ashes in a plain wooden box! You don't *have* to distinguish yourself for your country. And when you leave to join up, none of that talk about 'watching over the nation when I'm dead'—people say *they*'re the first ones to catch a bullet!"

The young man nodded to her and murmured, "Yes, I know, I know," in a subdued voice.

The little speech he gave at his send-off party was completely different, though.

"The long-awaited draft notice has come at last!" he bellowed. "As one who has been summoned as a soldier of His Imperial Majesty, I believe that to do battle and go to his death for his country is the dearest wish of every Japanese male. I too will do my duty as a member of the Imperial Army, with no thought of coming home alive. Goodbye, everyone!"

This was greeted with astonished applause by the people of the neighborhood who were present. The astonishment may well have been caused less by the content of the speech than by its volume. They'd never heard him talk in a loud voice before. Unlike his younger brother, Katsuyoshi, he was a quiet boy who always spoke softly, so much so that his mother was always saying, "Why don't you speak louder? You're a man, aren't you?"

No one had ever thought he could make a speech in such incisive tones.

What shocked H was not just the loudness of the voice, but the fact that he'd talked like something out of Tojo's *Senjinkun*. "He's lying," he thought. It wasn't true, for one thing, that he'd been looking forward to his draft notice. Now it had come, he must be putting the best face on things and trying to seem appropriately military.

As he walked along in the procession seeing the young man to the station, H was lost in thought. When he got home he promptly appealed to his father.

"I felt let down," he said. "Why did he say things different from what he felt? None of the family was at all pleased when the notice came. I know that people going off to join up are supposed to make that kind of speech, but I never expected that he, of all people, would say the kind of things they write in the papers."

His father's reply was unexpected.

"No—on the contrary, he may have said what he really felt but had never talked about till then."

"What? Why?"

"His mother and the others in his family don't want to lose him, they want him to come back safe—that's true enough, of course. I'm sure you've seen that for yourself, and he knows it himself, too. But at the same time he probably has this basic idea that it's a man's duty to give up his life for his country. I expect he'd been keeping quiet about it in front of his mother so as not to upset her. The thing must have bothered him, but on the day he left he spoke up. He may well have wanted to declare to himself and everyone else that the boy at the wood-form works was a real man now. I mean, once the draft notice comes you have to resign yourself to the likelihood of getting killed at any rate. I wonder, too, if he didn't want to prepare his mother for the worst with that talk about 'giving up his life for his country.' You see, they're pure-hearted, some young men like that...."

As he listened to this, H had a queasy feeling, almost as though he was going to throw up.

"It doesn't make sense what you say, Dad. Do you mean *I'm* not manly because I don't like war, then? Aren't I 'pure-hearted'? What's got into everybody lately? Are all men born just so they can die for His Majesty? Is that the only right thing? If it is, I hate it. There's something wrong somewhere."

H couldn't shake off the feeling that something *had* gone wrong, even though he himself couldn't have said just what. What they said at school, among the neighbors, in the papers—everything was veering slowly but surely off course. Even his own father, whom he'd always trusted, had lately begun saying incomprehensible, abstract-sounding things.

He dashed out of the house and headed for the shore. As he ran, he regretted not having brought his woolen scarf; there was a chilly wind, and he felt cold.

It was nearly December and the sea was rough. He didn't like the sea in winter, but somehow it seemed to fit with his present mood. He threw a stone at it, and then yelled "Waaah!" as loud as he could at the

153

white-topped waves as they advanced and retreated, repeating it again and again till his throat began to get sore. He felt unbearably depressed, but the tears wouldn't come.

As he gazed at the turbulent water, it suddenly occurred to him to wonder what was happening in the Japan-U.S. talks.

On November 15, the same day as the announcement that C-grade men would get their call-up papers, a special envoy, Saburo Kurusu, had been dispatched to America to help Japanese ambassador Nomura.

Everybody at school, fifth- and sixth-graders at least, was familiar with the name of "Envoy Kurusu," since even children at the time were caught up in the question of whether or not the Japan-U.S. negotiations would reach a solution.

Almost every day the newspapers carried articles dealing with the unstable situation between the two nations.

"Hopes Pinned on Kurusu Visit—Key to Peace or War," one headline would proclaim expectantly, only to be countered by reports of a speech in the Diet demanding that Japan should "stop being scared of America" and have things out once and for all. Another story reported that the war and navy ministers had declared they were ready for anything: both army and navy "were completely prepared for any eventuality."

Although H didn't properly understand what the newspapers said, he questioned his father closely.

"Might there be a war with America?"

"I don't know. They seem to be negotiating as though they want to avoid it if possible, but … They know that if they started a war now, Japan would be in even greater trouble, so I wouldn't think they'd rush into one without a great deal of thought, but …"

"'But …'? What does that mean? It's all 'buts.' I don't get it."

"How do you expect me to know something even the American president and Mr. Kurusu don't know?"

H had finally driven his father, usually a mild man, to irritation—though it may well have been exasperation, not so much with his son's persistent questions, as with a situation where neither a way ahead nor a way out was visible.

The public, it seemed, was coming around to the opinion that war between Japan and the United States was unavoidable, and a single spark might well set off a whole conflagration.

Almost all H's close friends shared the view that in a war with America Japan would win, since America lacked anything corresponding to the "Yamato spirit"; Japan ought not to waste time, but should go ahead and declare war.

H would have liked to argue with them. Did they think the Yamato spirit was enough to win a war on? Didn't they know America was the country that had built all those towering buildings he'd seen pictures of, whereas Japan had nothing taller than a few department stores? It wasn't just buildings, either—America was supposed to have enormous numbers of warships and planes, too.

But he kept his peace. To get away from the depressing awareness of being the only one to remain silent, he hunted around for some topic they could laugh about together.

"Do you remember," he reminisced, "a while ago there was an official directive telling baseball pitcher Stalkhin to change his name to Hiroshi Suda? The latest thing's even funnier: they're going to do away with movie stars' screen names. Tsumasaburo Bando's going to be Denkichi Tamura, his real name, so we won't be able to call him Bantsuma anymore. And Denjiro Okochi has to change back to Masuo Obe. It was in yesterday's paper."

"Why do they have to change the screen names everybody knows to names like that?"

"They say that in times like these even popular stars should give up using stage names and go back to the names their parents gave them so that they can concentrate on acting in a 'more serious' spirit."

"Why? Do they think you can't be a serious actor if you use a stage name? What a load of crap!"

The fifth-grade students were unanimous in condemning officialdom: "They're a bunch of idiots!" they said. "They make you too sick even to laugh at them!"

Two days later, on December 8 at seven in the morning, a tense voice came over the radio:

"We have an emergency report … we have an emergency report. An announcement from Imperial Headquarters Army and Navy Departments made at six o'clock this morning states that before dawn today, December 8, the Imperial Army and Navy entered into hostilities with U.S. and British forces in the West Pacific."

The broadcast came just as H was having breakfast. This is it.... As the thought flashed through his mind his hand shook, spilling some of the miso soup from the bowl he was holding. His father, who was drinking tea, had a fit of coughing. His mother said, "Is it war with America and Britain, then?" But H and his father sat silent, unable to reply immediately.

There was no information about how the fighting was going, but such considerations were outweighed by the initial shock of the sudden outbreak of war. All they could do, father and son alike, was repeat "This is it...."

At school, the sole topic of conversation was the outbreak of war.

"They said 'in the West Pacific.' I wonder where they attacked? They haven't given any details yet, have they?"

"I'm sure we're winning!"

"I wonder if the Combined Fleet sailed across the Pacific right close to America?"

The whole school was in a high state of excitement. One of the boys repeated the emergency report, skillfully imitating the tone of the announcer's voice.

The principal mentioned the radio announcement during morning assembly. "From now on," he said, "you must work even harder in school so as to be worthy of our soldiers at the front."

Shortly before noon another emergency radio announcement came over the school's loudspeaker system. It was rather difficult to catch, but the gist of it was that a naval air squadron had attacked Honolulu in Hawaii, sinking American warships in Pearl Harbor and inflicting huge losses.

At lunch break, H began to get stomach pains even before he'd eaten anything. He put up with them for a while, but soon couldn't hold out any longer and rushed to the toilets. It was considered humiliating for a boy to shit while he was at school. Unlike peeing, it meant going into one of the cubicles, which were normally used by the girls, so if your friends found you there you were liable to jeers of "Girly! Girly!" Ignoring this danger, H opened the door and went in. It sounded as if there was a girl in the next cubicle, but he couldn't hold out any longer and yielded to an impressively noisy burst of diarrhea.

Sometimes in the past he'd had diarrhea after eating something he shouldn't have eaten, but there was nothing like that to account for it this time. The only thing he could think of was the radio report that "before dawn today the Imperial Army and Navy entered into hostilities with U.S. and British forces in the West Pacific."

When he got home and told his parents about the diarrhea, his father simply said, "Me too."

"That makes two of us," said H, smiling for the first time since that morning.

His father too grinned ruefully. "It's not just human beings," he said; "animals get upset stomachs too if they've had a shock or are very tense about something."

They both continued to suffer from diarrhea until the early evening.

Hostilities between Japan and America had started in the early morning, so the morning papers carried no mention of them. But the evening papers, in two special editions, had huge headlines: "Empire Declares War on U.S. and Britain"—and printed the text of the Emperor's edict officially declaring a state of war.

Other headlines leapt up from the pages: "Do-or-Die Raid on Hawaii"; "Our Fliers Batter Honolulu, Sink Two U.S. Battleships in Pearl Harbor"; "Massive Raid on Singapore"; "Surprise Strike at Malayan Peninsula"; "Our Forces Launch Attack on Hong Kong"; "Massive Raids on Philippines"; "Dutch East Indies Declare War on Japan"; "Wake Island Already Occupied" … and so on.

The No. 1 Evening Edition detailed the reasons for launching hostilities. "Final Concessions Rejected by America," said the headline. Below it was a huge mass of print devoted to Japan's final ultimatum to the United States as published by the foreign ministry.

"It's too difficult for me," complained H. "What does it say?"

His father hesitated. "Do you want me to explain all of it?" he asked. "Surely the gist will do, won't it?"

"To sum up, at any rate," he went on: "Japan has been working hard to keep peace in the Pacific area and to secure world peace, but America hasn't responded in good faith. For example, it tried to interfere in matters between Japan and China. America has the mistaken idea that Japan is waging war in an effort to conquer China; it's giving aid to the Chiang Kai-shek government in Chungking, and engaging in other activities critical of Japan. On top of that, it's persuaded Holland to join in an economic blockade of Japan. Japan proposed a compromise whereby it would withdraw its troops immediately from the south of French Indochina, but that wasn't enough for America. Japan claims that America is ignoring the realities of East Asia and …"

"Is there still a lot left?" put in H. "You don't need to tell me everything."

"I'm cutting a lot out as it is," said his father, obviously fed up. "Shall I stop there, then?"

As he told H later, the United States was making it a condition that Japan should withdraw its forces from the whole of China and restore relations between Japan and China to their prewar state. The Japanese military had fiercely resisted this on the grounds that it would mean Japan's losing everything it had gained so far, leaving it stark naked, as it were—and talks had broken down. It seemed that this was one of the reasons for the frequent collapse of Konoe governments.

"They give 'maintaining peace' as their motive for declaring war," Morio said, "but reading the whole article, I don't think there were any real grounds for going so far. The *real* reason is that the economic blockade is too much for them. I imagine Japan's real motives are pretty obvious not just to America but to other countries too."

H was worried by the way his father was talking. "You'll be in trouble if people hear you talking like that," he said. "You're the one that ought to be careful, not me."

"I *am* careful. That's why I say it when your mother and Shige aren't here. The reason I'm telling you is that from now on all kinds of things are going to be happening, and I want you to look at them squarely and form your own opinions. I'm sure they'll put the squeeze on Christianity, for one thing. If you don't look out for yourself you'll go under. I don't want you to feel ashamed of yourself as a human being when this war's finally over. You'll have all kinds of things to put up with, but you'll manage as long as you know just *why* you're doing whatever you're doing."

Seeing the unusual expression on his father's face and listening to the things he said, H wondered uneasily whether he intended these words as a kind of parting message

A notice came to the church from the police asking it to cut back on the Christmas celebrations. The reason given was that December 25 was the day on which the Emperor Taisho had died, and it was disrespectful in the extreme to celebrate the birth of Christ on the same day. In fact the Emperor Taisho had died a full sixteen years earlier, and so far they'd never once been forbidden to celebrate Christmas. It was only because of the outbreak of war that they were suddenly being asked to give it up now.

Another source of distress for the Senoh family was that they had to ask Shige to leave.

"It's a sad business," Morio told him, "but the fact is there's no longer any work that gives me the chance to teach you or for you to help me."

Shige nodded in silence. On his last evening they gave a farewell supper for him. It was *sukiyaki*, but Shige didn't eat much. H felt sad, but ate Shige's share of the meat just the same.

17

Apostasy

H always looked forward to Christmas because it meant presents.

The presents were piled up under the Christmas tree at the church. After the service the names written on the packages would be read and the presents handed out. Usually, unable to wait, H would sidle up as close as possible to the tree, pretending to be looking at the decorations, and search for his own name out of the corner of his eye. Then he would try to work out from its size and shape what could be in the package.

From what he learned from foreign picture books, Santa Claus was supposed to come riding in a sleigh in the middle of the night on Christmas Eve and gently place the presents beside the sleeping children. But no one came to H's house; instead they got their presents from their pastor, the Reverend Hajime Kawaguchi.

Until H was six the pastor of the church had been Tokutaro Ueda, but even after he was succeeded by Pastor Kawaguchi the Christmas ritual had remained the same.

This year, as usual, H didn't have the patience to wait until he got home, but opened his package on the spot, revealing a sketchbook and watercolor paints. He was a bit disappointed; they weren't what he wanted, or even needed, since he could always get plenty of drawing paper and paints from his uncle in Onomichi.

He would have preferred a toy, and he envied young Moriwaki, in the grade below him, who'd been given a streetcar. Toys made of metal had completely disappeared and the streetcar was made of wood, but its shape and color weren't at all bad. He was trying to negotiate an exchange of sketchbook and streetcar in a corner of the room when his mother caught him at it and told him off.

Once the service and other related functions were over, there was a meeting of the grownups at which, they said, important matters were to be discussed, so the children were sent home first.

"It was a funny Christmas this year, wasn't it?" young Moriwaki said several times in a puzzled tone on the way home. "They've never done it with all the curtains drawn before."

H told him what he knew. "It seems the Emperor Taisho died on the same day as Christmas," he said, "so the police came and complained. They said it was disgraceful and that we must exercise self-restraint, so our people tried to make it not so noticeable as usual."

" 'Self-restraint'?"

"Stopping yourself from doing something you want to do."

"Will it stay like this?"

"I don't know, but it looks like it."

Moriwaki was going home by streetcar, so they parted when they got to the road where the streetcars ran. "I envy him going on the streetcar," said Yoshiko, who had been walking with them. "I wish our home was further away." The church was in Honjo 3-chome and H's home in Honjo 6-chome, so for them it was a journey of less than four hundred meters.

For a while after they arrived home Yoshiko played with her present, a cardboard doll with changes of clothes, but before long she dropped off to sleep. H himself sat waiting patiently for his parents to come home, wanting to hear what the "important matters" were that had been discussed. When they finally got back an hour or so later, they both wore sober expressions.

"The name of the church is to be changed," they told him. "From now on it's to be the 'Kobe Honjo-cho branch of the Christian Church of Japan,' not the Kobe Church of Nazareth. It was decided two months ago, in October, but they only told us the details today."

"Why? Didn't anyone object to having the name changed?"

"They couldn't," Morio explained. "Soon after the Tojo government was formed it decided to carry out religious reforms, so there's no arguing about it. An order's been issued saying that all the different branches of Christianity in Japan are to be lumped together under the name of the "Church of Christ in Japan." It's not just Christianity, either; they say the Buddhists have been ordered to amalgamate too. It seems that from now on everything that happens within the church, and the way it does its missionary work, will have to be reported."

While Morio was explaining all this, Toshiko kept her hands folded in silent prayer.

In sharp contrast to the atmosphere in the Senoh home, loud cries of "Banzai!" suddenly erupted from the house next door where H's friend Mita lived. As they discovered later, news had just come of the occupation of Hong Kong by Japanese troops.

The whole town was in a festive mood as a result of the string of Japanese victories, but the military were calling for "self-restraint" and had issued orders suspending the all-night operation of streetcars during the New Year's holiday, and banning New Year's decorations such as the pine branches normally placed outside the gate.

H had had high hopes of the rumor that there'd be a special ration of sugar and sweets to celebrate the fall of Hong Kong, but much to his disappointment it proved false.

The New Year's Day issue of the newspaper carried on its front page two large photographs issued by the navy ministry. Both of them were aerial shots showing Pearl Harbor under attack.

The captions said that they were "do-or-die" shots taken by navy planes at the height of the battle. They made a powerful impact, showing as they did some of the American vessels, drawn up in two lines in the bay, either hit and burning or beginning to sink. The photographs were described as "bird's-eye shots," a term that was unfamiliar to H.

Looking at the photos in the paper, H right away drew a "Bird's-Eye View of the Attack on Pearl Harbor" on a piece of drawing paper. It was fun to try drawing something from the point of view of a bird. Besides, he thought as he drew, the picture might be saleable.

At 9:00 A.M. on the third day of the New Year, radio broadcasts were interrupted by the stirring strains of the "Warship March," and there was yet another announcement from Imperial Headquarters: Japanese forces had completed the occupation of Manila in the Philippines.

A week later they also occupied Kuala Lumpur on the Malayan peninsula. The newspaper said that the British forces, surprised by the Japanese attack, had fled in panic, abandoning the town.

H was amazed at the success of the Japanese forces. Their strength astonished him because he'd always thought that since America and Britain, as advanced societies, were so far ahead of Japan, their weapons and military tactics would be more advanced too.

That evening, when Morio came home from delivering a suit he'd been altering to a place in Sannomiya, he muttered, almost as though talking to himself, "They say someone's chopped off the cross on the roof of the church at Oji."

The Oji church belonged to a different denomination, but it was a Christan church all the same. It stood by Oji Park, close to the Gokoku Shrine, a Shinto establishment.

"Why would they cut off a cross?" asked H, eager as always to know the whys and wherefores.

"Because they said it was disrespectful. The cross was higher than the Gokoku Shrine."

The latter, a local version of the Yasukuni Shrine at Kudan in Tokyo, was said to house the spirits of the war dead.

"I imagine they don't like it that any Japanese should believe in Christianity the same way as the Americans and British. They think it's disgraceful to worship Christ and not go to pay your respects to soldiers who died for their country. I expect cutting down the cross was a way of working off their resentment at that. Actually the ground slopes upward there, and a building standing on the slope can't help being higher than the shrine. Since the cross is the same as they have in America and Britain, simple people see it as a kind of symbol of the enemy. It's a tricky business."

H thought it was a tricky business, too.

Since they were now at war with the countries Mrs. Staples and the Reverend Aycoll came from, the latter had theoretically become "enemies," but neither his father nor his mother had stopped being Christians on that account, and the taunts of "Amen boy" had intensified at school.

Only the week before there'd been signs that someone had drawn a cross in chalk on his desk. Someone else had later rubbed it out, but H knew at once because it hadn't entirely disappeared. He had a good idea, too, of the identity of both the person who'd drawn it and the person who'd erased it.

The former was almost certainly Katsuzo, from Futaba-cho 10-chome; the latter, a boy known as Itchan. He asked Itchan about it on the way home from school, but Itchan denied knowing either who had drawn it or who had rubbed it out. He may have been afraid of retribution, though, since Katsuzo's father was a full-blown gangster, and his son was also much feared at school. If so, H couldn't make out why Itchan should have gone out of his way to rub it out at risk to himself....

He told his parents about it at the supper table that evening.

"I've an idea Itchan would like to come to church himself," his mother said. "Why don't you ask him when you have the chance?"

For a moment, the sheer wishful thinking of this sickened H, but almost immediately he gave a surprisingly understanding grin: after all, what could you expect from a woman who was always going on about God being love? She really was too much.

"There's something I'd like to talk about," said Morio once that subject was laid to rest. "Only you're not to say anything to anybody else about it." His expression was unusually serious.

"It's about what we as a family are going to do from now on. Japan's winning steadily at the moment, as you know. Our paratroopers have occupied Palembang, and Singapore's been forced to surrender unconditionally. The war's only been going for three months, but they say they've already sunk a hundred and sixty American warships and shot down fifteen hundred planes. If these announcements are true, things are going almost *too* well."

"Dad, what exactly are you trying to say?" H was impressed by the way his father could reel off figures of battleships sunk and so on, but it made him impatient: he couldn't see what it had to do with the future of their family.

"You'll soon see, so just be patient and listen. At this rate the war's going to go even better from now on. I don't know how long we'll go on winning, but the military and the police are going to be encouraged to put still more pressure on our religion. When that happens, I'm pretty sure that ordinary people will go along with them. Anyone who goes against the trend and is seen as thinking differently from everybody else is going to be labeled 'un-Japanese' or a 'traitor,' and may well be treated even worse than they have been until now. So I think we'd better be careful not to give the impression that anybody who believes in Christianity is an enemy."

"And when did you stop believing?" protested Toshiko, who'd listened in silence so far. "I didn't think you were that kind of person!"

"Now hold on a moment," said Morio, holding up a hand to interrupt the flow of protest. "I'm not saying we should stop being Christians. But if you go on in the same way trying to persuade other people to believe, there's going to be trouble—*that's* what I'm saying. A while ago the police told us to cut back on Christmas, but we didn't actually give it up, did we? We may have drawn the curtains so the light wouldn't show from outside, but we had our Christmas service just the same. From now on, I think, we'll have to keep an eye on what's going on around us in the same way. Back in the Edo period, when Christianity was being suppressed, there were people who became 'hidden Christians,' weren't there? Not that we have to go as far as they did to hide it...."

H knew about the "hidden Christians" of Nagasaki.

It was said that if they were caught they were hung on crosses and killed by having spears driven into them, or were burned alive. In order to detect covert Christians, Shogunate officials would make suspects trample underfoot small plaques carved with pictures of Christ or the Virgin Mary. Even though they knew that not to do so would mean exposure and death, many believers resolutely refused.

"Are Christians going to be tested by having to walk on pictures?" H asked anxiously.

"*I* certainly won't!" declared Toshiko. "Admittedly, not being Catholics we don't believe the same things as the 'hidden Christians,' but if that *did* happen I wouldn't do it!"

"You'd be wrong," said Morio. "It wouldn't matter even if you did. I wish you'd get it into your head that faith is something in your own heart, and that head-on resistance isn't the only way to preserve it."

H knew perfectly well that what Morio was saying was very important as a way to protect not only their family but their faith as well. Morio's next words, though, came as shock.

"I'm thinking of becoming a fireman—what do you say?"

This really took Toshiko aback; nor could H himself see the connection with what had gone before.

"This is obviously no time to go on with tailoring," Morio went on. "It's clear that unless I do something soon I'll be called up for work in a factory. That would mean I'd be put to work for days on end making army uniforms in a clothing factory. I thought that working for the fire brigade would be better than that. And as it happens, the station chief is keen to have me, too."

H knew the chief, a Mr. Okino, who was one of Senoh Tailors' oldest customers.

The Nagata Fire Station was on the other side of the main road across from the gas station where Girly Boy had hanged himself, so it wasn't far from H's home. When he was in fourth grade he'd been caught sneaking into the building to look at the fire engine, and it was the chief, who knew him by sight, who'd got him off on that occasion.

There were vacancies at the station, apparently, two of the younger firemen having recently received their draft notices, so there'd be no problem taking on Morio.

It was generally said that the chances of a fireman or policeman getting his call-up papers were small, though lately it seemed this wasn't necessarily so.

"I think it's a good idea—what about you?" Morio said to his wife.

"What *about* me? It's so sudden.... I mean, a fireman has to go jumping into burning houses, doesn't he?"

"The good thing about being a fireman," Morio went on, seeing Toshiko's reluctance, "is that you're on duty twenty-four hours every other day; the alternate days you have completely off, so I could work repairing or altering clothes."

"That would be nice," said Toshiko, more or less persuaded by this.

"There's one other thing I wanted to talk about," he went on. "It's about *you*. How would you feel about becoming head of the local neighborhood association? The thing is, Mrs. Tashiro at the cigarette shop, who's head at the moment, was saying her rheumatism is very bad and wondering whether you couldn't take over from her. What with air raid drills, arranging rations and so on, the job's going to mean a lot of moving about from now on, she said, and it's too much for an old woman. If you're not willing to put yourself out that much for the community, people are going to start saying things, you know. It'll help protect your faith, for one thing, so I think you'd better take it on."

"Oh, *yes!*" put in Yoshiko, who'd been listening quietly to all this. She could hardly have understood what was being said, but her decisive tone must have tipped the balance with Toshiko.

"Perhaps I'll give it a try, then. But though I could manage air raid drills and official business, I object to visiting Shinto shrines and so on with the rest of them. I can't pay my respects to gods I don't believe in."

"I thought you'd say that. But it's like the case of the hidden Christians I was just talking about, though you wouldn't actually have to trample on anything. Jesus would know you hadn't really lost your faith, and he'd forgive you."

Two weeks later Morio came home wearing a fireman's uniform, complete with helmet and puttees. He was too small for it, though: it hung loose on him and the sleeves were too long.

H was amused. "Are you supposed to be a hidden Christian?" he teased.

"Does it look so bad?" asked Morio with a grin. "You'll get used to it."

Government employees were not allowed to hold two jobs, and he couldn't carry on with his tailoring openly, so they shifted the sewing machine from the first floor, where it could be seen, to the second floor, and made that his workshop instead.

In order to move it, H pulled from above while his father pushed from below, but it was surprisingly heavy all the same. The eight-tatami room facing the platform for drying laundry that stood at the back, on the roof of the first floor, was to be the new workshop.

It was the room next to H's. Almost immediately he heard the sound of the treadle coming from next door and went to look. The fireman's uniform had already been dismantled and was in the process of being rapidly shortened and sewn together again.

For the first month after his father's new job started H refrained from going to the fire station, although he was in fact dying to go, hoping to get a look at the neighborhood from the top of the lookout tower that formed part of the station.

When H asked, his father refused adamantly.

"It's not a playground," he said several times. "You're not to come."

So H dropped in at the Nagata Fire Station on a day when his father was off duty, and asked Mr. Okino, the station chief, who complied with surprising readiness.

"I see," he said. "So your father said no, did he? Well, he's right, of course. But it's okay, I'll let you go anyway, provided you don't tell anyone. But don't get scared halfway up, now, and start crying."

And he let H go up, even sending one of the firemen with him. Several times on the way up, the latter warned him against looking down before he got to the top.

When they got there, the man on lookout duty seemed surprised.

"This is the Senoh boy," the fireman explained. "He's a pal of the chief's, so let him have a look around, will you?"

The lookout platform was swaying slightly, perhaps because of the wind. Looking down, H had a good view of the streets of Kobe. He could see the houses of Honjo-cho, but his own home was hidden by the roof of the rubber works in front of it. On the other hand, the buildings of the Nagara Primary School and the Takatori marshaling yards were clearly discernible. He could see locomotives, puffing smoke, going to and fro in the spacious yards, and another engine being turned around on a turntable. The sea off Suma gleamed in the sun, a few clouds floated in an otherwise clear blue sky, and Awaji Island seemed to loom close at hand.

"You'd never think there was a war on," he said. "I wish I was a fireman!"

"A lookout's job doesn't mean just sitting around enjoying the view," he was told. "You have to keep a sharp eye out in every direction so you can spot a fire even before they've reported it. It's hard work, I can tell you!"

H kept the fact that he'd been allowed up the lookout tower to himself, but only two days later word got to his father, who scared him by getting really angry for once.

"You're not to tell anybody under any cicumstances—not even your friends—that you went up the tower," he said. "It's a violation of the anti-spying law for anyone to go up so high, except for people who have special permission because of their occupation." H promised never to tell anyone.

On June 23, 1942, H had his twelfth birthday. His mother marked the occasion by using some of her precious sugar and red beans to make his favorite *zenzai*. Two days after that, news came from Tokyo of the arrest of Pastor Tsutada of the Church of Christ in Japan for "violation of the Peace Preservation Law."

"What's the 'Peace Preservation Law,' Dad?"

"It's a law that makes it possible to arrest people with ideas that might disrupt the state."

Morio, who had just got back from the fire station and was off duty, rushed off to the church without bothering to explain any further.

Even Pastor Kawaguchi hadn't heard the details yet, but it seemed that ministers were being arrested one after another all over the country.

"It seems they've made up their minds that since Christians seek the 'Kingdom of God,' they must be having 'dangerous thoughts'—rejecting the Japanese nation as ruled over by His Majesty the Emperor, and planning to change the 'national polity.' This is it, then!"

Morio seemed to sense that the mad rush into a "holy war" was finally becoming unstoppable. By now the situation was such that not only groups engaged in left-wing political activities but anybody connected with religion, even, could be had up for investigation under the Peace Preservation Law.

H felt he had understood his father's concern and he was horrified to learn that the situation in practice was taking a still more sinister turn.

Just as in the case of the young man at the noodle shop, the papers made no mention at all of the arrest of the Reverend Tsutada.

18

Neighborhood Associations

The 6-chome district was organized into four neighborhood associations, of which Toshiko was chosen to be head of No. 4. "Chosen" was hardly the word, though, since when the previous head, the old lady at the tobacco store, finally resigned, there'd been no one else to take on the job.

Even though she'd expected the work to keep her very busy, Toshiko was astonished at the way it went on increasing from day to day. But she uttered not a word of complaint, no doubt considering this to be a God-given opportunity to show people how a good Christian lived.

In the morning she would go to lectures on air raid drill, and in the afternoon she'd gather the neighbors together to share with them what she'd learned; then the evenings would be occupied with the pick-up and distribution of rations.

The most important thing for an association head to avoid was the suspicion of unfairness in doling out rationed items; it would never do if there were complaints concerning the relative size of the portions of dried fish or the way vegetables were cut and handed out.

There was a lot of official business to pass on too. The first matter in which H was asked to lend a hand was in drawing up a "Table of Air Raid Communications."

A pamphlet entitled "All About Air Raid Precautions" that had been sent around by the authorities was supposed to be distributed to the members of the neighborhood associations, but the print was blurred, since it had been done on poor quality paper, and H was asked by his mother to transfer it, enlarged, onto drawing paper.

"The 'Alert' siren wails continuously for three minutes.... The 'Air Raid Warning' siren sounds for four seconds and is followed by an eight-second pause, repeated ten times in all...." H wrote all these things in big characters and illustrated them with a picture of an airplane, which prompted old Mrs. Tashiro, the previous association head, to remark admiringly that it was "perfectly easy to understand, even for an old person." Puffed up by this, H went around personally distributing the leaflets to the fourteen households of the association, telling them to "stick it up somewhere where it's easy to see until you've got it by heart."

At school, too, the way to distinguish the sounds of different warning sirens was drilled into the children.

Coming across his mother shouting orders at the neighbors as he was on his way home from school, H felt a bit embarrassed, but passed it off with the reflection that it was probably better than going around singing missionary songs in a loud voice and beating a tambourine in the streets.

The air raid drills, originally held once a month, had recently been stepped up to once a fortnight. "Air raid drill" meant, in fact, practice in extinguishing fires. Each household had to send one member for this drill without fail, but most of those taking part were middle-aged women. There were very few men; the younger ones had almost all been drafted, and those who hadn't were away doing war work in the factories.

"It's the women who guard the home front" was the slogan of the day, and the general rule was to leave nothing to the men. So the housewives who came along carrying their buckets and sticks for beating out fires were a cheerful, energetic lot.

The sticks were bamboo rods with a bundle of rope bound to one end, rather like a broom. The rope was doused in water and used to beat out drifting fire flakes so as to prevent a conflagration from spreading.

Once the drill started the women would race about with ladders on their shoulders, climbing up under the eaves and dousing imaginary fires with water brought by bucket relay. Outstandingly energetic was the head of the association, Toshiko herself.

The neighborhood association that she headed was rumored to be the finest in the district, a judgment borne out by a fire drill contest held in the school grounds, where it led the field among the twenty or so associations taking part. Its overall mark for things such as the speed of its bucket relay, the amount of water used and the time taken to put out a fire, far outstripped that of the others.

When the supervising fire brigade official singled out their efficiency in splashing water around for special praise, the neighbors teased Toshiko: "No wonder!" they said, "—her husband's a fireman." On the other hand, perhaps because of her straightforward nature and the helpful way in which she always looked after other people's interests, she was never once discriminated against for being a Christian.

In short, as she herself would have put it, she was "loved."

"Your ma really goes for it, doesn't she!" joked H's friends. "They say she even fell off a ladder the other day." This was in fact true. H hadn't actually seen her fall, but according to witnesses she had landed on her butt, with the bucket still in her arms.

She'd been laid up with a bruised back for three days, during which time a procession of local wives had dropped in to see how she was doing. H was very pleased by this, not least because of the little gifts of sweet buns and other goodies so hard to come by in those days that they brought with them.

Another windfall of sweet buns that thrilled H came in the special rations distributed to mark the fall of Singapore. When talk of a special handout to celebrate the event first went the rounds, H had dismissed it as the usual unfounded rumor. At the time of the fall of Hong Kong, neither celebratory party nor special rations had materialized. This time, however, it was obvious that the rumors were true, since his mother had begun recording the number of members of each household on the special forms provided so that they could all receive their share. He knew what these special rations were to be, too, because the items involved were to be distributed via the neighborhood associations—saké, sugar and red beans, with the addition of sweet buns and rubber balls where there were children. The rubber-ball bonus was said to be a by-product of Japan's occupation of the rubber-producing areas of Southeast Asia.

For all H's avowed dislike of war, the enticement of such special rations convinced him that victory in war wasn't a bad thing after all—a lack of principles that demonstrated the efficacy of the government's policy of using special handouts to "raise the nation's will to fight."

In the days that followed, a steady stream of Imperial Headquarters communiqués announcing new victories came over the radio, always to the stirring strains of the "Warship March." The children eagerly anticipated another batch of special rations to mark each one.

On March 3, 1942, in two naval battles off Surabaya and Batavia, a total of forty-two enemy vessels were sunk, including six cruisers, eight destroyers and seven submarines.

On the ninth of the same month the Dutch East Indies surrendered unconditionally.

On the tenth, Japanese forces occupied Rangoon in Burma.

And on March 11 U.S. commander in chief MacArthur made his escape from Corregidor in the Philippines.

Aside from the radio, these victories were also proclaimed in blaring headlines in the newspapers.

H began to wonder if America and England might not surrender in the near future, and almost everybody else too seemed convinced that Japan would win the war. Morio's view, though, was rather different.

"I don't see *them* surrendering of their own accord," he said. "Japan should aim to work things around to peace talks from its own side. If the fighting goes on for a long time, Japan's going to have a hard job keeping up this string of victories. I mean, the other side has overwhelmingly greater resources."

Remembering the picture postcard of the skyscrapers in New York, H felt he understood: "Yes," he said, "Japan has to go around collecting statues of Kinjiro Ninomiya and temple bells just so it can make enough shells."

By this time, though, he was well aware that it wouldn't do to let others hear such exchanges, which could easily get you arrested under the Peace Preservation Law. After all, he reflected, "Walls have ears and *shoji* eyes...."

On April 18, just when the media were happily reporting how Japan was winning the war, something outrageous happened.

Around two in the afternoon an American plane appeared in the sky over Kobe, dropped incendiary bombs, and flew off again.

H was one of those who heard the roar as the plane flew over at very low altitude. It happened just as he was cleaning the corridor at school. The sound was different from any plane he'd heard before, so he dashed to the window and looked up, but the plane was no longer in sight. The boys who'd seen it, though, announced the fact proudly.

"I saw it—it was an American plane. The mark on its wings was a star with a circle in the middle. It was definitely an American Air Force plane."

"*I* saw it too. *I* saw the pilot's face—it was an American!"

"Come off it!"

"No, it really *was*!"

Another boy thought that the Japanese government had flown the plane to make air raid drill more like the real thing, and a lively argument ensued. H was disgusted at not having seen it himself.

When he got home he found that his mother, too, had only heard the noise of the plane.

Out on the street a group of neighbors were talking about it.

"Someone said she'd heard what they call an alert on the radio, but I didn't hear it."

"Somebody said the plane flew off to the west, in the direction of Suma, and somebody else said it went east—I don't know which is right."

"What's certain is that judging by the noise of the engines there was only one plane, not two."

They were still chattering excitedly when the air raid siren sounded.

"Listen to that! What's the good of air raid warnings when the plane's already gone?"

"Perhaps there's another one coming." The women hurried back to their own homes, but no more planes appeared.

At three o'clock that afternoon there was an announcement over the radio: "A communiqué from Military Headquarters, Central Japan. This afternoon two enemy planes carried out a raid on Nagoya, but damage was insignificant. Also this afternoon a single enemy plane raided Kobe and dropped incendiary bombs, but again there was no major damage. All members of the public are urged to redouble their fighting spirit and tighten up the nation's air defenses."

Everyone was aghast to learn that it had indeed been a real raid.

A dozen or so planes had flown over Tokyo too, and nine of them had been shot down, according to the announcement. The broadcast was followed by a song: "Who's Afraid of an Air Raid?" The song was still fresh, having been composed only four months previously, but H had heard it before. The words, which had struck him as unlikely to prove popular, ran:

> Who's afraid of a mere air raid?
> Now's the time for young and old,
> to rise and defend the skies—
> a mighty barrier of steel!
> Ours is the glorious task
> of defending our land.
> Come then if you will—
> we're ready, enemy planes!

Whether or not the military had directed that it should be broadcast at that particular moment wasn't clear, but since it was repeated four or five times, the effect at that point was the reverse of that intended.

The next day when H, who'd been wondering how the paper would report the raids, saw the headline "Who's Afraid of a Mere Air Raid?" he almost laughed out loud.

There were subheadings too: "The Neighborhood Association Spirit Beats the Raiders"; "Unshakeable Air Defense, Immovable Home Front"....

> On the afternoon of the 18th, there was the sudden wail of air raid sirens ... With a "Come on then, you sneaky enemy planes!" citizens were instantly at the ready, prepared to repel any enemy aircraft. They had been mentally prepared and well trained long since—not just the civilian air raid wardens, but the neighborhood associations, the womenfolk, the students at the national schools.... The first raids by enemy aircraft produced no panic. Each individual exerted his or her best efforts in his or her appointed task, keeping conflagrations to a minimum in a magnificent display of skills acquired by constant training....

H found the article puzzling since it was so far removed from his own impressions.

When his father came home from the fire station, his work finished for the day, he confirmed that he'd been to where the incendiaries had fallen.

It seemed he'd been summoned for emergency duty immediately the bombs had dropped. Four of them had fallen in the neighborhood of Matsubara-dori, south of Hyogo Station and near the central market. There was an anti-aircraft emplacement on Karumo Island, close at hand, but not a single shell had been fired. Pathetically, by the time they realized it was an air raid it was too late, and the enemy plane had already flown off.

The fires caused by the incendiary bombs were put out before they could spread very far, but it seemed that the members of the neighborhood association whose bucket relay tackled the bombs had been extremely upset and dismayed by the difference between the drills and the real thing. And no wonder, since no one had thought for a moment that there would ever be a real air raid.

They heard that someone had been killed in the raid, but both radio and newspapers failed to report this "one fatality."

"The newspapers are just a pack of lies!" declared H in annoyance.

"Well, you can't expect them to report anything awkward," said his father, the newspaper in his hand. "You'd do better not to expect the truth from them. It's partly due to censorship by the military, but the newspaper companies themselves couldn't keep going if they didn't show they were cooperating in the war effort."

"Then is most of it lies when Imperial Headquarters says we're winning the war?"

H was disturbed. Morio shifted uncomfortably as though reluctant to give him a straight answer, and said, "Well now, let's just say it *might* be better to take it with a grain of salt."

A week after that the paper carried a statement by Lieutenant Colonel Namba, chief of staff for the Central Japan military district.

Surely, H thought, Military Headquarters for Central Japan was the party responsible for not sounding an alert even when enemy bombers were in the skies over Japan? But Lieutenant Colonel Namba had something rather different to say.

The headlines over the article reporting his statement said: "Be

Ready for Raids"; "Surprise Attacks Inevitable"; and "Don't Let Up on Drills and Other Preparations."

> Unlike the Soviet Union and Germany, Japan is not linked with the enemy by land, so it is highly unlikely that raids will continue around the clock. Neither are many successive attacks in a single night likely. On the other hand, there is a distinct possibility of sudden surprise attacks. Thus Japan's air defenses must be considered from the viewpoint of dealing with such surprise raids.

> Next, since Japan's cities are characterized by dense concentrations of wooden buildings, I believe that it is vital to parry any first blow. To this end, we must be thoroughly prepared at all times; people must overcome the threat of the incendiary bomb by facing up to it. Most big fires are started by burning flakes, so it is important to beat out such flakes before the fire can spread. The only thing is that the reality is liable to prove daunting unless one is already mentally prepared for it. So it is essential to carry out drills with the confidence that the neighborhood associations can indeed put out fires themselves.

H asked his father what he, as a fireman, felt on reading this.

"Any air raids from now on," he replied, "are going to involve more than just a single plane coming and dropping a few incendiaries. It's all very well to talk about parrying the first blow, but if dozens of them came and dropped incendiaries and other bombs here, there and everywhere, there'd be fires starting up all over the city in an instant. If that happened, I don't imagine the neighborhood associations could cope. In air raid drills people use a bucket relay to pour water on a single source of fire, but in the actual event I don't think things would be like that. So far, no district has had the experience of a whole area going up in flames. I'm sure the fires would spread faster than they did after the Great Kanto Earthquake. Also, the roads might well be blocked by falling utility poles and collapsing houses, so that the fire engines couldn't get through."

"Then what would you do? How would you put the fires out?"

"To be honest, I don't think we could. At the fire station they've an expression for the kind of fire you can do nothing about: 'non-intervention fires.' The only places where the engines would turn out and try to do something would be at the factories producing military supplies; ordinary houses would be left to burn."

H had never been so shocked in his life.

"Then the fire beaters aren't any use?" he said.

"Surely you don't need me to tell you that if whole streets burst into flames, waving fire beaters about isn't going to do any good. If you see fires starting up in different places during a raid, the thing to do is to head in a direction where there don't seem to be any flames. If you're surrounded by flames you should soak a quilt or blanket with water, put it over your head, and make for where the fire seems to be least fierce. Three or four buckets of water aren't going to do any good, and it's stupid to think you can put such fires out by flailing about with a fire beater."

"Then why do they train people to do bucket relays and make them practice fire-beating if it's not going to do any good? I think it's awful of the Air Defense Staff to tell a lot of lies and make people in neighborhood associations all over Japan do that kind of training."

"If they told the truth it would cause chaos and take away people's will to fight by making them mistrustful of the military. They need some kind of magic formula like air raid drill as a way of getting everybody working together. Mind you, this is top secret!"

H almost wished his father hadn't told him all this. The thought of how he was going to view people going about their air raid drill from now on depressed him.

"You're not to repeat it to your mother either, under any circumstances. As head of the neighborhood association she has to take the lead, so it's better for her not to know. But if there's a raid and fires start, you're to see her to somewhere safe. I'll be away with the department myself, so I'm counting on you to take care of her. She's the kind of woman who'd act according to the training manual even if everything around her was a sea of flames...."

H tried to imagine what an air raid would be like, but the reality remained remote. Even so, he determined to remember what his father had just told him.

"Then what's the basic idea behind training at the fire department?" he asked, hoping it might give him something to hold onto.

"Ordinary fires and air raid fires are different, so we train for both. But as I said before, we wouldn't try to put out fires affecting just residential areas if there were widespread fires due to an air raid. The only exception would be if there was a danger of the blaze spreading to important facilities. When I say that, you might wonder what's the point of firefighting at all, but under normal circumstances we're out at the slightest sign of trouble, even if it's only a bit too much smoke from a fish someone's broiling."

"Well, that's something at least," said H. "Not that anybody'd ever dream of the place turning into a sea of fire unless there was a war in the first place.... It doesn't do to believe all those Imperial Headquarters communiqués about how we're winning the war, does it?"

It frustrated H that he couldn't say this to anyone except his father.

Although Japan was not only at war with America and Britain, but had been for some time with China too, until now there had been little sense of urgency among ordinary citizens. However, it looked as if the onset of air raids might have brought home the reality of war at last, since there'd suddenly been such a great fuss about air raid precautions.

At school, for example, there'd been a drill in taking cover in the event of an air raid warning. They were not to leave the school building while enemy planes were overhead, since it was safer inside a concrete structure. If there was time they were to go down to the first floor and lie down in the corridor. If they heard the whistle of a bomb coming they were to lie down immediately, press their hands against their eyes and ears, and open their mouths wide. This was to stop their eyes being blown out and their eardrums being broken.

All the boys from first grade to sixth had these instructions drummed into them over and over again. H, being in the sixth grade, the highest, had to practice leading the younger children to safer places. He approved of the bit about opening one's mouth and pressing down on one's eyes and ears: it might well work in the actual event.

A notice came from the municipal authorities directing neighborhood associations to prepare air raid dugouts in the streets in front of members' houses.

This was an official order, so they decided that everyone should turn out for the digging. Each small trench was to be one meter wide, 1.2 meters deep, and two meters long. In practice, one rather larger and deeper trench would have been better, but such a big hole in a public place wouldn't have done at all, so they were to dig a large number of smaller ones. The idea was, apparently, that if you got into a dugout during an air raid it would protect you from bomb blast—though it offered no protection, they were told, from a direct hit.

The association members were still sweating over the excavations when a stir was caused by the news that a Japanese submarine had shelled the American mainland.

"It was in the paper, you know. Serves them right for bombing us!"

"They say the shock has got the Americans quaking in their boots."

The newspaper had, indeed, carried an enormous banner headline: "Our Submarines Fire Huge Shells at Oregon—Repeated Bombardment of U.S. Pacific Coast." The article claimed that America and Canada, their bluff called, were in a panic, and that the incident had exposed the weakness of their defense patrols. The implication was clear: Japan had successfully avenged the recent air raids.

"Come on!" thought the young cynic. "If America's coastal patrols are weak, then who was it last April 18 that let a U.S. plane come and drop incendiaries but only noticed and sounded the sirens when it was too late? They talk about other people's weaknesses and forget all about their own."

Unable to vent his frustration, he'd been talking aloud to himself, finally prompting his father to say, "You'd better stop reading the papers. That way you won't get so edgy."

19

Gas Masks and Spies

Coming home from school one day, H found a pile of cardboard boxes on the step in the entrance hall. He knew immediately what was in them, since they had "Gas Mask Mark A" written on the outside.

"So they've come at last!" he said, and was about to open one when little Yoshiko stopped him.

"Mummy said I wasn't to let you touch them," she protested. Apparently Toshiko had gone out delivering masks to the neighbors, and had charged Yoshiko with seeing that no one touched theirs while she was away.

"Just a little look …," he pleaded, eager to see what gas masks were like. He'd been interested ever since he'd heard his parents discussing them a couple of months before.

A printed document entitled "On the Purchase of Gas Masks" had come from the city hall for further circulation, via the usual information board, to individual homes within the neighborhood association. This is what it said:

> It is recommended that each household within the areas desig-
> nated by the municipality should purchase one gas mask.
> Those desirous of doing so should enter their names, ages, and
> the style and size required on the appropriate form and apply
> as a body with other members of the neighborhood associa-
> tion. The masks will be distributed, beginning with the most
> important districts in terms of urgency, within a period of three
> months. The city is prepared to provide a subsidy depending

on individual households' economic circumstances. The purchase of gas masks is not compulsory, but in view of the increasing urgency of protection against attack from the air it is hoped that you will appreciate the circumstances and cooperate. *Ministry of Home Affairs, Air Defense Association, Kobe City Hall.*

Purchase was not compulsory, but the language was such as to make it difficult not to buy.

What bothered H was not so much his mother's wondering aloud whether *they*, being close to the oil tanks, were considered to be a district with a high degree of urgency, as the stipulation that each household should "purchase one mask."

"That would mean that in a poison gas attack some people in each family would survive and others be killed. There are four in our family, so we'll have to buy four masks, won't we?" H asked his mother, mistress of the family finances, peering at her anxiously.

"That's true," said Toshiko. "But," she added to her husband, voicing a doubt that bothered H too, "do you think these masks would protect against poison gas?" She'd heard from Morio that he'd worn a gas mask while helping put out a recent fire at the Sansui Chemicals factory in Higashi Shiriike.

"I suppose they *would* protect you against poison gas all right," he replied. "But," on a more positive note, "I don't think America would make a poison gas attack in the first place."

"Why?" exclaimed H and Toshiko simultaneously in shrill voices.

"With poison gas you never know in which direction the wind's going to disperse it, so it's not a very trustworthy weapon. Sometimes people quite a distance away get affected, and other times you can be really close without being harmed at all. Besides, it's not like incendiary bombs or explosives—you can't set fire to buildings or blow them up with it. It wouldn't be effective in any overall attack on Kobe, so I don't think they'll ever drop poison gas from the air."

He spoke with considerable conviction, and Toshiko and H nodded appreciatively.

"Well then, we don't *need* to buy gas masks, do we?" Toshiko said. "I mean, it seems they cost four yen eighty-eight sen each...."

She was expecting her husband to agree, but to her surprise he replied, "I don't see how we could do that. If *we* didn't buy one, nobody else in the neighborhood association would either."

"But surely it would be wrong to make people buy something expensive they might never use? Oughtn't we rather to tell the neighbors they needn't buy them because there probably won't be a gas attack anyway?"

"Now, you absolutely mustn't go saying that kind of thing!" said Morio, alarmed at Toshiko's naiveté. "You'd get dragged off by the special police in no time. They'd consider it behavior 'beneficial to the enemy,' you can be sure of that. So you're not to repeat outside the home the things we say here, whatever you do."

For a while the exchange between his father and mother continued on the same lines. H wanted them to buy some masks, but they did seem rather expensive, even to him—for four yen eighty-eight sen, an adult could see a newly released movie five times. So he had just resigned himself to going without them when, to his delight, it was finally decided that they'd buy four after all.

There were different sizes for adults and children, so they decided to order a No. 4 for H and a No. 5 for Yoshiko. "How much will mine cost?" H asked inquisitively. But his mother, who seemed annoyed at the decision, told him grumpily that it was no business of his. Sensing how she felt, H decided he wouldn't mention gas masks again.

Even so he'd been looking out for them every day, and now finally they'd arrived and were right there before his eyes.

Searching for a box labeled "No. 4" he suddenly shouted, "Ah, this is mine!" and was about to open it when his sister wailed, "No—you're *not* to!" and tried to stop him. But H brushed her hand aside and pulled out the mask.

It was heavier than he'd expected, with the chilly feel of cold rubber. The body of the mask itself was of grayish green rubber, and where the mouth should have been was a cylindrical attachment about ten centimeters in diameter and four centimeters thick, like a squashed-up tin can.

"I wonder if this would really protect you against poison gas?" H said, trying it on.

Yoshiko recoiled. "Don't!" she cried. "It makes you look like a kind of pig-monster."

It wasn't easy to breathe with the mask on, but that didn't stop H from happily going down on all fours and chasing after Yoshiko, making grunting noises.

Just then, their mother arrived home. "That's enough!" she exclaimed in a loud voice. "If you tear the rubber you'll spoil it."

"I was just practicing using my mask," H pleaded, hastily taking it off. "With everything, you have to practice...." But his mother wasn't so easily pacified.

At school, too, gas masks were a main topic of conversation. From what H heard, there was quite a difference between one district and the next: in some districts everybody had been compelled to buy; in others not a single family had bought any.

There were seven people in young Tamura's family, for example, but apparently they hadn't bought a single one.

Most of the boys were saying, "I wish they'd bought one for me!" Gas masks, it seemed, had a certain mystery about them, with all the allure of the novel and unknown.

"They wouldn't buy a child-size one for me, so I'd like to see yours," said one of H's classmates. "Bring it and show me tomorrow, will you?"

"Me too," said another. "You'll let me try it on, won't you?"

There were so many of them that H was in a fix, having been forbidden by his mother to take the mask out to play with. On the other hand, he knew he'd be labeled a "spoilsport" if he refused his friends. At the same time, he wondered who could have let on that his family had bought a gas mask for him. He was sure he hadn't told anyone himself, so he concluded that there must be a "spy" who'd got the information from someone in the neighborhood association.

He asked his father what he should do.

"If they're so keen to see it, why don't you take it and show it to them?" said Morio. "But mind you don't boast about it. And another thing—you're not to start spy-hunting. Everybody talks far too much about 'spies' already."

His father's tone was unusually surly, and H thought he understood why.

It was a fact that ever since members of the "Sorge international spy ring" had been rounded up in October there'd been an increase in the use of words such as "anti-espionage" and "spying" both in the newspapers and on posters stuck up around town.

During an "Anti-Espionage Week" held in July, the slogan had been "Use the Yamato Spirit to Wipe Out Spying!" and there had been a long article in the paper entitled "The Truth About the U.S.-British Espionage Network."

A subheading under the main title had talked about "A Spy Network Centering on Kobe."

> Kobe has long been the home of foreigners from many different countries, and as such is a source of valuable information for enemy espionage agencies. Taking skillful advantage of business and personal connections, they penetrate the families of those they have made contact with in order to use them as information sources. Many people have become enemy spies without even realizing how they are being used.
>
> The British agency recently exposed in Kobe took advantage of its longstanding, special economic status in the Osaka-Kobe area to engage in intensive spying. Typical espionage agencies included B. S. and Co., S. Raw Cotton, and the NK Trading Company. The British nationals who were formerly managers or employees of such companies are no longer out and about in Kobe, having either been deported or interned in detention camps for enemy nationals, but the espionage network they cunningly left behind still actively survives. It includes some nationals of countries such as Germany and Italy, with which Japan maintains friendly relations, and even some Japanese.
>
> It is often thought that the kind of information spies are after is restricted to top-secret economic and military matters, but the most ordinary, everyday matters can also be important to them, and it is essential that citizens should be constantly on their guard.
>
> For example, even data concerning the weather or the depth of the sea are useful to the enemy. There has, in fact, been a case where a man was arrested for measuring the depth of the sea while pretending to be fishing....

There was much more on these lines, but what astonished H was that even weather forecasts should be suspect. He remembered how the weather column had suddenly disappeared from the newspaper on the day Japan went to war with America and England—obviously, he now realized, to prevent leakage of valuable information.

Until then, the weather forecasts had continued even though Japan had long been at war with China. Perhaps China wasn't considered so advanced as America? Or was Japan more afraid of America? The stepping up of spy hunts would seem to suggest so. But he didn't give voice to these ideas, even to his father.

It was no wonder that Morio got nervous whenever he heard the word "spy." He had many American and British customers, and the whole family was on friendly terms with American and British people who had now automatically become "enemies."

He'd been thinking of taking H with him sometime soon to go and see the Englishman, Mr. Howard, who was in a detention camp at a place called Shirakawa, but by now such a thing would have been quite risky. It was lucky, in fact, that they hadn't gone, as was shown by an unnerving incident that occurred without warning one morning in late October.

Two plain-clothes policemen had appeared at the house.

"Are you Morio Senoh? We've a few questions to ask. Come with us, please." And they'd taken him away with them.

It was Morio's day off after a night shift at the fire station, so they must have known his hours of duty and the time he got home. Toshiko was out at the church, and H was about to go to school. Luckily a friend had come calling for Yoshiko, so she'd gone out already.

"You'd better not tell your mother and Yoshiko," said Morio as he left. "Tell them I've gone to Sannomiya on some urgent business."

"You let him go quickly!" H called after the policemen as they were going out, restraining an urge to attack them from the rear. "My father hasn't done anything wrong."

The policemen looked around but went out and shut the door behind them without saying anything.

H was thankful at least that they hadn't handcuffed his father, but wondered despairingly what they'd do if he was put in jail and didn't come home again, like the Reverend Tsutada. He waited a while in case his mother came home, then finally, afraid he'd be late for school, wrote a message and left the house at a run. Arriving at school out of breath and panting, he found the playground deserted and his fellow pupils already in their classrooms.

For a few moments Mr. Yamazaki eyed H in silence before asking, "Is there something wrong?" H was hardly ever late for class.

H gave a start; he'd been gazing vacantly out the window, beside himself with worry.

When he got home from school his father wasn't back yet. At dusk, he still hadn't returned.

"Where in Sannomiya did he say he was going?" pressed his mother, but all H could tell her was "He didn't say."

His heart beat faster as he wondered where his father was at that moment, and what kind of investigation he was undergoing.

They waited to have supper, but still he didn't come. This kind of thing had never happened before, and Toshiko was beginning to suspect that he'd gone out on something other than business. At last, around eight, he came home.

"Supper?" asked Toshiko.

"I don't want any," he said, and went upstairs.

H wanted to know what they'd asked him, but kept quiet and didn't follow him.

Nor did Toshiko, for once, ask what had happened.

About an hour later Morio called out to H: "Come up a moment, will you?"

"Do you still have that picture postcard of New York skyscrapers that Mrs. Staples sent you?" he began. "If you do, let me have it for a while. I have to go again tomorrow."

To H it was as though his heart had suddenly leapt into his throat.

"Was that postcard of mine the reason you were taken in?"

"No—you needn't worry," he said. "I'm sure it'll all be over by tomorrow night."

"Someone must have told the police about the card," exclaimed H excitedly; "otherwise, how could they know about a postcard in the drawer of my desk? There really *is* a spy somewhere, just as I thought. I'm going to hunt him out and pay him back for you."

"Now, stop it! I told you once, didn't I?—if you start looking for spies you'll end up becoming a nasty type of person yourself. There's no point in identifying him, anyway—you'd just make matters worse."

187

This irritated H: his father was doing his Christian act. He resolved that whatever happened he'd hunt out the informer and get him to admit his guilt.

The next day when he arrived at school he nearly fell through the floor with shock. On his desk, in white chalk, was written the word "SPY." The fact that his father had been taken in and interrogated by the police must be common knowledge already.

Who could he trust to talk to? he wondered. The good-natured Shogo was too timid; Toshio was only likely to spread the story around even further. He was deliberating along these lines when, through the window, he saw Hayashi going by in the corridor. Being in different classes they hadn't spent much time together lately, but Hayashi would make a reliable confidant and, being a "grand champion," could be depended on to send the culprit flying when he was found.

After class, in a corner of the shed where the PE equipment was kept, he told Hayashi about the incident and asked for his cooperation.

"Okay," promised Hayashi at once. "But we don't want it happening again, do we, so if I find him I'll thrash him, not just throw him."

This made H feel a little easier, but what Hayashi told him next shocked him to the core again.

"A rumor's been going around for some time that you're a family of spies, didn't you know? They say you've got a postcard with a photo on it that came from America. Do you really have one?"

"Who told you? I must know who talked about it. *He*'s the one who's a spy!"

" 'Who'? Any number of people were talking about it—I don't know who was first."

At this point H remembered that some time back he'd shown the card to Itchan.

"Do *you* have any idea who it might be?" asked Hayashi.

H didn't mention Itchan's name, partly because he was capable of taking care of Itchan by himself, and partly because of the shock of suspecting such a close friend.

He couldn't believe, even so, that Itchan was the kind of person to write "spy" on his desk. That meant suspicion must again fall on Katsuzo, who'd already been guilty of drawing a cross there. Either way, he wanted to make quite clear to the person concerned how much distress and inconvenience he'd caused. That would require some proof. Possibly there was more than one culprit. If there were a lot of them, he'd have to enlist the aid not just of Hayashi but also Mita and Hirai who sat on either side of him.

Dwelling on such things on the way back from school, he arrived to find his father already home. A flood of relief took all the strength out of his legs, and he plumped down on the step in the entrance hall.

"Don't you have to go anymore?" he asked in a husky voice. "Is it all right?"

"I think so. Look, here's your postcard back. But you'd better not go showing it to other people these days. There's no harm in it really—it's only an old picture postcard—but you can't be too careful."

"So it *was* this postcard that got you taken in?"

"No, the postcard was by the way. They did ask me who sent it, and about the church, but the main thing was my connection with Americans and British people before the war began. And they wanted to know whether I had any contacts with foreigners nowadays. They also told me that, in future, contacts with German Jews were to be treated as contact with enemy nationals, so I was to be very careful from now on."

As he listened, H felt an overwhelming resentment toward Itchan. He wouldn't be satisfied until, at the very least, he'd asked him what had prompted him to tell Katsuzo.

"I think it was Itchan who talked, and that bastard Katsu who wrote it," he told his father.

"Then who was it that showed Itchan the New York photo? If you hadn't shown it to him, there'd have been no cause for him to tell other people about it, would there? You shouldn't talk about Itchan being a spy. When was it, actually, that you showed it to him?"

"Just after I went up to third grade. We weren't at war with America then, so I said America must be a terrific country putting up buildings like that and so on...."

"Well then, all Itchan did was tell his friends the same things you'd said yourself, surely? If so, then it's not fair to attack him, is it? If anything, I imagine *he*'s the one who's feeling guilty about somebody writing 'spy.' You should be the one to put *him* at ease."

This time, H didn't feel he was just putting a Christian face on matters; on the contrary, he thought how much more decent his father was than himself.

He was glad his mother wasn't there, but if she'd heard the conversation she'd almost certainly have said that Morio was a "loving" person.

The next day H said to Itchan at school, "Let's go fishing for congers tonight. I'll come and fetch you after supper."

In summer the boys would often go down to the beach at night to catch eels. Attaching weights and bait to long pieces of fishing line, they'd whirl them round and round above their heads, finally flinging them as far as possible out to sea. Then they'd hook the near end of the line to a long bamboo pole stuck upright in the sand, and sprawl out on their backs on the beach. All they had to do after that was wait, listening to the sound of the waves breaking, until a conger took the bait. When that happened the bamboo bent and a small bell attached to it would ring.

After supper H went to Itchan's house to fetch him. He wasn't in. H thought perhaps he'd taken off somewhere, but found him sitting on the beach, waiting for him.

Together they flung their lines out to sea with all their might, then lay on the sand and gazed up at the sky.

H could sense from Itchan as he lay beside him that the other boy was on tenterhooks, wondering what H might have to say to him. Consciously trying to make his voice as gentle possible, he found it coming out a bit hoarse.

"I'm not angry," he said. "*I* showed the card to you, and talked to you about America. It was just that a war started—nobody's to blame. I've given up thinking of catching the fellow who wrote 'spy.' With you, I'll always be friends."

At this, Itchan suddenly started crying. "If I see any writing on your desk in future, I'll rub it out again," he said, which made H start crying too.

The tears blurred the stars filling the sky, making them seem all fuzzy.

That evening Itchan brought in two congers, but H didn't catch a single one.

20

A Train Journey

"Do you think you could get to my home in Hiroshima prefecture by yourself? You're in sixth grade now, so you'd be all right, wouldn't you?"

Intercepted by Toshiko immediately on his return from school, H was startled by the suddenness of the question. What lay behind it wasn't clear; even so, he shouted gleefully, "Of course I would!" The idea of going on a train by himself thrilled him.

It turned out that there was a condition, though: he was to take his younger sister with him.

"What? Do I *have* to take Yoshiko?"

But despite his disappointment he hastily accepted the terms; anything rather than lose this chance to go to the country.

"The country" in this case meant the village of Miyuki in Hiroshima prefecture, where both Morio and Toshiko had been born and raised.

H had been there two years earlier with his mother to attend a family memorial service, and on a number of earlier occasions too, but this would be the first time for the children to go unaccompanied.

Morio and Toshiko had reached the decision to send them alone because of rumors that in the near future restrictions on long-distance travel would make it difficult to get tickets. They probably sensed a growing threat, even to families like their own, in the form of investigations by the special police, religious oppression and so on, and wanted to give the children a carefree month in the country before it was too late.

H was all for setting out as soon as possible, but the date finally settled on was August 3, a Monday. They didn't have a church back home,

Toshiko said, so the children must attend at least two Sunday services before leaving.

Resigned to waiting till the third, H decided that at least he wanted to decide which train they should go by, and to buy the tickets himself.

Without more ado, he set off for the bookstore in Taisho-suji to check out the price of a railway timeable. It was thirty sen. H could have afforded this out of his own private savings but gave up the idea, since it would mean giving away the existence of those savings, and when he got home tried instead to persuade his mother to fork out.

"You can't look up trains without a timetable," he said. "I must have it, so let me have thirty sen."

"Why? You'd only use it once, wouldn't you? You don't need to buy a timetable specially."

H was disappointed: his mother was being stingy as usual.

"Actually I thought looking up things in a timetable would be good for my studies...."

"If that's the case, then why don't you go to the station and look them up there?"

H gave up trying to convince his mother and went to Takatori Station. Unfortunately, the only timetable they had posted in the waiting room was for the local electric trains. Takatori was a small station, and long-distance trains went straight through without stopping. To get to Hiroshima you had to change at Suma or Hyogo if you wanted a stopping train, or at Kobe, two stops back to the east, if you were going by express.

H thought of going to Kobe Station to check, but first, to make sure, he asked the man at the ticket barrier in the local station.

"I want to find out the times for a long-distance train. Do you have a timetable at the station here?"

"Indeed we do. I'll fetch it if you want to look at it here. Can you find the place you want to go to on the map? The numbers printed by the railway lines on the map show the page giving the times of trains on that line. If you can't manage it, I'll help you."

Taking the timetable, H sat down on a bench in the waiting room and began investigating.

Times for the main Sanyo line were on page nine. He was hoping to get a train around eight in the morning, so he traced the right place with his finger and found there was an express bound for Shimonoseki, at the southern tip of Honshu, that left Kobe at 8:40 A.M. The train in question was a night train leaving Tokyo at 8:40 the previous evening, and a mark showed that it had second-class sleepers attached. So it ran all night, taking a full twelve hours to get to Kobe....

Tokyo really *is* a long way off, thought H.

The train arrived in Fukuyama at 11:50, just before noon, so they'd be on it for three hours and fifteen minutes. At Fukuyama they would change to a Fukuen-line train, which took twenty minutes to Yokoo, the second stop. That meant they should be there just in time for lunch.

If they went on the slow train leaving at 8:37, they'd arrive at Fukuyama at 1:56 P.M., a full five hours' journey. H made up his mind that he wanted to go on the express. It wasn't just that it would get them there quicker, but that the two trains were drawn by different locomotives. The express was hauled by the C-59, a large, latest-model steam locomotive introduced in 1941, only a year before. Until then expresses had been drawn by the C-53.

H knew a lot about locomotives since the Takatori marshaling yards were a favorite playground of his....

"Haven't you found the train times yet?" said a voice.

Coming to himself with a start, H looked up to find that the station official who'd lent him the timetable had emerged from his office and was standing in front of him.

"Yes, I have—but maybe you could tell me something else: is this train here drawn by a C-59 locomotive?"

"I wouldn't really know. The steam trains all go through Takatori without stopping." H found this rather hopeless in a railway employee, but kept his feelings to himself and asked the price of the ticket instead.

"Now I can tell you *that*—that's my job! Hold on a moment." He went back into his office, sat down at the ticket window, and started flicking an abacus.

"From Kobe to Yokoo on the Fukuen line via Fukuyama, adult third-class single, is three yen sixty sen. Plus one yen sixty for the express ticket makes five yen twenty altogether. The fare for children is half that, which is two yen sixty. If you're coming back within a few days, though, it would be cheaper to buy a return."

For that much you could go to the movies eight times, thought H on the way home. It was more expensive than he'd expected.

"Where have you been all this time?" his mother demanded when he got home. "I was worried about you."

"I could have checked it at home if only you'd bought me a timetable. It takes *time* to find out at the station." This evasion omitted any mention of what he had in fact found out. He was pretty sure that it would be better to talk about that in front of his father, which would mean waiting till the latter came home the next day, an off-day.

The following evening his assumption proved to have been correct. As he'd expected, his mother obstinately opposed the idea of their going by express.

"You're children—what's all the hurry for? You don't need to go by express, surely? The slow train might take an extra hour and a half, but either way you'd be sitting doing nothing, wouldn't you? Surely there's no need to pay an extra eighty sen just to arrive a bit earlier?"

"It's not just that; that train is the only one drawn by the C-59, the big, new steam locomotive."

"I don't know about 'C-59s,' but you can't see the engine when you're on the train, can you?"

"Yes, you can. You can go and look at it every time it stops at a station."

"So it costs eighty sen just to see it, eh? Isn't that a bit expensive?"

He was no match for his mother, thought H ruefully; at this rate he was going to lose the battle.

He knew that what she said was reasonable enough. It would cost more than ten yen just to send the two of them there and back. Even so, he racked his brains for some counter-argument.

"If you and Dad were coming with us," he said, "the return fares would cost an extra twenty yen or more. You save that much because we're going alone. If you look at it like that, the express fare's cheap, if anything. We've always been by the slow train up to now, so I'd like to go on the express just once—*please*!"

At this point Morio, who had been listening to this exchange, finally spoke up.

"We should let him go on the express, just for once—it'd be something for him to remember." He turned to H: "But in that case you're to take proper care of Yoshiko once you get there."

194

"Right! I'll see there isn't anything to make her cry. Thank you, Dad, I'm really happy. Thanks a lot!"

With this stream of thank-yous, he aimed to deprive his mother of the chance to object again. The strategy bore fruit, and he duly went and got the tickets for the C-59-drawn express.

On the day of their departure he successfully blocked Toshiko's proposal to come to Takatori Station with them, and brother and sister set out alone. They got on the local electric train at Takatori and went to Kobe, arriving with a full forty minutes to spare before the long-distance train was due to leave. H walked about the platform with a self-satisfied air, comparing the wristwatch he'd borrowed from his father with the station clock. Yoshiko, who was trotting along behind him, seemed to be getting anxious.

"Hajime … you say you want to see the engine at the front of the train, don't you? What'd you do if the train started at one of the stations while you were up front looking at it? It'd be awful if you missed the train. I'm worried—I couldn't get there all by myself."

"Don't worry, I've made sure just how long the train stops at each station. Three minutes here at Kobe, then four minutes at Himeji and five at Okayama. So I'll have plenty of chances for a good look at the C-59."

"Did you find all that out by yourself?" she asked admiringly.

"Of course," H said with justifiable pride. "So you see, you *can* rely on me a bit, at least."

At 8:37, right on time, the C-59 drew into the platform belching smoke and steam.

Seen close to, it was quite enormous—far more impressive than when H had seen it in the Takatori yards. The driver and engineer got down and were replaced by another crew that stood waiting. Westward from Kobe was the main Sanyo line, while to the east it became the main Tokaido line, so there had to be a change of crew here. After a while the bell rang and H rushed back to the passenger cars.

Yoshiko had her head out of the window and was gesturing to him to hurry.

Inside it was rather crowded, but a kindly, middle-aged woman changed places so they could sit next to each other. Even so there were three of them, since there was an old woman too in the same seat, next to Yoshiko. Looking around, H saw that most seats had three people in them, with the grownups looking uncomfortably squashed. Nowadays, it seemed, you were supposed to do this whenever a train began to get crowded.

Less than ten minutes after leaving Kobe they passed through Takatori Station. H was interested to see how different the familiar scenery near their home looked when viewed from the window of a long-distance train.

Soon after that there was a loud clatter as passengers on the side facing the seashore drew the metal blinds down over the windows; on the stretch westward from Suma, where you could see the sea, it was forbidden to look out at the scenery. Seeing them do this impressed H forcibly with the power of the military secrets law. To act like this must have become second nature for grownups, since, to H's astonishment, they all stood up in unison as though at a command and voluntarily "blindfolded" themselves, so to speak.

He wondered, too, at the fact that not a single person looked puzzled or doubtful, even though some of them must be riding the Sanyo line for the first time.

With the windows covered on the south side, the interior went dim, and the absence of ventilation suddenly made it feel hot.

"What did they shut the windows for?" asked Yoshiko.

"If anyone saw a navy ship out there, it'd be against what they call the 'Military Secrets Protection Law' and the 'Anti-Espionage Law,'" H explained in her ear. "Anyway, you're not supposed to look at the sea."

"It's funny, isn't it?" said Yoshiko, smiling. "You can see the sea any time you like from near our house."

H almost smiled too, then remembered the recent "spying" incident and how their father had been questioned by the police, and the smile never materialized.

The train ran for a long time with the windows shuttered, but as they passed Akashi and approached Kakogawa they finally parted company with the coastline, and it was at last possible to open the shutters again.

H grew fidgety, realizing they weren't far from Himeji. The train was to arrive in Himeji at 9:32 and leave at 9:36, a stop of four minutes. As long as he ran the distance to the front of the train he could renew his acquaintance with the C-59. As they entered Himeji Station he jumped down onto the platform before the train had completely stopped, making a spectacular landing marred only by a station official blowing his whistle and yelling at him fiercely.

He'd have liked to get up into the driver's cab, but, discouraged by the official's yell, contented himself with gazing up at it from below, and returned to his seat even before the departure bell rang.

They'd been told to eat their breakfasts at Himeji, so they opened the packages. There were rice-balls with meat boiled in soy sauce inside— a rare treat these days—though H had actually wanted to buy one of the packed lunches they sold on the station just to see what they were like. Seeing the middle-aged man sitting across the aisle from them open a lunch box he'd bought on the Himeji platform and start eating, H felt a pang of envy. It was a "rising sun" lunch, the main part consisting of plain white rice with a single red pickled plum sitting in the middle, accompanied by a small fish boiled in soy sauce, a few bits of vegetable and some devil's tongue root. It didn't look all that tempting, but H would have liked to try it just the same.

When he'd finished eating, the man broke the disposable chopsticks and was about to put them and the empty box under the seat when H said to him, "Excuse me, do you think I could have the paper off your lunch box?"

"What, *this* paper?" the man said, startled.

"As a souvenir of the trip …," said H, which the man seemed to find still more curious.

"Well, *I* don't mind," he said, and gave H the paper that had covered the lid.

Thanking him, H smoothed out the creases. The paper had a picture of a thick iron chain across the center, with three round faces—a soldier, a factory worker and a middle-aged woman—in a row above it. "The Will! The Power! The Cooperation!" said the legend. "In all-out war, we all are warriors together!" It also gave the time the lunch had been prepared—eight o'clock that morning—and the price, which was thirty sen. Rather expensive considering what it contained, thought H. He also read the bits in small print saying "Please eat as soon as possible," and "Please leave the empty box under the seat"; then, when he'd finished reading, he carefully folded the paper in four and put it away in his case.

Yoshiko, who may have been embarrassed at her brother's asking a stranger for the wrapping paper on a station lunch, sat with her head bent, looking down, without saying anything.

The man across the aisle suddenly started to show an interest in H and to ask him all kinds of questions. What grade was he in? Why were they, two children, on the train together unaccompanied? Where were they headed for? ... and so on, the questions so detailed that H gradually got fed up and began to regret having asked for the wrapping paper.

Beyond Himeji there were a lot of the tunnels that punctuate the Sanyo line, and the passengers were kept busy closing the windows whenever the train was about to enter one. If they left it too late, smoke from the engine came pouring in and everyone was convulsed with coughs. The task of warning people to shut the windows was assumed, as a matter of course it seemed, by the most experienced traveler among them. As each tunnel approached he would give the signal, and everyone would dive for the windows—much more swiftly, in fact, than when they'd pulled down the blinds by the sea at Suma.

Watching the "man in charge of tunnels," H was impressed by his knowledge of the route. As the train entered a curve, even though there was no sign of a tunnel yet, he would say "Tunnel coming up!" He did it as though warning people about tunnels gave a purpose to his life.

People would hear his announcement, shut their windows, sit down again—and five seconds later the train would plunge into a tunnel. The timing was superb, and the man seemed very particular that his forecast should be neither too early nor too late. Someone remarked that there was usually at least one person like that in every car, so H wanted to go to the next car to check. But Yoshiko screwed up her face ready to cry: "Stay here," she wailed. "Don't go away and leave me—I can't open and close the window by myself."

"No, you really *shouldn't* leave your little sister alone," added the people sitting around them, so H had to stay put.

To travel on a train drawn by a steam locomotive was to resign yourself to a battle with soot and smoke. Even when the train left the tunnels behind and was running through level countryside there was no real letup. Sometimes the direction of the wind would make the smoke trail along close to the ground, whence it would leap in without warning through the window. So if you noticed smoke outside the window you immediately pulled down the mesh blind which was specially designed to keep out soot.

The smoke made him choke a bit, but H was content. He was on the express. Surrendering to the pleasurable sensation of speed, he was watching the landscape rushing past when he felt a sudden pain in his eye. He'd had his head out of the window, so he must have got some soot in it. The tears came, but the eye hurt too much to open.

"You mustn't rub it!" said the talkative man in the seat opposite, seeing him with a hand pressed to his eye. "Hold on!" He wetted the corner of a folded handkerchief with saliva and pushed his face close to H's. The fear of having his eye poked at and the unpleasant thought of the man's spit on the handkerchief made H go rigid. But the man had turned H's eyelid back and was examining it, when he suddenly exclaimed "Got it!" and gave the lid a quick rub. "There! Try blinking a bit. It doesn't hurt anymore, does it?" he said proudly.

"I think it's gone," said H. "Thank you." But even as he thanked the man, he was thinking that now he'd have to endure his talk with good grace all the way to Fukuyama.

At 10:56 they reached Okayama, where there was a five-minute stop. Sketchbook and pencil in hand, H ran up to the front of the platform. The engine was giving off great gasps of steam as if it were out of breath. H was about to start drawing it from the front, wanting to capture an angle impossible in the Takatori yards, when his eye met that of the engineer, who seemed to have been watching him. On an impulse H pointed a finger at the driver's cabin and gestured as though to ask, "I wonder if I could come up?" The man nodded. H was surprised: he'd never for a moment thought that the driver of a working locomotive would let a kid into the cabin. Swiftly, so as not to be seen by any station official, he ran up to a point directly beneath the cabin and had just got a foot on the lowest rung of the iron ladder when the driver stretched out a hand and hauled him up. More than likely he'd felt the same kind of sympathy for other boys who'd come to see his engine at Kobe and Himeji stations previously.

H was overjoyed at the idea that he was actually in the driver's cab of the C-59. "I can hardly believe it," he exclaimed. "I could die happy now!"

The driver smiled. "You should value your own life more," he said. He opened the stokehole door and showed H the inside, with its burning coal. The cab was cramped and hot. As the driver showed him first one thing then another, H reflected with satisfaction that at eighty sen the extra express charge had been ridiculously cheap.

For a while after returning to his seat in the passenger car H was in a kind of daze, but once the train had started he opened his sketchbook and drew the engineer's cabin as he remembered it. His pencil wandered with the swaying of the train, but he went on drawing regardless.

They passed through Kurashiki, and at 11:55 arrived in Fukuyama. For H, the three hours and fifteen minutes had passed like a dream.

They were to change to the Fukuen line here, but there was time to spare while the cars were connected to an electric engine, so they decided to wash their sooty faces. Passengers from the train were standing in a row in front of the long concrete trough on the platform, splashing and scrubbing at their faces with water from the taps there. Joining them, H and Yoshiko stood side by side washing their faces and the inside of their noses. Seeing the water dripping black from their faces, H said "I bet the inside of our lungs is black too!"

"Don't!" said Yoshiko.

Boarding the Fukuen-line train they arrived safe and sound at Yokoo, the second station. Uncle Yoshio, their mother's elder brother, was waiting for them at the ticket barrrier with a carrying pole.

"Nice to see you both!" he greeted them with a dazzling smile. The pole was so that when they'd recovered their baggage, which had been sent on ahead, he could carry it home over his shoulder. Walking fast in his wake they headed for the family home where their grandfather and grandmother were awaiting them.

"They said it's noodles for lunch today," said their uncle in his thick Hiroshima accent, and H suddenly realized he was hungry.

The heat was rising and there was a strong smell of the country from the tall summer grasses by the path along the embankment.

21

Summer Holiday

H's mother's childhood home was an isolated farmhouse situated about fifteen minutes on foot from Yokoo Station, at the bottom of the hillside on which the local Hachiman Shrine stood. At one time the spacious residence of the main branch of the family had stood next door to it, but no trace of the building survived now. It was there that his father had been born and brought up. At that time the two houses had been known respectively as the "main" and "branch" Mukaigoya, but since the disappearance of the main building the name had come to indicate his mother's old home only.

When H had visited two years previously, the storehouse had still been standing in the compound of the main residence, but now this too had been knocked down, leaving the white earthen wall surrounding the site to go to ruin.

Saddened by the sorry state of the place where his own father had once lived, H peered at the site through a gap in the wall. It was a vegetable patch now, with bright red fruits on the tomato plants.

"You mustn't go inside the wall," his Aunt Oiku had warned him; "the land belongs to someone else now." So H took care not to be seen as he got in through the gap. Oiku, the wife of Toshiko's elder brother, was basically a nice woman, but had a somewhat uncompromising tone, and H found her rather hard to get along with.

Looking around once he was inside, he found that the site was much larger than it had seemed from the outside.

The low mound with lots of large stones showed that there'd probably once been a fine garden here, with a man-made "hill"; the hollow in the ground had probably been an ornamental pond. H felt sure that his father would have been too good a child to fish for the carp that had lived in it....

To one side of the gateway there was a well without a bucket. He dropped a stone in, and, after a pause, there came a splash. Walking about near the well he found a bucket with a rope attached lying on the ground, apparently for use in watering the vegetables. The thought that his father had drunk water from this well when he was a kid made H suddenly want to drink some himself. He threw the bucket in and tried to draw up some water, but at first the bucket just floated and refused to sink. When, after much difficulty, he finally managed to get some up, it tasted disappointingly like any other water.

Near where the gate had been he found a litter of dry boards lying overlapping each other and with a powdering of whitish, dried mud. They were bent and warped into shapes suggesting that they were the remains of a riverboat.

It puzzled H that there should be a boat at a house that wasn't by the river.

When he got back, his grandmother was in the silkworm loft using a large cooking knife to chop up mulberry leaves for feeding to the worms. She was an active, cheerful old woman whose name was Chika, and she had had six children.

"Why don't you and Yoshiko have some watermelon?" she suggested. "It's nicely chilled." H went off to look for his sister.

Yoshiko was by the irrigation channel at the bottom of the slope from the house. Their grandfather, a slight, mild-mannered man called Jisaburo, was with her, catching small fish for her with a scoop. H lost no time asking him about the remains of the boat he'd found in the grounds of what had been the big house.

"They had to have boats in this area, because there've been floods ever since way back when. They've built up the embankment so there's not so much danger now, but until recently the paddy fields were always being swamped. A boat at the big house was useful at such times."

Those scattered planks were all that remained of the boat. It had been hung by ropes from the ceiling of the wide, roofed gateway for use in times of flood. With the main Mukaigoya cut off amidst the floodwaters, it would be lowered and put to use fetching supplies of drinking water, taking the children to and from school, and so on. Unlike the grownups, for whom floods were nothing but a nuisance, the children, it seemed, would be secretly overjoyed at this chance of going in a boat. Listening to his grandfather's story, H felt that he'd have enjoyed going to school by water, too.

There was one other thing he wanted to ask. His mother's name was "Toshi-ko," but everybody here referred to her as "O-toshi," and it puzzled him. His grandparents were always starting sentences with "Our Otoshi ..."

Admittedly "Otoshi" sounded a bit more old-fashioned, but the two names were really the same, with "O-" or "-ko" added to the basic "Toshi" to show that the person referred to was a girl.

He asked his grandmother about it, and learned something that his mother had always kept a secret. "Toshiko" wasn't in fact her real name; in the official register she was listed as "Otoshi."

His grandmother, though, warned him not to let Toshiko know he knew her real name.

"When she was a kid she was always crying because she hated it so much," the old lady said. "She said it was a rotten kind of name, because *otoshi* can mean 'dropping something.' And she went on hating it even when she grew up—decided of her own accord she was going to change it to 'Toshiko.'"

"Then why did you give your daughter such a funny name? Wasn't it a bit hard on her?"

"In the old days girls' names didn't often end in 'ko'; they preferred to put an 'O' at the front. Your Aunt Fujii's given name is Okame, isn't it? And there's one of your relatives, even, who's called Oshime."

Since *okame* could also mean "turtle" and *oshime* "diapers," H decided "Otoshi" was just about acceptable after all.

Aunt Okame was only a distant relative, but H felt particularly close to her, perhaps because he much preferred her son Tatsuo—"Tatchan"—to any other of his numerous first cousins. Tatchan was just one year older than H himself; they were not only close in age but temperamentally, too, so H got on better with him than with any of the others. Probably because neither of them had any brothers they were immediately on laughing and joking terms together whenever they met. Tatsuo's home was about twenty minutes on foot from Mukaigoya. He attended the communications ministry college in Hiroshima City, but was home at the moment for the summer holidays. Hearing this, H hurried through his lunch as fast as possible.

"It's the hottest time of the day just now," Aunt Oiku warned him. "Why don't you wait till it gets a bit cooler? If you must go, you'll have to take a hat."

"Don't worry, I'll put one on," he said in his best Hiroshima accent as he left. He was hoping to learn the Hiroshima dialect during the summer holidays, for which reason he intended to spend time not just with his relatives' sons but with the local children as well.

He was walking along the path through the paddies when Yoshiko came running after him calling, "Hajime, take me with you!"

"Here we go again!" he thought wearily.

"You're a nasty cheat!" she declared. "I thought you promised you'd look after me while we're in the country. If you're not going to take me, I'll write and tell them in Kobe, so there!"

"Of course I'll take care of you. But Mother said I was to make you have a rest in the afternoon, seeing that you're not very strong. That's *part* of looking after you, isn't it? Not taking you about in the daytime while it's hot, and making sure you have a sleep...."

They continued arguing until finally H managed to shake her off and set off running at top speed.

He could hear her crying behind him, but deliberately didn't look back. Lately she'd been getting surprisingly good at arguing, and already it was quite a job to fob her off with excuses.

As he raced to the top of the embankment, the view opened up all around. The river flowing below was the Takaya, which came down from the direction of Kannabe in the east. At the back of Tatchan's house there was another, bigger river called the Ashida, which was joined by the Takaya a little further to the west before flowing on toward Fukuyama.

It was hot on the path along the embankment, where there was no shade, but there was a pleasant breeze. Looking up, he saw clouds piled high in a deep blue sky. H liked summer clouds because of their suggestion of inner power. The clouds here, he thought, looked the same as those he saw on the beach at Kobe, but the breeze felt different.

In the dry part of the riverbed below the embankment he caught sight of some children putting a cow to graze. He hailed them in a loud voice: "Hello!" The children gazed at him in silence for a moment, then suddenly squatted down, scooped up some pebbles and threw them in H's direction.

Simultaneously they set up a clamor of "*Bugensha*! It's the son of a *bugensha*!" which H didn't understand.

He felt rather discouraged: he'd wanted to make friends, but the feeling hadn't got across.

He broke into a run. The sweat came trickling into his eyes and made them smart, but he went on without resting, his breath coming in great gasps. Running seemed to relieve the feeling of dejection a bit. As he was passing a temple he glanced at the wooden belfry standing in the precinct and saw that there was a bell hanging in it. In this area, apparently, they hadn't contributed their bells to the war effort yet. He felt like getting up onto the belfry and giving the bell a thwack with the pole suspended there for the purpose, but resisted the urge, remembering how the last time he'd come he'd rung the bell while in the precinct gathering fallen gingko nuts and had been soundly told off by the temple priest.

The gate of Tatchan's house came into sight. He was calling "Hey, Tatchan!" long before he reached it, but Tatchan must have heard him, since he came rushing out to meet him. "What a racket!" he said. "I could tell it was you coming a mile off."

Tatchan's mother, home from working in the fields out back, and his three younger sisters came trooping out of the house.

"Haven't you all grown!" said H, with an attempt at a Hiroshima accent and in such a grown-up way that everybody laughed.

"Hajime can talk just like us!" said Tatsuo admiringly in an even thicker accent.

"This summer holiday I'm going to learn the Hiroshima dialect properly," said H. "I want you to teach me."

"Hiroshima people don't all talk the same; there's a slight difference between here and Onomichi, and in Hiroshima City they talk a lot differently."

"I'll settle for here, then. As I was coming here some kids threw stones at me saying I was a *bugensha*. What's a *bugensha*?"

"A rich man. You're wearing a white hat with a white shirt and short pants, so I expect you looked like a rich kid to them."

"I don't want to be a *bugensha*, I want to be treated the same as the kids around here. I want to be friends with them—that's why I have to learn the language."

H spoke so earnestly that Tatsuo nodded understandingly and said, "I'll give you my old straw hat, then. And if you change into long pants and put on an old shirt, you won't look like a *bugensha* anymore."

Delighted, H got Tatsuo to lend him both the pants and the shirt.

"Tatchan," he said, "I thought you were going to the middle school near here, but you decided on a Hiroshima school instead—why?"

"Because we're not *bugensha*—that's why I'm going to the communications ministry school. If you go there you can get a job with the ministry as soon as you leave."

"You mean at a post office?"

"Yes—well, there are places like government offices too, bigger than ordinary post offices."

H was greatly impressed that Tatsuo should be studying by himself in Hiroshima and living in a dormitory.

"You'll be going to middle school next year too, won't you, Hajime? Where are you thinking of sitting for?"

"The prefectural Kobe Second Middle. But I haven't done any preparation, so I don't know whether I'll get through. I don't like studying just so I don't fail an exam. All the worse for me!"

"You'll get through. You're head of your class, aren't you?"

Talking all the while, they left their clothes in the house and went down to swim in the Ashida River at the back of the house. It was more difficult than swimming in the sea; the water was cold, the current was fast, and you didn't float so easily as in salt water.

On the way back to Mukaigoya they came across the children who'd thrown pebbles at H earlier. He called out to them again, in his best Hiroshima accent: "Hello, there! Nice weather we're having!" For a moment they gaped at the transformation—the straw hat and long cotton pants suddenly replacing the white hat and shorts, the sleeveless undershirt.

Then one of them pulled himself together and asked, "Where d'you come from?"

"Kobe," said H, running down the side of the embankment. "My name's Hajime, but you can call me H. Will you take me with you sometime when there's something interesting going on?"

The boy who seemed to be the leader looked around at the other three, and a brief glance passed between them. Then the leader said, "I'm Ryozo. We've got something secret on this evening—can you keep your mouth shut?"

"Of course, no problem! I never give away secrets."

"Then be at Dondonkoshi at eight tonight. But you're not to tell anyone, mind!"

"No, I won't—but where's Dondonkoshi? I don't know how to find it."

"You know the weir you come to if you go along this embankment toward Yokoo Station? Dondonkoshi's there, below the embankment."

H had no idea what they were planning, but he promised to be there.

After supper that evening he slipped out the back way so as not to be seen by Yoshiko and ran along the embankment, faster even than he had in the daytime. When he got close to the weir he saw a boy waving a flashlight in circles in his direction.

"You didn't tell anybody, did you?" said Ryozo. "If we get found out we'll be arrested."

"I didn't tell anyone," replied H, feeling a bit scared.

"Right. Let's start, then."

At a signal from Ryozo, another boy they called Shota took a handful of white powder out of a paper bag he had in a basket and scattered a large quantity of it over the water, which was placid here, held back as it was by the weir.

The moon shed so much light that the surface, white with powder, was clearly visible without the aid of the flashlight. A few moments later a large *buna* suddenly popped to the surface, soon to be followed by several more, all with their mouths wide open and gasping, till the surface of the water was thick with floating fish.

"What did you do? Did you spread poison? Will the fish die?" asked H, eager to know everything at once.

"The powder's lime, it's not a poison; but they come to the surface because they can't breathe. Lime doesn't get into the flesh, so if you gut

207

them you can boil them down in soy sauce for eating. They're good—
but it's prohibited, so ..."

Ryozo was glaring at H with an intimidating expression as though to
drive the point home. They would have given him a share of the *buna*,
but he refused it. Even if he'd taken some back with him he couldn't
very well have explained how he'd got hold of them.

H must have won their confidence, for he played with Ryozo and his
pals almost daily from then on. The ways in which the children amused
themselves here were interesting, quite different from those of the kids
in Kobe. One of them, for instance, was going to see a farmer let a bull
mount a cow so that it would have a calf.

Nor was it just the way the children spent their time; there was very
little here to suggest that Japan was at war. About the only thing was
the occasional procession of people, led by a banner-bearer, seen walking along the embankment on their way to Yokoo Station to see off a
newly enlisted recruit. And even those seemed few and far between
here....

One day, as H was on his way back from Tatsuo's place with Yoshiko,
they saw a mare with her foal grazing in the dry part of the riverbed
below the embankment. Seeing them H began singing a well-known
children's song in a loud voice: "Little horse, with your mother ..."

"Hajime," said Yoshiko, looking at him in disgust, "you're just like a
little boy!" And she began singing another, quite different song:

> On to victory we march—
> Junior citizens of His Majesty!
> The red blood of our parents
> Tells us we must die for him;
> The banner of our righteous cause
> Leads us into the attack....

"Hey, that's enough of that! Did you learn it at school?"
"That's right," she said, "didn't you?"
H didn't know the song. At schools, it seemed, they were starting to
teach third-grade children even that they should "die for the Emperor,"
which H himself didn't want to do. For some reason he suddenly remembered Girly Boy, who'd killed himself rather than die for the Emperor,

thus making himself "un-Japanese." H, though, had liked Girly Boy just the same.

Starting up "Little horse" again in an almost defiantly loud voice, he insisted that Yoshiko should join in too.

They'd been walking and singing for some time along the raised path between the paddies, when H suddenly heard a loud wail from Yoshiko behind him. Turning, he saw that she'd fallen into one of the sunken jars containing human waste for use as fertilizer that were installed beside the path. The bamboo frame of the straw cover had caught her before she could fall right in, but her lower half seemed to be immersed in the filth. Quickly he grabbed her hands and hauled her up, only managing with great difficulty to stop himself from going in too.

Yoshiko was quiet until her body was completely free, but the moment she felt safe she burst into tears. It wasn't surprising she should feel like crying, considering that she was almost completely covered in shit. Telling her to be quiet, H shoved her into the irrigation canal by the paddy field and started washing her with his hands. There wasn't much water, so this wasn't very effective. In no time his own hands were sticky, and the smell was awful.

When waste in the fertilizer pots in the fields got old, a film formed on the top and it stopped smelling as bad as when it was new, but Yoshiko must have stirred it up by thrashing around with her legs.

"We're nearly home," he told her. "I'll wash you properly when we get there. This is the best I can do here."

He calmed the still whimpering little girl, and together they hurried along the path, shedding great drops as they went. They arrived at the house to be greeted in an unexpected way by their grandparents and Aunt Oiku, all of whom started laughing. H took offense. Later, though, he heard that country children too sometimes fell in the fertilizer pots, and that whoever fished them out would say, "You're lucky—the fertilizer will make you grow up big!"

H duly recorded the "fertilizer pot incident" in his picture diary, though he hesitated at first, feeling guilty toward his sister. The picture showed Yoshiko crying as she walked along the path through the paddies, and the note he wrote beside it said, "Yoshiko cried because she smelled so bad, but her hands were too dirty even to wipe her eyes."

He could never show it to her, though, he thought.

In the event, Yoshiko herself said to him, "Hajime, did you write about it in your diary? I did, in mine. I wrote, 'For me, it was a smelly summer holiday.' You can write about it too, if you want to." H was relieved.

He enjoyed his summer holiday in the country. Twice they went on secret "fishing" trips again, and they did something else too, something still more secret. They actually spied on a dead body being burned. Following the funeral procession they hid in the undergrowth, watching while people piled up brushwood in a clearing between the hills and burned the body on it. The bands around the coffin burst amidst the flames and the dead person moved as though to get up, then collapsed again, which thoroughly scared them.

They saw a cow give birth, too. What astonished them was the way the new-born calf stood up immediately on its own legs.

At the local festival they saw a young man of the village, who was drunk, fight a man who'd come from Kannabe until both of them were covered with blood. Still more surprisingly, later on they saw the same two men drinking and laughing together.

H put everything in his picture journal. The days seemed to follow each other more quickly than in Kobe.

Tatchan was to go back to his dormitory in Hiroshima three days before H and his sister were due to leave. H didn't go to the station to see him off, but arranged instead to wave at the Fukuen-line train as it cut across in front of Mukaigoya. It was a good three hundred meters from the house to the tracks, but he clearly saw Tatchan waving too. Brother and sister went on waving until the train rounded a distant bend and disappeared behind the hills.

The day before they left H wrote down, in a horizontal row on a card, the names of the stations they would pass through. He knew them all from the timetable that Uncle Yoshio had bought him, thus endearing himself still more to H who promised to send him a postcard with a picture on it from Kobe.

Uncle Yoshio came as far as Fukuyama Station to see them off, and H and Yoshiko waved to him from the window of their train until he was out of sight.

The train home was the slow one which stopped at all the forty-three stations. H stood the long list of names against the window and crossed out the name of each station as they came to it.

On the way he let himself drop off to sleep. When he woke up he was alarmed to find he'd no longer any idea where they were. Looking at the list of names, though, he found that the stations they'd passed through while he was asleep had all been crossed out. The man sitting smiling in front of him had done it for him.

The two children finally arrived home exhausted, their faces still grubby with soot. Local trains were tiring.

To their astonishment, there were people digging an air raid shelter under the floor of the house.

"Hi! Back safe and sound, then?" Uncle Hadano greeted them, poking his head out from under the floor where he'd been shoveling up dirt.

Morio wasn't there, it being his turn to stay overnight at the fire station.

When his father got back the next day, H decided he'd ask him whether it was really any use digging an air raid shelter under the floor of a house. Personally he found it odd: if the house collapsed from a bomb or was set on fire by incendiaries, they'd be trapped under it. Surely that was more dangerous still?

In Kobe, he felt, the war loomed far closer and more distinctly than it had in the country....

22

Till Victory!

On his return to school after the summer holidays, H found that there'd been a momentous development. From now on, when Japanese was written horizontally it was to be from left to right, not right to left as it had always been. Moreover, the way the *kana* syllabary was used to indicate the pronunciation of the Chinese characters was to change also. The character meaning "law," for instance, whose pronunciation was at present shown as *hofu*, was henceforth to be *hou*, and the character for "bridge," now written as *kefu*, was to be *kyou*.

The boys gave voice unanimously to their doubts and dissatisfaction, creating bedlam in the classroom when the Japanese language and literature class came around.

"Why? Does it mean everything we've learned at school so far is going to be useless?"

"Does it mean we're going to be failed in the exams if we write things as we have until now?"

"*Kuwau*'s going to be *kou* and *chiuau*'s going to be *chuuou*, so all we have to do is write it just as we talk, don't we?"

"If so, then why did they make us write *kyou* as *kefu* in the first place?"

"Probably because that's what everybody'd always done."

"Well then, I don't see why they have to change it. *I* think grownups do everything just to please themselves."

Feeling that for once he should behave as was expected of the head boy of the class, H put up his hand with a question for Mr. Yamazaki: "Please sir, who decided on this and when?"

"There was a notice about it from the education ministry before the summer holidays, but I didn't say anything because I thought it would be better to tell you all after the second semester had begun. I thought I'd draw up a chart to make it simpler for you. As for why things have changed, the idea, it seems, is to spread Japanese to replace English in nations of the Greater East Asia Coprosperity Sphere, and to make it the language of the whole of Asia in the future. The only way you can teach Japanese to foreigners is to write it with the Roman alphabet. If you do that you have to write it as it's pronounced or nobody's going to understand, right? Another thing is, you can't write the alphabet from top to bottom as you do in Japanese: it's written horizontally, so you can only write it from left to right; it doesn't make sense if you write it from the right. So they decided that it would be better to take the opportunity and make everything consistent by writing Japanese too from left to right in future. It'll probably be confusing at first, but you'll soon get used to it. I personally think it's better, too."

Mr. Yamazaki's explanation was enough, more or less, to convince the students in the first class, sixth grade, of the need for the changes. But H himself felt that the idea of making Japanese the language of the whole of Asia was going too far. He knew an Indian, for example, who though he'd lived in Kobe for years still couldn't speak much Japanese, and for some reason seemed to stubbornly avoid speaking it even though he knew it would be more convenient to do so.

Three months after the decision to write Japanese from left to right in its horizontal form, confusion reigned even in the newspapers.

Every morning when he opened the newspaper H would look to see what had happened, and every morning he'd find chaos. One advertisement, for example, would be written from left to right and another on the same page from right to left.

On top of this, the ministry of education issued a directive saying that "words of enemy origin" were to be avoided where the names of plants and animals were concerned. This complicated matters still further. "Cosmos," the name of the flower, was "of enemy origin," so the phonetic transcription was to be replaced by two characters meaning "autumn cherry," while "kangaroo" became, of all things, "pouched rat."

The boys amused themselves by making up "substitute names," then getting the others to guess what they referred to; it was better to treat it as a laughing matter than to go on feeling irritated all the time.

Apart from the question of language, another annoying thing was that the campaign to round up anything made of metal had been stepped up still further.

The neighborhood association circulars were appealing to the public: "Let's rid our homes completely of metal. Every small scrap of iron goes to make weapons and warships that will carry us to victory!" The school's statue of Kinjiro Ninomiya had long since disappeared. Now even the metal mesh mats they used to scrape the mud off their shoes had been taken up and borne off, and it looked as though the iron bars they used in gymnastics were in danger too.

H had the uncomfortable feeling that his own rather rusty old bicycle was being eyed disapprovingly.

"Don't worry," his mother told him, "you don't have to hand over a bike you're actually using." Even so she seemed to find her own position awkward, since the authorities had directed that heads of neighborhood associations should "go around from house to house persuading people not to hold onto things unnecessarily."

"I can hardly tell them to hand over the pots they cook rice in," she said in an unusually plaintive tone. "About the only metal objects left for ordinary families to give up are things like charcoal tongs. I'm fed up—they're asking too much!"

They heard that in the next neighborhood they actually *had* been made to surrender their cooking pots. The situation was so bad that people were being pressed to give up anything, however small, that could possibly count as metal.

H hid his collection of metal buttons away where his mother, as head of the neighborhood association, wouldn't find it.

He had had an unaccountable fondness for gilt buttons ever since he was small, and whenever his father gave him one would carefully stash it away.

Every time Morio was asked to alter a uniform, whether military, police, railway official or student, it always came with its gilt buttons, and H would keep a beady eye open, knowing he'd be given any that might be left over when the job was finished. But now the manufacture of metal buttons had been totally suspended in favor of ceramic ones.

There was even an article in the newspaper calling on people to hand in their own metal buttons: "The button on your chest could be a bullet!"

With a guilty feeling of being "un-Japanese," H took his precious metal buttons, still in the cookie can he'd been using to keep them in, down into the air raid shelter beneath the floor, then dug a hole in the earth there and buried them safe from the eyes of others.

Children also went about collecting old nails and other scrap metal, making it a sort of competition, but gradually they stopped taking such stuff to school. At school it constituted a "contribution to the war effort," and they weren't given a single sen in reward, whereas if they took it along on the neighborhood's metal-collecting day they were paid.

H, whose foraging for metal took him far and wide, bore his finds on the prescribed day to the collection point, where there was a specialist who examined the iron or copper and fixed the payment for it. Old copper objects fetched five yen twenty sen for one *kanme*; brass, two yen twenty-seven sen. The price for iron depended on the degree of rusting, ranging from twenty to thirty sen for one *kanme*.

One day when Toshiko was away at the church, H took his finds to the collection point to find the woman from the tobacco store standing in for his mother as representative of their neighborhood association. The scrap iron he'd collected weighed 860 *momme*. This included, in fact, stolen property, since he'd removed some metal fittings from the wooden door of the priests' quarters at the Zenshoji Temple. To his disappointment he got a mere sixteen sen for the lot. He asked the woman from the tobacco shop not to tell his mother that he'd brought scrap along that day.

He had various other secrets, too. One of them was that he was skipping some of the special classes in which he was supposed to be preparing for the middle school entrance examinations.

The exams were due in the spring of the following year, and their homeroom teacher, Mr. Yamazaki, had determined which school each student hoping to go on to middle school should sit for. H himself was to take the exam for Kobe's Hyogo Prefectural Second Middle School. In Kobe, the First and Second Middle Schools were considered to be difficult to get into. Seven students in all from the Nagara National School were sitting for the Second Middle, Iwao Hayashi among them.

The reason why none were taking the First Middle School exam was that the city had been divided into east and west zones, students from the latter being allowed to sit for the Second Middle School but not the First, which would involve long trips to and from school. Besides these, there were two other prefectural middle schools—the Third and Fourth —in Kobe.

The number of students from Nagara National School who aimed to go on to middle school—exclusively for boys—or a girls' college was a mere one-fourth of the whole. The reason for this small figure was that quite a few of the families could not afford it, even though the boy or girl might have both the desire and the ability to do so.

In October the prospective examinees would stay on in the classroom after ordinary classes for extra study, though this wasn't compulsory.

H didn't like studying math; inscribing figures in his notebook, he would suddenly find himself for no particular reason thinking about movies instead. On one occasion the figures in some calculation or other had sprouted arms and legs, and he'd ended up doing a picture of a samurai swordfight, which had earned him a telling-off. It happened that at the time he'd been plotting to supplement the money he'd earned selling scrap metal with some of his secret savings in order to go to a period movie starring one of the most popular swashbuckling actors of the day.

During these extra classes H would often have stomach pains. "Sir," he would say, "my stomach hurts. May I go home?" And Mr. Yamazaki, who may have realized that the pains weren't genuine, would say with a smile, "What, again? Go on, then." For the benefit of the classmates he was leaving behind, H would go through the motions of pressing a hand to his belly as he left; otherwise, he'd have felt guilty toward them. He did not, of course, go home.

Glancing around the schoolyard on this particular occasion, he went into the shed where the gymnastic equipment was kept. Shingo was there, sitting on a vaulting horse, waiting for him as promised. H envied his friend, who was not taking the entrance exam and could amuse himself as he liked.

The two of them lifted up a mat, hid their school bags under it, climbed the fence by the east gate, which was closed, and jumped down into the road outside. If they'd gone out through the main gate there'd have been a danger of being seen from the classroom window. In accordance with a plan they'd drawn up four days earlier, they boarded a streetcar and headed for the movie district of Shinkaichi. Shingo, H's regular co-conspirator, was keen to see a comedy starring Enoken, a popular comedian of the day, and it was quite a job to get him to agree to see *Kurama Tengu*, a swashbuckling period movie, instead. He finally consented only after H had promised that they'd see Enoken next time and offered to pay half of Shingo's admission.

"So Shochiku-za's started putting on samurai movies, has it?" said Shingo pensively when they were sitting in the streetcar. Yes, thought H—now that movies produced in enemy countries were banned, the place had become somewhere to see Japanese movies. Previously it had specialized in foreign films, especially those from America and France.

"It seems German movies are okay because Germany's a friendly country."

"Yes, but where foreign films are concerned, I prefer American ones. I wonder why they can't show Chaplin? And things are getting tight even for Japanese movies, aren't they?" The two movie fans shook their heads over the situation like a couple of experts.

What was "tight" for Japanese movies was that the big movie companies such as Toho, Shochiku and Daiei, which up to now had had franchises where they showed their own films, were to be consolidated, and the distribution network was to be reorganized. They'd been forced into this as a kind of self-defense measure because shortage of film had dictated a cut in the number of movies they made. The tightness extended not only to the quantity of film used but even to the tone of the movies they did make, which were not given permits if they were judged to be inconsistent with national policy.

When they arrived in front of the Shochiku-za, H's heart started to pound. He was remembering the last time he'd come here with Shingo to see the American film *Destry Rides Again*, and how the girl at the box office hadn't let them in, not to mention scaring them with talk of the Guidance League.

This time they got in without any difficulty. Even so, they kept a wary eye open on the way to their seats, in case people from the league or others who might be teachers from other schools should be there.

The plot of *Kurama Tengu* told how the legendary goblin appeared in Yokohama in the period following the opening of Japan to the West and did battle with a man called Jacob and his henchmen, who were making counterfeit money in a foreign trading house. Jacob was a Jew, and it occurred to H that the Jews were being treated as villains in Japan as well as in Germany; otherwise, presumably, the film wouldn't have been considered "consistent with national policy." Even so, he admired Arakan's dashing swordplay as Kurama Tengu. His satisfaction wasn't entirely shared by Shingo, who still insisted that the Enoken film would have been better. H liked Enoken too, but had to admit that he found the occasional good swordfight stimulating.

"If you keep acting like you're waving a sword about," Shingo warned H as they were walking along the street after leaving the movie theater, "everybody will know straight off that we've been to see a film."

They didn't take the streetcar all the way to Honjo-cho 4-chome, which was nearest to their homes, but got off at Ohashi 9-chome, one stop before. One reason for this was that they thought they were less likely to be seen by the neighbors that way; another was that they had to drop in at the school.

Getting out the bags they'd hidden in the shed where the PE equipment was kept, they set off for home running, frantic because they were so much later than they'd expected. On the way, though, they met a procession of people carrying the ashes of a dead soldier from the station back to his home. However much of a hurry they were in, they were obliged to stop and bow silently in respect. The woman walking at the front, bearing in her arms the box of ashes wrapped in its white cloth, was Mrs. Nishida from Noda-cho, whom H knew by sight. He'd heard a report that her husband had been killed in battle, and now here he was—finally coming home, in the language of the time, as an *eirei* or "heroic spirit."

The couple were said to have three young chldren, but there was no sign of them in the procession.

Standing with head bowed, H reflected on the word *eirei*. It was funny: the *rei* meant "spirit" all right, but the character *ei*, meaning "heroic," was also in everyday use, especially in newspaper headlines, as a prefix meaning "British," so the word could just as easily have meant "the spirit of an Englishman." The Japanese language was difficult and tricky to handle. He remembered only the other day laughing with his friends over a newspaper headline reading "*Eiki gekitsui saru*" —"British Plane Shot Down." Unfortunately, the same two Chinese characters that here were read *eiki*, "British plane," were also those used to write "Hideki," the given name of Prime Minister Tojo, so that the headline could equally well be taken to mean "Prime Minister Shot Down."

When he got back to the house, his little sister was standing outside waiting for him.

"Oh, Hajime!" she exclaimed. "Something awful's happened! Mummy's found out that you cut your class. I've been waiting for ages, thinking I'd better let you know as soon as I could. Whatever will you tell her?"

H's mind immediately went completely blank, leaving him with no idea at all what to do. The question was, who'd told his mother he'd left the class, and when? His sister didn't know.

His first, provisional idea was to say that after spending some time with Shingo at his home, they'd both gone to the station with the others to fetch Mr. Nishida's ashes, and that they'd had to wait a long time.

As he opened the front door his mother appeared without warning and asked, to his horror, "So you went on the streetcar to Shinkaichi?" Apparently one of the neighbors had been on the same streetcar and had reported the fact to Toshiko. H fully expected to be given a thorough dressing down *and* made to offer up prayers of repentance to God. To his surprise, though, Toshiko pursued the matter no further.

Later he heard the explanation from his father. Learning that he'd apparently been to Shinkaichi, Toshiko had dashed off to the school to confirm the report. But Mr. Yamazaki had told her, "You'd do better not to put too much pressure on him or try to keep him shut up. You could safely let him see more books and movies. Even if you do, he'll be all right—and I'm fairly certain he'll get through the Second Middle School exam."

H decided that Mr. Yamazaki was a thoroughly good teacher. There was an extra item of good news that he'd given his mother, too: the movie *Sea Battles off Hawaii and Malaya*, soon to be released with the recommendation of the ministry of education, could be seen by children provided they were accompanied by a parent or other responsible adult.

The newspapers were becoming ever more preoccupied with the war, and air raid drills were being steadily stepped up in the towns. Even children were taught at school about the various types of incendiary bombs and their respective characteristics. Three different kinds were being dropped by America—petroleum, yellow phosphorus and electron.

The petroleum incendiary was about the size of a soft-drink bottle, and scattered a sticky oil that caught fire when it burst. The yellow phosphorus incendiary was a lump of stuff like the material on the striking end of a matchstick. The electron incendiary, which emitted a bluish white flame, gave off enough heat to melt metal. H's father had seen an actual specimen that had been sent to the fire station. It was about fifty centimeters long, he said, bigger than a soft-drink bottle. A bundle of thirty-eight of these was enclosed in a cylinder that opened up as it fell, scattering its contents in all directions. In residential areas with many wooden buildings, petroleum or yellow phosphorus bombs would probably be most commonly used; electron bombs in factory districts.

Imagining the streets around where he lived enveloped in flames, H felt scared. Even so, he looked forward to putting out at least two or three incendiaries with his own hands.

As air raid drills became more frequent at school, comparative frivolities such as music classes for sixth-grade students were dropped. But one day, for the first time in ages, Mr. Okuno the music teacher, who'd said he was very fond of the tenor Yoshie Fujiwara, hailed him in the corridor. H remembered telling him that he knew an aria from *Rigoletto*, along with "Leaving the Harbor" and "Lay Down My Spear."

"Did you know that the Fujiwara Opera Company put on a show at the Kabuki Theater in Tokyo?" Mr. Okuno asked almost proudly, his eyes sparkling. H, who hadn't heard about it, was astonished. However had they managed to do an opera at the Kabuki Theater when foreign songs were prohibited?

"Because it was an opera by a German called Wagner," explained Mr. Okuno. H was rather tickled: they'd managed to sidestep the prohibition nicely…. Privately, he vowed that sometime he would go and see an opera himself.

The *Rigoletto* aria wasn't the only kind of music H liked; he also liked jazz songs such as "Dinah." Foreign songs, unlike many Japanese pieces, cheered you up—and he needed something to cheer him up nowadays.

Normally Christmas, which wasn't far off, would have done that for him: it was the time of year when he usually felt *most* cheered up. The sight of the fairy lights on the church Christmas tree was itself enough to make him feel happy. He enjoyed getting presents, too. But it was impossible to celebrate Christmas in a very festive way at this time. The police and the military had got particularly bothersome lately, so this year again they were going to do things as unostentatiously as possible.

Opening the newspaper on his return from the Christmas service, his eyes lighted on a piece headed "Be Prepared for Air Raids!" It took the form of a discussion centering on Lieutenant Colonel Namba, chief of staff for the Central Japan military district. This Lieutenant Colonel Namba was the man who, after the first air raid on Japan proper, had stupidly talked of the importance of beating out burning flakes." Now he was at it again.

> Since Japan is surrounded by sea, we will often not realize that enemy planes are coming until they are actually over our heads. Thus Japan is particularly susceptible to raids out of the blue. Only in the most fortunate cases will it be possible to give an alert or air raid warning hours in advance; sometimes bombs will start dropping moments after a warning. This, in geographical terms, is one special feature of anti-air raid measures in Japan.

H sniffed in disgust: this was just an excuse for having issued an air raid warning after the enemy plane had aready flown off on April 18. But there was more to come:

> Even if air raids cannot be avoided altogether, it is still possible, if one is adequately prepared, to keep damage down to a minimum. And once the same thing has happened two or three

times it will become familiar. Depending on how you look at them, air raids are easier to handle than ordinary fires. Air raids may come suddenly, but they announce themselves with the sound of airplane engines. With ordinary fires, you never know when and whence they are coming, in which sense air raids are easier to cope with. What's more, you get used to them....

"Easier to cope with," indeed! The idea that such a man was in charge of a military district infuriated H. He thought of showing the piece to his father and asking his opinion but in the end said nothing and, folding up the paper, put it away in silence.

Lately the rhyme "Nothing for me / Till victory!" was to be seen on posters all over the town, and was being repeated again and again in the press and on the radio. It had been the winner in a competition for "slogans expressing the nation's resolve," held to mark the end of the first year of the Greater East Asian War. The author was said to be an eleven-year-old girl in fifth grade at a national school in Tokyo.

H was impressed by her skill, but couldn't help wishing there was no need for such slogans in the first place.

The boys soon started their own slogan competition. When one of them came up with "Restraint is in / Until we win," H followed it up with "Too much restraint / Will make you faint," and was set on by all the rest at once, who said it was an anti-slogan and he was "un-Japanese."

The numerals on the school clocks changed. This, too, came without warning. One day they found the figures 13, 14 and so on had been added in red on the dial as well as the ordinary figures from 1 to 12. From now on there would no longer be any A.M. or P.M., only twenty-four hours, as in the forces.

Learning that six in the evening would be "1800 hours," H felt that everything was getting to be more and more of a bother. Wondering what would happen to the railway timetables, he went straight to a bookstore to investigate. To his surprise, the new November issue, was titled not "Train Timetable" as before, but "Railway Schedules," and everything was printed according to the twenty-four-hour system. The price was unchanged at thirty sen, but the number of trains was considerably less than the previous summer. He was standing there flipping through the pages of this new "Railway Schedules" when the store owner demanded to know if he intended to buy it or not: "If not, you can put it down!"

A repeated offender on this score, H was always being driven out of bookstores. Thanks to his free look at the timetable, though, he'd learned that purchases of tickets would be restricted around the year end and New Year, when large numbers of people normally wanted to travel. So the rumors saying that travel would be restricted and that tickets would be hard to come by had been true.

It looked as though he wouldn't be going to the countryside in Hiroshima prefecture again for some time. "Nothing for me / Till victory"—the jingle came to his lips, but he chased it away with his own "Too much restraint / Will make you faint."

23

The Second Middle Exam

"We've all got to buy war bonds again," grumbled Toshiko, fresh from a meeting of the neighborhood association. As this implied, they'd already bought some, but now an official notice had come urging them to buy still more.

Toshiko dreaded the idea of going around from house to house again, as head of the association, trying to persuade people to buy. One bond cost twenty-five yen, close to one-third of the average office worker's monthly salary. This was definitely too much of a burden for individual households, and last time they'd decided in the end to fudge matters by buying one jointly.

H had got his mother to show him the actual bond that they'd bought previously. It was a piece of paper about half the size of a newspaper page, with a design resembling that of paper money printed on it.

"What do you have to buy printed paper like this for?" H had asked his mother wonderingly.

"Because it costs a lot of money to make war. There's not enough of it, though, so the government asks ordinary people to lend it some. That's what national bonds are. You can't get the money back whenever you like as you can with ordinary savings, but they're supposed to give you interest on it."

"When *will* they give you back the money you've spent on the bonds?" asked H.

"After we've won the war," Toshiko said. "If we lost, I don't suppose we'd get it back at all."

"*What?*" H exclaimed. Two ideas had occurred to him simultaneously: that they might lose their money altogether, and that Japan was hardly likely to defeat a rich country like America if it had to borrow money from its own people in order to keep on fighting.

National bonds weren't the only means being used to squeeze money out of people to finance the war. Taxes on all kinds of things had risen sharply, too. The price of cigarettes, in particular—perhaps because they were easy to tax—had gone up tremendously. Hikari—"Light"—cigarettes, formerly eighteen sen for a pack, had gone up overnight to thirty sen and "Golden Bats" to fifteen.

These increases didn't concern the children directly, but they all knew the new prices thanks to a popular variation of the celebratory "2,600th Anniversary Hymn." The original was:

> Praise ye now this happy morn,
> Bathing in the glorious light
> Shining from the Golden Bird
> That so long ago o'ersaw
> The founding of Japan.
> Ah, a hundred million breasts
> Pounding at the thought!

This had been amended to:

> Curse ye now this mournful morn
> Glorious "Lights" are thirty sen,
> "Golden Bats" cost fifteen too.
> Soaring high the "Phoenix Wings"
> Finally went to twenty-five.
> Ah, a hundred million breasts
> Groaning at the thought!

They'd been warned to be careful because they'd be arrested if the police heard them singing it, but in fact grownups and children alike all sang it in private.

What shocked H was that even Mr. Omori, the ex-army officer who was always talking about giving up one's life for the Emperor "for the sake of victory in the holy war," was to be heard singing "'Golden Bats' cost fifteen too" softly to himself. Even he must be privately dismayed by the way things were going.

There was another jingle surreptitiously doing the rounds, too:

> Prices up, not much to buy.
> "Don't do this" and "Don't do that."
> Who knows what they'll tell us next?
> Not to ask the reason why.

Stage names and foreign words had already been outlawed three years before, but recently there'd been an announcement saying that "British and American jazz, light music, and other frivolous music is to be done away with completely since it saps the nation's fighting spirit." To H's surprise, the list of music whose performance was prohibited included works such as "Dinah," "My Blue Heaven," "Old Black Joe," "Home on the Range," and "Aloha Oe." Apparently the list included a full thousand works that weren't to be sung anymore.

One thing that irritated the boys as they sang "'Don't do this' and 'Don't do that'" was that there seemed to be no rhyme or reason in the restrictions. For example, notification came that the foreign songs "Home, Sweet Home" and "The Last Rose of Summer," which had been banned at one stage, were now to be taken *off* the list on the grounds that they were "already a part of the people's daily lives."

Then what *was* it, H wondered, that constituted an "enemy song"?

His friends must have felt the same way, because they were always complaining about the pointlessness of vague prohibitions that were impossible to observe in practice.

"There was another thing that made me angry," said Shingo. "I heard that the ashes of that 'heroic spirit' turned out to be just a few pebbles. Mrs. Nishida was crying about it."

Shingo's mother, a member of the same neighborhood association as Mrs. Nishida, had gone along to the house to offer up incense to the deceased, and Mrs. Nishida had told her that when she opened the plain wooden box containing the "ashes," she'd found three pebbles wrapped in a cloth.

"When he was first called up, my old man always said he might well be killed. He was resigned to it," she'd said. "But to think that he should come home as a few pebbles … oh, it's too sad!" And she'd wept bitterly.

When Shingo's mother got home after hearing Mrs. Nishida's story, she'd wept angrily too. "They take away a family's breadwinner with their little slip of pink paper, and what do you get?—three pebbles! I know it was probably hard to collect bodies there where they were fighting," she said, "but think how bitter the soldiers who had to die in such a place must have felt. Why did we have to have a war like this?"

Notice came that the husband at the Kasugas', up the road on the other side from H's home, had been killed too. The ashes hadn't come home yet, but a notice saying "Home of a Heroic Spirit" had been stuck up next to the nameplate outside the front entrance.

For some time there'd been none of the Imperial Headquarters communiqués proclaiming war victories, but in the newspapers on February 2 reports of a victory in the Solomon Islands were given great prominence.

"Two battleships and three cruisers sunk!" they declared. "One battleship and one cruiser badly damaged. Three fighters shot down. Our losses: eight planes self-destructed and three missing."

The planes listed among the Japanese losses as "self-destructed" were probably ones that had tried to sink enemy vessels by deliberately crashing into them.

It seemed from newspaper and radio reports that there'd been a fierce battle in the islands of the South Pacific, far from Japan, but it wasn't clear whether Japan had won or lost it, since a week later the newspaper carried an article saying that Japanese forces had made "strategic advances" from Buna and Guadalcanal. A map in the paper located Buna and Guadalcanal just to the east of New Guinea. The meaning of "strategic advances," however, was obscure.

> 1. Since summer last year, our army and naval units in the South Pacific, checking and smashing stubborn enemy resistance, have been establishing strategic bases on important fronts in New Guinea and the Solomon Islands. This has been by and large completed, and they are now laying the grounds for the pursuit of new operations.
>
> 2. Our forces operating on Buna Island in New Guinea and Guadalcanal Island in the Solomons, which had been smashing persistent enemy counterattacks despite a shortage of manpower, have now achieved their objects and in early February

227

were withdrawn from the islands and ordered to advance in another direction.

H found the article's stream of difficult phrases hard to grasp, but after several rereadings decided that the real meaning was: "The enemy's forces being stronger than ours, we could no longer hold onto Buna and Guadalcanal and withdrew." In plain words, Japan seemed to be losing in that area.

At supper that evening he asked his father, "Does 'advancing in another direction' mean retreating?"

"Yes—well, I suppose so …," was all the answer he got. H was dissatisfied, having expected a clearer reply.

With most of the grownups in the neighborhood it would be risky to ask about such things, but H decided that the man at the charcoal store, at least, would give him a proper answer, and slipped out quietly to ask him. When he got there, though, H found someone utterly different from the man he thought he knew.

"Japan will never be defeated, absolutely not!" he declared angrily. "Anyone who thinks such a thing even for a moment is un-Japanese!" He spoke so heatedly that it made H, if anything, suspicious.

He read the newspapers every day hoping to find out what was really going on, but wherever he looked there was nothing but talk of Japanese victories and stories calculated to raise people's morale.

"You won't get through the Second Middle exam unless you stop reading the papers so much and study more," said Toshiko in her usual mothering way. "I know how difficult it is to get into that school!"

"I shan't get through unless I *do* read the papers," said H. "They say the exam includes questions about the war situation." It was true, too: Akio, the boy from the drugstore, who'd got through the previous year, had told him there were questions you could never answer without reading the papers.

"In last year's exam they were asked to explain the 'ABCD blockade.' Could *you*, Mum? A is America, B's Britain, C's China and D is for Dutch—that's Holland. They're the four enemy countries blockading Japan. If you don't know that much, you don't get through."

"You don't? I see," said his mother, and fell silent. H took the newspaper and went upstairs, where there were two eight-tatami rooms, the room where his father did his secret tailoring on his days off, and his own study room.

It was quiet when his father was at the fire station, with no sound of the sewing machine from the next room. On such days H was the only person on the second floor, so he could secretly read books he'd borrowed from his friends while pretending to study. He knew he ought to be working for the exam, but told himself with defiant optimism that he'd "manage somehow."

The final number of pupils from Nagara National School who were to take the Second Middle examination was seven. Hearing that Ryoji Shiga, a close friend, was to sit for Third Middle, H was shocked. Ryoji was a bright student and had been head of the class at one stage, but his teacher had apparently decided he should sit for Third Middle, which was considered much inferior. After class that day, H found him with his forehead pressed against the shelves on the first floor where they left their shoes, weeping. H was startled, but there was nothing he could say by way of consolation, so he slipped past pretending not to have noticed.

For the past two years, middle school entrance examinations had consisted solely of an oral exam, physical tests and a school report. The spoken examination apparently included questions on physics, math and the Japanese language. The math worried H, but he devised a strategy to make up elsewhere for his failings in that area.

Students at First Middle, in the east of the city, had a reputation for sober academic achievement, whereas Second Middle, in the west, seemed to go in for a rather heartier type, combining learning with more robust skills, and H had heard that the tougher-seeming candidates were more likely to get through. Well, he thought, I can manage *that* all right, and decided to answer the questions both briskly and emphatically.

On the day of the entrance tests, examinees were supposed to be acccompanied by a parent or guardian, so H's mother went with him. He was disgruntled, feeling that he could have gone by himself, but said nothing. The seven examinees from his school were to go in a group, so they and the adults accompanying them all bundled into a streetcar together. The stop for Second Middle, the eighth, was Goban-cho 2-chome, and the route was familiar to H since he always used the same streetcar to go to Shinkaichi, the theater district. Not, of course, that he mentioned the fact....

After getting down at the stop, they climbed a slope and came to where the Shin-Minato River was covered over with concrete. On the other side stood the white, four-story school building. H had seen it before when he came to get his application forms, but now that he was about to take the entrance exam he saw it with fresh eyes. Sunk into the wall by the entrance was a plaque inscribed with the official name of the school: "Kobe's Hyogo Prefectural Second Middle School."

To one side of the entrance stood a senior student holding a rifle and bayonet, with an ammunition pouch and sword dangling at his side, just like a soldier. He was a middle school student, no doubt, but the four years between him and H made him seem like an adult in the latter's eyes, and he felt a bit intimidated.

He was rather apprehensive as he entered the building: unlike the national school, it felt more like a barracks than a place of learning.

Although from the road it looked like a four-story building, the apparent first floor corresponded in fact to a basement, since the schoolyard was up a flight of steps from it. The classrooms on the building's second floor were the real first floor. It was a quite confusing structure.

The examinees gathered in the school assembly hall on the third floor, where they were kept waiting for a long time. Bored, H decided he was going to have a look around, but Hayashi stopped him. "You don't have to do it now, do you?" he said. "Wait till you've passed the exam—you'll have plenty of time then, surely." H decided he was right, and waited patiently.

It was an hour and a half before H's turn came. Entering the class-room that served as examination room, he found three teachers and an officer in military uniform seated at a desk facing him. The badges of rank on the officer's lapels showed him to be a captain. This must be one of the serving officers who, he'd heard, were assigned to every middle school, though he wasn't sure because he'd heard that there were other army men giving military training as well.

For the first question of the oral test, the teacher sitting in the middle pointed to an aluminum kettle and a traditional-style iron kettle standing on the table and said, "What are these made of? Tell us the names of the materials."

"The one on the left is aluminum, and the one on the right's iron, sir," began H in a loud voice.

The teacher looked rather startled. "Good strong voice," he remarked with a smile, "but you don't *have* to talk so loud. Then what about the rust on the aluminum one?" he went on.

"It's completely lost its shine, so it's oxidized all over."

"The aluminum kettle has twine around its handle, but the iron one doesn't. Why is that?"

"Aluminum is a good conductor of heat so it soon gets hot all over, including the handle, but iron is a comparatively poor conductor, so the handle doesn't get hot and the binding isn't necessary. On the other hand, it's a property of the iron kettle that once it gets warm it doesn't cool down as quickly as the aluminum one."

Next, the teacher on the right said, "Now, here's a mathematical question."

Here's where I fail if I'm going to, thought H, half resigned to his fate.

"There's a square tank holding water for fighting fires. It measures twenty meters all the way around and five meters deep. How much water does it hold when it's full?"

"One hundred twenty-five cubic meters," replied H, a certain relief mingling in his mind with surprise. Could this be the "difficult" exam he'd heard so much about?

"Well, then—Japanese forces have advanced into the South Pacific area and are fighting there. What are the reasons, and what do we have to do to win this war? Give us your own opinions."

Probably this is the crux of the oral exam, H thought, nerving himself.

"In order to preserve peace in Asia," he began, "Japan wanted to create a Greater East Asia Coprosperity Sphere, but America mistakenly saw this as an attempt to dominate Asia. It banned exports of iron and oil to Japan, and drew in England and Holland as well in order to set up the ABCD blockade. The Greater East Asian War began when Japan lost patience with this unreasonable behavior.

"The reason why Japan advanced into the South Pacific was to liberate the nations that were colonies of America, England and Holland,

and to remove the threat to Japan by securing sources of oil and rub- ber. To win the war, every individual must possess the determination to smash the American and British fiends and to conserve resources. I feel it is important to be aware that conserving is the same as producing. I'm afraid that was rather long, but I think that's about it."

He watched their reactions to gauge whether or not he ought to add a little more.

All four of the teachers were gazing at him with equally dumb- founded expressions. Then the round-faced teacher in spectacles gave a vigorous nod of satisfaction. It seemed to say "Right! That went well." And H thought to himself, "I'm a cunning devil, though I say it myself!"

The phrase "smash the American and British fiends" had been adopted by the war ministry a month previously as its "slogan for final victory." According to the newspapers, posters bearing it had been dis- tributed throughout the country, so H hadn't hesitated to use it in his answer. In fact, though, he objected to the phrase. The word used for "fiends" was written with Chinese characters meaning, literally, "demons and animals," but H, calling to mind the faces of the American and British people he was friendly with, found nothing in them that sug- gested either.

Yet he'd been so keen to impress the examiners as a solid "junior cit- izen" that he'd used that very phrase himself. Even though he'd done so out of desperation, he still felt that he'd betrayed his friends just the same.

As for the reasons why Japan was at war, he'd simply repeated what the newspapers had said, which didn't represent his own views at all. He felt a little guilty at this effortless transformation into a typical, mili- taristic youth. Admittedly his father had said, "It doesn't matter if you trample on the cross," but H had his doubts as to whether *this* was what he'd really meant. He had a slightly queasy feeling that he wasn't so much a "hidden" Christian as an out-and-out apostate.

Voicing such views, however, had made him realize something for the first time. While some of his elders might be in earnest when they said everything was "for the sake of His Majesty the Emperor," or that "the Land of the Gods is immortal, totally invincible," there must be a considerable number, he suspected, who said it because they were afraid to say anything else.

It was slowly dawning on him that he was no longer a pupil at national school, but a middle school student now, not far removed from the world of adults, and it occurred to him that there'd be hard times ahead.

On the way home the boys exchanged views on their chances. H declared, rather conceitedly, "I'm not worried—I'm sure I passed." The exam had been that easy.

The physical training test on the second day involved putting the shot, bar work and vaulting. In the bar work they were tested to see whether they could do a forward upward circle on the highest bar. H managed this without trouble, but not the vaulting, in which he got stuck astride the horse at the fifth level. Following this there was a physical examination in the assembly hall in which they stripped to their underpants, removed their shoes and, standing on straw mats spread in one part of the hall, had their height, weight and other vital statistics measured.

The names of those who'd passed were to be announced at 1300 hours two days later. Again, they were to be accompanied by parents or guardians. When the gate at the foot of the steps leading to the west building of the school was opened, the crowd of examinees rushed in a body up the steps and diagonally across the sports ground, making a beeline for the gymnasium where the numbers of the successful candidates were posted. Bursting in breathless and panting, each searched among the numbers for his own. H's number was there: 147. Hayashi had passed too. Over people's heads he could see Koji Maeda leaping up and down: he'd apparently got through as well.

Leaving the gymnasium they found Sadao Takami, Hideo Mochizuki and Yasuo Kawada waiting for them, smiling. "Kajiyama's gone home," said Mochizuki. After that, nobody mentioned Kajiyama again.

Of the seven pupils from Nagara National School who'd taken the examination, six had passed, a pretty good showing. The successful candidates and the adults accompanying them were subsequently assembled and given information about orders for school uniforms, regulations concerning traveling to and from school, and other such matters.

Students coming to school by streetcar were forbidden to come as far as the Goban-cho 2 stop just below the school, but were required to get down at a point some two kilometers away from the school. To walk long distances every day, they were told, was good training for the future, when they'd be soldiers. On alighting they were to form up in double file and march off with the senior students at their head.

If they encountered a teacher or senior student in the street they were to halt and salute. New students were advised to practice the various methods of formal greeting in their own homes.

After leaving the school the others all called in at a tailor's in Nagata to order their uniforms, but H went home with his mother. He'd no need to order a uniform since his father would make it for him.

If he'd had it made elsewhere, a student uniform in mixed rayon fabric would have taken forty clothing coupons. Since the allowance was one hundred coupons a year, there would have been little left after buying socks and underwear as well.

H asked his father specially to make the lapels a bit higher than usual. Much to his satisfaction, the cloth, perhaps because his father had got it in some time previously, was good quality, like that used for officers' uniforms. The buttons unfortunately weren't gilt but ceramic. The boots, too, were only pigskin, with little pits all over them, but they were laceups and looked smart when he tried them on.

Since the boots were new he put them on indoors without worrying about the tatami and practiced over and over again binding his legs in puttees. Watching him, Yoshiko said, "It's like you're practicing to go into the army, isn't it?"

"I might be, at that," he said with a wry smile. "At middle school they have army officers who give you military training, so in a way it's a school for soldiers. They say the training's tough."

That was the thing that worried him. He'd heard people say that the senior students were a pretty brutal lot and would hit you as soon as look at you, like non-commissioned officers in the forces.

The rumors had been right. On the day of the entrance ceremony there was a senior student standing on sentry duty in front of the school gates. Curious, H asked to have a look at his rifle, and got struck across the face without warning for his pains.

"What did he need to do that for?" thought H angrily.

24

Kamikeru

One day soon after, a bunch of older students burst noisily into the classroom. The new boys were scared, wondering anxiously on what pretext they were going to be hit this time, but were relieved when they found that the seniors were only recruiting for the clubs. New students were all required to select one of these clubs—rugby, baseball, sumo, judo, fencing, gliding, bayonet fencing, shooting, riding....

H was disappointed to find no painting and sketching club. Hayashi, as might have been expected, joined the sumo club. His reputation as the "grand champion of Nagara" had apparently preceded him, and he'd been singled out by name for recruiting.

H chose the riding club, since he'd long wanted to try riding a horse —added to which it seemed likely not to entail as much hard work as other clubs, and might actually be enjoyable.

He'd already applied to join the riding club when a senior student came in asking for him by name—"Is Senoh here?"—and introduced himself as "Sugita, third year, from the rifle club." Remembering that it was a fourth-grader in the same club who'd struck him without warning on the day of the entrance ceremony, H tensed himself ready to take on the newcomer, determined not to be hit again, this time by a third-grader.

But the other showed no sign of wanting to hit him. "I've come to recruit you for the rifle club," he said. "Seems Furuta's taken a fancy to you—told me to bring that guy Senoh to the armory."

H sensed danger: there was no telling what might happen to him if he went.

"I don't like being hit just because someone's taken a fancy to me."

"Can't you distinguish between hitting someone because you hate them and hitting them because you've taken to them?"

"No, I can't. Either way, I don't like being hit. And besides I've already applied for the riding club, so write me off for the rifle club, please."

"Okay, I understand. I'll tell Furuta-san what you said," the third-grader replied, and went out.

The next day, though, the classroom door opened and in came Furuta himself.

The new students in the classsroom backed away nervously. Furuta was already notorious as the senior who'd struck a first-grader without warning in front of the main gate. H just stood there, almost wetting his pants.

"Don't look at me like that! I'm not going to hit you today. I came to ask you why you were so interested in the gun. Why did you want me to show it to you?"

"I just wanted to see what sort of mechanism could fire bullets."

"Was that all?"

"Yes, that was all."

"I see. You know, we could teach you that if you joined the rifle club. And you'd improve your marks for military training, too. If you ever decide to quit the riding club, come straight to us. We'll be expecting you."

He left without saying anything more. H felt himself wobble at the knees in relief. He almost found himself thinking, despite his first impression, "He *might* be quite a nice fellow...."

A week later he went to the riding ground for the first time, under the wing of a senior in the club.

The club's paddock lay near the Gion Shrine, a short way up the Arima Highway to the north of Hirano, the terminus of the municipal streetcars. Surprisingly enough, only four new students had joined the riding club. With one of them, Muneo Ogura, who said he liked sketching, H soon became friendly. A relative of Ogura's had been a riding man so Ogura himself had a pair of riding boots, though admittedly secondhand.

Some of the older students had leather boots too, but there were others who bound their legs with cloth puttees as a substitute. The new students were all wearing puttees, but they'd been told that these wouldn't do once they actually started riding. It seemed there was a danger, if a gaiter came loose and unwound while you were on horseback, that it could get entangled in the horse's legs.

"Anyway, puttees will be all right for some time to come," they were told. "You won't be doing any riding."

Puttees were, in fact, quite unnecessary, since for days on end they did nothing but work cleaning out the stables and washing down the horses. Having joined the riding club in the hope that it would be easy going, H felt let down.

"So you thought you'd get to ride right away?" said Oi, a senior student, laughing. "You idiot!"

The Hirano Riding Club provided riding grounds for other groups besides the Second Middle club, and the horses too were owned jointly with other clubs. The stables housed fourteen horses. On the third pillar from the right as you went in was a tag saying "Koyuki," meaning "Light Snow." The horse indicated by the name tag was a chestnut, but his face was flecked with white, like snow. For students new to the riding club, to suffer on account of this horse was apparently a kind of rite of passage. Belying the gentility of his name, he had an unpredictable temperament. Anyone who unwittingly turned his back on him was liable to have his shoulder suddenly bitten from behind, and to walk behind him without taking proper care invariably meant being kicked. For these reasons he was known by the nickname of "Kamikeru"— "Bite-kick"—and was an object of fear.

On the day of their first encounter, H himself was startled by a sudden chomp on his shoulder. Oi-san had, admittedly, told him to be careful of Koyuki, but not *how* to be careful. It seemed very much as though the horse and the senior students had just been waiting for a chance to have a go at the newcomers.

On joining Second Middle, H at once noticed two things that were different from the national school. One was the strict insistence that younger students should submit to the older students in everything. This vertical relationship hadn't existed at his previous school. The other was the use of surnames in addressing each other. For the first time H found himself called "Senoh," which didn't displease him since it made him suddenly feel more grown-up.

Even so, the first-graders who were as yet unfamiliar with each other, would feel their way cautiously, so that "Yokota-kun" would only gradually and with some effort become plain "Yokota."

Yokota, who was more worldly-wise than H, flattered the middle-aged man called Sawamura who managed the riding ground by addressing him as "Instructor Sawamura, sir." H determined to share in the benefits that seemed to accrue from this—specifically, the private instruction in riding techniques that the senior students didn't teach them—by doing the same.

"First of all, you must make the horse respect you. Horses keep a close eye on human beings, and they won't let anyone ride them who's bad at it or scared. You have to make friends with them, but if you try too hard to please them you'll end up their servants for life. To get a horse to take you on his back, you've got to make him feel it's okay for him to do so. This place is a stable, so there are plenty of quiet horses who'll carry anyone; but Kamikeru's different—he's an uppity beast. If you can ride *him* you're doing fine."

"Instructor Sawamura, sir's" explanations were easy to follow. The senior students never talked to them like this; perhaps, H suspected, they were afraid that if the younger students got on too fast they themselves wouldn't be able to put on superior airs.

When he cleaned out the stables H paid particular attention to Kamikeru. On entering he'd go immediately to stand in front of him, fix his gaze on the horse's face, and without glancing away pat his cheeks with the palms of his hands and say, "Good boy, good boy!" If the animal bared his teeth and made to bite him, H would rapidly pull the reins apart with all his strength so that he couldn't move his head, continuing to stare at him all the while.

He repeated this process, without trying anything else, for days on end, until Kamikeru finally calmed down. Then one day on entering the stable he deliberately ignored Kamikeru and began seeing to the other horses first. Kamikeru snuffled loudly to remind H of his existence.

Leading Kamikeru out to the paddock, he was giving the reins to Oi-san when, without warning, Kamikeru bit the older boy. What surprised everyone even more was that Oi-san, who'd always been proud of his prowess on Kamikeru, was so alarmed by the sudden bite that he fell over. Mr. Sawamura laughed at the sight. Annoyed at being rejected and humiliated by Kamikeru in front of everyone, Oi-san told H not to bring him out to the paddock again.

H felt sorry for the horse, although he needn't have. After that, it seemed, Mr. Sawamura took to riding Kamikeru for quite long distances outside the grounds when the Second Middle students weren't there. On such days Kamikeru was particularly amiable, as though to let H know he'd been out for a long ride, and H felt he'd like to take him out himself someday.

Mr. Sawamura may have sensed this, because he began secretly letting H and Yokota ride the horses on days when the seniors weren't there. It seemed there were hidden affinities between particular people and particular horses. Yokota had taken a liking to "Tristar," a horse with three white spots between his eyebrows, and had struck up a friendship with him.

Even on days when there was no riding club practice, the two boys would make cleaning the stables an excuse to come to the riding ground for instruction by Mr. Sawamura.

At first, just to mount was quite a task; since the stirrups were too high for them, they had to use a low wooden fence to step up on in order to straddle the horses. Once on the horse's back, though, it was fun looking down on your surroundings as though you'd suddenly become a giant. Kamikeru would let H mount him, but when they started walking would deliberately bump himself hard against the fence around the paddock, with H's leg getting squashed in the process. The horse knew perfectly well that this hurt like hell, but to let out a cry would have been to admit defeat.

Determined not to be beaten, H persevered in the battle of wills with Kamikeru, thanks to which he could soon ride him quite well. Occasionally the grip of his knees was too weak and he fell off, but Kamikeru didn't take advantage, and never under any circumstances stepped on him where he'd fallen.

"You'd think we joined Second Middle just to learn to ride," the three of them—H, Yokota and Ogura—were joking with each other one day as they were cleaning out the stables, when Mr. Sawamura came rushing in.

"C in C Yamamoto's been killed in action!" he shouted excitedly.

"You're sure? *That* Yamamoto?"

It was, indeed, Admiral Isoroku Yamamoto—Commander in Chief of the Combined Fleet, the man who'd directed the attack on Pearl Harbor and was revered not just among the military but by the public at large as a national hero.

"I'm sure. I heard the Imperial Headquarters communiqué giving the news on the radio just now."

Mr. Sawamura paced restlessly about the stable for a while as though not knowing what to do, then just as suddenly rushed out again.

Once they'd more or less recovered from the shock, the three boys decided they'd better go home for the moment, and left the stables.

Arriving home, H found his father back from the fire station. He already knew of Admiral Yamamoto's death, and told H that Admiral Mineichi Koga was to succeed him as commander in chief.

"This is it!" he said. "If Japan doesn't negotiate a ceasefire pretty soon, it's going to be slowly dragged down to defeat. Even in an ordinary fight there comes a time when it's best to call it a day, and that's still more true of war. If Japan doesn't quit soon, it's going to be crushed out of existence."

Morio had been keeping pretty quiet recently, and H was surprised to hear him speak out like this.

"If you ask me," he went on, "the fact that they announced the C in C's death *after* his successor was appointed means he was actually killed quite a while ago, but they've been keeping it a secret. In the meantime, you can be sure American forces will have been advancing steadily, so it's probably safe to assume that an attack on our home ground isn't far off. We had notification from Air Defense Central Headquarters yesterday about what they call 'Reorganization of Defense Zones in Air Raids.' From now on, fire engines from west Kobe are going to answer calls from as far away as Amagasaki. You can't help feeling that the bombing of the main islands is going to start in earnest very soon now."

H felt sure that what his father said was right.

In morning assembly at school the next day, Principal Sakai read aloud the "Imperial Message to Students and Schoolchildren," then followed it with an address on the death in action of C in C Admiral Isoroku Yamamoto. For a whole day the boisterous clamor of Second Middle gave way to the silence of mourning.

Nor was the death of Admiral Yamamoto the only shock. Ten days after that news, late in the afternoon of May 30, the strains of "Down to the Sea" came over the radio. Whereas any Imperial Headquarters communiqué announcing a military success was invariably preceded by the "Warship March," "Down to the sea" always heralded gloomy news.

What it signified this time was that the entire garrison on Attu Island had died in a final, suicidal onslaught on enemy positions. H, who remembered an article in the previous day's newspaper triumphantly reporting "the sinking of seven American battleships and other vessels in the vicinity of Attu Island," was utterly nonplussed. Just what was happening?

The front page of that day's paper was almost exclusively devoted to the "Glorious Annihilation" on Attu. "Garrison Commander Yamazaki, Officers and Men Die to a Man in Heroic Night Attack," it said. "Whole Garrison, Without Requesting a Single Reinforcement, Takes on Vastly Superior Enemy Force and Goes to Glorious Annihilation." The word used was *gyokusai*, referring to a last-ditch effort made in the expectation of certain death for all.

Although the newspaper extolled the Japanese forces' gallantry in "not requesting a single reinforcement," H thought it more likely that, quite simply, they'd known no one would come to their aid even if they did request it. Taught never to allow themselves to be taken prisoner, they'd had no alternative but to die in that final assault. The thought of the bitterness they must have felt, abandoned to their fate on that isolated island in the distant Aleutians, was intolerably painful to H, but there was nothing he could do except gaze vacantly at the tears spilling onto the pages of the newspaper in front of him.

At school, too, *gyokusai* was a prime topic of conversation.

The doubters who felt that the Japanese lines were perhaps over-extended were overwhelmingly outnumbered by the "Land of the Gods" faction, who held that an expansion of the front was unavoidable now that Japan was no longer fighting just China, and that Japan could never be beaten so long as its forces had the warrior spirit to sustain them and didn't shrink from *gyokusai*.

According to the replies he'd given in his entrance interview, H should have belonged to the "Land of the Gods" party, but his real feelings were just the opposite, so he refrained from joining the argument.

A few days later Yokota came up and whispered in his ear, "Not long now—the day's fixed for carrying out the plan!"

H's heart beat faster. The "plan" was to take their horses out for a long ride, without permission and without telling the senior students. They were to put it into effect, it seemed, in three days' time, when the senior students were going to do war work at the Kawasaki Heavy Industries factory and wouldn't be coming to the riding ground.

"But let's not tell Ogura," said Yokota. "I'd feel bad toward him if we got caught—he's a serious student, not one of the bad boys."

If Ogura wasn't going to join them, H would have liked to borrow the high boots he used for riding, but kept the idea to himself.

They could hardly get the horses out unseen by Mr. Sawamura, so on the appointed day Yokota brought along, as a means of winning him over, a bottle of whiskey that his father had brought back from overseas.

Whiskey was a precious commodity that no grownup would willingly have parted with.

"It's okay," said Yokota. "The old man told me to do what *I* wanted to do." Whether or not this extended to swiping his whiskey wasn't clear, but the offering certainly had a stunning effect.

"This is for you, sir," said Yokota. "In exchange, will you please let us have the two horses? You can trust us absolutely not to do anything silly."

For a moment Mr. Sawamura looked taken aback, but then he nodded and smiled. What was more, he lent them riding boots and spurs, and even whips. Literally smirking with delight, they saddled and mounted the horses in front of the stable, then took a turn around the paddock before going outside. They heard Mr. Sawamura's voice behind them saying "No galloping, now!" but just raised their hands in response without looking back.

Going down the slope in single file, they emerged onto the Arima Highway. The Tenno River ran alongside the road, so they decided to go north as far as the point where they could get down into the dry part of the riverbed. Kamikeru seemed to want to go faster, but H checked him with a slight tug on the reins, since they were on a main road and cramped for space with horse-drawn carts and trucks passing. Looking around he saw that Yokota too was keeping a tight rein.

To be going for a long ride on Kamikeru was like a dream. The sky was clear, and they could hear the waters of the Tenno running on their left. H was happy: it didn't seem like wartime at all. For the moment he'd forgotten all about the suicide assault on Attu and the death of C in C Yamamoto.

Drawing level with him, Yokota said, "Let's go down to the river just this side of Kanekiyo Bridge." H agreed: it should be easy to get down there.

Without waiting for an order from the reins, Kamikeru was already turning onto the path down to the river. It was as though he'd been listening to what they said, and H found himself smiling. Probably the horse had been there with Mr. Sawamura on previous occasions and was familiar with the route.

Dismounting in the riverbed, H and Yokota took off their horses' saddles; then they took off their own boots and, barefooted, led the horses into the shallows. Yokota had had the foresight to bring a collapsible cloth bucket, which he'd hung behind his saddle, and they took turns scooping up water so that they could scrub down the horses' backs and legs with a brush. Kamikeru looked pleased, as though this too was part of the expected routine.

They spent rather too much time by the river so they had to come back at a trot.

Back at the riding ground they found Mr. Sawamura with a red face, having apparently partaken of the whiskey. He checked the horses all over, then said, "Right—they're nice and clean, so just wipe off the sweat. Then when you've done their hooves you can go home. I'll see to the rest."

In theory, no one should have found out about their excursion. Two days later, though, the secret was out.

The two of them were summoned to the riding ground, surrounded by five seniors, and given a beating. Their noses bled, but they'd been at fault so they didn't complain. In the end it was decided to expel them from the riding club. But they still wondered how they'd been found out. Manager Sawamura would hardly have talked of his own accord; the hard-to-come-by whiskey he'd been given had effectively sealed his lips,

Only later did they learn that on the highway during their ride they'd passed the owner of the bookstore that stood by the streetcar stop. Members of the riding club often dropped in on their way to or from the riding ground, and he'd apparently commented to a senior on the rapid progress being made by this year's first-grade students, which had let the cat out of the bag.

For a while the two of them went around with hands pressed to purple swellings on their cheeks, but they'd enjoyed the long ride outside too much to regret it. Although Ogura had had no connection with the incident, they heard later that he'd opposed their expulsion and made a plea for clemency on their behalf.

Not long after that—though it was unconnected with their dismissal from the club—the survival of the club itself was endangered when a number of seniors were caught smoking on the hill behind the paddock. Unlike the other clubs, the riding club was far from the school itself, and for some time there'd apparently been complaints that it was difficult to keep an eye on its members. Unluckily the seniors had been up on the hill smoking on a day when a teacher came to the ground for a spot check, and had been caught red-handed.

A rumor said that the manager, Mr. Sawamura, had given them away himself, and H was inclined to believe it, since relations between the Second Middle riding club and the manager were distinctly cool.

Three months later the club was done away with. It wasn't clear whether this was an indirect result of the smoking business, or because the worsening war situation had made horseback riding impossible for students who were being increasingly pressed into work in the factories or fields.

Then again it may simply have been that, in comparison with the judo, fencing, rifle and other clubs, the riding club was seen as a frivolity irrelevant to the war.

Either way, the Second Middle riding club disappeared, but H went to visit Kamikeru a number of times even after that.

25

Instructor Tamori

As H got used to the feel of the school, he gradually realized that the seniors were not all intimidating but varied from individual to individual, and that the teachers too all had their own little peculiarities. With advice from seniors he'd become friendly with, he drew up and secretly circulated a table of the teachers' nicknames.

Since these referred to physical characteristics or peculiarities of behavior, there was nothing particularly interesting or funny about them for people who didn't know the originals, but among students in the school they were a source of much amusement.

Mr. Kawano, the math teacher, was "Grasshopper," because he looked like a grasshopper when he bowed, with the upper half of his body kept rigid. Mr. Sumitani was "Valjean," because when he was in a good mood he'd relate episodes from the story of Jean Valjean in *Les Misérables*. "What, you haven't heard him do it yet?" the seniors would say, to the chagrin of still uninitiated first-graders. "You should—he's really good at it!"

Mr. Anezaki was "Anekan," because he taught *kanbun*, classical Chinese. The principal's nickname, "Pokemon," meant simply that he was small and reminded them of a pocket monkey.

Instructor Tamori, in charge of military training and one of the most feared men in the school, was called "His Lechery," which caused considerable hilarity among H and his classmates when they heard the reason for it from a senior student.

"Instructor Tamori may have a square face and a sour expression, but actually he's a lecher," he said. "He'll say to a student, 'You've got a sister, haven't you? Just bring along a photo next time you come.' He knows these things because he checks with the school register where it gives details of students' families. So you'd better look out if you've got a sister yourself! He prides himself on being an army lieutenant, but in fact he's a lech-tenant....

"Even so, he always acts the strict military man—gives his students lectures full of talk about 'His Imperial Majesty, who's ever so graciously done this or that,' which he mentions only with great hesitation. If you ask me, the thing he really ought to hesitate about is bringing up His Majesty at every opportunity for his own purposes. It contrasts so much with the other side of him that people started combining the two and calling him 'His Lechery.' Be careful, though—he'd half kill you if he heard you saying it! To use 'His Lechery' is more dangerous than *lèse majesté*. Anyway, if he once takes against you then I'm afraid you've had it!"

The first-graders had laughed when they heard the first part of this, but fell into a scared silence by the end of it.

In fact, H himself had "had it," having already been "taken against" by Instructor Tamori.

Their first encounter had been in the classroom where the oral entrance exam had taken place. He was the military man who'd nodded vigorously with such an air of satisfaction on hearing H's account of the Greater East Asian War. So his first impression of H had unquestionably been favorable; he might even, in fact, have been partly responsible for H's being accepted.

He'd probably remembered H's face from that one episode, because he'd smile faintly whenever they passed each other in the corridor.

Ultimately, though, he turned out to be a man to be feared.

One morning, meeting him in front of the main gate of the school, H had come to attention and saluted. In doing so he dropped the sketchbook he'd been carrying under his arm, and when he made to pick it up the instructor held out a hand to see it. As he took it and turned the pages, his expression suddenly changed.

"What the hell is this?" he shouted.

A naked woman reclined on the open page. "It's a copy of a Manet painting," replied H, but the instructor had apparently never heard of the artist and took the name to be the Japanese word *mane*, meaning "imitation."

"What do you mean, 'copy of an imitation'!" he yelled. "Are you making fun of an instructor?"

The copy in question had been made from a Manet nude included in a collection of reproductions that he'd been shown at Ogura's house. Ogura's father was fond of art, and the bookshelves were full of expensive albums of this kind. H envied his friend, but Ogura told him he could come and look at them any time, so he'd sometimes call in on the way home from school. From time to time they'd give him supper, and occasionally he'd stay the night.

H liked looking at attractive pictures of nudes. But though he wasn't indifferent to the charms of the female body, there was more to it than that. Turning the pages, spellbound, he'd soon felt that simply looking wasn't enough, and had begun making quite careful copies with a pencil in his sketchbook. It was one of these that had so angered Instructor Tamori.

H explained in as much detail as possible, but Instructor Tamori refused to be mollified.

Since this took place in front of the main school entrance, the other students arriving at school eyed them dubiously, saluting nervously and giving them a wide berth as they entered the building.

"Right—I'll take care of this!" declared the instructor finally. "Come to the staff room at the end of the first class." And putting the sketchbook under his arm he went off rapidly, the way he walked suggesting that he was still quite angry.

Instructor Tamori was not the school's only military instructor; there were two others besides him. Every middle school included "military training" in its curriculum; since this was given to all students, the one serving officer officially attached to each school wasn't enough, and other, reservist officers were taken on as teaching staff. These reservists wore uniforms and carried swords at their sides the same as the serving officer, so outwardly the two types were indistinguishable.

The serving officer at H's school was Instructor Tamiya. Instructor Tamori was only a reservist, but bore himself more arrogantly than Instructor Tamiya, boasting that he'd had experience of actual fighting

247

in China. Instructor Tamiya, who had no such experience, always seemed to feel rather inferior on this account.

The other reserve captain in Second Middle besides Instructor Tamori, Instructor Hisakado by name, had been a watchmaker in civilian life. Interested in art and music, he was a decent, humane sort of person and was trusted by the students. Although the training given by the three instructors was the same, the three of them had considerably different personalities.

The friends who heard that H had been summoned to the staff room by Instructor Tamori accompanied him anxiously to the door. "Remember, don't contradict him," they whispered in his ear, "or there's no telling what he might do!"

At the entrance to the room, H announced in a loud voice, as though in a barracks, "Hajime Senoh, first grade, Class 2, summoned by Instructor Tamori!" This was according to regulations. A few of the teachers in the staff room raised their heads and glanced at H, probably feeling sorry for him,

"I'm coming in," he went on, closing the door behind him and going up to Instructor Tamori's desk.

"You—" Instructor Tamori began, "you tried to fob me off this morning by saying this here was a copy of a famous painting, didn't you? So let the other teachers have a look at it. Go on—go around and show them what kind of pictures you've been drawing!"

"Yes, sir, I'll show it to the other teachers," H repeated dutifully. Advancing first to Instructor Hisakado's desk, which was next to Instructor Tamori's, he opened the sketchbook at the page with the picture of the nude.

"Well!" exclaimed Instructor Hisakado. "Manet's *Olympia*. Did you do it yourself?"

Next, H showed it to Mr. Hata, the physics teacher, who was writing at his desk on the opposite side.

"Manet?" he said, looking up at H.

"Yes, Manet, sir."

At that moment H happened, most unfortunately, to glance in Instructor Tamori's direction. Their gazes met.

The other seemed to see H's look as saying contemptuously, "There, you see—the other teachers know who Manet is, don't they? Nobody else mixes up Manet and *mane*, do they?" That hadn't been H's intention, but Instructor Tamori was convinced that he'd been made a fool of in the staff room in front of all the other teachers. Seizing hold of H's lapel with one hand, he suddenly struck him a blow on the face with his fist.

"It's got fuck all to do with Manet or anyone else!" he yelled in a rage. "You were drawing nudes! The kind of bloodless bastard who does pictures like this while our soldiers are fighting on the battlefield is un-Japanese! If you want to do pictures, why don't you draw weapons or something? I'm going to knock some military spirit into you if it kills me!"

It hadn't satisfied him to hit H once, apparently, and he dealt him another blow on the other side of his face.

Then he gazed around the staff room. "Do you call yourselves *teachers*," he demanded in a loud voice, "to let a middle school student get away with drawing a female nude and bringing it to school? If you've any ideas on how to handle a boy like this, I wish you'd let me know!"

The other teachers averted their eyes, looking down at their desks.

The angry voice went on and on even after the second class began and the rest had gone out, leaving the staff room empty except for the two of them. H wasn't finally released until shortly before the other teachers, their classes over, came back to the room again.

Instead of going back to the classroom where his friends were anxiously waiting, he went up to the roof of the school building. Mount Takatori was visible to the west beneath a cloudy sky. The bleeding in his mouth had stopped, but the pain remained, mingled with sadness. Kobe Second Middle, the school on which he'd pinned so many hopes, ought not to have been like this. On the day of the entrance ceremony he'd looked up at the framed calligraphy in the assembly hall which read "Plain and tough. Self-respect and self-control," and had recognized it with delight: it was the phrase, the senior students had told him, that summed up the spirit of the school. A carelessness about external graces combined with a passion for freedom, a spirit of self-discipline rather than supervision by others—these, he'd been told, were the characteristics of the Kobe Second Middle School. The many artists and poets among its graduates would seem to bear witness to this.

The principal's address to the new students had referred to the tense wartime situation they faced, then touched on the school's distinguished history and urged each of them to cultivate an awareness of himself as a young individual.

One of the things H had wanted to confirm in his first explorations after joining the school had been the presence of a painting that was supposed to hang in the principal's room. He'd heard that it was *Dancing Girl*, by the well-known painter Ryohei Koiso.

When H, having obtained permission, knocked at the door of the principal's room and announced his name in a loud voice, the principal let him into the room at once. The picture was bigger than he'd expected.

"What a picture!" H exclaimed admiringly.

"The school has a painting by Kaii Higashiyama too," said the principal.

"You mean the *Winter Hills* hanging in the assembly hall, don't you, sir?" said H. "I saw it."

"Do you paint? If so, I hope you'll become famous enough in future to donate a painting to the school yourself."

Ryohei Koiso was from the class of 1922 and Kaii Higashiyama from the class of 1926. H himself would be class of 1948, so they were far and away his seniors in years and experience. Besides these two, the principal told H, the alumni of Kobe Second Middle included artists such as Shin Furuya from the class of 1917 and Tadao Tanaka from the class of 1921, and others outside the world of art itself such as the poet Iku Takenaka, a close friend of Koiso-sensei.

When he'd taken the exam for Second Middle, H had been hoping to join the art club and do sketches from plaster models, which he'd never done before. In that way, he thought, he'd be able to prepare to become an artist while studying at school. When he actually entered the school, though, he'd found that classes in art had been dropped and that the art club no longer even existed. Worse still, the school had become a place dominated by a swaggering military man who'd bawl you out for doing a copy of a Manet painting.

It was as though he'd entered a military academy rather than the Second Middle of his dreams. H went up onto the roof and, making sure no one was around, yelled "To hell with His Lechery!"

That day didn't see the last of Instructor Tamori's bullying, though.

"They tell me your father and mother are Christians," he sneered. "Do *you* go to church too? Do you know it's the religion that Americans and Britishers believe in? How do you pray when you pray to your God in church? Can you pray that Japan will win the war, as people do when they pray at Shinto shrines? I don't see how you can pray to the same God as the Yankees and their friends. Your God is sure to side with the countries that have most people. When you get home, tell your parents that if they're Japanese they ought to quit being Christians."

In his mind, H was shouting back at him: "What about the Germans you're so fond of, you fool—aren't most of *them* Christians too?"

The military training classes were hell for H, not because the training itself was tough, but because there was so much that was irrational or humiliating. You'd suddenly be asked about something you hadn't been taught yet, and if you couldn't answer you'd be punished by being forced to do extra pushups or turns around the sports ground. H put up with it by chanting repeatedly in his own mind: "To hell with His Lechery!"

He even inadvertently said "His Lechery" aloud at home, so that his mother said reprovingly, "Whatever are you saying!"

He'd heard that His Lechery was the son of a pawnbroker in Motomachi, so he asked his father—who at one time had been apprenticed to a tailor's in that district—whether he'd ever heard of Instructor Tamori. To his surprise, the Tamori Pawnshop had been the third house up the road from Shimazaki Tailors, where Morio had learned his trade.

"Now you mention it, there *was* a son at the pawnshop. So he's a lieutenant now, is he, an instructor? When I was an apprentice, the people at the pawnshop often gave us clothes to mend. Next to the pawnshop there was another shop with a sign saying Motomachi Antiques, but actually that was run by the Tamoris too. The so-called 'antiques' were all things that had been pawned at the shop next door—home altars, cameras, old clothes, everything you could think of. They'd bring the old clothes along to Shimazaki's to have them mended so they could get a bit more for them. They used to knock us down to a minimum on the charge for repairs, so the apprentices did the work as part of their training. Looking back on it now, it was useful practice for us."

H was annoyed to find his father remembering the Tamori Pawnshop with affection, not to say gratitude.

"At a pawnshop you're supposed to be able to assess the value of anything people care to bring you, don't you?" he said. "But that fool of an instructor doesn't know anything—he didn't even recognize a picture by an artist everyone else knows about. Anyone trained by him would be so misinformed that he'd get killed as soon as he went to the front."

He made a resolve: if this was going to go on, he'd get himself killed by Instructor Tamori in front of all the others. Every day he went to school prepared to do single-handed battle with His Lechery. He was painfully aware that Ogura and Yokota were worried about him, but he didn't want to get them involved.

H had finished his lunch box and was looking up at the eucalyptus tree in front of the west building, and sketching it, when he caught sight of Instructor Tamori out of the corner of his eye. He pretended not to have seen him, hoping he wouldn't come his way. But he came up to H and gazed at the sketch briefly, before saying, "So you've given up doing women and are on to eucalyptus trees now, eh?"

H felt almost sick. He knew what would happen if he said what had come into his mind, but he went ahead and said it anyway.

"I don't know whether this one's male or female, but I thought there'd be no problem with a tree...."

As he'd expected, the words were hardly out of his mouth when he was kicked with a booted foot, and the next moment he was struck across the cheek. With the courage of despair he went on:

"Did it make you feel better to hit me? A student's strictly forbidden to protect himself even if he's hit—so go on, hit me until you're satisfied."

So saying, he shut his eyes and gritted his teeth against the shock of the next blow from the enraged "sensei." But the blow failed to materialize. Puzzled, he opened his eyes cautiously: the instructor had turned his back and was walking away in the direction of the main school building.

Before going back to the classroom, H called in at the infirmary and got them to look at his mouth. There wasn't much bleeding, but the flesh was torn. More than his face, his chest was painful where the boot had landed, so he was told to lie down and rest for a while.

He was just thinking that he might not be able to take much more of this when reinforcements appeared.

The door of the infirmary opened and Furuta-san, one of the fourth-grade members of the rifle club, came in. Yokota was with him—maybe it was he who'd told Furuta that H was in a bad way—and they were followed by Sugita-san, in third grade, and Kitami-san, in second grade.

"Stay where you are," Furuta-san told him as he tried to sit up. "They say Instructor Tamori's been 'looking after' you. It'd be dangerous to provoke him any further. Come and join the rifle club—we'll protect you. The club's under Instructor Hisakado's supervision, so even Tamori can't interfere with its members. Instructor Hisakado himself says he wants you as a member; he says he'll stand by you whatever happens. If you don't like it you can always quit. Come to the armory later."

They went out. As Sugita-san, the last to go, was closing the door, he looked around briefly and winked at H.

H was in two minds, since learning to fire rifles was so directly connected with warfare, but decided that someday he'd at least drop in and take a look at the armory, which was the rifle club's base.

According to the newspapers, the ministry of education had sent a notice to schools saying that summer holidays were to be done away with at national and middle schools.

> We must not allow ourselves to be affected by the heat of summer at such a time of national emergency. Strictly disciplined group training must be carried out so as to raise the students' fighting spirit. Middle school students in particular should be trained just as though they were in the forces, and the summer holidays devoted to thoroughgoing seasoning as "tomorrow's soldiers." In addition, all students should be given aggressive instruction in swimming so as to enhance the effectiveness of the "Nation of Swimmers" campaign.

The school lost no time in launching ten days of swimming training on the beach at Suma.

Shocked to hear that the teacher in charge on the first day was to be Instructor Tamori, and fearing for his own safety, H went to see Furuta-san in the armory.

The armory, a sturdy-looking building of unpainted wood, had large double doors which opened to reveal, directly ahead, broad stairs leading up to the second floor. Inside, the building was chilly and smelled of oil. On either side of the staircase on the first floor, rows of rifles stood in their racks.

H announced himself: "Hajime Senoh, first grade, Class 2!"

"So you've come!" said Furuta-san's voice from somewhere in the back. "Come on in."

Behind the staircase three seniors were dismantling and cleaning rifles. One of them looked H up and down with a smile and said, "So this is him, is it?—the Senoh who defied His Lechery all by himself!..." H was relieved to find the seniors not so intimidating after all.

"May I have a look upstairs?" he asked.

"I'll take you," said Furuta-san, and led the way.

The second floor too was lined with rows of rifles.

"There are four types, aren't there?" H said.

"You notice things, don't you! This one here's a Tamura rifle, adopted in 1880. This one's called the Type 30 infantry rifle. It was adopted in 1897, the thirtieth year of the Meiji era, and used in the Russo-Japanese War. It won't fire anymore, but it's good enough for training beginners."

Seeing a gun that seemed somehow familiar, H stretched out his hand.

"That's the rifle they call the 38; it's the infantry rifle that's in use at the moment. Do you want to try holding it? It weighs one *kanme*— more accurately, 3,950 grams." H found it heavy, but didn't say anything, dreading the prospect of being bawled out and told that this was "the rifle our troops have to carry about with them every day" as they fought.

"Do you know why it's called a 38?" he was asked.

"Is it because it was officially adopted in the thirty-eighth year of Meiji?" he ventured timidly, remembering being told a few moments before that "Type 30" was a rifle adopted in the thirtieth year of that era.

"That's right. You knew, then?"

"No...."

"All right—you're doing okay," said Furuta-san, softening suddenly for no apparent reason.

H calculated how many years ago "Meiji 38" was—forty! Were they really still fighting with such an ancient weapon? He wondered what kind of gun the American troops were using....

"What's this one like the 38 but shorter? Is it for children?"

"Don't be silly, they don't make rifles for children. That's the Type 38 cavalry rifle. It's short and light, so it's just right for training new students."

H began to feel an interest in guns. He'd like to try dismantling them and even actually firing them. He resolved to join the rifle club.

"Well then," said Furuta-san, "you can come along tomorrow. We'll take care of you."

He smiled, and H found himself smiling back.

Little did he know how tough the training lying in store for him was.

26

The Rifle Club

August would normally have been the time for summer vacation, but H and Yoshiko were both at school.

Almost every day H went to work in the school fields with a party led by Mr. Murobushi, while Yoshiko went to the beach at Suma for swimming lessons with other members of her grade from the national school.

Two years earlier H would have had plenty of time for recreation, and not just in the summer holidays either. These days, though, there was little time left for play, even for the younger children. Their free time had all been taken up by air raid drills, "spiritual drill" and suchlike activities. A glance around the school or the immediate neighborhood was enough to show just how much things had changed.

This extended even to the age at which military service began. The minimum age for boys to volunteer as cadets had been lowered by one year. According to the papers, this was "in order to make it possible for boys to join the army at fourteen, immediately on finishing the supplementary course at school."

H himself would reach that age the following year.

"You're a soldier as soon as you volunteer," H said to Hiroshi Akao as they dug in the school fields. "It must be tough, being a soldier alongside the adults when you're only fourteen. I mean, think of the training we get in the rifle club—if you were a *real* soldier, I'm sure it'd be much heavier going."

"It's heavy enough as it is, without being a soldier," said Akao irritably. He was working at H's side, putting manure in the places H had dug.

It was hard work, no doubt about it, almost every day digging the soil or carrying human and other waste in buckets hanging from a pole slung over your shoulder. Besides the ache in their backs and shoulders, the work itself was demeaning, being shouted at by Mr. Murobushi and called a "bunch of idiots" as he grabbed up a handful of horseshit and showed them how to stick it in the ground.

"Anyone would think we'd got into Second Middle just to handle shit," the boys would mutter in disgust.

Told one day that there would be no farm work the next day, they looked at each other with expressions of relief. But to their disappointment, the next moment they were told they must come to the school instead, since there was work to do there.

The work in question was to tidy up and clean the school auditorium, which had been used for examinations for the Naval Academy. It had been used twice for the same exam since H had entered Second Middle, and was due to be used again in two weeks' time for an exam for prospective army tank men. Not only was the auditorium being used for army and navy exams, but the school itself was increasingly frequented by actual soldiers.

The walls of the school corridors were plastered with posters urging them to take exams for the Naval Academy or the Army Officers' School. Alongside these posters was another, larger one proclaiming "Smash the American and British Fiends!"

A rumor got around that schools were soon to stop giving English language classes on the grounds that it was illogical to go on teaching the enemy's language at middle school when American and British music had already been banned.

The source of the rumor was Shiro Maruyama, whose father had got hold of the information at the prefectural office where he worked. Possibly because his eldest brother had been killed while in the navy, Maruyama, who was hoping to get into the Naval Academy, burned with a particular hatred for the enemy.

The Maruyama report, a piece of news that had not yet appeared even in the papers, spread like wildfire throughout the school.

The only way to find out the truth of it was to ask Masanobu Matsumoto, the English teacher.

Mr. Matsumoto had barely closed the classroom door behind him when several students put the same question: "Sir, is it true there aren't going to be any more English lessons?"

"I hope at least that none of you have believed the rumor and thrown your textbooks in the waste basket," he said. Then, having made them laugh, he added with a serious expression: "There does seem to be a rumor to that effect, but it's not official yet, so you're to go on studying without letting it upset you. It's useful to know the other side's language —'Know thine enemy,' they say, don't they? What worries me more at the moment is this tendency to discard anything that's considered 'enemy culture'.... Anyway, the way things are I don't know how long we can go on with our English lessons, but personally I intend to go on teaching you English until that time comes. So I want you to look on each class individually as something valuable, something to be cherished. All right?"

There was a chorus of "Yes, sir's," from the class, but the atmosphere was somehow tense, as though Mr. Matsumoto had put his own safety at risk in order to tell them something very important.

H took a liking to Mr. Matsumoto from that moment on, and gave a mental seal of approval to what he'd heard about Second Middle having good teachers.

They were sweeping out the classroom after lessons when Sugita-san of the rifle club peered in through the window and shouted, "Meeting in the armory—pass it on to the other classes!" and ran off again. H went to the neighboring classroom to contact Yokota, who, the day after H had joined the club, had declared that he might as well do the same.

When they got to the armory they found two platoons of soldiers drawn up in the yard. They were from the Central Japan Unit 4126, but their clothing and the way they were standing showed at a glance that all the men—between one and two hundred of them—were new recruits.

A lot of them, moreover, were already approaching middle age; even the few younger men among them looked below par in both height and strength. So they've started calling up the grade-C men, thought H.

What startled him was the information that the unit had come to return rifles that they'd borrowed from Second Middle. H wondered why.

"Why does the school have to lend the army its rifles?" he asked Sugita-san.

"Our rifles were originally ones that the army sold off or lent to us, so we have to cooperate when they say they need them. But don't start asking why they came to borrow them in the first place. You've got to be careful—things like that come under the heading of strategic secrets."

He wouldn't explain any further, but H deduced that there must be a shortage of rifles.

He got the impression that the unit of new recruits had called in at the school, borrowed the rifles, and then been made to shoulder them on a training march over a considerable distance before calling in again at Second Middle to return them. They all seemed pretty exhausted.

Once they'd returned the rifles, the soldiers drew up in a line and marched in file down the steps to the west gate and out of the school.

The members of the rifle club carried the returned rifles to the benches in the armory, where they wiped each one off with an oily rag. It took less time than H had expected since the rifles hadn't been fired, so it only involved wiping off the outsides, which were dusty and damp with sweat from the soldiers' hands.

On receiving the report that the task was finished, Instructor Hisakado came in and said "Well done, lads," to the club members. H, who'd heard that he was interested in sketching, would have liked to ask him about it but kept quiet, deciding that here in the armory, where Hisakado was strictly an army captain, was no place for such trivial matters.

He could hear what the instructor and Furuta-san were talking about at the back of the room.

"Who's responsible for training the first-graders who've just joined?" Hisakado was asking.

"Sugita, sir."

"Do you think they could manage a night march?"

"They're not properly trained yet, sir, but I think it could be done."

"Well, tell him to see they don't hurt themselves, anyway."

From this exchange H gathered that sometime in the near future there was to be one of the notoriously hellish "night marches" he'd heard about.

To a bellowed command, they saluted Instructor Hisakado as he went out. Then Furuta-san made a brief speech:

"Sugita-san will be in immediate charge of you. And there'll be no slacking even if the going gets rough. You're not to hold it against the older students, either—they don't put you through it out of ill will. If you've got any complaints you can come and talk to me. But I won't tolerate any wingeing. That's all."

Rifle club training took place almost every day—not just after classes, either, but immediately after they got back to school from doing farm work too. Nor was there any holiday on Sundays.

Sundays they got up at dawn and went by the first streetcar of the morning to assemble at the Minatogawa Shrine. Dedicated to Kusunoki Masashige, it was a favorite place of worship for the people of Kobe.

It was a tradition of the rifle club that its members should sweep and tidy up the shrine precincts. This was done every week on Sunday morning, come rain or shine, and members were not allowed to shirk the task under any circumstances.

Once assembled, the boys made obeisance at the main building of the shrine, then got bamboo brooms from the shrine office and scattered throughout the grounds to start sweeping. The area that H was responsible for was that around the so-called "tomb of Kusunoki Masashige," which was an unusual shape in that the gravestone rested on the back of a large turtle.

The inscription said, "Here, alas, lies the faithful retainer Masashige." H had been told by an older student that the script was done by the celebrated Mito Komon.

The sweeping done, H would join his hands briefly in respect before the tomb. He felt sorry for Masashige, who'd died in battle, fighting to the end out of loyalty to the Emperor even though he knew he was bound to be defeated. He hoped that the present "Greater East Asian War" would never end with a battle to the bitter end similar to that which had once taken place there in Minatogawa.

Sweeping the shrine precinct always involved a struggle with sleepiness, but it was far easier than the "belly-crawl" drill that formed another part of club activities.

This consisted in crawling along the ground, keeping as low as possible all the while, with your rifle held horizontally in both hands; you advanced shifting knees and elbows alternately, which soon caused the elbows of your jacket and the knees of your trousers to fray against the hard earth and small stones. If you raised your head even slightly as you moved forward, a senior student would take a sideways swipe at it with a wooden rifle of the kind used in bayonet fencing. This didn't hurt much, since you were wearing a metal helmet, but the loud clang made your brain swim.

"It's tough," they were told, "but whether you're killed in battle or not may depend on whether you've learned to do this properly." The older students didn't just hit the younger ones on the head; they joined in the "belly-crawl" themselves, which made it more bearable for their juniors.

The rifle club's marches, too, were pretty tough—far tougher than the marches that the whole school would go on from time to time—since they were intended as training for marching in full battle gear.

This meant carrying a rifle weighing four kilos, with a pack containing a ten-kilo sandbag on your back, a bayonet and four ammunition pouches each containing thirty rounds at your hip, and a helmet on your head.

In the early days, just eight kilometers was enough to have you tottering with fatigue.

"They should have a change from nothing but marching," Instructor Hisakado said suddenly one day. "Let them do a bit of target practice for once."

H and Yokota exchanged a look and a wink. They'd thought they wouldn't be allowed to actually fire the rifles until they were in second grade, and the prospect of shooting with live ammunition while they were still in the early days of training was an unexpected thrill.

"It's real ammunition all right," said Furuta-san, "but it's the kind with not much powder and a bullet with a flattened head, so it doesn't go very far. That means you can use it in the school grounds; you don't have to go specially to the firing range."

H had seen the older students firing rifles on a small range surrounded by a wooden fence that stood in a corner of the school grounds.

"When you're firing with proper ammunition, the target's a hundred meters away," said Furuta-san; "with this stuff the distance is only ten meters. But the effect is the same as with proper ammunition. In ten minutes I'll give you each a rifle. For now—di-is-*miss*!"

Saluting Furuta-san, the eight first-graders dashed off to the urinals.

"It's a grind, but it's fun, isn't it?" said Yokota as he stood peeing next to H. "His Lechery's stopped bothering you, too!"

It was true that since joining the rifle club H had been blessedly free from assaults on his person.

The rifles they were to use were in a closet under the stairs in the armory. It was kept locked with a sturdy padlock, being a kind of "armory within an armory." Inside stood a row of twelve Type 38 infantry rifles. The reason why the closet was so well secured was that it held rifles still "in actual service," with the imperial chrysanthemum crest engraved on the barrel still undeleted. It was these rifles that were used for firing practice with live ammunition. They were taken particular care of compared with the other rifles used for training; if you peered down a barrel, not a trace of powder was detectable on the gleaming spirals inside.

"You're to make sure you leave them in the same condition after you've finished using them," they were told. "As for the actual firing, I've told you before that once you've loaded your gun, you're to put on the safety catch, rest the gun, and not put your finger on the trigger until you get the order to fire. You can have ten shots each today, so mind you take good aim!"

The rifle that H was given was a type called a Mark IV. They went down the steps in front of the armory and walked across toward the firing range in the corner of the grounds.

"That Mark IV has a habit of hitting the target a bit high and to the right," Sugita-san told H in a low voice as they walked, "so you should aim just a bit below the bull's-eye and to the left."

For H it was the first time he was to fire a real rifle, so he was rather tense and missed the target completely the first two times. Even so, thanks to the advice about the rifle's idiosyncracy, he did well.

"You're good, considering it's the first time," said Instructor Hisakado. "You should be more careful not to snatch at the trigger, though. There's a saying that you should pull the trigger 'like frost falling on a dark night'—that means squeezing it lightly and gently. And one more thing: don't take aim for more than five seconds. If you hold it any longer your eyes blur and the rifle begins to waver. If you can't fire within about three seconds you should take aim again. All right?"

"Very well, sir!" replied H, who was experiencing something—a sense of being intensely alive, perhaps—to a degree he'd never felt before.

He'd never thought for a moment that aiming at a target and scoring a bull's-eye could be such fun. At one time, when he was in primary school, he'd had a passion for firing rubber bands at matchboxes. That had been fun, but scoring a hit on a target with a real rifle was far more thrilling.

Autumn was already well advanced, the rice harvest over, when the "night march" for which the rifle club was notorious finally took place.

They were to set out from Hirano at 2300 hours and march throughout the night, in full battle gear, all the way to Arima, twenty kilometers away, with a pause for battle training somewhere en route. Since the starting point was not the school but Hirano, each of them was to leave home in full battle gear, which meant that they had to get their rifles and other equipment at the armory and take them home with them.

Toshiko was appalled to see her son come home looking like a soldier, complete with rifle.

"What does *this* mean?" she complained loudly. "Is that a *real* gun? You could fire with it, couldn't you? You could *kill* someone with it, couldn't you?"

Unfortunately it was his father's day at the fire station, and H himself was hard put to explain things.

"Firing doesn't mean firing at *people*," he said. "If I didn't do this training now I couldn't stay on at the school. You don't have to worry—I don't have any live ammunition."

The cartridges in his ammunition pouch were dummies—blanks—he explained, but the mere presence within the house of a real rifle was enough to horrify Toshiko.

H had a short nap around dusk, then got up at nine and ate his supper with one eye on the clock.

He was joined at the table by Yoshiko, who for some reason had insisted that she wanted to eat with her elder brother.

It was still a bit early to leave, but he put his boots on in the entrance hall, wound his puttees round his legs, shouldered his pack and stood up. His mother stood gazing at him with the tearful expression of someone seeing her son off to the war. Even Yoshiko looked anxious, and H left the house in some embarrassment.

When he got on the streetcar, driver and passengers alike, not unsurprisingly, looked a little shocked at the sight of a middle school student boarding a streetcar at that late hour in military outfit complete with rifle.

When H got off at the Hirano stop, some members of the party were still to come, but he could see Instructor Hisakado's cigarette glowing and fading in the darkness. Those locals who weren't in the know seemed to feel uneasy at this gathering of middle school students in full military gear in the street at night. Some opened their front doors to look, only to close them again as quietly as possible. "Seems they take us for another February 26 Incident," someone said, and everybody laughed.

At precisely 2300 hours, the platoon set off in double file for Arima. Furuta-san and the other fourth-grade students had started thirty minutes earlier to act as a mock "enemy" and were to lie in wait for them on the way.

The commander of the platoon was Sugita-san, a third-grade student. It seemed that the fourth-graders wanted to let members of the next grade get some experience in leading others. The second squad, which H was in, was led by Matsukawa-san from second grade.

On the right, somewhat north of the entrance to the Arima Highway, lay the fields where the school's riding club had kept its horses. As they passed by, H poked Yokota, who was marching in front of him, in the back. Yokota too must have remembered the episode of the long ride, for he nodded vigorously.

By the time they got to Tennodani they were already flagging, though they'd only been marching an hour and a half. "Come on, now!" bellowed Sugita-san. "There's another fifteen kilometers to go yet!" and he started singing the "On to the Distant Foe" song. The boys all followed suit, the platoon commander singing one verse himself and his "men" repeating it after him:

> We march on through unending mud;
> No food at all for three full days.
> Rain splashes off my helmet.
> My faithful horse has neighed his last;
> While he lies there, I cut a lock
> Of mane and take it as I leave....

Singing along with them, H wondered to himself why such a dismal piece should be an army marching song. It was the sort of thing that brought home the miseries of the battlefield, until you almost lost the will to fight altogether. But still the song went on, to the measured tread of booted feet.

> All my cigarettes are gone,
> My matches damp and useless:
> A cold and hungry night's ahead....

The song ended, and they marched in silence for a while. It was then that Matsukawa-san said, "That song was written by a man called Yoshie Fujiwara—have you heard of him?" H jumped, almost as though he'd had a sudden electric shock: it was the same man who had sung "Woman is fickle" from *Rigoletto* on the record. A fateful reencounter, he felt.

They'd been marching for two and a half hours, but still they were allowed no rest.

"We'll soon be at Minotani," said the squad leader, Matsukawa-san. "That's just about halfway to Arima. The really hellish part's still to come, though...." Then, after they'd marched another two kilometers or so, they were finally allowed a break of fifteen minutes. But hardly had they sunk down by the roadside with sighs of relief when they were suddenly attacked, from somewhere ahead and to the right, by the "enemy."

They could hear the crack of rifles firing at them out of the darkness, and even, alarmingly, see the flash from their barrels.

The platoon scattered into the paddy fields on the left and threw themselves face down, releasing their safety catches as they did so. H estimated the distance at about two hundred meters, though in fact it may well have been rather less. Although he knew that the "enemy" consisted of Furuta and other senior students all well known to him, he found himself feeling scared, as though they were a real enemy.

"Squads 1 and 2, move around to the left!" came the platoon commander's voice, so H started to belly-crawl forward, taking care as far as possible not to raise his head. As he crawled over the harvested field, the rice stubble scratched painfully at his face.

Squad leader Matsukawa signaled silently for them to stop. They lay still, hardly breathing. Then, not far away, there were indications of movement, and soon after that they spotted "enemy" forms, crouching low, shifting their positions.

"Fire!" At the squad leader's order they squeezed the triggers. No bullets flew, since their cartridges were blanks, but the powder was real enough to produce both noise and light. It felt as though they were really firing at each other, and H was scared.

After a "battle" lasting thirty minutes or so the enemy disappeared. Forming ranks again, the platoon marched off along the Arima Highway.

Their heads were reeling with fatigue. The desire to sleep was overwhelming; try as they might to keep awake, their eyelids developed a tiresome habit of coming together of their own accord. The sand in the packs on their backs was so heavy that H had half a mind to dump his.

At last, below the gate of the Tamonji Temple, they were allowed a proper rest, some five hours after they'd first set out.

Taking off their packs they flung them on the ground and collapsed onto the road, lying with their rifles in their arms. H, who was gasping with thirst, drank some of the water from his flask. While he was drinking Sugita-san said, "Last year there was a fellow who dumped his sand on the way. When we got to Arima, though, the packs were weighed and he was given all hell. I don't suppose any of *you* have cheated on the weight of your packs, have you?"

Yokota, who was lying next to H with his eyes closed, gently prodded him in the side. When H turned to face him, he was pointing at his own pack with a tragic expression. "I'll have to find somewhere to fill it up with sand again," he murmured. But to break ranks and put more sand into his pack while the older students weren't watching was of course impossible.

At the command to move off they got to their feet and started marching again sluggishly, still overpoweringly sleepy.

Twice H fell asleep as he walked and tumbled into the irrigation ditch by the paddies. The first time Instructor Hisakado hauled him up by the hand, but his pants were already soaking. By now, every one of them was covered with mud.

It seemed as if the morning would never come. Not only were rifles, packs and ammunition appallingly heavy, but their legs seemed to be no longer their own and were ceasing to obey their commands.

When the long night finally faded and the sun began to rise, the houses of Arima were visible further up on the other side of the road between the hills.

H was just thinking that the end was in sight, when "enemy" troops appeared on the road ahead. It was Furuta and his comrades, wearing the white armbands signifying "hypothetical enemy." Six upper-grade students, got up as the "enemy," were rapidly bearing down on them, the bayonets on the rifles they grasped in both hands gleaming viciously in the morning sun.

Turning, platoon commander Sugita yelled "Attack!" and they broke into a run. But they were reeling with fatigue, and when they tried to give a menacing battle cry they could hardly manage anything more than an ineffective croak.

The distance between them and the hypothetical enemy narrowed till it was only five meters, when both sides halted and, giving vent to animal-like snarls, went through the motions of stabbing each other in the chest with their bayonets. Seeing a senior student's bayonet lunging at him, H was seized with a genuine fear, as though he were really being stabbed....

At last the battle training was over. Their sandbags, fortunately, were not weighed, and Yokota's eyes were moist, perhaps with tears of relief.

As though in a dream, H heard Instructor Hisakado's voice saying, "That will be the end of the night march."

The next moment everything went blank and he toppled over.

27

Blood Types

H hadn't known that even members of the same family could have different blood types.

Not just H but almost everybody at that time was more or less indifferent to the existence of blood types; they didn't know, for example, that in a blood transfusion the compatibility of the blood used could mean the difference between life and death.

They only began to take an interest in the subject when the papers carried an article advising people to find out their own blood type in case they were hurt in an air raid, and a neighborhood association circular came around on the same subject.

"All Family Members Should Find Out Their Blood Types," it said in big letters at the top. "Everybody should wear a cloth tag on his chest bearing his or her name, address and blood type," it went on underneath. "The blood type in particular should be written clearly and in large script. It may save your life!"

From then on, the question of blood types became a common topic of conversation.

Children in school were to be checked there, but grownups who didn't yet know their own types could have themselves checked on days when the mobile "Blood Type Survey Squad" came around. This squad moved around the town, stopping and setting up its tent here and there as it went. It came to Nagara National School, for instance, and pitched its tent in the school grounds. On that day large numbers of people who'd applied through their neighborhood associations came and awaited their turn in a long line.

Having your blood type checked was a perfectly simple matter involving nothing more than taking a drop of blood from the lobe of the ear and dropping it on a glass slide coated with some transparent liquid, which changed color after a while. The color told you the blood type, it seemed, and the woman in a white coat who was standing by would announce "A," "O," or whatever the case might be.

They all had theirs checked—H's father at the fire station, his mother by the mobile squad, and H himself and Yoshiko at school—thanks to which the whole family learned its blood types for the first time. H's father was AB, his mother O, and Yoshiko and he, B.

Although H had known that you died if you lost one-third of the blood in your body, he'd been shocked to find out that even your parents' blood could kill you if it was the wrong type. His mother, though, declared with a blissful expression, "Don't worry—*my* blood wouldn't kill you. O-type blood can be given to anyone, it seems. So you can leave it to me." She actually quoted the Bible for good measure: "They say 'It is more blessed to give than to receive,' don't they?"

H had his doubts: not just whether O-type blood could really substitute for other types, but whether his mother was really O-type at all. The reason was that Mrs. Shimizu over the way had declared that the tests weren't to be trusted. Two years previously, when she'd been operated on in the hospital, she'd been told she was A-type, but the mobile tent people had said she was O. When she got them to recheck, they told her she wasn't O after all, but A.

The story had made H uneasy: it was awful to think that a blood transfusion might actually kill someone who would have survived otherwise....

Blood types were a popular topic at school, too. One of his friends, Tomita, who enjoyed telling people things they didn't know, proudly imparted a brand new piece of information that he'd got hold of somewhere: you could tell a person's character by his blood type.

"Take a fellow with type-B blood," he said to H: "he'll get mad if he doesn't get his own way, but the next day he'll forget it and be all smiles. What do you say—that's right, isn't it?"

Four or five of the others who knew H was type B looked at him and burst out laughing.

H was annoyed. "It's absurd to say that all Bs are the same," he protested. "My little sister's a B too, but our characters are quite opposite."

"You can be a lot alike without being just the same, can't you?" the other replied. "They say Japan and Germany both have a lot of As and Os, and *they're* kind of similar, aren't they? They say it's Italy that has all the Bs."

H wondered how Tomita could possibly have the statistics for Italy, but the rest of them all listened admiringly. "So Italians are B-type, eh? They *are* a bit undependable, come to think of it!" And they burst out laughing again.

H called to mind several Italians that he knew, but couldn't believe they all had similar characters. The one thing they seemed to share in comparison with the Germans was that they were more happy-go-lucky—which was why he liked them. So he didn't mind if they really were the same B-type as himself....

Only a few days later, however, something shocking occurred that was calculated to make any B-type person feel rather small. Italy, a member of the Tripartite Alliance along with Japan and Germany, had put out the white flag and surrendered unconditionally.

H had already read articles saying that U.S., British and Canadian forces had landed, first in Sicily, then on the Italian mainland, but he'd never thought Italy would give in as quickly as this.

Principal Sakai told them about Italy's surrender at morning assembly on September 10.

"I'm sure a lot of you know about this already, but I'm afraid that Italy has surrendered unconditionally to the American, British and Canadian allied forces. Actually, though, it isn't the whole of Italy that has surrendered, so you mustn't allow this to upset you too much. It's rather complicated, so I'll explain further. It was in the time of the fascist government led by Mussolini that Japan, Germany and Italy concluded a tripartite agreement linking them in a kind of brotherly relationship. Unfortunately, however, Mussolini was betrayed by a politician called Badoglio and forced to step down, so that Italy now has a Badoglio government. The 'unconditional surrender' has been made by the

Badoglio faction and certain elements of the armed forces. Mussolini, who was our ally, has not surrendered. The German leader, Hitler, has apparently made a speech saying that Badoglio not only betrayed his own country, but tried to bring down Germany with it too. However, he says, nothing has changed within the Tripartite Alliance, and no enemy can ever daunt the German nation. That about sums it up, I think. I want you, too, to devote all your efforts to winning this struggle, in the same spirit as the soldiers who are fighting in the field."

Considering that Italy had surrendered, H thought admiringly, the principal had put a good face on things.

Around dusk that day there was a major earthquake in Tottori prefecture. Damage was said to be considerable, especially within Tottori City. Natural disasters come without warning, and Italy's surrender, too, had been as sudden and unexpected as some great natural upheaval.

A few days later, news came that Mussolini, who had been taken into custody by Badoglio's supporters, had been rescued by a German parachute unit. Once again, the classroom was agog.

An appendix to the news came in the form of a report saying that Mussolini had organized a fascist cabinet and transferred his capital from Rome to Milan.

"Wow!" exclaimed one of the boys. "To rescue an ally using a parachute unit is quite something, isn't it? A and O types *are* dependable after all. Italy's got too many B-types to be much good, though."

"What's that got to do with it?" H demanded irritably. "It's got no connection with blood types, has it?" He was imagining how fed up the Italians living in Kobe must be feeling at the moment.

Nor was it just his fancy: they had, in fact, been driven into a state of isolation. A week or so after the Italian surrender, some trousers that Morio had been asked to repair for Signor Antonio were ready, so Morio went to call on him, partly to return the trousers and partly to see how he was doing.

Antonio wasn't there, though.

"I'm not sure," a neighbor told him in a quiet voice, "but I suspect he's been taken to Shirakawa."

The foreigners living in Kobe were of many different nationalities, but since the war began they'd been classified, according to their nationality, into "friendly" and "enemy" aliens. Germany and Italy being axis nations, it was permitted to associate with their nationals in the same way as before; on the other hand, Americans, British, Dutch, Canadians and Australians, who were enemy aliens, were kept strictly out of the way in concentration camps.

Shirakawa, situated about eight kilometers up the Myohoji River from H's house, was the local concentration camp. Although the name "Shirakawa" suggests a river, it was in fact the name of a pass over the hills behind west Kobe.

Long, long ago, it was said, the hills in this area had lain beneath the sea, proof being that you had only to scratch their slopes to uncover fossilized shellfish. For H it was a familiar spot as he'd been there several times in his primary school days on school outings-cum-fossil-hunts.

Since the beginning of the Greater East Asian War, however, he had been to the Shirakawa camp area just once. He'd wanted to see it because Mr. Howard, the Englishman, had been sent there. If you were caught in the neighborhood, though, there was every danger of being taken for a "spy seeking to contact enemy aliens under detention," so he'd been careful to arm himself with hammer, brush and a small bucket to make it look as though he were going to collect fossils.

Taking care not to approach too close to the camp, he'd climbed to a high spot which gave an overall view of the area and, lying down, peered out from behind a rock. The camp, with its rows of wooden, single-story structures, was surrounded by wooden posts driven into the ground at two-meter intervals, with barbed wire stretched between them. Looking more closely he could see another, smaller enclosure encircled by more barbed wire within the camp. It looked as though ordinary civilians and prisoners of war were being kept separate.

H had heard a rumor that British troops taken prisoner in Southeast Asia were kept here. He'd seen such prisoners in the streets of the town —tall, lanky men marching in formation in the charge of a small Japanese soldier with a rifle. The difference in physique was very noticeable, just as H had so often heard.

The man at the ironworks on the opposite corner from H's house knew where the prisoners were being taken.

"They put them to work in the shipyards," he told H. "Seems they're good, hard workers."

"Do you think Antonio and his family will be put in the camp?" H asked his father.

"I wonder. He's not actually an enemy, so I just don't know."

After a few anxious days he heard a report that Antonio had come back home again.

Apparently all Italians, diplomats and ordinary people alike, had been checked to see whether they had any personal connections with the Badoglio faction. As a result of this, those cleared of suspicion were not put in the detention camp. Even so they were to be placed under surveillance and forbidden to move about as freely as hitherto.

When Morio showed up with the trousers, Antonio had apparently told him that they'd better not see each other for the time being.

"He looked kind of sad," Morio said.

H felt sad too. Kobe was slowly but surely becoming a different town....

The town itself had changed, and so had the appearance of individual houses, since the glass of every window and sliding door was crisscrossed diagonally by strips of paper about three centimeters wide, which had been pasted on to prevent them from shattering and scattering fragments during bombings. The gleaming white buildings of H's school, too, had undergone a sad change, having been painted in irregular patterns of black and gray so as not to present a landmark for enemy planes.

As H and his schoolmates approached the school gates walking in formation, the older student acting as squad leader would give the order "In step!" and they would march on swinging their arms in a military fashion. But for all this splendid show, it was depressing to look up and see the school buildings daubed in drab colors. Even when they got there, classes had been shortened to an absolute minimum while the time given over to farm work and military training was steadily, and most annoyingly, increasing.

"It's a swindle, making us pay school fees just to carry night soil and work in the fields."

"Even if you get into college you can't really study—you get called up as a 'student soldier.'"

The complaints were justified. Any real study was out of the question by now.

The October 21 newspaper had a headline saying "Smash the British and American Pigs! Student Soldiers in Impressive Parade," with a large photo of schoolboys, rifles on shoulders, marching in formation through the rain. The paper also carried the complete text of the exhortatory address made by Prime Minister Tojo. It was the same stuff as usual— "Forward along the path of eternal justice! Crush your counterparts on the enemy side!"

H had never cared much for Prime Minister Tojo, a feeling that had grown steadily since he'd entered Second Middle. Perhaps it was because he reminded him of Instructor Tamori....

Tamori's training sessions were universally disliked, unlike those given by Mr. Hisakado. There was always something that rang true in what the latter told them.

"The closer a human being gets to his limits," he'd said, "the more he tends to act instinctively. You should always bear that in mind. If, for example, you're firing from the cover of a tree, you automatically stand so that your left side, where your heart is, is sheltered from the enemy. So far, so good. But when you move forward from shelter you mustn't rush out without thinking. The enemy is already waiting with his eye on the place where you'll appear, and it's stupid to play into his hands. So when you emerge from shelter you must do so from the left—the opposite of what you'd do instinctively. And you shouldn't come out standing, but should keep your body low so as to pass beneath the point the enemy's aiming at. Train yourselves to avoid danger by not moving automatically."

Instructor Hisakado not only taught them logically but didn't hit any of his students either, so he was popular with the boys.

Instructor Tamori, who was forever going on about "the spirit of the fighting man," would have them run round and round the sports ground or do repeated pressups, all to no purpose. The fine-sounding lectures he gave in the classroom were equally offputting.

Coming into the classroom one day holding a newspaper, he brandished it in a self-satisfied way over his head and demanded: "Have you lot seen the newspaper? Hands up all those who've read this morning's paper!"

H had read it, but didn't put his hand up.

The instructor looked them over and then said, "Well then, I'll read it to you." And he began reading: "The headline says: 'From National School to University, All Are Preparatory Schools for the Army.' Next comes a bit reporting how a bureau chief from the war ministry explained to the Diet the revisions being made to the Military Service Law and described what lay behind the army's decision. 'The age limits for military service have been extended to cover men from twenty to forty-five. The same system has been in force in other countries for a long time. In Britain the ages are from eighteen to fifty, and in America too it starts at eighteen. In Japan, the Military Service Law has already been revised, so a lowering of the age limit can be legally enforced any time the necessity arises. From now on we must abandon half-measures and see that proper, organized military training is given not just at boys' schools from national school to university level, but at schools for girls too. With military education, it is no longer enough in the present situation simply to instill the idea of defending the country as in the past. Every school must provide training that will serve as a preparation for its students to go into the forces.'"

At this point Tamori suddenly yelled, "Atten-*shun*!"

"Each one of you," he proceeded, "is already a soldier in the forces commanded by His Majesty the Emperor. From now on, there must be none of this spineless stuff about being 'only middle school students'!"

His usually florid face suffused still further with blood until he looked like one of the "red demons" of popular myth. The boys all assumed wary expressions and kept their eyes down in case they attracted his attention and were singled out for something by name.

In the staff room, too, many of the other teachers took care not to catch Instructor Tamori's eye so as to avoid as far as possible any clash of opinions. They'd no stomach for getting caught up in futile arguments about lofty principles.

There was one other teacher, though, who made fun of Instructor Tamori. This was Mr. Tan Watanabe, who taught English grammar. A corpulent figure, with a huge, pot-bellied frame barely covered by a *kokuminfuku* that threatened to burst in a shower of buttons, he looked like a character in a comic strip. In fact he had a quick temper that kept his students constantly on edge, but was popular even so because his classes were interesting.

However cold the weather, whenever he came into a classroom he'd say, "Let's have the windows open—change all this germ-laden air for something good and fresh!" Being so fat he was forever mopping at the sweat with his handkerchief, even in winter, but his students were horrified by the way he'd open all the windows, sending a chill wind through the room.

He and Instructor Tamori were instinctive enemies. If they happened to pass each other in the corridor, Wantan—as he was known—would immediately greet his colleague with some sarcastic quip such as "On the ball as usual, I see," or "How I envy you your energy!" Whether his timing allowed of no reply, or whether he had some hold over Tamori, he'd never once, oddly enough, sustained a counterattack.

Truth to tell, Mr. Watanabe was a natural foe of H's too. H had a strong suspicion that he'd been the fat man sitting on the far right, scrutinizing him closely, during the entrance interview. Possibly at that time he'd felt that H was an unpleasantly precocious brat. Anyway, he often picked on him in class, and if H couldn't answer would say, "This won't do, *will* it?" and twist his ear painfully. Wantan never slapped a student across the face, but the "ear-twist" was punishment enough. If you tried to back away you only succeeded in pulling your own ear and making it hurt still more.

His friends in the same class would tease him about it. "Senoh, your ears have got bigger since you came to Second Middle," they'd say. By now he'd been given the "ear-twist" so many times that he was beginning to suspect it was true.

"AB—Watanabe-sensei's blood type is AB!" shouted Tomita, rushing into the classroom after class one day. By now he'd set himself up as a virtual authority on blood types. H had no idea what kind of disposition AB people were supposed to have, but think as he might he couldn't find anything in common between Wantan and his father, who was also an AB.

"And I'll tell you something still more interesting," Tomita went on. "His Lechery is an O—that's the same as Instructor Hisakado!"

This created an uproar.

"But the two are completely different!"

"It's just not true you can tell people's characters by their blood types!"

Tomita stood helpless in the midst of this storm of criticism. Eventually the fuss about blood types died down, to be replaced in a few days' time by another topic, the annual march, an event that involved the whole school.

This "whole school" march, which took place at the beginning of December every year, was a march from the school to Tarumi and back, a distance of some twenty kilometers. The route took them straight to the west, along the national highway, through Suma and along the coast to Tarumi.

The day came and the weather was fine, though there was a cold wind. The first contingent, the fifth-grade students, set out from the school at 8:00 A.M., to be followed at ten-minute intervals by the fourth-, third-, second- and first-graders in that order.

The distance was more or less the same as that night march to Arima, but the going this time, by day and without packs or rifles, was incomparably easier than that "hell" had been. Once they were past Suma they could see Awaji Island beyond, and the sea between was windswept and covered with white-crested waves.

Everyone was exhausted by the end of it, but no had one dropped out, not even among the first-grade students. It clearly wasn't such a tough march, but four seniors, H heard, had taken a train back, probably simply for the thrill of eluding the teachers' watchful gaze. Unfortunately they were found out and were severely reprimanded by Instructor Tamori.

That year, 1943, was almost over when, on December 21, an Imperial Headquarters communiqué announced the *gyokusai* of Japanese ground forces on Tarawa and Makin islands. For five days a force of three thousand, commanded by General Shibazaki, had fought fifty thousand enemy troops, finally perishing to the last man.

The newspaper carried remarks by General Yano, who was a contemporary of the dead commander: "General Shibazaki told me that since Tarawa Island, where he was going, was in the very front line of the Pacific fighting, he felt much as Kusunoki Masashige must have done when he went into battle at Minatogawa. Whatever happened, though, he was resolved to give it all he had."

More talk of Masashige, thought H. That means another one left to his fate.

The man at the charcoal shop had much the same view. "They may not say it straight out, but Kobe people know too much about Kusunoki Masashige. Privately they're fed up with people who use the name to cover up what's actually happening in the war."

H heard his parents talking about it too, saying that the church would have to be even more careful about Christmas this year than last, coming as it did right after a *gyokusai*. It made him realize that he hadn't been looking forward to Christmas as much as before. Perhaps it was the awareness that he wasn't a child anymore, combined with the generally tense atmosphere around him. It was getting more and more difficult to protect the church against the continued attacks on Christianity as an "enemy religion." The papers had even reported the activities of an organization in Osaka aimed at getting Christians to renounce their faith.

Pastor Kawaguchi himself had started working at the Nodahama Ironworks, perhaps as a way of avoiding being conscripted for war work in a munitions factory. Every day he arrived home in his oily overalls just in time to take the evening service.

On the day of the Christmas service he gave off a faint odor of factory oil even as he preached his sermon.

28

Live Ammunition

"Second-grade students in the rifle club are to go to the firing range tomorrow morning," came the message. "Assemble in the armory after school today." H and his classmates, however, were due to do farm work at Maruyama, so they went to tell Instructor Hisakado that they were afraid they wouldn't be able to manage it.

To their surprise he told them it was all right: they'd been let off the farm work. They suspected that this was a piece of clever maneuvering on the instructor's part, but they were wrong. There'd been a meeting of the teaching staff, as a result of which the school authorities recognized that training in the rifle and bayonet drill clubs was important enough to take precedence over farm work.

After class, H fetched Yokota and went with him to the armory. There they found Instructor Hisakado but none of the senior students. The seniors in the third and fourth grades were all doing war work at the Mitsubishi Heavy Industries and Mitsubishi Electric works, so there were no students in the school apart from the first and second grades.

"Tomorrow, second-graders will fire with live ammunition at the Ochiai range. You're to treat the rifles you used the other day to fire live, miniature cartridges as your own guns and keep them in good condition accordingly."

At this sudden announcement that they were to fire with real ammunition there was a flurry of talk and they looked at each other, pleased yet rather uneasy at the same time.

"Don't worry, I'm getting Furuta and Sugita to come with us—their shift is off duty at the works tomorrow. It's live ammunition, but all you have to do is what you've been doing in training up to now. So I'm going to give each of you his rifle, and that's all for now."

Their instructor opened the rifle locker under the stairs, and the boys went in and took out their own guns. Today, the idea that they were at last to fire with real ammunition gave an extra keenness and solemnity to the way they went about cleaning them. The instructor must have sensed this; H was busily scrubbing at the inside of the barrel with a rag soaked in oil that he'd fastened to the end of a cleaning rod when he was told, "Don't overdo it and get the inside all coated with oil, now!"

The next morning they were in high spirits, having been released from both farm work and Instructor Tamori's training. "I bet His Lechery's fed up," they told each other as they marched in formation, rifles on shoulders, toward Minatogawa Station on the Shinyu line. "There are times when even he can't go against Hisakado."

The latter, who could hear what they were saying, stayed silent, making no move to check the talk. All of a sudden, though, a voice called out, "No talking while marching!" The voice was that of Yukawa-san, a third-grade student. Yesterday the instructor had said nothing about Yukawa taking part, and the boys took a sour view of his presence. The third-grade students were divided into two groups which in alternate weeks went either to the Mitsubishi Denki works or stayed at school for classes. Yukawa had been working at the factory until the day before, so from today he should have been in school. He must have taken the day off from classes in order to accompany them.

H and his classmates felt less at ease with students only one grade up from them than with seniors in the fourth and fifth grades. H had once said as much to Sugita-san, who was in fourth grade.

Sugita had laughed. "We were the same, too," he said. "The fellows who were quite a bit older were nicer to us than those immediately above us. You see, you're no longer taking it out on the new boys just because you were bullied when *you* were in their position."

H had felt a bit ashamed, remembering how, when he himself had just entered second grade, he'd been pleased at the idea of having juniors in the form of that year's newly arrived first-graders, and had rather overdone the "taking them in hand" bit.

Leaving the train at Suzurandai Station they marched by a deliberately roundabout way to the Ochiai firing range.

The range was in a kind of valley, hemmed in by hills on both sides. The firing platform was a slightly elevated piece of flat ground, and the targets were a hundred meters away: they stood there, three of them in a row, looking as though they'd sprouted out of the ground, far away on the other side of the slight dip in the valley lying between them and the firing platform.

"To begin with we'll go over to the targets so I can show you what it is you have to aim at," said Sugita-san. He took them along a path that dipped down, then followed a course along the valley that would be absolutely safe from any flying bullets.

"Actually," Sugita said smiling significantly, "it's not so far if you go via the hollow between the firing platform and the targets." H didn't understand at first the significance of this smile, until he realized that the "shortcut" meant a route that went beneath the path of the bullets, so that you could only take it when there was no firing in progress.

Climbing a steep slope up from the path along the valley, they reached the entrance to a deep concrete trench. The trench, dank with moisture, was 1.6 meters wide, just enough for one person to stand with arms outspread, and about 2.5 meters deep. That left plenty of room above your head even when you were standing. H felt almost as though he were in the dungeon of some fortress; when he showed surprise at the depth, Sugita-san laughed and said, "It *has* to be deep. The bullets come flying this way, so if you weren't in a trench like this you might get hit."

The trench, apparently, was known as the "observation trench," since it was used for observing the holes where bullets had hit the targets. Seen from the firing platform a hundred meters away, the bull's-eyes on the targets looked barely as big as peas, but from here you could see that they were actually black circles nearly thirty centimeters in diameter.

The score for a bull's-eye was ten. If you hit the first of the concentric rings around the bull's-eye you got nine, and so on down to the white part outside the rings where you scored nothing.

The targets were big, painted on pieces of paper the size of a sliding door, and pasted on boards.

Two boards with the paper pasted on them were joined vertically and pierced by a spindle in the center on which they could be revolved, so that one of them was visible above the trench while the other was waiting down below. The role of the markers was to prepare the targets and let the marksman know where his bullet had hit. Even the bull's-eye was barely visible from where he fired, much less the hole made by his bullet.

Looking up at the target from inside the trench, the markers could clearly see the hole made by each bullet, and would point to the spot using a long pole with a disk attached to the end so that the marksman, seeing where his bullet had gone, could adjust his aim for the next shot.

"This pole with a black disk attached is called a 'saucepan lid,' probably because it looks like the black knob on top of a saucepan. Sometimes the saucepan lid doesn't stop still over one spot on the target but waves from side to side; that means the bullet has missed the target altogether and gone off somewhere, leaving no hole that the markers can find. For the man who's fired, that 'bullet hole unascertainable' signal is a serious disgrace. So take aim carefully before you fire, or you'll find yourself being labeled 'saucepan lid.'"

The Ochiai range that day was reserved for the use of the second-grade students. The eight of them were split up into two parties to act alternately as marksmen and markers. Yokota was happy to find himself in the same party as H.

H's group was ordered to start by acting as markers. Sugita-san and Yukawa-san were to stay with them in the trench, while the other four second-graders, who were to fire first, left the trench and climbed back up the way they'd come to the firing platform on the mound.

As he stood waiting in the trench, H was bitten all over the face and hands by mosquitoes, which seemed to be breeding in the puddles left by rain at the bottom of the trench. Itching madly, he was scratching furiously at himself when Sugita-san said, "They'll start firing any moment now." Wondering how he knew when there'd been no sound, H noticed that a mirror like the rear-view mirror in a car was installed over the trench. Sugita-san, who'd been keeping an eye on it from down below, had apparently seen one of the others waving his arms to signal that they were ready to begin.

They waited but no bullets came. When, after a while, there was still no sound of a rifle being fired, Yukawa-san shouted "No bullet hole ascertainable." At this, there came the sharp crack of a rifle and the whistle of a bullet—but no hole appeared in the target. "You, Senoh, give them a good wave with the saucepan lid," Yukawa-san said, so H raised the pole with the black disk over the top of the trench and waved it from side to side.

The next shot was "bullet hole unascertainable" too. It must be awfully difficult to hit the mark, H thought uneasily.

"Shall I tell you why he's missing?" said Sugita-san. "He's too long in taking aim. If you do that, your eyes blur and the rifle itself starts wavering. He's probably scared because it's the first time. He's so tense he tugs on the trigger, and the bullet swings off the mark."

This was what Instructor Hisakado had told him, and H felt encouraged, realizing that all he had to do was fire in the same way as he'd done at miniature cartridge practice.

As the second marksman started to fire Sugita-san said, "Yukawa, you'd better take the next two and get off to the firing platform; then bring the two who've already fired back to the trench. I'll bring the other two myself."

Emerging from the trench in the wake of Yukawa-san, H and Yokota realized that the path they were taking to the firing platform was different this time from the one they'd come by.

"We go this way—it's the shortcut," said Yukawa-san. H and Yokota looked at each other uneasily, realizing that this "shortcut" meant passing under the bullets flying overhead.

"It's okay," said Yukawa-san with a smile. "No one's been killed yet! It may be right under the line of fire, but the part we go through is sunken ground, so provided you keep down low you won't be hit. This is an experience everybody's put through."

"Does Sugita-san know we're coming this way?"

"*He* does—but you're not to tell the instructor. This isn't training as supervised by Instructor Hisakado, it's *special* training."

With this, Yukawa-san set off at a trot crouching low. Since there was no help for it H started to run after him, but just then there was a tremendous crash—a sharp crack, echoing and reechoing—and with a sound as though the air were being ripped apart, a bullet passed over their heads. Alarmed, H flung himself flat on the ground. His heart had risen suffocatingly close to his throat, and at the same time he realized that he'd wet his pants. Yokota, who'd been running about five meters ahead of him, was lying motionless on the ground too. H wondered with a sickening shock if he'd been hit. Yukawa-san was beckoning to them to come on quickly, so he crept forward a little at a time on his belly. As he came up with Yokota, H shook him and whispered urgently "Hey!"

"I'm scared!" said Yokota.

H too was frightened out of his wits at the thought of another bullet coming flying over. This, he realized, was what "belly-crawl training" had been all about. He was reflecting that it certainly had its uses when again there came the crash of a rifle being fired, and the bullet went overhead with an odd, drawn-out whine.

"That one was a 'bullet hole unascertainable,'" said Yukawa, suppressing a grin. "The bullet was traveling upward. That kind of sound means it's risen above the valley. Keep an eye on the markers' trench—you'll see the saucepan lid being waved." He was quite right: they saw the saucepan lid emerge from the trench and sweep vigorously from side to side. H was impressed that Yukawa, who was only one year senior to himself, should be able to tell by the sound alone.

The reason why the sound of one of the shots had duplicated itself as though any number of shots had been fired was, of course, that it was echoing between the hills on either side.

This realization calmed him down a little, and it occurred to him that although the bullets were in fact going over their heads, being in a hollow might well mean there'd been no need to crawl along the ground at all.

"You wouldn't get hit even if you didn't crawl, would you?" he ventured to Yukawa.

"You'd probably be all right," the latter replied, "but it's better to go on your belly. It's always stupid to stand up and run. Remember that bullets sometimes ricochet, too." For some reason, he sounded rather annoyed. The direction in which a bullet ricocheted was unpredictable, depending as it did on the configuration of the ground where it first struck.

This scared H again, and he resumed his "belly-crawl" position. By the time they'd covered the ground between the markers' trench and the firing platform and were approaching the mound on which the latter stood, more than a dozen bullets had passed over their heads.

On the way up the mound to the firing platform, Yukawa stopped and turned toward them.

"Don't think the idea was just to give you a hard time," he said. "If you come up against live ammunition in the future, this experience should help you to survive. Whatever happens, never panic. The man who doesn't have a cool grasp of the situation is the one who gets killed. A pointless death is a dog's death—you don't want to die like that."

As he spoke he was beating the dirt off their clothes with his hand, discreetly ignoring the wet marks on their pants. H decided that he'd been wrong, after all, to dismiss Yukawa as just another self-important senior....

They arrived on the firing platform to find that the fourth student had just finished firing. Once again, H was impressed—this time by the fine sense of timing shown by Sugita-san in sending them out of the trench when he did, and by Yukawa-san for having them crawl there by the shorter of the two routes.

Instructor Hisakado and Furuta-san surveyed the two of them from head to foot in silence, then grinned briefly, probably noting the wet pants. Both seemed to be aware that they'd come crawling along the shorter route. And yet looking down from the firing platform you could see nothing at all of the shortcut or the depression around it, which was natural enough since if it had been visible it would have meant it was liable to be struck by bullets.

Carrying his Mark IV rifle, H got up onto the firing platform ready to do his own live-ammunition firing. He raised the bolt, pulled it toward him, and stuffed five cartridges into the chamber. As he closed the bolt, the metallic clatter made him start. Since the sound itself was familiar enough from training, it may have been that today it emphasized the fact that the gun was loaded with real bullets. He immediately put on the safety catch so that the gun wouldn't fire even if he touched the trigger, but his heart was pounding nevertheless.

At a command from Instructor Hisakado H got into a horizontal position ready for firing.

Taking off the safety catch, he waited for the order to fire. He knew that his Mark IV tended to fire high and to the right, but didn't know just how far low and to the left he should aim. To start with, at any rate, he decided to try aiming simply at the low left.

At the command "Fire!" he gently squeezed the trigger with his finger. The crash and the shock were stronger than he'd anticipated. At the moment of firing he felt the barrel leap, so he was afraid the bullet might have gone quite high. When you were on the platform firing you couldn't hear the sound of the bullet as it went; you only heard that whistling noise if you were under the bullet's path.

He waited anxiously. Where would the saucepan lid point when it emerged from the markers' trench? Or would it just wave from side to side? The saucepan lid rose up from below till it covered the black bull's-eye in the center, and stopped.

H stared in disbelief. "It's a bull's-eye," said Instructor Hisakado, who was watching through binoculars.

To put the bullet through the very center of the target at one's first shot was a fluke. H was not so much pleased as shocked and embarrassed.

"The way you took aim and fired were both fine," said Furuta-san. "Now take good aim and fire again the same way."

"It's all very well to say 'take good aim,'" H felt like saying, "but I'm firing quite a bit off the mark, not at the middle, so I don't know what's going to happen." But he kept quiet.

H's second shot scored six, the third—to his surprise again—nine.

Wondering what would happen if he aimed at the bull's-eye without adjusting for the gun's deviation, he fired the fourth shot taking normal aim. As a result the bullet hole was far off to the upper right of the target, and his score was zero.

There was a gasp of disappointment from the others around him, and puzzled looks asking why he should suddenly miss entirely after putting a succession of shots in or near the center.

H didn't tell them that he'd aimed directly at the bull's-eye, feeling he might get his ears boxed if he explained exactly why he'd missed.

His fifth and last shot scored seven. "To score a total of thirty-two when you're firing live ammunition for the first time in your life—that must be a record!" he was told. "You're brilliant! That single zero must have been because you snatched at the trigger." This rather tickled H, who knew the real reason, but he just said "Right, I'll be more careful from now on."

Poor Yokota had three "bullet hole unascertainables."

"Where the devil are you aiming?" demanded Furuta-san loudly. "You've got to search—find the right place for yourself. You'll never hit the target unless you get the hang of how your rifle works, rather than just taking aim and firing."

Not one of the rifles, in fact, would fire accurately without correction. H was surprised yet again at this revelation of what the Type 38 infantry rifle, which was said to be very accurate, was like in reality.

H's Mark IV, unlike the rifles used for drill purposes, had been selected for its high degree of accuracy. What about the rifles carried by the soldiers at the front, then? In the thick of battle were they calmly making allowances for the idiosyncrasies of their guns as they fired? Or were they just letting rip? The question preoccupied H....

Perhaps because Furuta's comment had taken effect, Yokota scored a two with his fourth shot and a respectable five with his fifth.

It seemed he'd at last realized he had to aim quite a bit to the right. After Yokota had finished, Furuta-san had them watch him fire with the same gun. With his first shot no bullet hole was "ascertainable." They watched in silence to see what would happen next, but he justified his reputation by gradually approaching the center from the third shot on. Even so he got nothing better than a seven.

When the flattering references to H as a "crack shot" died down, Furuta-san scared him by coming up, clapping him on the shoulder, and saying, "If the enemy should come ashore for a showdown on our territory," he said, "people like you are going to make all the difference."

On three occasions after that they had a chance to fire with live ammunition. Sometimes, in fact, they fired as many as thirty rounds at one go, which puzzled H. Ammunition was supposed to be precious— even the forces didn't have enough—so it seemed strange that they should let middle school students use so much.

Perhaps, he thought, they were secretly getting ready—as Furuta's remark had suggested—for a final battle on the main Japanese islands? In the event, that might actually be far more effective than training people like the middle-aged rookies in Unit 4126, who were now housed in part of the school. But the idea of having such expectations pinned on him dismayed H. Though he could never tell Instructor Hisakado or the senior students about it, using live ammunition had made him realize something about himself. When it came to it, he really couldn't fire at another human being. Not only that: if the bullets came flying in his direction, he knew he'd just drop to the ground and lie there motionless. To shoot and be shot at was a horrifying idea ... and yet, why should he enjoy firing so such?

Although H had realized he was a coward, he still couldn't deny the pleasure he got from firing a gun. Maybe it was something instinctive? After all, most people enjoyed firing at a matchbox with a rubber band twisted over their fingers. In that sense, at least, there was nothing so bad about the simple act of firing a gun.

H's original aim in joining the rifle club had been an overriding desire to escape from Instructor Tamori. By now, though, he was putting up with the rigors of the training because he enjoyed shooting. Through actually firing them, he had discovered an interest in guns.

The trouble was that, depending on what it was aimed at, a gun could become a deadly weapon. He knew, for example, that his Type 38 infantry rifle was, in itself, nothing more or less than a device designed to kill the enemy, and the paradox bothered him.

He decided to put a question to Instructor Hisakado: "Has there been an order from the army that students should be trained to become marksmen?"

"Even if there has," the instructor said, neither denying nor confirming the suggestion, "I don't want any students of mine to get killed through carelessness, so *my* aim is to teach you things that will help you protect yourselves if the eventuality arises."

The troops of Unit 4126 would watch morosely as H and his fellow club members did firing practice at the miniature cartridge range in the school grounds or deployment training with rifles. They themselves weren't even getting the kind of military training that these middle school kids were getting, much less experience in firing rifles. H couldn't begin to understand why they had been called up in the first place.

One day, as H and his friends watched, the same troops were drawn up on the sports ground and then moved to the west side of it where they began, in groups of four, to dig holes. They were the kind of one-man foxholes, some eighty centimeters in diameter, popularly known as "octopus pots."

A good twenty holes were being dug at intervals of some five meters, so the sports ground was soon pitted all over.

One of the second-graders watching exclaimed sarcastically, "Octopus pots for the final battle on home ground!"

As to understanding the kind of tactics that required holes to be dug in a school playground in readiness to meet the enemy, H was at a complete loss.

He was to find out a week later. They were tactics of a truly mind-boggling nature.

29

Octopus Pots

The "octopus pot" dugouts were completed, and the training of the troops began. This consisted quite simply in getting in and out of the holes, which they did turn by turn for a period of two hours or so. They carried no rifles, and it wasn't clear what was the point of training them to jump into and crawl out of the "pots," but it was repeated again and again nevertheless.

Finally at noon the troops took a break in order to eat their rations. At the time, some thirty of them were inside the holes where they'd been dispatched, and these, it seemed, were supposed to eat their rations inside the holes—"it seemed," because from where H and his classmates were watching they couldn't hear what the troops had been told. The men got into the "octopus pots" with their rations and didn't come out again.

Since there weren't enough holes for all of them, the remainder sat on the bank on the north side of the sports ground with their bamboo canteens and started eating.

A soldier's canteen was normally made of metal but, presumably because of the shortage of metals, these troops had been issued with tube-like sections of bamboo cut from a particularly sturdy variety. Their rice was cooked all together in one large pot, so there was no need for them to prepare anything themselves, and a makeshift bamboo canteen was good enough.

The boys unpacked their lunch boxes likewise and, sitting on the ground under the eucalyptus tree, ate their meals of "substitute rice" with pieces of pumpkin and sweet potato. But they were far more interested in what the Central Japan Unit 4126 was doing.

Feeling rather contemptuous of the unit soldiers, they made comments and poked fun at them unreservedly.

"What do they have to eat their meal in a *hole* for? They sure make them do some funny things!"

"Training for living in a trench, d'you think?"

"Then what about when they want a pee or a crap?"

"In a *real* war there'd be times when you couldn't come out for ages, so I expect you do it there in the hole."

"But it'd get like a cesspit! You couldn't stand it—even if it *was* your own shit."

H, though, had seen something to beat everything else for sheer oddity. "There were two platoons drawn up outside Hyogo Station, all carrying bamboo canteens and water flasks like these. What was really funny, though, was that they each had a couple of pairs of straw sandals hanging from their belts."

"Bamboo ... and straw sandals," sighed Fukushima, whose father ran a shoe factory. "It sounds like foot soldiers in the Middle Ages!"

It was true that the quality of the army's equipment seemed to have been getting steadily poorer. Not that all units were using bamboo and straw sandals—H had seen troops on the move who were, reassuringly, fully equipped and carrying rifles. But it was equally true that such encounters were becoming less and less frequent.

Its peculiar "octopus pot" training over, Unit 4126—that sad symbol of the decline—fell in and marched off the sports ground, taking with it spades and thick hemp ropes.

"They're going to demolish houses," said Miyamori, watching them go. "Probably in Meiwa-dori, on the coast side of Hyogo Station."

"Demolishing houses" referred to the job of knocking down and clearing away, by official order, houses in the immediate vicinity of munitions factories and other important facilities. Such areas were officially dubbed "compulsory evacuation zones," and the aim was to create fire breaks to protect the facilities in time of air raids.

Miyamori, whose home was close to Meiwa Street, knew that a whole swathe of buildings adjoining the Kawasaki Rolling Stock works, the Kawanishi warehouses and other installations had been designated a "compulsory evacuation zone" and was being knocked down.

"I feel sorry for those men," someone said. "You'd think they'd been called up just to work as navvies." But something similar could have been said of the students as well, since H and his classmates were themselves due to take part in "compulsory evacuation" operations in the near future.

As if to emphasize the resemblance still further, it was decided that the "octopus pots" dug by the troops were to be used in Instructor Tamori's training.

"Just as I said," said Yokota, "I'm sure there's a secret agreement between the army and the school." (The large amount of live ammunition that had been doled out to the rifle club seemed to tie in with this.)

Instructor Tamori's class began with their being drawn up in front of the octopus pots on the sports ground. They glanced at each other surreptitiously, wondering what they were in for now.

To begin with, at a command from the instructor several of them went to fetch equipment for the training from the farming tool shed. To their surprise, this consisted of a cart of the kind usually drawn behind a bicycle. Piled in the cart were about a dozen straw mats, folded into squares about thirty centimeters each way, roughly the same size as a baseball base, and bound fast. Pointing to them, Instructor Tamori explained the nature of that day's drill.

"This cart is an enemy tank, and these square things are anti-tank mines. I'll explain the operation we're going to practice today. It's called the 'anti-tank mine tactic.' What it comes down to is that you lie in wait in a foxhole until an enemy tank comes along, then when it arrives you crawl out of the hole and throw the mine under the tank so it runs over it. The thing you have to be most careful about in this operation is to take good note which way the tank's moving and retreat into your hole immediately you've thrown the mine. If you don't you get blown up the moment the mine explodes. If you succeed in blowing up the enemy tank, I'll wave this yellow flag and blow once on my whistle; if you screw it up, I'll give two blasts. Anybody who gets the two blasts can consider himself blown to bits. The secret of success in this exercise is to act resolutely, with the idea 'it's him or me.' That's all. Any questions?"

H and his fellows listened to this explanation in horror. As for questions, there were none to ask: what it boiled down to was "Get it right or be blown to pieces."

They were to get into the foxholes in batches of eight while the others watched, then change places.

H was in the second eight. To his immense relief he was not chosen to be the "tank driver."

"Driving" in practice meant running along pushing the cart from behind.

To see the cart as an enemy tank was asking too much. Nothing could look less like a tank as it came bumping and swaying along with someone pushing it from the rear. They resisted the urge to laugh, knowing that to do so would bring all hell down on their heads. In the event, though, the worst happened. On the trial run, Okubo, who was supposed to be the tank driver, fell over. The sight of a great fellow like Okubo falling flat on his face and the cart going ahead on its own was so like something out of a comic strip that they all burst into helpless laughter. His Lechery, naturally, was apoplectic with rage.

"Don't you lot have *any* idea what war's like?" he raged. "This isn't a game!"

They were resigned to being physically abused, but to their surprise got off with a lecture, possibly because the instructor was so eager to get on with his "anti-tank mine tactic."

Clutching their anti-tank mines, the first party of eight leapt into the row of foxholes stretching from left to right in front of them. As each boy disappeared completely inside his hole, then popped his head halfway out again, the effect was so like a group of marmots that the rest of them again had to struggle to restrain their laughter.

Seeing the cart being pushed toward him, Yuzawa jumped out and threw his mine under it, but was late getting back to his foxhole, and the instructor gave two blasts on his whistle.

The "tank" retreated the same distance as it had advanced, then moved forward again. This time it curved to the right as it came, so that Fukushima, expecting it to come in his direction, drew his head in to wait a few more moments. As a result the tank was right on top of him before he stuck it out again, and the mine burst at a minimal distance.

Again there were two blasts on the whistle.

Each time Instructor Tamori gave the two blasts, it meant another of them was blown up, until in the end, of the eight anti-tank do-or-die units, five had been killed by the explosions. "Killed"—but they had destroyed their tanks. Or that was the theory. In actual warfare it was unlikely that tanks could be blown up so easily, and "dead" and "survivors" alike all looked somewhat skeptical.

Then it was the turn of H's party to get into the foxholes. He jumped into his hole clasping the bulky, cushion-like pad of matting that was supposed to represent a mine. The hole was small and fitted him closely. Looking around him, all he could see immediately in front of his eyes was the surface of the earth, scarred with the marks of a shovel. Looking up, he could see the yawning circle that was the sky. Perhaps because this was the first time he'd ever seen the sky as round and framed in this way, he had an odd sense of isolation. As he stood waiting, the feeling that there was nobody else close by added to his desolation. H wondered why he should feel so uneasy when the next foxhole was only five meters away.

Several small holes had been gouged in the side of the foxhole—footholds, he realized, to help you climb out. Wondering in what order to put his feet in them, he raised himself and, furtively putting his head out of the octopus pot, looked toward the next one. As he did so he saw another face peering around with a similar, uneasy expression.

Although he doubted whether a simple drill like this—pretending that a cart was an enemy tank—could be of any use, and knew too that drill and actual warfare were quite different things, he had a very real vision of himself being blown up holding a land mine.

The fear was different from the terror he'd felt when crawling beneath flying bullets. To crawl had been the logical alternative to dying a pointless death. But in this situation there was no safety in staying in the foxhole either. After days on end of standing still, he reflected, the urge to get out of the hole might become so overwhelming that you screamed and leapt out. That would be foolish, he knew: you'd be shot on the spot. And though to anyone watching the sally might well look like a sudden, death-defying attack, they'd be wrong. It would just be the inability to stay put any longer; the person most immediately concerned wouldn't even have considered the reality of death.

He was vaguely turning over such things in his mind when he suddenly realized that the "tank" was all but upon him. Hastily hauling himself up out of the foxhole, he hurled his "mine." Almost simultaneously he heard two blasts on the whistle. But then he saw that the yellow flag was being waved too: he had died an honorable death in action. H had a sudden urge to laugh.

It was a sense of the stupidity of the exercise that predominated, but at the same time all kinds of other things too had begun to seem stupid to him....

The "anti-tank mine tactic" over, Instructor Tamori gave his summing-up, but for the most part H heard only the sound of his voice without taking anything in.

Later he heard from Yokota that they were to repeat the same procedure after class the next day, so that Unit 4126 could see it. According to His Lechery, it would be a disgrace to show them anything too amateurish, so today's had been just a preliminary drill. "And I bet he wants to show off a bit in front of the unit's officers," Yokota added.

Hearing this, H rushed off to see Instructor Hisakado.

"I've a special request, sir. Could you, if at all possible, send the second-grade students on a march after class tomorrow? And could you tell Instructor Tamori so that he lets us off drill after class? *Please!*"

"I was watching you through the window," Hisakado said with a smile. "All right then—as you say. Tomorrow we'll go on a march outside."

The following day's march included only a handful of second-grade students, and they set off in full gear carrying rifles. To their surprise, the destination proved to be a low hill next to the Maruyama farm. It wasn't far from the school, and even when they got there all they did was go to sleep, without any drill to speak of. The place they chose to sprawl out in was a windless dip in the ground that held the warmth of the sun.

In the middle of their nap an air raid alert sounded; then thirty minutes later intermittent blasts of the siren signaled an air raid warning. Even so, Instructor Hisakado gave no order but remained lying on the ground, gazing up at the sky, so the others followed his example. The sky was blue and it was pleasant.

School regulations laid down that "In the event of an air raid warning, students may leave the school and take shelter according to their own individual judgment," so what they were doing was well within the rules.

Another factor may have been that the instructor, seeing a formation of B29s flying over the sea from west to east, had judged that the target of today's raid was not the built-up areas of Kobe.

The thud of anti-aircraft guns was heard, and they could see puffs of white smoke blossoming in the blue sky as the shells burst, but as usual there were no hits.

"Anti-aircraft firing's a difficult job," said Hisakado. "If only the shells could chase after the aircraft they might score a hit, but ..." H was mentally agreeing when he noticed the B29s dropping something black.

"Look! That's stupid," he said with a laugh. "What's the point of dropping bombs over the *sea*?"

"Those are mines," said Hisakado. "Dropping them into the sea's the whole point. You don't hear any bombs bursting, do you?" He was quite right—they couldn't be bombs after all.

"I've seen a mine explode," someone said. "There were no enemy planes around, but suddenly there was this great noise and a huge column of water shot up in the air out at sea. A boat had hit a mine dropped by the B29s. A guy from fifth grade told me he'd seen a boat hit a mine, too, and sink out at sea off the Mitsubishi Heavy Industries yards."

"I heard about it. He said he'd seen a submarine they'd only just launched sink with a terrific explosion."

They must all have been privately wondering what was going to happen in the war, but since the rifle club was looked on as being at the very heart of the school's military training, there was no question of voicing doubts.

The all-clear sounded and the party fell in, ready to return to the school.

As they approached the school gates, the order "March in *step!*" was given, and they went in proudly swinging along—a crack unit, brisk and alert, that no one would have suspected of having just enjoyed a nap at Maruyama.

Stowing their guns and equipment in the armory, they went out onto the sports ground to find the area around the octopus pots deserted.

Back in the classroom they found Okubo and Fukushima deep in conversation.

"Has something happened?" H asked.

"One of the guys threw himself at the tank in earnest and got hurt," they said.

H thought at first they must be joking, but soon realized that it was true. It wasn't a second-grader who'd got hurt, however, but one of the soldiers.

First, the students had been made to go through the same training with "anti-tank mines" as the day before, while the soldiers of Unit 4126 watched. Next, the latter were to repeat the exercise in place of the second-graders. The commander of the unit had taken over from Instructor Tamori, while the troops got into the foxholes just vacated by the students. The latter, though, had felt uneasy when they saw how clumsy the soldiers were.

Just as they'd feared, quite a few of them were unable to gauge when the cart—the "tank"—would arrive, and poked their heads out of their holes after it had gone past, while others barely managed to heave themselves out of their foxholes at all, much less throw land mines.

Gradually, they told H, a kind of unspoken pity for the soldiers had begun to spread among the students watching.

The unit commander, irritated by his troops' clumsiness and possibly conscious of the watching students and school instructor, had lined up the troops in front of the octopus pots and started yelling at them: "D'you call yourselves soldiers? How d'you think you'd manage against real enemy tanks? What you need is more of the kill-or-be-killed spirit. So hold the mine against you and fling yourself at 'em! Don't bother about getting back to the foxhole—you should think of this as training to act as human mines. If any of you still don't think you're up to it, we'll carry on training until dark if necessary!"

It was after that that the accident had happened. As the cart was coming directly for him, an elderly soldier came out of his foxhole and flung himself straight at it.

"There was a big crash and I saw the blood spurting. And would you believe it—His Lechery suddenly got up and started waving the yellow flag. And it wasn't even one of his own pupils! The students and soldiers all stared at him, so he shouted in a loud voice, 'That was what I call a *real* anti-tank assault!' That kind of thing was for the unit commander to say, surely? It makes you sick!"

The soldier on the ground may have had concussion, because he

297

didn't move, and when some of the other troops hauled him up, his face was all red and streaming with blood. The accident put an end to training for that day.

"Military training is supposed to be an anticipation of actual fighting," H.L. had apparently declared before dismissing the students. "So you shouldn't let a little accident like this upset you." They'd all saluted their instructor, then dispersed, carefully avoiding his gaze.

"His Lechery trudged off to the teachers' room by himself," said Yuzawa. "I'm sure the accident bothered him, actually. From behind he looked kind of depressed. I've never seen him like that before. And there isn't anybody he's really close to, even in the teachers' room. He's probably lonely."

It was true, H reflected: H.L. was always by himself. For some reason the thought evoked a strange picture—a picture of H.L. all alone in an octopus pot. He could see him, patiently putting up with the solitude in the foxhole, looking quite different from the usual, pompous figure; and it occurred to him that, just possibly, *this* was the reality of that middle-aged man called Shintaro Tamori....

He said nothing, though: Fukushima and Okubo would only tell him not to be a fool.

When he got home he found Yoshiko alone in the house.

"Mummy's gone to the church," she began, talking rapidly as though she'd been waiting for him. "She said Pastor Kawaguchi got his call-up papers. She said when you came home to tell you to let Daddy know, then come to the church yourself."

Calling in at the fire station, H found his father had gone to Okurayama for some kind of general training session or something.

All the way to the church H was chewing the fact over in his mind: so the pastor was to become a soldier....

The Reverend Kawaguchi went off to join the forces four days later. Apparently he'd been conscripted into the navy—which H thought was at least a little better perhaps than the army. While he was away, his wife Yoshiko was to act as minister in his stead.

H had been rather depressed recently; it was as though his own personality was riddled with holes like the octopus pots that pitted the sports ground.

The following day, "H.L.'s anti-tank drill" was suddenly suspended. Whether this was the instructor's own spontaneous decision, a recommendation from the school authorities or an instruction from the army wasn't clear. What was certain was that this particular kind of training was over for good, and that quite a number of students, even in second grade, would never have to undergo it.

Some would have liked to try it and regretted that it was now no more than a memory, but the majority opinion was represented by Yuzawa when he declared, "That kind of training's completely pointless. It was just a crazy idea of His Lechery's, the stupid bastard."

A few days later an odd rumor reached H's ears: that Instructor Tamori's violent speech and behavior, and his unnatural taste for hurting other people, had been due in the first place to his wife's leaving him.

It had all started, the rumor said, when he came back from the front to find his wife having an affair with a young man working in the family business. His rage had been so violent that the two of them had eloped, fearing for their own safety.

"Is the story true?"

"Seems so. I heard it from a senior student who knows all about it."

"One of the teachers knows about it, too. I expect it was only his being a fellow teacher that kept him from mentioning it before."

So the gossip went. There was one student, even, who talked as if he'd known about it all along. H himself thought the rumor was suspect though, since he'd never heard it until then. In fact it had not begun to circulate until immediately after the "octopus pot affair." Such a completely unheralded development was odd.

If the rumor was fabricated, it was probably a product of longstanding resentment—possibly a pent-up desire for revenge—harbored toward Instructor Tamori by his students.

If, on the other hand, it was true, it would somehow help to understand why the instructor had persisted in playing the "military man" they knew so well, forever putting on a bold front and never letting others see any weakness. He might even be in the kind of unstable state where to let others see his inner resentments and weaknesses would have meant total collapse.

As H toyed with these ideas, it seemed to him almost as though

Instructor Tamori was somehow shrinking. He no longer seemed an adversary to be taken too seriously.

That wasn't to condone his unnatural persistence in bullying the weak or his violent behavior, but it did mean that he had ceased to be such an object of fear.

Before long H didn't care much whether the rumor was true or false, since the strong resentment he'd once felt had given way to a feeling that the man was a lonely, pitiful figure. Possibly, as the war situation grew increasingly critical, he was desperately feeling that he should do something, without knowing what that something was.

The other students too may well have noticed a sense of urgency and bewilderment in the instructor, for the rumor fizzled out within a couple of weeks. And along with it a change had occurred within them too: they were no longer particularly afraid of His Lechery.

30

Zosui and Evacuation

In town, eateries had appeared here and there where you could get a bowl of *zosui*, a kind of porridge of rice and vegetables, for twenty sen without surrendering an "eating-out" coupon.

The drawback was that each shop was allowed to serve no more than a few dozen people, so in order to get a bowl you had a long wait in line before lunch. The veteran Omori, who'd apparently been around sampling them, declared pompously, much as though he were an inspector himself, "At the place in Udezuka 9-chome, you can't make your chopsticks stand up in the stuff. If they go on like that they'll soon be ordered out of business."

The failure of chopsticks to "stand up" that so annoyed Mr. Omori referred to the fact that if you stuck your chopsticks upright in a bowl of *zosui* and they didn't topple over, it was up to standard; but if they toppled over it showed the place was thinning the stuff down more than was officially allowed. In short, they were either unscrupulously watering the mixture down or putting on the black market some of the rice and other ingredients that should have gone into it.

The consistency of the *zosui* was thus a matter of major concern for customers, who before starting to eat would perform the rite of standing their chopsticks in it to make sure for themselves.

Normally, if you wanted to eat out you had to apply for special eating-out coupons in place of your ordinary ration of rice, and present them at the restaurant; only then were you permitted to eat rice with your meal. So you either had to take some rice about with you in a bag or carry eating-out coupons on you.

In theory the daily ration of rice was two *go* three *shaku* a day, but by now the rice was often replaced in fact by wheat or noodles, and even that tended to be delayed. Allocations of non-basic items such as fish and vegetables were also diminishing compared with a year previously.

The newspapers were carrying a series of articles entitled "How to Make Do on 'Decisive Battle' Food"—that is, how to stop thinking of rice and rice substitutes as an essential part of any meal and make do with other things. Thus: "1. The straw of the rice plant is edible, too. You powder it, mix it with powdered *hijiki* or other seaweed and flour, and knead it to make noodles. 2. If you cut up and dry the skins of sweet potatoes, pumpkins or mandarin oranges, dry them, and grind them in a mortar, you can make dumplings or 'steamed bread' at any time."

Another article dealt with "Edible Insects": "Bee grubs, or the grubs of the dobsonfly, dragonfly and long-horned beetle are all good to eat and nourishing if you boil them in soy sauce or roast them with a little oil," it said. H had eaten bee grubs and locusts, but resolved on no account to eat rice straw. However, since everyone was hungry, they manfully tried anything that seemed even remotely edible. Even so, they were irritated by official propaganda that declared, as though trying to cover up the government's incompetence, "Shortages of foodstuffs mean a shortage of ingenuity! Let's get by on 'decisive battle' food!"

Now an apparent sudden change of policy, aimed perhaps at placating troublemakers, had permitted the establishment of these restaurants where one could eat without "eating-out coupons." A surprised but pleased public began to form lines in front of the new eateries. Unfortunately the delights of *zosui* were unavailable to those without the time to line up. H, being in school, was one of them, but he was desperately eager to try it. If you went and stood in line taking a pot with you, they would give you enough for one person to take home, but H's mother refused to go and line up for him. "You don't need stuff like that," she declared. "What we make at home is much better."

As it happened, a chance to try the *zosui* came along unexpectedly soon, thanks to a rescheduling of air raid drill. Normally held after school, one day it was switched to the morning for the convenience of the instructor from the Nagata Fire Station. Hearing that the bucket relay drill was so energetic that a number of students regularly got soaked and were given special permission to go home early, presumably in case they caught cold, H dashed into the toilet and deliberately splashed water all over his trousers. In the event, all students in third grade and below were allowed to go straight home as soon as fire drill ended that day anyway, so he hadn't needed to do anything so foolish.

Once outside the school gates he rushed off at top speed in the direction of Hyogo Station, unfazed by the clamminess of the trousers clinging to his legs, his destination a former sushi shop near the station that had gone out of business because of official foodstuff controls and later reincarnated as a *zosui* eatery.

Two other boys went with him—Tomita, the boy who was always bursting with information, and Ishizuka, the bookseller's son. Tomita had brought an encouraging report saying that lines were short at this particular place and that if you lined up again after you'd eaten you could get another helping.

When they arrived, breathless and panting, at the former sushi shop, there was already a line of about thirty people.

Joining it right at the end, H and his friends did "paper-scissors-stone" to decide their own order in the line. To his relief, H, who was usually the loser on such occasions, won for a change. The shop had already been open for some time so Ishizuka, who was furthest back, went inside to find out whether the gruel would last until his turn came around. He came out grinning. "I got shouted at," he said as he rejoined the line. "They said they'd no idea how many servings were left—when the pot was empty, that was it!"

It was so cold that they stamped their feet continuously while they were waiting. H in particular, with his wet trousers, was shivering and sniffing noisily to stop his nose dripping.

When at last they got inside the shop and got their hands on the warm bowls of food, their spirits rose. Steam was rising from the *zosui*, which came about four-fifths of the way up the bowl. Like everybody else, H started by sticking his chopsticks in upright. The porridge was sloppy and barely supported them, but they didn't topple over so it passed muster. Just to see what would happen he tried putting the chopsticks in at an angle, whereupon they slowly keeled over.

The *zosui* itself contained pieces of giant radish and sweet potato along with the half-liquefied grains of rice. Perhaps because they'd used soy sauce substitute, it was both watery and burned-tasting at the same time, so H didn't enjoy it much.

"It's not much good, is it?" he murmured in Tomita's ear, only to be told off for being too fussy.

Even after he'd eaten he didn't feel full, but he hadn't the heart to go and line up again.

Leaving the shop, H and Tomita dropped in at Ishizuka's house to eat the packed lunches they'd brought from home. While they did so H put his wet trousers to dry on the *kotatsu*, but it was too late to stave off a cold, it seemed, and that evening he developed a fever.

Back at school after a day off, he was waiting for the second class to begin when four senior students suddenly came into the classroom.

"You're to leave everything as it is and go out into the grounds in double file, taking nothing with you," one of them said. "Okay—*move!*"

They'd no idea what it was all about, but outside in the grounds they found the other students already lined up as though for morning assembly. Once the whole school had gathered, the vice-principal, Mr. Kameoka, got up on the dais.

"Yesterday, a very unfortunate event occurred," he began. "A packed lunch disappeared—I'm reluctant to say 'was stolen'—in a third-grade class. Now, I know you're all hungry, but it's disgraceful that a packed meal should disappear at a school like Second Middle. I'm having a spot check made at this moment on your belongings in the classrooms. To ensure objectivity and fairness, a student from a different class is also looking through the belongings of the fifth-grade students who are carrying out the check."

There'd been other inspections before this too—"spot checks of belongings"—to find out, for example, whether they had any cigarettes. Sometimes they'd even had their pockets turned inside out to check for grains of tobacco. This latest one, though, was much more humiliating and unpleasant.

When they got back to the classroom nobody said a word. In the end, nothing was found that day.

As though to lighten the atmosphere, Okamura, who had an elder brother in fourth grade, brought up a completely different subject.

"Seems that third- and fourth-grade students are going to be sent to work at Mitsubishi Electric."

"Indefinitely?"

"For just a week to begin with. How long it'll go on after that I don't know."

"I wonder whether we'll go when we move up into third grade," someone said. "It'd be better at least than carrying dirt or working in the fields." Nobody, it seemed, enjoyed going with Mr. Murobushi to work on the farm.

"They do say, though, that you get a ration of the sweet potatoes once they're ready to harvest," said Okamura. "I bet old Murobushi'll be back in favor with you once *that* happens." He laughed at his own sally. Perhaps because there was very little to laugh about at that time, everybody seemed to laugh more at things that weren't even particularly funny.

Ishizuka, with whom H had struck up a friendship since they'd gone to eat *zosui* together, lived in Irie-dori near the Mitsubishi Electric works. His home was a small bookstore handling both new and secondhand books, and his father was always to be seen seated at the back of the shop. When H had first met Ishizuka he'd sensed a resemblance to some animal or other he couldn't quite place, but on meeting the father he'd realized what it was: a giraffe. The father wore spectacles on his giraffe-face and was thin, tall and weedy. He was said not to be very strong, which was perhaps why he hadn't been called up.

Whenever H dropped in on his way home from school, Ishizuka's father greeted him with a smile, so H never felt guilty about browsing among the books on the shelves. In the past he'd occasionally been to the public library at Okurayama, but this was better: there was no filling in of slips of paper for each and every book, and he could take down any volume he saw in front of him at his own leisure.

What pleased him even more, though, was that Ishizuka's father would sometimes tell him things he'd read in the paper which H himself knew nothing about. H's family took the *Asahi Shimbun*, while at Ishizuka's place they took the *Mainichi Shimbun*, and from time to time the reports in the two papers would differ. He'd shown H the *Mainichi* for February 23, for example. "Here, read this," he'd said. "It's something that'll interest you."

"Victory or Destruction?" said a horizontal headline in big characters. Beneath it were subheadings, printed vertically: "This is how bad the situation is! Bamboo spears are not enough. What's needed are planes, air battles over the sea!" The main text read:

> Two years and two months since the commencement of hostilities, the enemy's rollback actions against the dazzling early victories of our forces have led us to a point where we face either victory or destruction.
>
> The Greater East Asian War is a Pacific War, a war of the seas. Our greatest enemy is approaching from over the Pacific. The outcome of a maritime war must be determined on the sea, not along the shores of the main islands. If ever the enemy encroaches on our home ground, all will be over.
>
> The fact that since Guadalcanal we have been obliged to draw back our front lines, together with the death of all our troops on Attu and the similar slaughter in the Gilbert Islands, can surely be blamed above all on the fact that, quantatively, Japan's maritime air power is inferior.
>
> One cannot use bamboo spears to fight an enemy who comes on the attack in planes. Ultimately, the outcome depends on fighting power.

They're right, thought H as he read. Here's someone who's telling the truth.

The same day's *Asahi Shimbun* carried an Imperial Headquarters communiqué saying "An attack on the Truk Islands by an enemy task force has been repulsed. 4 warships, including an aircraft carrier, and 54 planes were destroyed. Our losses were 18 vessels and 120 planes." It also gave prominence to an article stating that henceforth Prime Minister Tojo would personally fill the post of Chief of the General Staff. There was no sign, though, of any article on the lines of the one carried in the *Mainichi*.

H felt the *Mainichi Shimbun* was the better paper because it said clearly what it thought. From then on, he decided, he'd call in at the Ishizuka store most days on his way home from school and have them show him the *Mainichi*. But neither the next day nor the day after that were there any more articles like that first one.

"I imagine the military did take exception to that article after all," said Ishizuka's father.

Three days after the publication of the article on "Victory or destruction" and the inadequacy of bamboo spears, the strains of "Down to the Sea" came over the radio. This was usually an ominous sign, and that day's Imperial Headquarters announcement did in fact bring unwelcome news: yet again, a Japanese force had died to the last man.

On two islands of the Marshalls group, 4,500 Japanese troops had perished doing battle against two enemy divisions. If one read carefully, it was clear that they had been subjected to fierce attacks by an enemy task force for some time, and that they had made their final desperate charge on February 6. The Imperial Headquarters announcement had come on February 25, nearly twenty days later. It was only too obvious that the doubts cast by the *Mainichi Shimbun* on the way things were going were being confirmed. The article had hit where it hurt most.

At morning assembly the following day, Vice-Principal Kameoka called for "a moment's silence to pray for the repose of the valiant souls who have perished to the last man on the Marshall Islands." This was followed by the usual exhortation from the principal. It was, for once, remarkably brief.

Not long after H and his classmates entered second grade, they were informed that First Lieutenant Tamiyama, the resident military officer attached to the school, was to go to the front.

Instructor Tamiyama, whose long face and red complexion had earned him the nickname "Redhorse," was popular among the students for not putting on airs. He himself had reportedly volunteered in person to go to the front. According to rumor, he'd opted for the front line as a gesture of defiance against repeated snide references by Instructor Tamori to "people who have no experience of actual fighting." It was generally agreed among the students that this rumor was probably true.

A send-off gathering for Lieutenant Tamiyama was held in the school auditorium with the whole student body in attendance. Not long after that, a teacher called Ichimura, known as "the Ghost," and another called Hanada, nicknamed "Amma," also got their papers.

"I don't know what things are coming to," someone said one day. "They say baseball and tennis are being banned. Do you think it's because they're enemy sports?"

"I expect so," said another boy. "Even if they change the name of tennis to *teikyu*, it's still an English game originally."

H was just wondering whether there could really be any basis to the rumor when it was indeed proved to be true. A notice had apparently come from the ministry of education saying that baseball and tennis were to be banned at all schools from national school level to university.

The school's tennis courts were to be dug up and used for growing vegetables. Much to the students' annoyance, Mr. Murobushi seemed actually to be pleased at this increase in cultivable land.

The field in the school grounds that had once been the tennis courts was planted with sweet potatoes, and the patch on the roof with yet more sweet potatoes and onions.

A still greater shock was to come from the education ministry. On top of its earlier order mobilizing schoolchildren and students for war work, it now proposed to convert the schools themselves into factories.

The ministry notice declaring that school buildings would be made over into factories, "as a means of increasing production of military supplies," came on June 16. On the same day there were air raids in the northern Kyushu area. The principal target, apparently, had been the Yahata Iron and Steel works, but there had been considerable damage to ordinary houses in the vicinity as well.

The feeling was growing that raids on the main islands were beginning in earnest.

In Kobe itself there were factories all along the coast, stretching westward from the Kawasaki Aircraft works to Kobe Steel, the Kawasaki Shipyards, Kawasaki Iron and Steel, Mitsubishi Heavy Industries, and Mitsubishi Electric, and there were important port facilities too. Besides these there were plenty of other places of military importance, such as the Rising Sun oil tanks and the Takatori marshaling yards, near H's own home.

People with relatives in the country were beginning to leave the city, taking their families with them.

On July 17 every household finally received, via the schools, a notice from the education and home affairs ministries announcing the mass evacuation of children. In order to protect them from the air raids, all youngsters in third to sixth grades at national schools were to be compulsorily evacuated. Children with no relatives or friends to take them in would be evacuated en masse at the responsibility of individual schools.

They asked Toshiko's family in Hiroshima prefecture to take Yoshiko, who was eleven at the time and in fifth grade.

The following day an Imperial Headquarters communiqué announced that the Japanese garrison on Saipan had fallen in a last-ditch battle. The papers had for some time been reporting fierce fighting on the island; now it too was gone.

Careful reading of the accompanying article revealed that on July 7 the Japanese forces there had launched an all-out attack in which every one of them had perished.

H felt like shouting: "Show some sense of responsibility, Tojo! Where do you think you're taking Japan?"

It seemed very doubtful that his feeling had got across, but even so, one week after the debacle on Saipan, the Tojo government finally announced its resignation.

"The people who object to Tojo have finally succeeded in bringing him down," said Ishizuka's father when H dropped in at the store. "But it's already too late. Even assuming we're going to carry on with this war, the enemy isn't going to pull his punches. The attacks are going to get fiercer and fiercer." He sighed.

On the morning of August 4, the first batch of mass evacuees left Nagara National School, their destination a place called Izushi.

Neither H nor Yoshiko knew what Chinese characters were used to write the name "Izushi," nor that, even though it was in Hyogo prefecture like Kobe, it lay far to the north near the Japan Sea, nor that it was the birthplace of the priest Takuan, who had given his name to a very homely type of pickled radish.

The boys, it seemed, were to stay at the local temple and the girls at the Izushi girls' school.

Yoshiko had a couple of wicker baskets in one corner of the room, and her mother was helping her get together clothes, underwear and other necessities ready to pack and send off to the country. There was a limit on what could be sent: two packages per person.

Yoshiko wanted to find room for the dozen big floral-pattern plates that Mrs. Staples had given them. They meant a lot to her, and she was anxious to protect them from possible damage in the air raids. Her mother carefully wrapped them, one at a time, in pieces of clothing before putting them in the baskets, dividing them between the two.

"I imagine they'll handle the baggage pretty roughly," warned Morio, who was watching. "They may get broken, so you'd better be prepared for the worst."

It was decided they should leave the silver knives and forks behind in Kobe. Yoshiko had objected to taking them, saying it might give her grandmother a shock if they used them in front of her.

They very seldom used the knives and forks these days, but H, who was fond of them, declared he would keep them well polished so that they didn't tarnish while his mother and sister were away.

The packing done, Yoshiko's departure was delayed. Never very strong at the best of times, she'd picked up some bug and had to go to bed. She fretted because she was supposed to join her new school in time for the second term, but her temperature refused to go down, and it was two weeks before she was better.

Her departure was finally fixed for August 30, just in time for the school term, and the evening before that they used the knives and forks at supper for the first time in ages. The meal consisted of "steamed bread"—homemade with cornmeal in it—and shellfish soup, with some pumpkin too, on a plate. The shellfish were short-necked clams that H had gathered on the beach.

As always they said grace before the meal, but today Toshiko lingered particularly long over her prayer.

"You'd think it was the Last Supper!" exclaimed H, disgusted by the air of ritual.

"That's enough of that!" said his father reprovingly. "This isn't the last time—we *shall* see each other again." At which, to H's alarm, Yoshiko burst into tears.

It happened that just at that moment the news of the fall of Paris to the allied forces was coming over the radio: "The German strongholds that were defending the city have finally fallen in the face of fierce attacks by superior enemy forces." It was clear, even here in distant Japan, that Germany's situation was pretty shaky.

It had been decided that Toshiko should accompany Yoshiko to her destination in the Hiroshima countryside. Morio was on duty at the fire station that day, so H skipped his first two classes and went to Suma Station to see them off. They were taking the 8:54 local which stopped at Suma. Watching it draw in, H recalled the day when he and Yoshiko had gone together unaccompanied to Hiroshima. Yoshiko may have been thinking along similar lines, because she said, "Come and see me, won't you, Hajime?" But H, who doubted if it could be managed, merely grunted. It was no longer possible to buy train tickets so easily, and a certificate would be needed if he was to get one.

The train only stopped in Suma Station for ten or fifteen seconds, and H had to shove his mother and Yoshiko up onto it in a hurry. Their car seemed to be quite crowded, probably because so few trains were still running. The two of them got inside all right, but couldn't get close to a window, it seemed, and the train started before he could get a last glimpse of their faces.

He stood waving until the train carrying them finally disappeared around the curve of Suma Bay.

A middle-aged woman, who'd probably just seen off a close relative going to join up, was weeping in the shadow of a pillar on the platform.

Running up the stairs and down again to the next platform, where the electric trains stopped, H stood and waited for his own train.

He'd probably be jumped on for being late the moment he got to school; for that he was prepared, but the last thing he wanted was to be caught out by Instructor Tamori.

Getting off the train at Hyogo Station, H ran flat out all the way to the school. On the way he spotted the tail end of an army unit march- ing up the hill. Catching up with it he found it was Unit 4126. The atmosphere at school had grown oppressive ever since the unit had been quartered in the school's judo and fencing clubs. As he passed it he wondered whether the club would be lending its rifles again for the soldiers' drill.

When he reached the school gates, machinery was being unloaded from a horse-drawn cart in boxes printed with the name "Mitsubishi Electric." So the day was approaching when the school would become a factory....

A postcard arrived saying that, of the floral-pattern plates they'd sent to the country, "two arrived broken."

31

Sweet Potatoes, Canned Crab

Having seen Yoshiko safely to her family home in the country, Toshiko herself stayed there a while before coming back to Kobe. H was glad to see her back, not least because she brought with her rice, eggs and chicken, all of them precious commodities that would have been confiscated if the police had discovered them on the way.

He made himself an omelette with chicken in it, using, for the first time in quite a while, two whole eggs. The taste spreading over his palate and the subtle aroma gave him intense satisfaction. "I'm sure I'll sleep well tonight, and have pleasant dreams," he told himself as he went to bed. But once again he was awakened in the middle of the night by the air raid sirens.

His mother was muttering a prayer softly to herself as she put the remaining eggs in the air raid shelter beneath the floor. Hearing her, he shared her concern for those precious eggs.

There was only one B29 that night, and it passed over the city at a hgh altitude without dropping any bombs.

"Don't you think we'd better eat the eggs and chicken as soon as we can?" he suggested the next morning. "You never know whether we'll be alive tomorrow or not."

To H's surprise, Toshiko agreed. "That's true," she said, and though it was only breakfast time she made a lavish *oyako domburi*, topping the rice with two eggs and plenty of chicken. H wanted to get started on it as soon as possible, but his mother launched into a lengthy grace in which he had to patiently join; it was, after all, made with stuff she'd brought back for all of them. There were still four eggs left, he reflected as they prayed.

The extra time spent over breakfast meant a danger of being late for school, and H left in a hurry. He missed one streetcar, but finally caught up, panting heavily, with the usual procession of school-goers close to the school gates.

As they walked, his friends were discussing the sound of the previous night's B29. On several occasions they'd been played records at school to help them recognize the sound of enemy planes, but the real thing, they agreed, had made a louder and heavier noise. Probably the impression had been different because the sound of a single plane flying at night was more distinct.

"It made a kind of regular moaning sound, didn't it?"

"I expect we'll be hearing it a lot more from now on. The garrisons on the islands to the south are being attacked and steadily wiped out."

Talking noisily they reached the school gate, to be informed that there were no morning classes.

"Second-grade students need not go to their classrooms after morning assembly, since they are required to help carry some machine tools from Mitsubishi Electric that have been delivered. They are to assemble, without taking off their puttees, in front of the shoe lockers at the rear of the entrance hall."

The boxes containing the machine tools and machinery were a dead weight, and the classrooms into which they carried them acquired an instant reek of machine oil not unlike the smell of the armory.

They were given no time to rest, but were ordered next to join the first-grade students who were digging up sweet potatoes in the school grounds. The area where they grew had once been the tennis courts. A breeze hinting at autumn was already blowing from the hills, but a hot summer sun still lingered, so they were soon sweaty and muddy as they dug. The work itself was laborious, but they were delighted whenever they pulled at a runner and a string of potatoes emerged.

The sweet potatoes were bigger than they'd expected. As they dug, Mr. Murobushi was complacently giving a lecture on the history of the sweet potato and the different strains, but his students were too absorbed in getting up the potatoes themselves to listen.

The potatoes they gathered were laid out in bundles of three in a single row on the dirt of the schoolyard. Since they varied in size, the way they were rationed out was a matter of serious concern; there were only three each, but their worth for the individual was far more than the phrase implied. Mr. Murobushi explained how they were to be shared out, and this time they hung on his every word with an almost comical intensity.

"First- and second-grade students are to fall in and march in single file along the row. At the command 'Unit—*halt!*' you're to stop where you are, and each of you is to take the potatoes at his feet. You're not to move once you hear the order—you stop, without fail, right where you are. Understood?"

There was a chorus of "Yessir!" and at the command "Forward—*march!*" they moved forward anxiously, eyes glued to the ground, each hoping, whenever he noticed some large potatoes coming up, that the order to halt would come when he was just beside them.

"Please," H himself was praying, "let me stop by *those!*" But to his disappointment the command "Unit ... *halt!*" came just as he'd gone two paces past the ones he'd had his eye on. It was Mr. Murobushi's fault, he thought, for dragging out the order so long.

What he got in the event was one big fat potato and two puny little ones. Even so, he had to agree that the method of sharing them out had been fair enough.

The senior students who were away doing war work in factories soon got wind of the fact that the potatoes in the grounds had been distributed among first- and second-graders, and complaints reached the authorities that it shouldn't have been done in their absence. But there were still, of course, potatoes left on the roof for distribution to students in third grade and above, and the first- and second-graders were mobilized again to dig them up for the seniors. This time, though, their hearts weren't in it. They'd already received their share, and regret that this time there was nothing in it for *them* made the potatoes, unfortunately, seem all the more desirable.

As they were working Yokota gave H a meaningful look. Then, as H watched, he chose a moment when Mr. Murobushi's back was turned to throw the sweet potatoes in his hand down from the roof with a swiftness and decisiveness that renewed H's admiration for him.

As soon as the work was over, Yokota and H rushed down the stairs and ran to the spot where they calculated the potatoes would have fallen.

What they found was a great disappointment: the precious potatoes had splattered into little pieces. On reflection this wasn't surprising, but their minds had been so set on the idea of eating them that they hadn't taken time to think of such details. Still, a sweet potato was a sweet potato, so they hurriedly gathered the fragments and divided them up. The dirt sticking to the pieces didn't matter; washed and cooked with rice, they'd make an excellent gruel....

The whole school, teaching staff as well as students, was looking forward to the next allocation of sweet potatoes, this time from the Maruyama farm. Unfortunately it would mean two each at the most if all the students and the staff as well were to have a share, and Vice-Principal Kameoka was seriously worried....

There was a great earthquake in the Tokai area on December 7, and a day later an order came for them to do war work at the anti-aircraft emplacement on Karumo Island, off the west of Cape Wada. The work might be hard, but H and his schoolmates decided that it was worth it: they'd be given their midday meal, and they'd heard that as they left they'd also get one bean-jam bun each.

The work consisted in bringing sandbags and piling them up around the site of the anti-aircraft guns. The bags were heavy and their backs ached, but as they'd hoped they were given rice-balls made with real white rice for lunch. The soldier's life had a lot to be said for it.

During the break after lunch they were given a talk about anti-aircraft guns, with someone actually operating one for them.

"It's no good aiming directly at an aircraft in flight. By the time the shell's traveling toward the plane and has reached the right height, the plane's not there anymore, it's gone on ahead, and the shell explodes after it's gone. So you aim in front of the plane—which is difficult, too, because how far ahead you fire depends on the height, and you have to set your sights differently in every case."

It sounds much more difficult than firing a rifle, thought H. "So as soon as you see a plane you have to calculate the height and speed on the spot, do you?" he asked.

"That's right, son—you've got it. And another thing: the exact height the shell explodes at is important too. The best thing of course is a direct hit, but the blast will still destroy the plane as long as it's close enough. But even at an angle that should take it to the plane's fuselage, you won't bring it down if it explodes underneath it. It's really difficult to score a direct hit, so what you have to do is watch where your shells burst and adjust accordingly."

His account made H realize clearly, not just how difficult it was to score a hit with an anti-aircraft gun, but also that if the B29s started coming over in huge numbers they'd be forced to stand by helplessly, powerless to do anything. That worried him more than anything. He wanted to ask what they'd do in such a case, but prudently decided to keep quiet.

In the late afternoon, after they'd finished piling up the sandbags, they were set to feeding the pigs. The pigs, they were told, were eventually for eating, once they'd been properly fattened. "You get *pork* here?" one of the boys said enviously. "I wonder if we could keep pigs at school?"

But that was too much to hope for. A quick check of the bucket containing the pigs' food revealed vegetable peelings and leftover rice. Apparently you couldn't keep pigs unless conditions were good enough to produce edible waste.

As they were leaving they were given two bean-jam buns each, which they sank their teeth into immediately outside the gate. The sweetness was enough to make you weep.

The piling of sandbags resumed the following day, but H himself was given the task of cleaning out the pigsties on the grounds that "the pigs seem to like you." H was inclined to agree. When he went into the sty and made snorting noises, the pigs chorused in pleased response, even coming and butting against him.

It seemed that the non-commissioned officer at the emplacement had taken note of this interesting rapport between H and the pigs, and the following day he was singled out by name to clean out the sties again. His friends jokingly called him "the swineherd," but since he enjoyed playing with pigs much more than piling sandbags, the actual cleaning didn't bother him. The idea that the pigs would end up being eaten by somebody else annoyed him, though; he would have liked to eat them himself.

At morning assembly one day as the year was drawing to an end, it was announced that of ninety-six students who'd taken the examination for Yokaren, fifty-three had passed. "Yokaren" was an abbreviation for "Naval Reserve Cadets," and they were the objects of general admiration. There was even a popular song beginning "Seven buttons / Cherry and anchor"—a reference to the seven shiny brass buttons, each with a design of cherry blossom and anchor, on the front of their uniforms. Almost twenty students had passed from H's year alone; one of them, Shiro Maruyama, was ashamed and annoyed because he'd had to drop out after all on account of fierce opposition from his father.

1945 arrived, and the New Year's break was scarcely over when the boys from second grade were mobilized to go and help carry firewood and charcoal in the grounds of Hyogo Station. An air raid alert sounded while they were working, and shortly after it a full warning. Looking up they saw B29s flying in formation from east to west, each plane leaving a fine white trail like smoke behind it. "Those are 'vapor trails,'" someone said.

The squadron, tracing white lines in a deep blue sky as it flew, was beautiful in its own way. For some reason the anti-aircraft emplacement on Karumo Island remained silent; perhaps the planes were too high. A short time passed, and a second squadron flew by in the same way, in the direction of Osaka. Raids by B29 bombers were gradually becoming a feature of everyday life.

In the early hours of the fourth the warning siren sounded again. Hastily H tugged at the black cloth shielding the electric light to bring it down still further. This was something you had to be careful about; apparently the slightest leakage of light was visible from up in the air. It was said that even striking a match was enough to provide a target for the bombers. In the neighborhood next to theirs, someone had been marched off to the police station for allowing light to show from a window during an alert—which, he'd been told, was "as bad as spying for the enemy."

When the alert sounded H was already in his clothes with his puttees on, but he checked on the essentials he kept close by just to make sure. To the padded air raid hood he'd added a metal helmet, since his father had told him that that gave more effective protection. He'd filled his water bottle before going to bed, but checked it once again. He tested his flashlight. His gas mask had developed a small tear and was useless, so he decided not to take it with him. Although they'd been recommended to buy them by the city hall, they appeared to have been shoddily made.

H had a suspicion that the other precautions they were always being told to take were about as useless as the gas masks, but he'd decided to make the preparations that made sense to him at least.

The following night he was again aroused by an alert, but the planes, which were coming in over the sea off Kobe, seemed to be skirting Osaka on their way to Nagoya. He later learned that that night's raid had indeed targeted Nagoya. As for the planes that came to Kobe, then flew off again without dropping any bombs, he supposed that they were engaging in a war of nerves. There'd been a number of these dummy runs in the past month, but he'd decided not to get too worked up about them, and by now was inured to the repeated alerts. Even getting up when the sirens sounded had begun to seem a nuisance.

In February, though, these sorties by enemy planes finally began to seem more like real raids than a war of nerves.

No alert had been sounded, but H heard the drone of a B29 one day, so he went outside and saw a single plane in the sky. It was followed the same afternoon by an air raid warning, so maybe it had been a reconnaissance plane.

February 4, a Sunday, also happened to be Morio's day off, and he'd gone to church with Toshiko. On being told during the service that there'd been an air raid warning, he rushed off to the fire station. If a warning sounded, men of the fire brigade, wherever they happened to be, were supposed to report for duty as quickly as possible and take up emergency stations.

When it arrived, the formation of enemy planes was bigger than any H had seen before. He was supposed to have school that afternoon, but decided instead to stay at home. Toshiko was going around the houses of the neighborhood association urging them to check up on their firefighting equipment.

H ran upstairs to the laundry platform and gazed in the direction of the noise. With a loud thudding, the guns at the Karumo Island emplacement had begun firing at the formation of B29s, but were failing miserably to score any hits, the white barrage of smoke formed by the shells as they burst seeming to fall considerably short of the enemy planes.

The bombers continued on their way unruffled, still in tidy formation, dropping bombs as they came. Leaving the planes, the black specks grew steadily bigger until they landed and exploded with a tremendous roar, sending up columns of black smoke. The explosions, H was sure, were coming from the direction of the closely packed Mitsubishi Heavy Industries, Mitsubishi Electric and other factories.

Third- and fourth-grade students from Second Middle, who were on Sunday duty, were almost certainly doing war work at those two factories.

The raid was a heavy one. Possibly it had been aimed specifically at factories producing military necessities, since the bombs contained ordinary explosives, not incendiaries. As the first wave of B29s was followed by a second, Japanese fighters could be seen climbing rapidly to plunge into their midst. They looked awfully small, rather like sparrows tackling eagles.

After a while there was a puff of white smoke, and H shouted "Got him!" thinking a wing had been torn off one of the B29s. Unfortunately, it was a Japanese fighter plane. Twisting in a slow spiral, the fuselage fell in the direction of Mount Takatori, leaving a long trail of white smoke. Probably it had been a Zero.

"Where've you been?" demanded Toshiko when he came downstairs from the laundry platform. "I looked in the shelter out in the road but you weren't there either. I was so worried! I expect your father's over in Wadamisaki, so let's pray for him to get back safely. Come on—you too!"

H offered up a silent prayer, and not just because he'd been told to.

The ominous drone of the B29s grew steadily louder. It seemed they were coming down lower in order to pinpoint their targets better. Mingled with the fierce pounding of the anti-aircraft guns came the high-pitched buzz of Japanese fighters, but it was impossible to tell from the vicinity of H's house the location and nature of any damage. For a while things got quieter, but then the drone peculiar to B29s came again, and ten or more appeared, coming his way.

Moments later it seemed that a shell sent up by the Karumo Island emplacement had hit one of them. Spewing smoke from the place where a wing joined the fuselage, it broke formation and began to fall. H hoped to see parachutes opening as the crew escaped, but the plane disappeared from view behind the roofs of the houses opposite.

Fairly late that evening Morio came home safe and sound. With his face blackened, and still clad in a fireproof suit of thick black quilting, his appearance startled Toshiko and H.

"I have to go back to the station again," he said. "I just called in for a moment." As he spoke he took a succession of blackened cans out of his pockets and lined them up on the step in the entrance hall. They were oddly misshapen, swollen till they were almost spherical.

"It's canned crab," he said. "We put out a fire in a munitions factory warehouse, but even after it was out the cans of food kept on jumping about and popping. These are some of them. The man in charge of the factory told us we could have them, but to eat them as quickly as possible because stuff in cans swollen up by heat soon goes bad. Don't worry, now—I haven't been looting burned-out ruins! Just get them eaten before it's too late."

"Canned crab," thought H. "The stuff's around if only you know where to look for it...."

The sight of her husband safe and sound, plus the windfall of twelve cans of crab, cheered Toshiko up immediately. "We can't eat all this by ourselves," she said gaily: "I'll pass on some to the neighbors."

Here she goes again, H was thinking: "more blessed to give than to receive."

Morio, though, put his foot down: "No!—no giving them to other people!"

His grounds for objecting were quite different from H's, but H could fully appreciate them.

"It'd be all right if you could share them out fairly among a lot of people," he went on, "but it's not a good thing to create a gap between those who get some and those who don't. Use your head. The people who don't get any aren't going to be very happy. It's a good thing to be kind to others, but sometimes it hurts people. You're not to give any away, okay? Well, I'm going now—we've still got to put away the hoses —and I may not be able to get back tonight."

Toshiko grumbled to herself for a while after he'd left, but H, who was eager to open the tins and eat some of the crab, got some small dishes and a can opener out of the dresser. Right away, he stuck the blade of the opener into one of the scorched, swollen cans. There was an alarming hissing noise, but the crab inside was unspoiled. He tried a mouthful and was almost overwhelmed by the long-forgotten flavor. He worked his way in silence through three cans, relishing every mouthful.

Going to school the following day he was relieved to hear that although the Mitsubishi Heavy Industries and Mitsubishi Electric works had been damaged, all the third- and fourth-grade students were unharmed. At the same time he realized clearly that from now on Kobe was going to be pretty much a battlefield. The raids had, in fact, claimed their first victim among the students of Second Middle. A third-year student had been critically injured when a bomb had fallen on his home in Motomachi 1-chome, and they subsequently learned that he had died.

The school was full of talk about what had happened in the raid, but accounts differed according to where the speaker had been, and it was soon clear that no overall picture of the situation was to be had without gathering a large amount of information.

Hearing a rumor that Ishizuka's home had been damaged, H looked for him, but his friend wasn't at school. Worried, he decided to call in on the way home to see if he was safe. As he approached he could see from a distance that the Ishizuka bookstore was still standing, but going closer he found that the glass sliding doors were broken and part of the roof twisted upward. Peering into the store he saw shelves leaning at angles and the books from them scattered in piles on the floor. The house had suffered in the blast from a bomb that had been intended for the factories but had gone astray and landed nearby.

Ishizuka and his father were working together tying the books up with rope. His mother and younger sister seemed to be packing clothes at the rear of the house. "Nobody's going to read books anymore, so we're getting out into the country," the father told H.

Their destination was a place further inland from Himeji. "I've a friend who runs a bookstore in Himeji," he said, "so I thought I might let him have these. But I don't think we can manage to carry everything, so I may well sell some by the roadside for whatever I can get. Not that I expect to find any takers. Anyway, we hope to move within the next couple of weeks."

H was disappointed to be losing a new friend so soon. He'd been helping them for a while when the bookseller said, "Here—you can take these if you'd like them," and pointed to a bundle of Iwanami paperbacks. H was delighted, but said "Thank you" quietly, with a little bow of the head, feeling it would be wrong, in view of the Ishizuka family's circumstances, to seem too happy. They lent him a bicycle, so he tied the forty-odd volumes to the carrier and pedaled off home. Once the house was no longer in sight, he couldn't help relaxing into a happy smile at the thought of all the new books he'd just acquired.

As he was passing by Sugawara-dori, he encountered a horse-drawn cart coming from the factory district. The top was covered with oil-stained sailcloth, and he sensed at once that they were carrying a victim of the bombing.

There was another body, though not of anyone connected with the school, laid out in the school's reception area. It was that of the fighter pilot who had been shot down while engaging the B29s. He had crashed in the hills behind the school, H was told, and it wasn't until the next day that they'd recovered the remains. As he passed the room that was now being used for the lying-in-state, he stopped for a moment and bowed his head briefly in silence.

By the next day the man's comrades had come from his unit and taken the "heroic spirit" back to the base.

A few days later H found that the single plum tree left on the bank beneath the steep hillside on the north side of the school grounds was in bloom. Normally he had no interest in flowers, but the sight of the blossom brought him up with a start. It was as though, by announcing the arrival of spring, it was showing its supreme unconcern for things such as air raids.

From various parts of the school came the sounds of work in progress. In the assembly hall and the Class 5 classroom, parts of the floor had already been taken up—wooden floors, apparently, were no good for installing factory machinery on.

H and his friends had received notices saying that the order mobilizing students for war work was being applied to them. This apparently meant that when they went up into third grade they were to work in the school's factory, which they'd heard was to start operating on March 19. Until then they were to practice cold-chiseling under the supervision of a factory hand. The training consisted of placing a chisel against a steel plate, which was held in a vice fastened to a massive work bench, and hammering it so as to cut through the plate. A skilled hand could hit the chisel accurately with one mighty swing of the hammer, even with his eyes shut, but for beginners it was no easy matter.

Almost without exception the students hit their own fingers, yelling in pain as blood oozed through the skin....

32

Air Raid

H awoke to the protracted, three-minute wail of the siren signaling an air raid alert.

The clock said a little after one in the morning. That made it March 17. As yet, H hadn't any inkling of what that day had in store for him.

His father, who was sleeping next to him, got up at once and pulled on his trousers, then started winding his puttees around his legs. Since there were alerts almost every night, nobody changed into nightwear anymore but went to bed in their underwear, so that at any time they only had to put on pants and a jacket to be ready to dash outside.

H was so sleepy that he went on lying there with his eyes shut. He was exhausted from being woken up almost every night by the sirens, and if it were at all possible he would have liked to stay where he was. It was cold outside, and if he left the futon he wouldn't be able to warm himself up and get back to sleep again when he returned after the all-clear sounded.

Even when his father shook him, he still didn't get out of bed. "I know, I know," he said. "There'll be plenty of time after the next warning's sounded."

But his father seemed worried. "Tonight's raid is going to be on Kobe," he said as he put on his helmet and made for the entrance. "Osaka got it badly four days ago, so it's Kobe's turn now. You're to look after your mother—I'm counting on you!"

H got up as he heard the door close and turned on the radio. "An announcement from Central Military District Headquarters," came the usual voice. "An alert is now in effect. Enemy planes are flying northward over Enshu-nada. Tonight's force seems to be a large one, so proper precautions are advised. Other enemy planes are flying northwest over the sea off Tosa. It is believed that tonight's raids are aimed at large cities. Please take proper precautions. I repeat …" and so it went on. There must be a considerable number of planes for them to call it a "large force," thought H.

Toshiko was in the kitchen filling pots and the rice cooker with water. H himself drew water in a bucket and carried it upstairs. There were already two barrels full of water on the laundry platform, but he left some more there just in case, remembering what his father was always drumming into him: "If a fire starts, the best thing at first is water. If the flames start rising higher than your head, get out—fast!"

It was 1:56 A.M. when the warning siren started.

H went out into the road to have a look around at the neighbors. He could see Mr. Shimizu from over the way throwing something that looked like a box wrapped in straw matting down into the shelter they'd dug in the road. Watching him, H remembered that he himself had something precious he'd hate to get burned—the forty volumes of Iwanami paperbacks they'd given him at the Ishizuka bookstore, which were still in the closet where he'd put them. He'd meant to read them, but as yet they remained tied up, unread.

He put the two bundles of twenty books each into the indoor shelter they'd dug under the floorboards.

Wondering how he could save the books even if the house went up in flames, he had a sudden idea.

He surrounded each bundle with bags of sand intended for putting out incendiaries, then topped them with a "lid" in the form of jars of fermented bean paste brought from the kitchen. It was a gamble, but it was the best he could do. As he was scrabbling about under the floor trying to hide them, he became aware of the drone of a single B29.

"What are you up to?" he heard his mother's voice say. "Don't you know they say indoor shelters are dangerous?"

As H emerged, the area outside the window facing the street was suddenly flooded with light. It was as bright as the midday sun, a strange, bluish-white glare unlike anything he'd ever seen before. He rushed out into the road to locate its source and looked up at the sky. Three tremendously bright balls of light were swaying gently down to earth: flares, suspended from parachutes.

If flares could light up the streets like this, all those strict warnings against letting even the slightest amount of light escape had been a total waste of time.

Having released the flares, the B29 went off without dropping either incendiaries or explosives.

Almost immediately afterward came the drone of a whole squadron of them. It was the first bombing wave. Countless narrow bands of light crisscrossed the sky as searchlights sought out the ghostly shapes, and there were repeated thuds as anti-aircraft shells burst. But there was no buzz of Japanese fighters going up to meet the invaders.

The second wave of bombers came in from the skies over Awaji Island. The noise of their engines grew steadily louder, suggesting that they were lowering their altitude as they came in to attack.

Just as the droning seemed to be almost overhead there came a rushing sound like a sudden downpour of rain, and the incendiary bombs came pouring down, sparkling like fireworks. The sight of these clusters of fire falling from the sky was stirring—in a strange way, beautiful. So this was one of the nighttime incendiary raids he'd heard such a lot about, thought H as he gazed up at them.

The incendiaries spread out as they fell and the rushing noise grew louder and louder. The time that actually passed must have been short, but it felt oddly drawn out. Then suddenly it occurred to H that they were coming his way. Aware that there was no real escape from such a rain of fire, he nevertheless dived into the house to protect himself from a direct hit.

The next moment there were repeated thuds as the incendiaries struck the ground all around.

The back yard outside the kitchen was flooded with light. He heard his mother cry out, "One's landed out back!" Rushing through the tatami-floored best room in his boots, he found an incendiary embedded in the concrete, spurting fire. It was a petroleum bomb, the type that sprayed sticky oil all around to spread the fire.

"You take care of this," he shouted to his mother, "I'm going to have a look upstairs!" He raced up the stairs.

He'd heard a loud crash up above. As he'd feared, an incendiary had smashed through the tiles of the main roof and embedded itself, spouting fire, in the tatami of the eight-mat room at the front of the house. The walls of the room and the wooden frames of the sliding glass windows were already on fire, but H fetched a bucket of water from the laundry platform and flung it at the flames. One bucketful was not enough to douse them, but they seemed a little less fierce, so he dragged a thick quilt out of the closet, the kind used to cover the sunken fireplace, drenched it with water from the barrels on the laundry platform and, taking it up in his arms, flung it over the bomb. Then he fetched several more buckets of water from the barrels and flung them around the room, until before long the flames were out. He wasn't sure whether the incendiary under the quilt was completely extinguished or not, but he hurried downstairs anyway.

His mother was standing in the back yard. "I put it out!" she said proudly. "Just like in the drill!"

"That's because it was just in the right place, I expect," said H. "It would've been quite different if it had gone through the ceiling and into the closet."

"It was God's grace!" came the prompt response.

H ran upstairs again anxiously, but the fire in the big room was out.

Even so, there was a red glow beyond the laundry platform. The house out back was on fire.

The back of the tobacco store to the south was in flames, too. It was still less than ten minutes since the incendiaries had started falling.

It seemed to H that it would be dangerous to stay in the house any longer. Before fleeing, though, he felt they should at least carry his father's prized Singer sewing machine down from upstairs and put it outside.

He yelled to his mother. There was no reply, so he looked down into the back yard from the drying platform and saw her throwing water on the wooden fence at the back, which had caught fire from the next house.

"Stop that and come upstairs—quick!" he shouted.

He tried lifting the sewing machine and found to his surprise that he could carry it by himself. So this is why they say "In a fire, your strength becomes superhuman," he thought to himself. Nevertheless, it was impossible to get it down the stairs without help. Just then his mother came up, so together, one in front and one behind, they lowered the machine one step at a time till they finally reached the entrance hall.

When they slid open the front door they saw that the Shimizus' house over the way was in flames.

They trundled the machine as far as the crossing a little way up the street. So far, so good: they'd managed it, thanks to the wheels fitted to the legs. But they soon realized that the castors were too small to allow them to take it any further, and decided reluctantly to leave it in the road and make their getaway unencumbered. Looking toward the hills they saw the Nagara market, about eighty meters to the north, enveloped in flames. There were fires between them and the sea, too, but the flames seemed just a little less fierce there than at the market.

"Okay," H said, "let's make for the sea. I'm just going back to get a futon. You stay here."

He dashed into the house, where the fire had already reached the kitchen. Dragging a quilt out of the closet, he got outside again as quickly as possible and soaked it in water from the fire tank. Returning to the crossing with it, now much heavier than before, he flung it—without warning—over his mother's head and shoulders.

"Oh, it's cold!" she shrieked, staggering.

"It's better than getting burned to death, so don't complain!" H shouted, irritated. It would have been quite impossible, in fact, to get through the fires ahead without a wet quilt over your head.

"I can't see to walk!" his mother complained in a tearful voice, but H got under the futon too and decided to make a run for it with the wet quilt covering both of them.

Looking back occasionally as they went, they saw the ironworks on the side where they'd left the sewing machine and the noodle restaurant both beginning to burn. But wherever they looked they could see no sign of any of the neighbors. They'd all fled long before.

There was someone shouting in the distance, but apart from that the only sounds were the crackling of the flames, the roaring of the wind that sounded like a hurricane, and the crash of houses collapsing.

They were hurrying toward the shore with the futon over their heads when three people came running through the smoke in the opposite direction.

"No, not that way—no!" they shouted as they went past. "Komaga-bayashi's on fire too, so you can't get to the beach."

"Nagara market's on fire too," H yelled after them, "so it's no good going that way either!" But his voice, drowned in the noise of the fires all around, may not have been audible.

"Let's go through the Rising Sun refinery onto the beach at Suma," H urged, tugging at his mother's hand. "Come on, this way!"

"Wait a second," his mother said, halting in her tracks. "The national bonds I tied around me under my clothes are slipping." She was deter-mined that the national bonds the members of the neighborhood asso-ciation had bought together should be safe.

"A fat lot of use bonds will be if we get burned to death," said H, waiting impatiently.

After retying the cloth around her waist, Toshiko got under the quilt again. "Right, let's go!" she said.

When they finally arrived at the entrance to the Rising Sun refinery, the barred iron gates were shut. H had thought they were always left open, but he'd made a serious miscalculation.

Looking back he saw flames rising from a house in Honjo-cho 7-chome; the fires were getting closer and closer.

As he was rattling at the bars of the gate, a soldier with a bayonet on his rifle came running up.

"Open up, will you?" said H.

"You'd be in danger here too," the man said from inside. "There's no telling when the oil tanks are going to blow up—I'd like to get out myself! You'd do better to get away from here as soon as you can. Why don't you follow the fence along that way?"

There was in fact no other way left, H realized. The path skirting the concrete fence surrounding the Rising Sun compound was about a meter and a half wide and had a deep ditch running along the other side.

Turning to his mother, he found that she was leaning against the gate with hands clasped and head bowed as though in prayer.

"This is no place to pray," he told her. "Wait till we get to somewhere safer." But she didn't move. "Come on, pull yourself together," he said shaking her, but her body remained limp, swaying as he shook her. He slapped his mother across the face.

At the second or third slap she finally came to and opened her eyes.

330

"I was praying," she said, which was a lie, since she'd quite obviously fainted.

Come off it! thought H angrily, but controlled himself and hauled her to her feet.

"Now we have to run," he told her. "If we can get safely all the way along this path we'll be in the open ground next to the Rising Sun. But we have to go past the back of the rubber factory and the west exit of the Nagara market on the way. I can't see them from here because of the smoke, but if the fires have got there first, we've had it. If we can run faster than the fire is spreading we'll be okay—but that means going at full speed. This quilt will get in the way so I'm leaving it behind, all right? We'll just have to run without worrying about falling sparks. Can you do it? I can't pull you along by the hand, so you'll have to manage on your own."

H was in a hurry to get moving, but he talked to his mother patiently, as though to a child..

"It's all right, I can run," she said with a smile. "I used to be a marathon runner." H thought this a funny time to be smiling, but he simply said "Let's go, then," and set off at a run with his mother desperately bringing up the rear.

They could see fire spurting from the windows of the rubber factory ahead.

Then the drone of the B29s grew louder, and the third wave of bombers approached. H and Toshiko ran on. If the next attack should be ordinary bombs, not incendiaries, it might be safer to jump in the ditch and lie low. But he chose to go on running: he'd decided to trust to tonight's being an incendiary raid, and leave the rest to fate. They just had to get past the rubber works before the buildings collapsed and blocked their path.

A tearing noise came as the incendiaries started falling. Once more a rain of fire descended on the whole area as though someone were casting a fiery net over it. From all around them as they ran there came the thud of incendiaries embedding themselves in the ground. H was afraid of a direct hit by a falling bomb, but still he ran on.

This time the bombs weren't petroleum but electron incendiaries, which burned fiercely, spurting out an intense, bluish white flame.

Their chief characteristic was the intense heat they gave off, so the aim was probably to set fire to factories and warehouses rather than ordinary houses.

The blasts of hot air aggravated their breathlessness. Looking back, H found his mother was lagging behind. He marked time briefly to let her catch up, then started running again. He calculated that if they went on at this speed they'd be able to get past the rubber factory, which was gradually being consumed by fire, before the buildings collapsed.

The area to the right on the other side of the ditch was Nagata 6-chome. The whole of the 7-chome area through which they'd just passed was already burning. The flames reached high, and houses were collapsing noisily, sending pillars of fire and burning flakes into the air each time. 6-chome was on fire too, but the flames hadn't yet got near the fence along which they were running.

Suddenly H's mother, running by his side, must have caught her foot on something, as she fell over. H wondered if she'd reached her limit, but the next moment she was on her feet again and smiling a little sheepishly. She's beyond me, he thought, looking at her in wonder.

"We made it," he told himself as they reached the other side of the rubber works: it wasn't far now to the grassy open space. But still they had to get past the back of the Nagara market.

"Keep going—we'll soon be there!" he shouted, turning to his mother —or rather he *meant* to shout, but his throat was so dry that nothing intelligible came out.

"What's that?" she asked, so he just waved to her to keep on running.

They only just made it past the Nagara market though they could see that it was already ablaze.

Then finally H must have relaxed, for he tripped over the rail of a siding and fell flat on his face. But he was happy—stretching before his eyes was grassy earth. Now no fire could come after them from behind, nor were there any buildings to collapse and block their way.

He lay still for a while, sprawled on the ties between the two rails.

This vacant lot was the place where he'd played baseball and caught insects in his early years at primary school. He felt a wave of emotion at the idea that the place they'd finally made their way to was a stretch of ground familiar to him ever since his earliest years.

His mother, who'd fallen slightly behind, came up gasping and asked anxiously what had happened. "I'm okay," he said. "Why don't you lie down here and have a rest?" She too stretched out on the ground.

Mother and son lay side by side, cramped between the rails but with a rising sense of contentment.

A considerable number of other people were there too, squatting here and there in the open space. There were surprisingly few they knew by sight, but the woman from the vegetable stall in the market was there with her son. He heard her and Toshiko calling to each other and congratulating each other on getting out safely .

At that moment a moan came from a spot about ten meters away.

"He was hit in the shoulder by an incendiary just a while ago—got his arm torn off," the woman from the vegetable stall told them. "There's no doctor, and nothing anybody can do the way things are here."

H went over to see if there wasn't something he could do to help. The groaning was coming from a boy from Aoba-cho, close to where they were now. H didn't know his name, but judged he was around the same age as Yoshiko; he must have stayed on in the city when the others were evacuated. His mother sat in silence, holding him tight to her, but the blood was pouring from him at an alarming rate.

H almost fainted at the sight. Squatting down he managed to get a grip on himself and, unslinging his flask from his shoulder, handed it to the woman. She took it with a slight bow and tried to give some to the boy, but it trickled from his lips unswallowed. Then, after a while, there was silence.

The boy had died from loss of blood. "Now it won't hurt anymore," H told himself.

Once the boy's moaning had ceased, the open area was quiet save for the sound of houses burning. They watched in silence as the neighborhood went up in flames, their faces red in the flickering light of the fires.

From time to time they saw flames shoot up from the roof of the rubber works. The tin roof curled up, came loose, and was carried into the air by the upward drafts; obviously, if H and his mother had come a moment later, they'd have been in even greater danger. Nor would they necessarily have been safe if they'd got to the vacant lot earlier, since someone who'd taken refuge there had in fact been killed by a direct hit. Basically, there was no telling where was safe.

Rejoining his mother, H drank some of the water in his flask and, as he did so, felt the cold for the first time. He was still wet through with a mixture of sweat and the water that had dripped from the futon.

Hearing someone at his side say, "I wonder if I could have a cup of your water?" he turned and saw an elderly man, a stranger.

"Which neighborhood do you come from?" he asked as he handed over the flask.

"Namimatsu-cho 2-chome" the old man replied. That was the district immediately south of Takatori Station.

"Do you know if Honjo-cho 3-chome was burned down?" H asked, hoping to find out if the church was safe or not.

"I don't think it was on fire when I came through on my way here," the other replied, "but I'm not sure. You see, the sky was red over that way too."

Toshiko was all in favor of going straight to the church, but H stopped her as fires were still burning in various parts of the town. One thing that struck him was that she hadn't once said "I wonder what happened to our house." Probably she was resigned to its having burned down.

Coming to Kobe from Hiroshima prefecture in their youth, his father and mother had worked, pinching and scraping, until finally they'd got their own tailoring business. Now this raid had reduced it to ashes. H was filled with pity at the thought, and at a loss for words of comfort.

It was 5:15 when the all-clear siren sounded. "Well then, let's get off to the church," said Toshiko and made to get up, but H stopped her. "We'd better wait till it gets a bit lighter," he said. As he spoke, a woman his mother knew by sight came into the vacant lot with a young girl.

"So you're safe!" called Toshiko.

"Yes, but our house burned down."

"At least *you* weren't hurt, though."

"You're right. We'll just have to start over again. No point in regretting what's already done, is there? Cheer up and get going is what I say! If only there was a bit more to eat...."

There's another tough 'un, thought H.

Hearing her say that the road with the streetcar tracks had been passable, he got up. As his mother stood up too, she groped for his hand and showed no sign of letting go. It was the first time it had happened since he'd reached adolescence, and he was a bit embarrassed, but didn't pull his own hand away even so.

Dawn was breaking, and they began to get a slightly better view of the city. In some places smoke and flames, fanned by a strong north wind, still crept low along the roads, but the street where the streetcars usually ran was safe. It occurred to him that if the road was like this a fire engine could get by. His father was probably out at Wadamisaki.

Beyond the smoke he could see the area of Honjo-cho 3-chome lying unscathed. The church too had escaped the flames.

"We must be grateful," said Toshiko. "God heard our prayers and kept us from harm!"

"Grateful, when your own home has just burned down?" demanded H.

"Oh, yes!" she said. "I mean, neither of us is hurt...."

I give up, thought H, but left it at that.

When they arrived at the church, the pastor's wife came out to welcome them. "I was praying," she said. "I'm so glad you're safe. Come on in, now!" Both Toshiko and H were black with soot and covered with mud into the bargain.

She heated some water for them, and they wiped themselves all over. After that, the noodles she prepared for them were hot and tasted good.

33

Aftermath

H was running hither and thither amidst a hail of incendiaries. Strangely, out of the flames there came the sound of people singing a hymn and an organ being played. "I wonder why?" he thought as he ran. "Does it mean I'm close to Heaven? Is this the end?" With which he woke up to find he'd been dreaming.

For a while he didn't know where he was, then realized that they'd been given lodgings on the second floor of the church. He could hear a hymn being sung in the church hall downstairs; since it wasn't Sunday, there must be a special service. He looked at the clock—well past noon already. He was desperately hungry.

Judging from the silence now in the hall below, the service had finished. He crept down the stairs, taking care not run into any of the congregation, and went into the kitchen to look for something to eat.

There were steamed sweet potatoes on a plate on the table. He was in luck. He was stretching a hand out toward them when he sensed someone behind him. Startled, he looked around to see the pastor's wife standing there smiling.

"Have as many as you like," she said.

"Thank you," said H gratefully, and taking her at her word ate three of them straight off.

Toshiko came into the kitchen. "I was talking to Shinzo Tanaka," she said to her friend. "He'd been to see the house. As we'd expected, it was gone, burned down."

H suggested that they should go together to the site, but his mother flatly refused. So he decided to borrow a large bucket and trowel and go himself, thinking to dig up and retrieve any crockery or pans that might have survived the fire and bring them back.

"I don't expect there'll be anything left, though," he told his mother as he left the church, for fear of raising her expectations.

He was anxious to go and inspect the ruins, but besides retrieving any kitchen utensils he was concerned about what had happened to the sewing machine they'd left in the roadway.

And one more thing: he wanted to put up a sign on the site saying "Both safe."

On the way to the house he made a slight detour to another place he wanted to see: the Mampukuji Temple. As a mischievous brat he'd put himself in the temple's debt on many occasions, having gone there regularly every autumn to steal its persimmons. The old-style wall around the precinct stood as it always had, but he could see at once that the persimmon tree had been burned, for it was sticking up above the wall like a blackened bone. Worse still, the great roof of the main temple building was no longer to be seen, having evidently collapsed into the flames as the temple burned.

Dazed, H walked along by the wall and out into the street where the streetcars normally ran. In front of him there was nothing but a burned-out waste as far as the eye could see. From the street where he stood down to the sea, there was nothing to hinder the view. The flames had clearly consumed the whole area without so much as a single drop of water from the fire engines to check them.

So it had been one of those "fires left to burn," thought H, remembering the phrase his father had taught him. If you did that to a built-up area of wooden houses, the whole lot was, quite literally, turned to charcoal.

He could see smoke still rising here and there, and from time to time a gust of air would come, possibly triggered by heat lingering in the ruins, and a stale, scorched smell that he'd never smelled before permeated the streets.

The only things left standing amidst the desolation were blistered and blackened utility poles and the tall chimneys of public bathhouses. One chimney in particular, bearing the legend "Honjo Bath," reared stark and solitary out of the scorched earth, unnaturally prominent.

Now that he could take it all in at a glance, H was surprised to see just how small and insignificant was the district in which he'd lived. Until just the day before it had seemed so much bigger.

Next to the bathhouse on the north side, a blackened barber's chair lying on the ground among the ashes showed where the hairdresser's had been; on the south side of the same bathhouse lay a large refrigerator, pitifully deformed by the flames. This had been the charcoal man's store. H wondered if he and his second son had got away safely; so far there was no signboard saying whether they were safe or not.

It was an eerie scene, with the houses in the neighborhood all vanished and a deathly hush prevailing.

What was really strange was that he could see almost no one from the neighborhood looking around among the ruins.

Perhaps, though, they'd been there long before H and, finding the ruins still too hot to enter, had gone back to their temporary places of refuge.

As he passed by the remains of the Nagara market, smoke was rising from the still smoldering debris. The ground was pitted with marks where incendiary bombs—a startling number of them—had landed.

H was trudging on toward his house when he saw white butterflies fluttering over a burned-out site ahead. Rising upward one after another, they were swirling high into the air.

Breaking into a run H approached the place, only to discover that they were rising from the very site where his own home had been.

What had looked from a distance like butterflies were in fact unburned pages from his Iwanami books, swirling up into the air on currents of wind. The scene, with white cabbage butterflies dancing round and round above the overall black of the ruins, was dreamlike, fantastic.

Approaching for a closer look he found that the fire had apparently got into the shelter too, for the cloth of the bags of sand with which he'd surrounded the books was completely burned away. He could also see, though, that the miso pots he'd stood on top of the piles of books had held out admirably. Thanks to them, the central parts of the books had somehow managed to survive. But they weren't really books anymore; burned away around the outside, the two square piles had become two cylindrical bundles of paper. It was this paper that he'd seen floating up into the air on the breeze—white flakes ... the very souls, he felt, of the books.

For a while he stood gazing in fascination at the dance of the "butterflies." As he did so, the familiar aria from *Rigoletto* rose to his lips with what seemed startling irrelevance: *Qual pluma al vento ...*

Cheerful and rhythmical, the song was utterly at odds with the scene before his eyes, yet at that particular moment it seemed somehow sad, an appropriate expression of his own feelings.

Coming to with a start, he realized that he hadn't yet taken a look at the sewing machine. He went to the crossing where they'd abandoned it, in the roadway close to the utility pole, and found it lying there, sadly changed.

The iron legs were standing upright, but the body of the machine lay scorched and blistered at their feet. Since the wooden boards had burned away, it was natural that the body should have fallen, but the effect was still unspeakably pathetic.

With pain in his heart, H wondered how his father would feel if he saw the sad end it had come to.

It struck him again that for his father, who saw tailoring as his vocation, this sewing machine must have been akin to life itself. And with the realization came the nagging worry that, though all this time had passed, his father had still not come home.

He'd intended to salvage from the ruins any pots and pans that seemed usable, but that was still out of the question. The site was even hotter than he'd expected, and quite impossible to investigate.

H resigned himself to coming back again at dusk. Picking up a piece of unburned board he found in the outside shelter, he wrote on it, "Toshiko and Hajime Senoh are safe and at the church in Honjo-cho 3-chome," and stuck it in the ground near where the entrance hall had been.

He was about to leave when he heard a voice say "So you're safe! What about your mother?" Turning, he saw the woman from the tobacco store standing there. She and her family, she said, were all safe and sheltering at the Nagara National School. Almost all the neighbors had taken refuge there.

"What—you managed to get all the way to the school?" H asked in amazement.

"That's right. You could get out all right as long as you went east."

Apparently all the eastern area from Noda-cho 6-chome, where the school was, to Shoda-cho 1-chome, was unscathed—a zone a full five hundred meters wide and one kilometer long.

His astonishment grew. He'd thought the whole city had burned to the ground, but he'd been wrong. Since it was impossible to get a bird's-eye view of the city in the middle of an air raid, he'd known only what came within his own narrow field of vision. He realized now that he and his mother should probably have made their escape to the east, too.

Yet in fact, at the time when they were actually preparing to get out, the road leading toward the Nagara National School had been blocked by flames. It would almost certainly have been impossible to move along it to the east. Did this mean, then, that the others had left home and headed for the school grounds almost as soon as the air raid warning had sounded?

He remembered now that when he'd finally succeeded in putting out the incendiary that had fallen on their house, he'd noticed the house at the back as well as the tobacco store already in flames. So the neighbors must have got out without bothering about extinguishing incendiaries or anything. No wonder there'd been nobody about in the streets!

He groaned inwardly at the realization. That was what *they* should have done. Discretion would have been the better part of valor....

The kind of bucket relay they'd practiced so many times in the neighborhood association's fire drill might be some help when there were only one or two sources of fire, but in a raid like that they were completely useless.

In a situation where the sky was raining incendiaries and there were several dozen simultaneous sources of fire, the correct advice was "rather than trying to put the fire out, think of your own safety and get out." This was even more true when, as had actually happened, the raids came in waves, with fresh clusters of incendiaries coming down all the time. What was one supposed to do in such circumstances? Neither the newspapers nor the neighborhood association circular had ever said anything about *that*.

The article that was repeatedly carried in the newspapers said that incendiaries were nothing to be scared about; they could always be put out provided the usual bucket relay was carried out as taught. The important thing was the conviction that the neighborhood associations *could* put them out: a feeling of hopelessness was more dangerous than any bombs as such.

The real object of H's resentment wasn't so much the enemy who'd dropped the incendiaries as the people who all along the line had consistently avoided telling the public the truth, fobbing them off with a pack of lies—namely, the government and the army.

He was irritated too by his own failure in judging the situation. He hadn't followed the advice of his father, a fireman, who'd warned him that once the incendiaries started falling bucket relays wouldn't be of any use. If they behaved according to the drill, they'd be in danger, he'd said. Seeing a couple of incendiaries there in front of them, H and his mother had naively set about extinguishing them. Admittedly, they'd succeeded, but there'd been a lot more than just those two....

H decided not to tell the woman from the tobacco shop that they'd stayed behind in the house putting out fire bombs.

When she said, "There are other people from around here at the school—why don't you come and stay with us out of danger? We'd be glad to see you," he nodded and mumbled something, but didn't really want to go.

He didn't realize it at the time, but he was ashamed of how he'd behaved. The people who'd fled, the other members of the neighborhood association, had been the wise ones; he and his mother the fools....

He decided to retrace their footsteps, to find out more about the raid and what had happened to the places they'd come through as they fled.

As he walked through the streets gazing about him by the light of day, the realities of the raid became apparent.

From the crossing where they'd left the sewing machine he and his mother, with the wet futon over their heads, had first gone about a hundred meters south toward the sea. The houses on both sides of the road, he now confirmed, had been completely razed.

By the roadside, covered with straw mats, lay the bodies of two people who'd been burned to death. A carbonized arm was poking out from between the mats. One of the two seemed to be an adult, the other a child, but their sex wasn't clear.

The actual number of people killed by the fires but still lying undiscovered in the ruins of houses or in narrow alleys throughout the district must be much greater.

This was the area where a creeping bank of fire and smoke had obscured the view of what lay ahead. They themselves could well have ended up burned to death around here....

It was here, too, that they'd passed the three people fleeing from the direction of the beach, and here was where they'd been told, "No, not that way ... you can't get through!" It was this warning that had made him choose to turn right into the road leading to the gates of the Rising Sun refinery.

Walking there now, however, he was startled to find that Komagabayashi-cho was in fact intact. The report of its being on fire had been false. The people they'd passed had certainly been fleeing from the direction of Komagabayashi-cho, so why should they have been under such a delusion?

It was too late to speculate on what might have been, but supposing—just supposing—he and his mother had fled in the direction of Komagabayashi, they would almost certainly have been spared their terrifying brush with death.

But he resolved to say nothing of such things to her.

Retracing the path they had taken along the Rising Sun fence, he came across the futon they'd left behind still lying on the ground. Although it had been so wet then, it was dry now and caked with mud.

More surprising still, though, were the marks etched in the ground where incendiaries had landed.

This wasn't of course the first time he'd seen the places where fire bombs had fallen, but he was appalled at the sheer number that had landed here. In some spots they were stuck in the ground at distances of only five meters or so apart. Even assuming they hadn't all fallen at the same time, it was a wonder that he and his mother had managed to dash through without sustaining a direct hit.

He took another, closer look to see what kinds of bombs these were. As he'd thought, they were the electron bombs dropped by the second wave of raiders. Slimmer than the petrol bombs, they were hexagonal rods about five centimeters in diameter, and it was these that had been spurting that fierce, bluish white fire. H realized now that these second-wave incendiaries had been dropped in the same area and right after the first-wave petroleum bombs. No wonder the area had been razed so thoroughly.

The buildings of the rubber works that had threatened to block their way had steel frames, so they had retained their general contours. The roofs, though, had collapsed in the fire, and the iron girders, twisted in the heat, seemed to be poking fingers up at the sky.

Of the Nagara market, which had consisted entirely of single-story wooden buildings, nothing remained save an irregular series of charcoal humps.

He went to have a look at the vacant lot. By now there was no one left there, but on closer inspection he found electron incendiaries stuck smoldering in the soil. It was one of these that had struck the boy, and there was a blackish stain at the spot where his blood had soaked into the earth. H joined his hands in silent prayer for the repose of the dead, and left.

As he walked in the direction of the fire station where his father worked, he reflected that it was a wonder, considering the number of incendiaries that had fallen in that piece of open land, that more people hadn't been killed by direct hits.

"Hey," exclaimed Mr. Tada, who knew him by sight, when H showed up at the station, "you must have just missed your father. He's only just left."

H heaved a sigh of relief: so his father *had* got back safely. "If you run you might catch up with him," Mr. Tada added.

He ran—not as they'd run during the air raid the night before, but happily, looking up at the sky, and the bucket in his hand with the trowel inside it gave out a loud metallic rattle as he ran.

With this sound in his ears he thought, "If the raids had still been going on he wouldn't have been home today either...."

As he approached the place where their house had once been, he saw his father standing, his back to him, amidst the desolation.

He'd never seen his father looking quite like this from behind, and something made him check the impulse to call out. Approaching quietly he said, "It's had it."

"It has, hasn't it?" said his father simply, without turning around.

343

After a while he asked, "Nobody hurt?"

"We're all right."

"Really?" said his father—"that's good," and fell silent again.

H avoided looking at him directly, since it seemed he was crying.

Holding his bucket and trowel, H stepped into the burned-out site. It was still rather hot, but cooler than when he'd come earlier. Standing where the living room had been, he pushed aside fallen tiles with his trowel. In the aftermath of a normal fire the charred posts that were once pillars would have remained standing, but there were no pillars here, nothing but ashes.

Digging with his trowel among broken bits of tile and the fire-crumbled plaster of what had been walls, he found, near the place where he judged the china cupboard to have been, a bowl with melted glass stuck to it and another which was broken. He also managed to dig out a few unbroken plates, but they were scorched black and he wasn't sure whether to put them in his bucket.

Digging further, H found an object sticking upright out of the ground like the shoot of a plant just emerged from the soil. It was his fork—the fork that had been kept for his personal use.

He recognized it at once because one of its prongs was missing. Feeling as though it had been waiting there for him, he stretched out a hand and grasped it, then immediately flung it down with a yelp of pain. It was hot.

His hand hurt a lot. Opening his fist, he saw three red weals.

He'd been foolish to use his bare hand to take hold of a silver fork that had been in a fire. Scooping the fork up, soil and all, with his trowel, he put it into his bucket, where it fell to the bottom with a dry clatter.

H had first become acquainted with knives and forks when he was in second grade at primary school, some seven years earlier. It had been an odd relationship: at times he'd disliked, almost hated them; other times he'd felt an intense affection.

It grieved him to see this fork, once almost a part of himself, all black like this. The knife that went with it was probably buried somewhere nearby, but he gave up the idea of looking for it; no amount of polishing with tooth powder would ever restore it to its former glory.

Dangling the bucket, H went over to the remains of the outside shelter and dropped the fork into the hole. Then, using the trowel, he covered it with earth. His father stayed outside, watching what he was doing without himself stepping into the ruins.

H remembered being told by him, "Whether people eat with a knife and fork or with chopsticks is a matter of culture. You have to recognize that there are different cultures, and respect them as such."

As he went on shoveling earth onto the fork, it was as though he was saying goodbye to a culture.

"Don't you think we could use the pans and the rice pot?" his father called, breaking his silence at last.

H thought they probably could, so, taking care this time not to get burned, he drew some water in the bucket and dashed it on the area where the kitchen had been, to cool it down. There was a hissing sound and steam arose. H hadn't realized that the site of a fire held the heat for so long.

He unearthed such utensils as looked at all usable and put them in the bucket, though the idea of what his mother might feel when she saw them made him hesitate rather about taking them back.

At the same time, he also felt he had to let her know how things really were. There was another thing, too, that bothered him, and that was whether he should let his father see the Singer sewing machine that had been so precious to him.

He wavered, but decided that here again it was better to tell the truth. "We wanted to save the sewing machine. We got it down from upstairs, but couldn't manage to take it when we got away. So we left it there in the road, but it got burned just like everything else. Do you want to see it?"

"Yes, I do," his father replied immediately. "Where is it?"

"By the utility pole at the crossing over there," H said, pointing. His father hurried over toward the wreck of the machine. Crouching down, he started feeling it all over, then suddenly said, "I'll take this back with me."

Surely, H thought to himself, he's not got any funny idea, at this late stage, of donating it as scrap iron to the government? But that wasn't it.

"If I get the rust off, polish it and oil it, it may work."

H doubted it, but he put the body of the machine in his bucket and picked it up. It was heavy.

345

Puffing and grunting, they carried the bucket and trowel, the legs of the sewing machine, and the pans and big rice pot back to the church.

As they opened the door, Toshiko came rushing out. "Oh, you're alive!" she cried, bursting into tears. "I was so worried. I thought you might have been killed. Oh, but I'm glad, so glad! I was praying you were safe!"

H, who'd found it odd that she hadn't once mentioned his father, realized that she'd been quite deliberately controlling herself.

For days on end Morio polished and oiled the sewing machine until at last he got it to work.

He'd replaced the boards that had been burned away with pieces of wood from old apple boxes. For the belt, he said, he'd helped himself to the rubber from an old bicycle tire. When, with a rhythmical clatter, he finally started sewing up a tear in a pair of trousers, H broke into spontaneous applause.

"It's all thanks to you for getting it out," said Morio kindly. "If it had stayed upstairs it would have burned beyond repair."

It was very touching to see something once given up for lost come back to life again....

34

Friends

H set off for school to report that he'd been bombed out.

There were no streetcars running yet, so he had to walk. It was only about three kilometers to the school, easily manageable within an hour, so walking presented no problem.

He'd left the church and started walking when quite suddenly he remembered Akutagawa Ryunosuke's *The Three Treasures*, and felt he'd like to know whether Haruo Ota, who'd lent it to him, was safe or not. It was rather off the route to Second Middle, but he turned in the direction of Noda-cho 7-chome, where Ota's house had stood. His first encounter with the book had been in fourth grade at primary school, only a few years back, but now it felt like the distant past.

He'd heard that the area to the east of the Nagara National School had survived the fires, and the report was correct: he could see its buildings rising abruptly beyond a waste of ashes, still standing just as he remembered them. As he went closer he saw that Ota's house too stood untouched. He felt a sense of relief: both Ota and *The Three Treasures* were safe—but for the moment he'd no desire to encounter either of them.

He looked at the pine trees in the garden and the roof of the residence from over the wall, then turned back before he got to the gate.

He'd been afraid that Ota's mother might suddenly appear through the gate. If she'd spotted him, he'd have been invited inside, commiserated with at the loss of his home, and almost certainly given clothing and other essential items. He didn't want that to happen; still less did he want people to think that he'd come with some ulterior motive.

Either way, he didn't want to meet anybody whose home had survived. The difference made by a single night—whether one's house had disappeared or remained intact—was too great. It was probably why some of the lucky people looked rather embarrassed in front of those who'd lost their homes, almost as though they felt they owed them something. So H went straight by Iwao Hayashi's home in Kubo-cho, too, which had also survived.

As he got near the Shin-Minato River, again the houses were gone: the area bordering the river on both sides had burned down. The buildings of the Kagura Primary School bore sooty marks showing that they'd been on fire, and peering through the school gates H caught sight of a large number of charred bodies covered with straw mats laid out in the schoolyard. Nobody had got around to cremating them yet. Among the blackened bodies there were some that were red and bloated, apparently people who'd been caught in the smoke and suffocated.

H was not particularly scared by the sight of dead bodies. Far more unbearable, it occurred to him as he passed, was the sight of people suffering and in pain, with blood streaming from them.

The area surrounding Hyogo Station, on both the hill and the sea sides, was completely leveled. Here too there were a lot of bodies that had not yet been cremated. So this is war, he thought as he gazed over the seemingly endless sea of destruction.

Not surprisingly, Irie-dori, where the Ishizuka bookstore had stood, was razed to the ground. Ishizuka's father had been right to get out while the going was good.

H had never dreamed that the familiar road between Hyogo Station and his school could change so utterly. Power lines dangling from charred utility poles dragged along the ground, and debris from the ruins of collapsed houses had spilled out into the road, making it difficult to get by. Here too the only things left upright were the tall chimneys of bathhouses and small factories which still thrust into the sky.

The buildings between Sanban-cho and Goban-cho, which had survived the fire, obscured the view of the school, and H felt anxious. Halfway up the slope he met a senior student coming down. H saluted and asked if the school was safe.

"Don't worry, it's still standing," said the other, and told H that he was on his way to contact the Mitsubishi Electric works at Wadamisaki.

When H told him that the whole of that area had been flattened, the other shook his head.

"One part burned down," he said, "but not the whole lot. They're still operating. It was a lucky thing," he added as he went off down the hill, "that they made people evacuate the buildings around it and knocked them down to make a fire break."

So the "compulsory evacuation of houses" had been of some use after all. At the time H had felt it was tough on the people concerned. They'd been turned out of their homes by an arbitrary order declaring that they fell within a "compulsory evacuation area" and ordering them to leave within a week. But that had, at least, served to protect factories and other important facilities from the spreading fires.

At the top of the slope he found Second Middle's buildings standing unscarred. As a result of the various detours he'd made, it had taken him not one hour but two to get there.

Although the building itself was unharmed, the interior presented a very different spectacle compared to three days previously.

The corridors and the area around the lower-level entrance hall were overflowing with people. Those gathered there appeared to be local residents, but the only things they seemed to have with them were the pitifully few personal belongings they'd escaped with and any crockery and pots and pans they'd dug out of the ruins.

A middle-aged woman sitting there with her two children told him that so far they'd received neither food rations nor treatment for their injuries.

Opening the door of the staff room H found Mr. Matsumoto, who raised a hand in greeting and exclaimed, "Good to see you safe!" He'd been worried by a report that the area where H lived had burned down.

Next to a map on the wall there was a sheet of paper with the names of students who'd been burned out of their homes, but apparently they'd not yet traced the whereabouts of everyone.

"No classes today," said Mr. Matsumoto. "And students who've been burned out don't have to come to school for the time being. You'd better come again when things have been cleared up at home."

"There isn't any clearing up to be done at my place," said H, "so I want to come to school."

The teacher smiled. "You'll only be rounded up to do war work. Why don't you take a bit of a rest?"

To tell the truth, H didn't feel comfortable about being put up on the second floor of the church and having the pastor's family and congregation doing things for him. He almost felt he'd be happier coming to the school and living with the people camping in the corridors, though he had enough sense to keep such self-serving notions from his mother and the people at the church.

Opening the door of the classroom and going in, he found Yuzawa, Fukushima, Okubo and Nishioka talking animatedly together. To his relief, they were all friends he could behave naturally with.

Catching sight of him Nishioka immediately demanded, "Did your place get burned down too?"

"Yup. But I wasn't hurt, and Mother and Dad are both safe," he said, noticing as he spoke that he'd called Toshiko "Mother." Indeed it was some time since he'd thought of her as "Ma" or "Mummy."

"Did you know that Yokota's house burned too?"

H hadn't known.

"And on top of that they got a notice, just the day before the raid, saying his father had been killed. He was on a ship, you know. The very next day their house burned down. Poor people! It makes you really sorry for them."

With a pang, H remembered something Yokota had once told him. "As my father was leaving," his friend had recalled, "he said to me, 'I may not come back, so live your life just as if I weren't here. You're a man, so you've got to take care of your mother and sister. But as for what *you* do, please yourself. Don't bother about trying to please the teachers at school. Do what *you* feel you want to do.'"

"Just like the famous 'parting at Sakurai,'" Yokota had added with a cheerful smile. "You know—Kusunoki Masashige and his son Masatsura."

Feeling an overwhelming sadness, H tried to imagine what his friend, who'd always been so full of life and mischief, would be doing now.

"They say Sugita-san in the rifle club lost his house too," said Okubo, "and his mother's in serious condition with burns all over her body. It's awful for him, what with his father being away in the forces too...."

The talk about Yokota and Sugita was too much for H, and he finally gave way to the tears that hadn't come even when his own home went.

"Anyway," put in Nishioka, perhaps trying to coax H out of this somber mood, "it's something that *you're* safe, isn't it? The incendiaries were pelting down when *I* got out, too. I thought afterward it might have been all that stupid training under Instructor Tamori that saved my life."

This raised a laugh, so Okubo added quickly, "It might have been, at that! I'd thought all that octopus pot drill was a complete waste of time, but it looks as though it was useful for protecting yourself in an emergency, at least—though I'm not sure you could destroy a tank that way. But don't let His Lechery hear what I said, whatever you do—I'd hate to give him any reason to feel smug!"

This earned another laugh. It was a long time since they'd laughed like that.

H remembered what the newspapers had said ten days previously.

"Did you see the *Asahi Shimbun*?" he said. "It was putting out headlines like 'Any Battle on the Main Islands Bound to Succeed—Many Times the Enemy's Fighting Power'; and 'Any Enemy Landing Will Be Smashed—Tide of Battle to Be Turned Overnight.' Do you think they really believe that? I mean, *they* were the people who said that incendiaries could be put out by bucket relays. Or is it because they wouldn't be allowed to publish otherwise?"

"I'm sure the newspapers aren't allowed to tell the truth," said Yuzawa. "Do you know what they said about the Kobe air raid?"

H, who hadn't seen the papers recently, was eager to know.

" 'Imperial Headquarters has announced that approximately sixty B29s carried out a bombing attack on Kobe. A considerable number of fires were started in the city by the bombs, but they were almost all got under control by 10:00 A.M.' "

"What?" exclaimed H in surprise. "Is that all?" To dismiss everything in a bare two or three lines was a bit much....

"That was all they said about the damage. But they did say that 'courageous counterattacks from our side brought down twenty bombers and inflicted damage on almost all the rest.' "

"Lies!" put in Okubo angrily almost before Yuzawa had finished. "We didn't shoot down all that many!" He spoke with conviction, having watched the whole raid until morning from up on Mount Ege.

It didn't take Okubo's anger to convince them: by now hardly any of them believed the Imperial Headquarters communiqués, which announced with monotonous regularity that damage had been minor and Japanese successes great.

Although H had had no faith in the newspapers for some time past, he was particularly anxious to get hold of the edition reporting the March 17 raid.

"All right—I'll cut that bit out and bring it along," said Yuzawa, but it was the whole paper for that day, not just a cutting, that H wanted. He had a feeling that somewhere in that gap between the newspaper articles and what he himself had seen lay the whole truth about the war.

"All right then, but the whole newspaper for the eighteenth will come pretty expensive," said Yuzawa jokingly. "How much can you afford? Not that I can expect much from someone who's just lost everything in a fire!"

Just then Hayashi came into the classroom. "I was looking for you," he said, spotting H. "I saw the notice where your house used to be, saying you were safe, so I went to the church and they told me you'd gone to school. Anyway, I'm glad you're okay. Here—it's not much, but I brought some clothes and notebooks and things in case they'd help. Your mother told me you were really brave putting out incendiaries...."

Mother's been talking out of place again, thought H, embarrassed, though he was grateful for the clothing and writing materials.

"I don't think it was brave at all," he said as he accepted them. "It was plain stupid. We ought to have got out much earlier. What about you, Hayashi? What were you doing during the raid? At home?"

"Actually, our place didn't catch fire in the end, but we'd already got out as soon as the alert sounded. My father was on guard that night at the Red Cross where he works, but before he left home he told us that in a big raid it was always better to get out quickly. It was Kobe's turn to get pasted, he said, so we'd better get to some safe place as soon as possible. So we left, me dragging my mother by the hand. My father knew how badly Tokyo and Osaka have been hit, so he was warning us not to get any stupid ideas about being brave...."

"How far did you go?"

"We ran all the way to the municipal sports ground at Nishidai. We'd got steel helmets on, of course."

"Nishidai? That's a good two kilometers, surely?" The more H thought about it, the more he was impressed by Mr. Hayashi's concern for his family and the good sense with which his son himself had acted.

"Discretion really *is* the better part of valor, isn't it?" said Okubo. "Though I expect Sumiyama-san would get mad if he heard me say it."

Yuzawa nodded. "Sumiyama-san's so full of the Yamato spirit he'd probably take a swipe at anyone he heard so much as mention running away."

H, who'd had personal experience of being hit in the face by Sumiyama, had an immediate vision of his angry countenance.

"I mean," added Yuzawa, "Sumiyama-san said he'd stayed put—tackled an incendiary at the height of the raid and threw it in the river. You couldn't talk to a guy like that about 'discretion.'"

In the matter of putting out incendiaries H could match his record, but the convictions behind the action were different in the two cases. Sumiyama had fought with the bomb as an embodiment of "the enemy."

Sumiyama was tall and sturdily built. He often boasted that his name "had three mountains" in it—a reference to the fact that all three of the Chinese characters with which "Iwao Sumiyama" was written contained the element meaning "mountain"—and his presence was, in fact, rather large and overbearing. His one aim was to get into the Naval Academy, which meant that in spirit he was already a military man through and through.

"To give up one's life in defense of one's country is the dearest wish of every man in Japan," he would declare. "It's not a question of victory or defeat, it's a question of how much one personally can do in the service of Japan!"

It seemed that, apart from H and a very few of his immediate associates, almost all the students at Second Middle held the same opinions.

It was during a discussion of *gyokusai* in the classroom that Sumiyama had hit H. The former had said that rather than be taken alive he'd prefer in the last resort to die taking a couple of the enemy with him. He spoke almost as though for him the whole point of life was to die in this way. H had looked a little doubtful, and Sumiyama, noticing his expression immediately, had demanded, "Couldn't *you* do it, Senoh?"

"Don't you think it's bad strategy for everyone to kill themselves?" countered H, and had instantly received the full force of a blow on the chin.

"I'll knock that un-Japanese spirit out of you!" Sumiyama had shouted, blazing with anger.

Ever since then H had done his best to avoid him. But recently the atmosphere had been subtly changing. For some reason Sumiyama had loosened up and begun to show a kind of friendliness toward H, the very student who in theory at least was the most distant from him. Although he knew that H was the son of a Christian family, his admiration for the latter's performance in the club and his prowess with a rifle must have convinced him that H was a kindred spirit. Since H on his side relied on the club as a cover for his own personal opinions, this meant that his deception had worked. But still he was scared of being exposed.

They were exchanging anecdotes related to their fear of Sumiyama when, to their horror, the subject of their conversation himself came into the classroom.

They waited warily, assuming he'd come to complain about something, but they were wrong. To their astonishment he'd brought some undershirts and pants to give to H. Among the undershirts were some that had belonged to his elder brother, who'd been killed on the South Pacific front, and H had mixed feelings about accepting them.

"I'll be going into the navy sooner or later, so I shan't need any clothes of my own," Sumiyama said. "I'd hung on to these as a keepsake because they belonged to my brother, but I suppose it'd be better for someone who's still alive to use them, so I'd like you to have them."

Hearing this, H decided to accept with gratitude. He had a feeling that although the other boy was pursuing a course directly opposite to his own, in some way there was an odd kind of empathy between the two of them.

His friends there in the classroom, who knew a lot about both of them, watched the scene in blank amazement.

At that moment H realized very clearly under what circumstances it was possible for him to accept something from another person with a pleasantly straightforward feeling of gratitude.

Put at its simplest, he could feel grateful for it if the other person brought it along for him spontaneously, but he hated to go and ask for anything. For the first time he realized that this apparently very simple distinction was extremely important to him.

He was aware of the underlying contradiction: that to insist on such a trivial point could make life extremely difficult for him. But he decided defiantly that he must be awkward by nature, and that he'd better cover up as best he could something he himself, even, didn't really understand.

As they left the classroom, having all decided to go off to their own homes, they said to each other simply, "Take care, then!" But if Sumiyama hadn't been there they might well have said, "Make sure you get away in time! Don't go getting killed—we don't want any 'absent friends' the next time we meet!"

H was going down the steps from the sports ground at the school gate when he bumped into Ogura coming the other way. Ogura's house hadn't burned down either, but his father too had insisted that they get out before the incendiaries started falling.

"I hear your place got wiped out. Here," he said, handing H a sketchbook and watercolors he'd brought specially, "why don't you use these?"

H was happy: it was good to have friends.

When he got back to the church and opened the front door, he was met by the sound of a hymn. That wasn't surprising in a church, but it made him feel uncomfortable. As he tiptoed upstairs so as not to be heard, he was telling himself he was the wrong kind of person to be putting up here. Despite the shortage of food, they'd taken in the whole family, and members of the congregation were helping them in all kinds of little ways. But still H felt ill at ease. It was all the more painful in that everybody was so overwhelmingly kind and helpful.

In spite of losing everything they had, Morio and Toshiko were happily settled there, never uttering a single word of complaint about their lot. Perhaps they felt they'd finally reached a kind of spiritual home. Whatever the case, it was most impressive.

People who have something to believe in are really tough, thought H with a mixture of exasperation and admiration.

His mother in particular was delighted at being put up at the church. "You can hear the organ being played and hymns being sung," she said, "and you can pray in the meeting hall. It's *wonderful*."

H himself, though, was begining to feel the strain.

One reason was that since entering Second Middle he'd stopped attending church, and had been trying to escape the image of "a child of God" that had been imposed on him. He couldn't help feeling uncomfortable about actually living in the church.

The incident that had finally prompted him to forsake his religion had been a prayer that a woman called Mrs. Yoshimoto had made one day during service.

"Lord," she'd prayed, "protect us from the bombs of enemy aircraft. Please let Japan win this war. Give it the strength never to be beaten by America and England. Amen."

Though in fact no Christian himself, H had felt disgusted by this prayer, and had walked out of the church rather than put up with it in silence.

Surely you shouldn't pray to God for things like that, he'd argued angrily in his mind. What would happen if Christians all over the world asked God for things just to suit themselves? Christianity isn't the kind of religion that aims at practical benefits for the individual, is it? If you want to pray about the war, surely the only thing to do is to ask God to end it and bring peace!

He'd challenged his father too: "Why didn't the minister tell her it was wrong? It goes against what the Bible says, doesn't it?"

But his father hadn't been able to come up with any clear answer. "Well ...," he'd said, "seeing the authorities have got it in for Christianity as going against national policy, to pray like that might help to protect the church. And besides," he'd added, nonsensically, "Mrs. Yoshimoto's got a husband at the front...."

H found this reply evasive and altogether unsatisfactory.

Such being his frame of mind, it was a trial for him to live in surroundings where the sound of hymns coming from downstairs was clearly audible.

Quite apart from that, they could hardly go on letting the church put all three of them up indefinitely.

As the result of a family conference they decided that since Morio couldn't make a living if he gave up working at the fire station, he'd continue to live in the church and commute from there, but that Toshiko and H would go and impose themselves on Toshiko's old home at Miyuki in Hiroshima prefecture, to which Yoshiko had already been evacuated.

35

Machine-Gun Strafing

The alert had sounded, but H set out for school anyway in order to get the application forms necessary for switching schools.

Recently the sirens had been sounding every day, and people no longer gave up going out just because of an alert; unless an actual air raid warning sounded there was little sense of tension.

It didn't mean that they weren't scared of raids anymore; they simply felt it was enough to decide what to do on the spot, once enemy planes were actually in sight. It was not the incendiaries but the explosives that were particularly frightening. If you heard the sharp whistle of a bomb coming down, you promptly leapt into the nearest dugout. If there was no dugout close at hand you dived for a ditch and got down low. If you hesitated because of sewage in the ditch, you caught the blast of the bomb, and you'd had it. Even with an incendiary, of course, if you got a direct hit it didn't matter where you were—but that was just a matter of bad luck.

The streetcar carrying H had reached the Higashi Shiriike crossroads when it suddenly stopped at a place that wasn't an official stop. The air raid warning was sounding, and regulations said that in such an event the car was to stop so that the passengers could take shelter. The doors were opened, and the passengers scattered to take cover in the dugouts at various points in the main street.

H got into a dugout, then decided to get as far away as possible from the street with the streetcar tracks, having a hunch that if he stayed where he was he might get a direct hit.

The feeling had little practical justification, except perhaps for the fact that the factory district wasn't far away. Either way, he felt it was safer not to think too much, but to move swiftly in accordance with animal instinct. Whether the instinct was right or not was a matter of fate.

H ran north in the general direction of the school, along a road bordered by scorched ruins on either side, thinking as he ran that if an enemy plane appeared he would immediately find a suitable spot and lie low.

From time to time as he ran he looked back up at the sky in the direction of the sea, since any split-second decision would require a clear idea of the direction the enemy planes were coming from, which had so far always been from the sea, never over the hills. Coming in either over Awaji Island in the west, or from the direction of Osaka in the east, they flew along the Kobe shoreline, which stretched from east to west.

He was expecting to hear the drone of B29s at any moment when there came the buzz of a fighter plane, and he saw it silhouetted against the sunlight, flying just above the peak of Mount Takatori. Since no enemy plane ever appeared from over the hills, he knew at once that it was a Japanese fighter. Moreover, it was a Shoki, the very latest model.

The Shoki was a crack interceptor fighter developed even later than the Zero, and H comfortably assumed that it was going up to tackle the B29s before they got to their destination.

The next moment, though, the fighter executed a half turn and came hurtling down. An earsplitting whine bore down upon him, and at the same time there came a loud *rat-tat-tat-tat*. Astounded, H fell flat on his face right where he was and stayed put.

The plane that swept by just over his head was an enemy plane, not a Japanese fighter.

Watching it fly away, H realized that it was a Grumman F6F carrier-based plane. He'd never before seen an enemy aircraft as close to as this. He remembered seeing in the newspaper a special feature, with photographs, on "How to Distinguish Enemy Carrier-Based Planes." The Grumman F6F had been among them, along with the Curtiss SBC2C dive-bomber and the V-Sikorski F4U. It was an improved version of the F4F, it said, with a stubby body and square wingtips which looked as though they'd been cut off. The wingspan was thirteen meters, and it had a pair of air-cooled engines, so that in flight it looked like the

Japanese Shoki fighter. It had a 12-mm. machine gun on each wing, and could carry a 200 kg. payload.

H was walking on, wishing to himself that he'd had a better look at the enemy's very latest fighter, when he heard the whine of engines again.

The Grumman had come back. Instinctively H broke into a run at right angles to the plane's path.

As he ran he looked for cover. Spying a large concrete tank holding water for firefighting not far away, he tumbled down behind it.

"A plane's guns point in the same direction as it's flying, so anything lying directly ahead is in the line of fire," Instructor Hisakado had told them. "So to avoid the fire you run at right angles to it."

The bullets from the Grumman's guns passed by in a line about five meters in front of his eyes, raising sprays of dirt as they struck the ground. H's whole body went rigid at the sight of an actual machine-gun strafing in close-up. He realized that he was soaked in sweat; even so, he hadn't wet his pants.

The only human being running among the ruins had been H himself, and anyone looking down from above would have realized that he wasn't military personnel. Despite that, the Grumman had come after him spraying its machine-gun bullets. Maybe the pilot had seen it as a kind of game, like someone firing at a rabbit running across open ground in the country.

To his surprise he heard the sound of engines approaching yet again. The enemy plane had come back.

H felt a surge of anger at this persistence in chasing one single human being. But there was nothing for it but to take responsibility for his own safety, and the best way of doing that, he judged, was to remain motionless behind the object screening him. He was sure that the concrete tank was too thick to let any bullets through.

The noise of the Grumman grew louder and louder, and he saw it bearing down on him from directly ahead. Hastily ducking behind the tank, he made himself as small as possible. The next moment everything else was blotted out by a tremendous roar and the sound of firing. H's body quivered in the noise and the tremendous blast of air. The plane had passed directly over him. For a moment everything, to his horror, had gone dark, but it had been the Grumman's shadow....

Stealthily H peered out, making sure that the plane was disappearing into the distance, then went around to the other side of the tank.

Thinking the plane might come back yet again he lay low for a while, waiting for another attack, but the Grumman had gone for good.

He was startled to find a bullet partly buried in the concrete of the tank. If it had hit him he'd have been killed outright.

A 12-mm. machine-gun bullet! He touched it with his finger, hoping to extract it, but it had gone in too deep to be moved.

Once the enemy plane had gone, there was no sound. Today, a raid by a carrier-based plane had elicited not a single shell from the anti-aircraft emplacement on Karumo Island. H knew it was impossible to take aim at a plane flying in at such a low altitude, but he felt rather disgusted even so.

Today's raid had been all for him. It was almost as though he'd taken personal charge of the war. He nearly laughed out loud at the thought, and wondered whether the upper echelons of the military had been aware of the stupid situation....

He trudged on along the road through the ruins in the direction of the school, his mind overtaken by a kind of partial blank.

On the way, the long shadow of a chimney stretched across the road. He'd never seen a shadow like it before. He'd passed back and forth along the same road any number of times in the past, so he knew the district well, and the sight of this odd, unfamiliar shadow was all the more surprising. The source, of course, was a chimney that had been left standing alone after the building it was part of and the other buildings all around it had gone up in flames. Seized with a feeling that it would be wrong to tread on the shadow of a chimney that had had such a narrow escape, he leapt across it in a single bound.

He walked on for a while and was just coming to the Nagata crossroads when the all-clear sounded.

Finally reaching the school he found Hayashi there too, in the teachers' room. His house had been spared, he told H, but his family had decided to evacuate to a place called Toyooka—in the same prefecture as Kobe but on the Japan Sea side—where his mother's childhood home was situated. He was to switch to the Toyooka Middle School in a week's time.

"*I'm* going to the Seishikan Middle in Hiroshima prefecture," H told him. "I don't really want to go, but I can't let them put me up at the church indefinitely, so it can't be helped."

"One to the north, one to the west," said Hayashi. "We'll miss each other, but we'll hang in there, eh?"

It seemed that several other students, none of whom H knew very well, were leaving Kobe too.

On the day H and Toshiko boarded the train to go to Fukuyama, Morio was on duty at the fire station, so Uncle Hadano carried their belongings to the station and saw them off instead.

For H and his family, Uncle Hadano was rather like the "Long-Nosed Goblin of Kurama." In the film of that name the goblin, who was really Kanjuro Arashi in disguise, would always appear riding on his horse whenever someone was in extreme distress. Uncle Hadano appeared, not on a horse but on a bicycle. He'd come through muddy waters at the time of the great floods, and he'd come to help when they'd had to dig air raid shelters. So to H he was a kind of second father.

Uncle Hadano lived alone in Myojin-cho 2-chome, about three kilometers from H's home in the direction of the hills. Since he worked in the civil engineering department at the city hall, he'd sent his family into the country while he himself stayed on. The decision to stay in Kobe hadn't been solely his own, since a notice from his superiors had said that "in order to safeguard the city there would be restrictions on transfers of able-bodied males."

It was for the same reason that Morio was sending Toshiko and H off into the country and staying on himself in the city.

On the day that H and Toshiko were to leave for the country, they had breakfast earlier than usual. The gruel with dried stalks of sweet potato plants in it was a sad affair, and H was just thinking to himself that in the country they'd be able to eat as much white rice as they liked when his father said, "It's difficult to get hold of train tickets these days. I wonder when we'll see each other again?"

Restrictions on travel had got tighter and tighter since the raids started, and by now it was a job to get hold of tickets at all. To buy them for long distances, for example, it was necessary to have proof that you'd been bombed out or a document certifying that your journey was necessary. They'd only been able to buy tickets for this journey because they had a permit and a certificate saying that they'd lost their home and were evacuating to the country.

The train that H and Toshiko were taking was the slow local train leaving Suma at 8:54 A.M. It was the same train that Yoshiko had gone by when she'd been evacuated, one of the few trains still running now.

They got to Suma Station with twenty minutes to spare, so H went by himself down to the beach. Now that he no longer knew when he'd next be back in Kobe, he felt an intense longing for the sea, and spent the time scooping up sand in his hands or picking up pebbles and throwing them into the water.

"Hey!" Uncle Hadano called from the platform. "The train'll be here in a minute!" H brushed off the sand and ran toward the station. The platform continued straight on from the beach, so he was in plenty of time.

As he saw the locomotive drawing into the station puffing its white steam, he grasped Uncle Hadano's hand tightly. Then they got on the train, H giving his mother a heave up from behind to help her inside.

They tried to make their way inside the car, but it was far too crowded. As the train moved off Uncle Hadano ran along after them waving, but they soon lost sight of him.

At Himeji they finally managed to get inside the car, and at Okayama Toshiko got a seat. By the time they reached Fukuyama at 14:13, H had been standing, squeezed in a swaying mass of bodies, for a good five hours, and he was tired.

Changing to the Fukuen line at Fukuyama, they arrived at Yokoo to find H's Uncle Yoshio and sister Yoshiko waiting at the ticket barrier. With a loud cry of "Hajime!" Yoshiko flung her arms around H and burst into tears.

"The same old crybaby as ever!" said H, but he was close to tears himself.

Though they claimed to have occasional air raid warnings even there, to H Fukuyama seemed as peaceful as ever, with no feeling of wartime urgency about it. Yoshiko too, with all the adults there—Grandma, Uncle Yoshio and Aunt Oiku—to make a fuss of her, seemed to be leading an easy and contented life.

Even so H felt uneasy as, standing in the garden of the single-story house in its idyllic setting, he surveyed his surroundings. Would he be content to lead a placid life in such a place? He wasn't at all sure, and it worried him.

The next day he took the train to Fukuyama and went to the Seishikan Middle School.

The school stood right next to Fukuyama Castle. It had originally been a domain school, founded to educate the children of samurai in the service of the Fukuyama *daimyo*, so it had a reputation in the area as one of the more distinguished prefectural middle schools.

As he went in through the school gates, the wooden main building was visible beyond the yard. It was quite old but, unlike Kobe Second Middle, the glass in its windows was not broken, and the wood-floored corridors were polished to a handsome shine.

Classes were over and silence prevailed inside the building. H was walking along a corridor, finding the silence somehow oppressive, when he heard the sharp cries of people practicing fencing and the fierce clash of wooden swords. There was a fencing club at Second Middle where H himself had practiced occasionally, but things here felt rather different. The peaceful atmosphere pervading the school as a whole, combined with the sharp sounds of *kendo* practice, conveyed a sense of moral rigor reminding you forcibly that this had, after all, been a samurai school.

Opening the door of the teachers' room, he declared in a loud voice: "Hajime Senoh, from Kobe Second Middle School. I was bombed out in Kobe, and have come to ask to be taken in as a third-grade student at the Seishikan Middle School!"

There were several teachers there, and they all looked at H with expressions of surprise. One of them came up to him and asked, "Your house was burned down by incendiaries, then? Tell me, can you really put out incendiaries with buckets of water? If it's possible, I wish you'd tell us how."

So even here, in this old castle town, they were beginning to feel the threat of air raids....

"It's true you can put out incendiaries with buckets of water provided there aren't too many of them," he replied. "Some neighborhood associations in Kobe managed it with bucket relays, but that was in districts where not many bombs fell. If a lot start falling, it's safer to get out rather than have ideas of putting them out."

"I see," said another teacher, who seemed to be the vice-principal. "I hope you'll talk to the other students about your experiences in the Kobe raids. I'm sure it would put you on good terms with them in no time."

At that moment H suddenly decided, without quite knowing why, that he'd give up the idea of switching to this school and go back to Kobe instead. He didn't understand the reason himself, but something told him that this school would be too "proper" for him ever to feel comfortable there. The feeling seemed to have been taking shape ever since he'd heard the cries and the clash of wooden swords as he was walking along the corridor; it was nothing that he could have explained plausibly to anybody else.

He excused himself somehow—he hadn't yet got together all the papers necessary for switching schools; he hadn't brought his seal with him; he'd come again another day—and got out of the room.

Leaving the school building and walking across the grounds, he felt appalled at what he was doing. Did he really intend to go back to Kobe and the raids? Even so, he still thought it would be better to follow his intuition.

The long and short of it was that H, much to everyone's astonishment, announced that he was returning to Kobe.

"You'll be killed if you go back, Hajime!" cried Yoshiko. "Don't go—stay here!"

Toshiko was vehemently opposed to the idea. "Go back?" she demanded. "How do you think you'd get a ticket? Are you going to *walk*?"

It would certainly be difficult to buy a ticket, and H was figuring out ways of getting over that difficulty.

There were two possibilities. One was to buy a local ticket not subject to controls, then get off at the other end and buy another one, progressing in short stages till he reached his destination. That would mean frequent waits for infrequent connections, and spending a night in a station waiting room, the whole journey taking at least two days. The other, more resourceful method was to write to Uncle Hadano and get him to cooperate. He would send H a telegram saying, "Received conscription papers stop return Kobe forthwith stop Father," and H could use it to obtain a certificate of need to travel.

H wrote a letter with this request and sent it by express mail. As he was buying the stamps and sticking them on the envelope at the post office counter, he said a silent prayer to his "Long-Nosed Goblin" uncle to help him.

He was determined to go back to Kobe, whatever anybody said.

During the few days that it took for a telegram to come from Uncle Hadano, he persuaded them to let him eat his fill of decent rice to fortify him for what was to come. They killed a chicken for him, too, and he feasted on such delights as chicken sukiyaki and *oyako domburi*.

Toshiko kept demanding how he was going to eat, going to Kobe all by himself, but H no longer paid much attention to his mother's views; their parent-child relationship had changed definitively on that night of the air raid.

H told neither his mother nor anybody else about his strategy for buying a long-distance ticket. He kept it a secret because he was sure that if his mother heard about the plan she would immediately take steps to frustrate it. At the very least, she would send an express letter back to Uncle Hadano. That was the kind of person she was.

Four days later a cable came from Kobe. Hearing the postman call "Telegram!" Toshiko looked as though she would collapse, thinking it must be a notice that her husband had been killed or injured in an air raid. H tried to tell her there was nothing to worry about, that it wasn't that kind of telegram, but she insisted on seeing the message for herself. Reading it, she was still more alarmed, since the message was exactly as H had dictated: "Received conscription papers stop return Kobe forthwith stop Father." Having assumed that her husband would never get his papers, she burst into tears with the shock.

"This cable's a lie," H hastily reassured her. "It's just a trick to buy a ticket." But it took considerably more than that to explain matters to his mother and Yoshiko and finally calm them down.

H then went to the station to buy a ticket, taking the cable with him. "There's only me to see my father off when he joins up," he pleaded with the station employee in the ticket office, showing him the cable and the certificate saying that he was a raid victim. "If I don't go back to Kobe immediately I shan't be in time." This got him a ticket to Kobe with surprising ease. His strategy had been a great success.

H was convinced that this had finally made him a dyed-in-the-wool sinner who could never enter the church again even if he went back to Kobe. He had already, in fact, written to Uncle Hadano asking to be given a room in his house.

His mother and Yoshiko saw him off tearfully as he boarded the train for Kobe.

On the way, not long after leaving Okayama, the train stopped. The signals were against it, apparently because there had been an air raid warning. It had been standing there for a while when there came a sound familiar to H: the engines of a carrier-based Grumman. He looked out of the window, but though the noise continued he could see nothing of the plane itself. The noise swelled, then passed just overhead, but much to his relief there was no strafing. "I was worried," said a man sitting next to H in a thick country accent. "I heard of a train being machine-gunned a couple of days ago."

The train stopped again in the vicinity of Akashi, not far from Kobe, but again they were spared a strafing.

Alighting at Suma Station, H took a streetcar and got off in front of the fire station. His father, who was putting hoses out to dry, looked astonished when he saw H. Unable to find any way of explaining his return, H simply said, "I've come back after all." With equal simplicity his father nodded and said gently, "I see."

Then, after a moment, his father surprised him by saying, "I'll soon be finishing work, so will you wait for me? I'd like to go to the photographer's and have a photo taken of us standing side by side. I want to send one to your mother and Yoshiko—all right?"

H sensed vaguely what was in his father's mind. In silence they walked to the photo studio in the road leading to the Sumadera Temple. The photo, it occurred to H, might well be the last one they'd ever have taken....

When they left the studio the sky to the west was red with the sunset. H went back to the church with his father to inform them of his return to Kobe. He also told them that he was going to stay with Uncle Hadano.

There was something that still worried him, though: he'd decided, purely to suit himself, that he was going to live at Uncle Hadano's place, but he still didn't know whether the man would have him or not.

Not wanting to go to Uncle Hadano's place of work, he decided to go to his house instead and wait for him to come home. He sat down on the stone steps in front of the house to wait, and was still there after dark when Uncle Hadano came back on his bicycle.

Almost as though he'd known H would come that day, he showed no sign of surprise, simply remarking "You must be hungry" as he took the bike under his arm and unlocked the front door to let H in.

Saved, thought H. But the question of how to explain things when he went to school the next day still bothered him. He hardly thought they'd accept him back without a murmur as his father and Uncle Hadano had done.

36

School Factory

H's sudden reappearance at Second Middle went more smoothly than he'd feared.

When Mr. Matsumoto, the head teacher of his grade, met him in the teachers' room, he smiled and said, "Well—back again? I'm afraid you'll find there aren't many classes, though, because third-grade students too have to work in the factory now. Do you still prefer Second Middle, even so?"

"Yes, I still like it better here," said H. It was true there were teachers he found unpleasant and seniors he couldn't respect, but he honestly thought, flattery apart, that it was a good school.

"Right," said Mr. Matsumoto. "Then I'll send Seishikan Middle a letter of apology from us. Actually, there's one other student, too, who's come back in the same way as you."

Feeling much easier, H left the teachers' room and was running up the steps when he encountered Ogura, Nishi and Uchida coming the other way. The three of them were known as the "Yumeno Three," because they all lived close to each other in the Yumeno district.

"Oh-oh! You've come back, have you?" exclaimed Ogura, his white teeth flashing in a smile.

"Some people *want* to come back and get themselves killed," teased Nishi.

"The school's turned into a factory while you were away," said Uchida. "Shall we take you on a tour of the works?"

The school had indeed begun to look like a real factory, with machinery in the assembly hall and several of the classrooms.

The fourth-grade students, who until now had been going to work at the Mitsubishi Electric plant in Wadamisaki, had stopped going there and were working at the school's machines instead, so the place was livelier than before.

The products being turned out at the school, H was told, were "motors used in raising the periscopes on special submarines." He was also told that this was a "military secret" and not to be mentioned to outsiders.

For H, though, the "military secret" bit didn't ring quite true. At least sixty-odd of the small motors, some twenty-five centimeters in diameter, were being assembled every day at Second Middle alone. It seemed highly unlikely, to say the least, that an equal number of "special submarines" were being turned out daily.

One of the fifth-grade students was openly skeptical about the talk of submarines.

"I know, because I was doing electrical fittings for submarines at the shipbuilding yards," he said. "There's no way they could make sixty special subs every day. To my mind, it's impossible. So those mini-motors aren't for raising periscopes; they want students to believe they're making such things, and that it's a military secret, just to raise their morale—it's just a management strategy, if you ask me!"

This only strengthened H's own suspicions when he heard it.

From the spring of 1945 H and the other third-graders were to be incorporated into the school factory work force.

This was divided into a large number of separate squads, whose chief assignments were engine lathe work, motor assembly, spring manufacturing and processing, and insulator production. H was put in one of the squads assembling motors. Each group was made up of three students, and was supposed to compete with the others in seeing who could produce most.

H's squad consisted of himself, Joji ("George") Fujita and Heizo Hirobe. Fujita was in fact H's senior by one year, but he'd been off school for a year and had joined the same class as H in third grade.

Sensing a kindred spirit, H soon made friends with this Fujita, who had an indefinably brash quality that set him apart from the others. His nickname of "English"—cumbersome for a nickname when translated into *Ingurisshu*—derived from the fact that his mother had, according to rumor, been an Englishwoman, and that Fujita himself could speak English as well as he spoke Japanese. H marveled at the way he calmly used English when everybody around him regarded it as an "enemy language."

They were soon on close enough terms for H to call him "George." Although he couldn't speak English like George, the two of them had several things in common. One was that, though their mothers were both Christians, the sons were both unabashed atheists.

The other member of their squad, Heizo Hirobe, was usually known as "Heichan." His father was a craftsman who carved *ramma*, the decorative openwork panels fitted over the doors in the best rooms of traditional Japanese houses. Heichan, as might have been expected, was clever with his hands and good at intricate work. He was a rather serious boy, with none of the self-consciously rebellious spirit of George and H, but he entered easily into a friendship with the other two boys in his squad.

Since all three of them were good with their hands, they set out to make at least three motors a day if possible—not from any newfound awareness of themselves as "warriors of industry" but purely from a desire to give themselves more free time.

Apparently the members of other squads too were privately planning to step up production, but this proved more difficult than it seemed since inspection of the assembled motors was very strict.

If the "mass production" was too successful, they only got their motors sent back with a cross, indicating "reject," chalked on them, so they had to be careful. The sticking point in the inspection was the precision with which the copper-wire coil was fitted into the motor. Since even the slightest error meant that the motor would not rotate properly, the strictness was necessary. Even so, those responsible for the checks, being students from the same year, were resented and referred to as "military police."

H and his workmates made a thorough study of how to fit the coils. Soon they were highly skilled workers where this process was concerned, turning out five motors a day with no trouble at all.

The two extra motors were not submitted for inspection that day, but treated as valuable "savings" and concealed by removing a board at the side of the dais in the assembly hall and putting them underneath it. The members of the other squads knew about this, but never betrayed them to the supervisor or helped themselves to their finished products.

There was in fact none of the competitiveness that the factory people had counted on. On the contrary, each squad produced precisely three motors a day, the secret lying in the fact that when one squad turned out a reject and got behind, another squad would let it have a finished motor of its own.

This was typical of a school that, ever since its founding in the Meiji era, had always had an unusual sense of comradeship.

Every three days the finished motors were loaded onto a large hand-cart and taken to the Mitsubishi Electric works. The student responsible was envied the perks of this job, which included the chance to idle on the way to the factory and the occasional windfall of bread from the factory workers' meals.

Sometimes, though, he was exposed to danger. On two occasions a student was the target of machine-gun strafing by a carrier-based plane, just as H had been. Recounting how he'd cleverly escaped being shot, Nemoto of the rugby club would proudly display the machine-gun bullet dangling at his chest. The tip of the bullet was flattened, and the base had been drilled so that a cord could be passed through it; he'd got a worker he was friendly with at the Mitsubishi factory to do it for him, he said.

H knew that the bullet from the Grumman that had chased him was probably still embedded in the concrete tank among the ruins, but had no inclination to go and get it, not wishing to be reminded of the horror of that occasion.

Apparently a woman had been killed in a similar strafing near Hyogo Station, but no mention of the incident was made in the papers, so it was known only to those who'd witnessed it.

Tomita, the student who prided himself on being a source of information, had made an analysis of these visitations by carried-based planes.

"The way they keep coming these days shows that enemy aircraft carriers are in the seas not far from Japan," he pronounced. "The point of the low-altitude flights by Grummans is reconnaissance; the strafing is just a bit of fun on the side. Almost certainly they're taking photos of targets still left in Kobe, so there'll be a big raid before long, you'll see!"

H tended to agree with him. He'd had a feeling for some time that it wouldn't be long before Kobe was completely reduced to rubble. He'd asked himself whether there was anything he wanted to do before Kobe disappeared, and was dismayed to find that all he could think of was "seeing a movie."

But then, perhaps it wasn't really *so* strange.... To eat as much as you liked and to go to see a movie were the two greatest luxuries imaginable at that particular time.

The chance to manifest these desires was to come unexpectedly soon.

The school informed them that a special grant was to be given to students who'd been bombed out, and that such students were to come to the office bringing their seals.

The amount of the allowance was ten yen. H was delighted: with ten yen you could go ten times to see a movie at a top first-run movie house.

He decided he wouldn't tell either his father or Uncle Hadano about the money. He was elated at his unaccustomed—for those days—affluence.

On his way home from school, among the ruins at the Nagata crossing, he saw an elderly man sitting by the roadside selling books.

Stopping to have a look, he found quite a few volumes of the Iwanami series, the same ones that had flitted off like white butterflies from the ruins of his home.

"It's dangerous to sit here," he told the old man. "You'll make a target for strafing."

"That's why I want to get rid of them as soon as possible," the other replied. "Why don't you buy some?—you can have them cheap. We're moving out to the country, so I'm getting rid of things we shan't be taking." H was delighted, and decided to knock him down as far as possible. One-star volumes in the Iwanami series were twenty sen each, so Maupassant's *Une Vie*, in three volumes, would be sixty. Gide's *La Porte Etroite*, a two-star volume, was forty sen. Stendhal's *Le Rouge et le Noir*, a four-star book, was a full eighty sen.

"Will you let me have ten volumes for one yen?" he pressed. "If so, it's a deal."

"Right!" said the old man, agreeing with surprising readiness. H chose ten volumes, telling himself that this time he'd bury them some-

372

where where they wouldn't get burned. He'd no idea when the war was going to end, but when it did, he'd dig them up and read them at his leisure.

Myojin-cho, where H was now living, lay at the foot of the hills further up the Myohoji River from Itayado, and a huge cave shelter had been carved out of the hillside bordering the built-up area. On the other side of the river there was a makeshift office and laborers' quarters for carrying out more work of the same kind, so it seemed they were planning to build still more cave shelters in the neighborhood. Uncle Hadano had told him there was actually a plan to move factories into the caves.

The residents of Myojin-cho had official permission to use the nearest of the huge shelters, so H decided he would bury his books there. This time he carefully piled earth on the wooden box in which he'd put them.

The books safely buried, the next thing was the movie. Movie-going, though, entailed considerable risk, though of a different kind from machine-gun strafing.

The entertainment quarter in Shinkaichi had been completely destroyed, and the only theaters within range were three that had survived in the Taisho-suji district. They were showing movies as usual, but the area was one where the Guidance League's eagle eye was omnipresent. Since very few movie theaters remained intact, the scope of the league's net was restricted and its focus correspondingly concentrated. The chances of getting caught were greater than before, so you needed the reaction-time of a ninja to make your escape.

Several students of Second Middle had been caught, confined to their homes, and suspended from classes. The punishment was particularly stiff in that they had taken sick leave from factory work in order to go to the movies.

H asked George to go with him. He refrained from tempting Hirobe, who was too serious for such escapades.

When H offered to pay for both of them, George was immediately all for it. The movie house they chose was the Takatori-kan, to the west of the Takatori market. Standing apart from the main amusement quarter, it was a seedy establishment showing films that—as in most other local theaters—were two years past their release date. H felt at home there, though; this was where he'd seen Chiezo Kataoka in *Miyamoto Musashi* and Enoken's *Isshin Tasuke*.

When he'd seen *Miyamoto Musashi*, the celluloid had been so worn that the screen looked as if it were in a snowstorm, and the showing was frequently interrupted when the film broke. H put up with it, though, because admission was only half that at other movie houses.

On his way to school H made a detour in order to find out what was showing at the Takatori-kan. It was *Muhomatsu no Issho*, a film he'd wanted to see for some time.

H knew the plot of the film well, having read the advertisements and reviews when it had been shown two years previously.

The setting was Kyushu in the Meiji era. A man known as Muhomatsu, a rickshaw driver, becomes friendly with an army man and his family. The officer, however, falls ill and dies, leaving a wife and a son. Muhomatsu is, in fact, in love with the wife, but after the officer's death he looks after her and the boy without ever confessing his true feelings.

Arriving at school, H told George he'd decided on *Muhomatsu no Issho*. "Let's slip out tomorrow at lunchtime," he said. "We can ask Hei-chan to cover for us by getting some of the 'savings' out." The "savings," of course, were the already-finished motors that they'd stashed away.

At lunchtime the following day they climbed over the fence at the west end of the sports ground and started running in the direction of Nagata.

"People will notice us if we run," said George. Right as usual, thought H, and slowed to a walk. Wherever possible they wove their way through burned-out districts, since there was less danger there of meeting some-one who knew them by sight than in one of the surviving districts.

"Don't they have to stop the movie if an alert sounds?" George asked anxiously, but H reassured him. Strictly speaking, regulations said that they must stop screening within thirty minutes following an alert, but more often than not nowadays an alert was followed immediately by the all-clear, so they went right on with the show, taking care not to be caught by the police, until an actual air raid warning sounded.

About forty minutes' walk brought them to the Takatori-kan in Kaiun-cho 2-chome. Admission was forty sen.

The theater was only two blocks away from Honjo-cho 3-chome, where the church stood, and there were lots of people who knew H by sight in the neighborhood, so he kept a fairly sharp lookout.

Muhomatsu no Issho was already about halfway through, but the story wasn't difficult enough to be incomprehensible on that account, so they went on in.

"It stinks!" muttered George as soon as they got inside.

"It's cheap, so don't complain!" H whispered back, though he thought it smelled too. It was, certainly, a dump compared with the Shuraku-kan and Shochiku-za in Shinkaichi, but in a sense anywhere you could get to see a movie was like a palace nowadays.

Dragging an unwilling George with him, H advanced to the front seats nearest the toilet. The view wasn't good so close to the screen, but the seats were safe compared with those in the center and rear. Nearer the exit, you could easily get caught by the Guidance League; here, if you smelled danger, you could always nip into the toilet, lock the door, then make your escape via the window. H explained this to George in a low voice, but though his friend nodded, his eyes, disturbingly, remained fixed on the screen.

Besides watching the screen, it was necessary to take an occasional furtive glance at the seats behind them to check for anyone who looked like a Guidance League member.

To keep a simultaneous eye on both the screen and the back of the place was tiring, and didn't do much for concentration or appreciation, but H was thrilled just by the idea of being at the movies.

On the screen Tsumasaburo Bando, in the leading role of Muhomatsu, was beating a drum. Keiko Sonoi, the actress who played the widow of the army officer, was beautiful. H found himself wishing that, in the same way as the boy in the movie, he had an older man like Muhomatsu, an admirer of his mother's, whom he could rely on. But then it suddenly occurred to him that in fact he did: his own Muhomatsu was Uncle Hadano.

The thought produced a thrill of emotion—it might really be the case. There was evidence to suppose so. Mr. Hadano had once lodged with them, before H was born—that was all—yet ever since then he and the family had remained closer than ordinary relatives. He'd kept a constant eye on H's family, not just when it was in difficulties but at all times. It didn't seem quite normal, and H had the feeling that even now

Uncle Hadano's fondness for him resembled Muhomatsu's relationship with the boy in the movie.

But there was one big difference: the wife of the major, with whom Muhomatsu was apparently secretly in love, was a stunning beauty, not the least bit like H's mother; nor, for that matter, was his mother the kind of woman men fell for in the first place. Mentally he apologized to Mr. Hadano for even entertaining such a notion.

Dwelling idly on such things as he watched the movie, H had relaxed the watch he was keeping on the back seats, but suddenly he sensed something wrong: there were two men at the back who seemed to be looking around at the other patrons instead of watching the film.

"Let's go!" he hissed at George, grabbing his arm. Keeping as low as possible he quietly opened the door to the toilet. Then, pushing George into one of the cubicles, he dashed into the one next door and slid the wooden bolt to lock it. "Get out through the window!" he called, then himself took hold of the edge of the window frame and clambered up. The window was small and high, so it was more difficult than he'd thought. Looking down as he thrust himself through the window with the intention of jumping, he found it was unexpectedly far. George had got himself halfway out of his window but now he too was stuck.

Giving up the idea of jumping from the position he was in, which would mean landing on his head, H decided to get back inside and go through the window feet first. George had apparently had the same idea, for he too disappeared back inside.

H was on tenterhooks, expecting a bang on the door behind him at any moment.

He finally got his lower half outside, but it was still not possible to jump unless he got a bit further out. George too was wriggling desperately in the next window. Finally H steeled himself, let go his grip, and jumped.

He landed safely enough, but slipped and fell. George landed and slithered in the same way. The spot was right next to the outlets where the "honey-bucket" men came to take away the accumulated waste, and the ground all around was, not surprisingly, filthy.

Both boys, besides plumping down heavily on their backsides, had got their hands all sticky into the bargain.

"Hell! What a stink! Out of the shit and into it, too." There had been no intentional pun, but it was so apt that they laughed even as they screwed up their faces in disgust.

All the while H couldn't help wondering just who the people had been who'd slipped into the theater behind them.

Bending forward, the seats of their trousers still smeared with shit, they walked along, keeping close to the movie house, and peered out from the alleyway into the main street. A truck was parked in front, and a string of people were being brought out and shoved into the back. The two men hadn't been from the Guidance League, then, but from the still more ominous "Emergency Labor Enlistment Squad." The "enlistment" was a euphemism, for in fact it was press-ganging. If they'd been caught the school would of course have been informed, and they themselves would have been carried off forcibly to a "compulsory evacuation" site and set to work knocking down houses. Nor would it have been possible to complain or refuse to go with them, since anybody happily watching a movie at such a time of national crisis was considered to be free from the pressures of work and with plenty of time to spare.

"Safely out of the shit!" H said to George. They'd been lucky—lucky enough to make the pun possible even though they were still covered with the stuff. A neighbor had once told H that he'd been forcibly removed while watching a movie and taken to the police station, and today's experience had borne out the story.

H was more relieved at not being caught than he'd been at escaping the machine-gun strafing. As to why the experience should be more frightening even than the threat of imminent death, it was probably, he reflected, because being loaded forcibly onto a truck and taken to the police station felt somehow even more unfair and insulting to the intelligence.

They lay low in the alleyway until the truck had started and moved out of sight. Finally they were safe. Immediately, the smell clinging to their persons became intolerable.

George was quite angry, glaring at H with eyes that said "It was all *your* fault!"

The only thing they could do was go in search of a tap where they could wash themselves. H had the idea of going to the Takatori market, which wasn't far away. Somewhere at the rear of the market there ought to be a hydrant.

Walking on warily in their miserable state, they eventually found a tap outside the back of the market.

Hurrying to turn on the water, they washed their hands and then took off their pants. Water alone wouldn't get the shit off however hard they ran it, so they scraped at it with bits of wood they found on the ground.

H helped George with his, but his friend continued to be so bad-tempered that H finally got irritated in turn and said with some force, "Think yourself lucky you weren't taken to the police station, and quit grumbling!"

Before long the water splashing over them had a calming effect and they could begin to smile again.

The tap, they figured, must be there because it was at the back entrance of a fish shop. A board from a box marked "fish" had in fact been used to repair damage to the wooden wall of the house.

Just at that moment the back door opened. A woman looked out and let out a squawk at the sight of two boys naked from the waist down.

The two friends were equally startled. Leaping up, H and George clamped both hands modestly over their crotches.

37

Prisoner of War

On one memorable occasion, the third- and fourth-grade students working in the school factory were given a special issue of two bread rolls each by the Mitsubishi Electric works.

The six boys who went to the factory to pick up the rolls were fourth-grade students, one year senior to H and his friends, and a rumor got about that fifty rolls had vanished into thin air as they were bringing them back to the school.

H and his classmates had no idea that such an incident had occurred, since they themselves had each been handed the two rolls promised them, and they were puzzled when they heard about it three days later.

In short, the factory had informed the school that there would be six hundred rolls, and if the number had been as many as fifty short there would naturally have been a big fuss that same day. But there hadn't been, so how could fifty of them possibly have disappeared? It was a strange business and shrouded in mystery.

They could hardly ask their seniors directly just what had happened, but neither could they be indifferent to a rumor that "rolls seemed to have disappeared on the way."

Then, however, Okubo came along excitedly bearing a piece of information that couldn't be dismissed lightly. "I've found out!" he declared. "The fourth-graders who went to get the rolls ate them on the way. Someone at the works said he'd seen them at it!"

"Are you sure? If it's a false report, you'll be in for it!"

"I'm sure it's not false," said Okubo positively. "I got it direct from one of the factory hands. He said he'd seen them from a window going along the road pulling the cart and munching the rolls as they went. It's no mistake—I even got their names!"

Among the six names was that of Yoshioka, a member of the rifle club. H was surprised, but at the same time felt a new respect for him. It rather tickled him that Yoshioka had been shameless enough to wolf down the rolls so openly, even though he knew that he'd be found out, the number they were to fetch being fixed in advance.

In time the outlines of the affair became clearer. It had all started when the factory had mistakenly given them seven hundred rolls, a hundred more than they were supposed to get. Realizing with delight what had happened, the six of them had devoured half the extra rolls on the way back. The fact that they'd left half the surplus untouched was later to prove a piece of good fortune.

The truth had first come to light with a call from the factory. "We made a mistake and gave them a hundred rolls too many," they said. "Please share them out as you think best among your people."

Oddly enough, the students who'd diverted the extra rolls—which would normally have got them a week's suspension from classes at the very least—were not so much as told off. The "Case of the Missing Rolls" was allowed to pass into oblivion without further fuss—the reason being, it seemed, that when the mistake first came to light the teachers had already divided up the remaining fifty among themselves, so that they too had unwittingly become accomplices to the crime.

The whole affair caused much hilarity. Even its teachers, it was felt, did honor to the true traditions of Second Middle....

A consensus was reached that from now on all credit went to anyone who could get extra rolls out of the factory; and with that, the strange affair came to an end without having harmed a soul.

A couple of weeks later a date for another issue of rolls was announced.

Once again, it was fourth-grade students who were to go and fetch them, much to the envy of the third-graders. There were so many fourth-graders who wanted the job that they reportedly drew lots to decide who should go.

That afternoon H got a message from Instructor Hisakado telling him to come to the armory immediately.

He went, wondering what was up, and received a highly mystifying assignment.

"You are to go alone to Mitsubishi Electric at Wadamisaki, in full gear minus backpack and taking with you a 38 rifle. When you arrive you will enter via the west gate and go to see a manager called Tokita, to whom you will hand this letter. Then, when you have received the envelope containing the reply, you will join up with the fourth-grade students transporting the rolls and come back to the school. When you leave the factory you will fix your bayonet, and if anything untoward occurs on the way use it to intimidate the offender and protect the vehicle carrying the rolls and its attendants. Whoever asks, you are not to divulge the purpose of this mission. That's all."

H would have repeated what he was supposed to do but, feeling a little confused, ended up asking for a recap. Put simply, it seemed he was to dress up in full gear with rifle, go alone to the factory, hand over a letter and take care of the rolls on the way back. Since the purpose of the mission was secret, apparently, he was not to tell anybody about it—but there was no way he could have told them about something he wasn't clear about himself.

"Mr. Matsumoto and the manager at the factory have been told, but there's no need to tell the other students or teachers, all right? Okay!—off with you, then."

With which command, H left the school.

Just as he was about to cross the streetcar tracks at Goban-cho, an alert sounded. Anxiously he wondered what he should do if a Grumman appeared. If he was caught running through the ruins got up as he was, he'd quite certainly be mistaken for a soldier.

He'd had quite enough of providing a target for strafing planes. He was carrying a rifle, but the bullets in the ammunition pouch at his waist were dummies for practice use only, with no powder in them. Even if he were to fire at an enemy plane there'd be nothing but the click as the hammer fell—no bullet.

H decided that if he heard the drone of an enemy plane he'd dive out of sight into a ditch.

He wavered between trying to get to the factory before a full air raid warning sounded and playing safe by giving the factory a wide berth. But having heard that the factory had a fairly sturdy shelter, he decided to follow orders and get there as soon as possible.

As he hurried on he pondered the meaning of the order to use his rifle and bayonet to guard the cart carrying the rolls on their way back to the school. One possible answer to the riddle was that the unusual escort was intended as a silent warning to the students that, though the six responsible for the buns' disappearance last time hadn't been accused, if a similar situation arose again they wouldn't get away with it this time.

Or perhaps it was an intimidatory measure to discourage looting by residents of the neighborhood? Only a few days earlier there'd been an incident in which locals had surrounded a cart carrying pieces of wood from a house that had been knocked down to make a firebreak, and had made off with posts and planks. The reason why the cart—also, as it happened, being drawn by Second Middle students—had been targeted was that rations of fuel such as charcoal and firewood were dwindling. That incident, too, had apparently been dealt with privately in talks between the head of the neighborhood association and the school, without calling in the police.

So the role assigned to H that day might well be to forestall any more such incidents. Whatever the case, though, it was a heavy responsibility, and he didn't feel happy about it.

Arriving at the factory he reported at the west gate guardhouse that he'd come to see a manager called Mr. Tokita. There were two guards there, both of them far older than H's father.

"Come inside and wait," said one of them, getting on a bicycle to go and fetch Mr. Tokita. While he waited, H asked to be allowed a brief look inside the factory grounds.

Inside, all was silent, unlike the last time he'd been there. He felt uncomfortable: there was an ominous feeling, almost as though the factory had died. He asked the guard the reason for the hush. "It's a power failure," he was told. "The machines aren't working."

But then, as H was wandering around, the sirens suddenly blared an air raid warning. There were sounds of urgent movement inside the factory, and people came spilling out of the buildings and scattered in all directions, probably to take up their firewatching stations.

H could barely keep still, imagining himself being blown to pieces here in this factory. It was the first time an air raid warning had frightened him so badly.

He felt sure that the factory district he was in was the target of today's raid. It was strange that it should have been spared in the last raid, on March 17, and the enemy would almost certainly be wanting to make quite sure this time.

The sound of the enemy aircraft was instantly recognizable to H as that of carrier-based planes.

The thunder of a fierce barrage came from the anti-aircraft guns on Karumo Island, which was adjacent to Wadamisaki.

He looked up, but all he could see from where he was standing with factory buildings on both sides of him was a narrow strip of sky that gave no real picture of what was happening up there.

"There's a big shelter directly ahead on the right," the guard told him. H thanked him, but declined to go; he didn't want to go too far inside the factory.

Getting half inside an open dugout next to the guardhouse, he watched the rectangular strip of sky above. He was getting rather impatient at Mr. Tokita's non-appearance.

He heard voices outside the gate shouting, "A hit! Got him, got him!" and "Ah, he's coming down!" but could see nothing from where he was. Then he heard someone say, "His parachute's opened."

It seemed that an enemy plane had been shot down and the pilot had bailed out. H wanted to leap out and have a look, but made himself stay put, since Mr. Tokita should be there any moment.

A military police sergeant, presumably one of the MPs stationed in the factory, rushed past directly in front of him. He glanced at H, but H, who had always disliked the military police, kept his head bent, avoiding his gaze.

Eventually the manager turned up, riding pillion behind the guard who'd gone on his bike to fetch him. He apologized politely to H for keeping him waiting.

H handed over the letter that Instructor Hisakado had given him. Tokita opened it immediately and started to read, but just then the same MP came running back, seemingly in a panic, and stopped in front of H.

What he said was so unbelievable that H doubted his own ears. Irritably, the MP repeated it:

"I am proceeding to take into custody a member of the enemy forces. You are ordered to accompany me in the operation!"

" 'Ordered'?—but I'm a student, a pupil at Second Middle," H mumbled.

"What do you mean, 'pupil,' you bastard!" screamed the MP. "Are you disobeying an army order to go and capture an enemy airman? You've got a gun, haven't you? Are you scared to fight like a *real* soldier?"

H decided he'd better do as he was told, though he also felt like saying he could hear perfectly well without being yelled at. He didn't fancy the latest turn of events at all, but resigned himself to the inevitable.

With a brief bow to Mr. Tokita, he followed the MP out of the gate. Noticing that the sergeant seemed to be armed with nothing more than a shovel, he gradually realized what he was going to be made to do.

The road between Mitsubishi Electric and the Mitsubishi Shipbuilding yard extended along the railway sidings as far as the sea, and then continued right out along the wharf where the ships came in.

At the far end of the wharf an American airman was to be seen trying to extricate himself from his parachute. It was still half open, and he seemed to be in danger of being dragged into the sea by the breeze.

The man was being watched with open curiosity by a number of workers from Mitsubishi Electric and the shipyard, who were standing silently along the walls on both sides, scared perhaps at being confronted in the flesh with a specimen of what they'd always known as "American and British Fiends." They were pressed flat against the walls, probably to avoid the bullets that might fly if there were a shootout.

H envied these spectators lined up on both sides: he was sure they'd witnessed everything—the moment when the Grumman was hit and began to fall, the airman's escape from the plunging aircraft, the opening and descent of the parachute, even the landing at the end of the wharf.

Wishing he'd seen the parachute open and come drifting slowly down, H keenly regretted having got into the dugout by the guardhouse to wait for Mr. Tokita.

With his rifle at the ready, he slowly approached the American airman, together with the sergeant. The former was squatting, hauling in the cords of his parachute. His hands stopped moving and he looked in their direction. He was younger than H had expected.

When they were about thirty meters away, the sergeant suddenly gave the order, "Load—*gun!*" His voice came out strangely, somewhere between an order and a shriek of distress.

"That's all very well," H felt like saying, "but these are *dummies*— you won't get any bullets out of these!" He kept quiet, though, and clattered busily with the bolt, then adopted an appropriately menacing stance as though he'd loaded the gun.

Startled by the metallic sound of the rifle apparently being loaded, the airman got to his feet. He was tall and well built, but the blue eyes that watched their movements flickered uneasily.

The sergeant seemed equally uneasy. The start he gave when the enemy suddenly moved was quite apparent to H, standing at his side. By then, though, H himself had lost any sense of fear.

The one thing that bothered him was that the airman might have a gun concealed somewhere on him.

Since American servicemen lacked the psychology that enabled their Japanese counterparts to kill the enemy and then kill themselves, there seemed little likelihood under the present circumstances that he would draw a pistol and fight. H tried, even so, to look as intimidating as possible—though, since the other must have seen at a glance that H was only a boy and that the little Japanese soldier was armed only with a shovel, he still obviously felt a bit tense.

H dithered, wondering how to say "Put your hands up!" in English. So he ventured "Hand up!" and the man promptly raised his hands.

Relieved, H barely stopped himself from saying "Thank you."

It seemed incredible—almost like something in a movie—that he should be face to face like this with the enemy. Another thing he found hard to believe was that this young foreigner standing with arms raised and a frightened expression was a member of the American forces they were fighting and had been piloting a Grumman.

Whether this was the same man who had chased him around the streets or who had killed a woman near Hyogo Station, he would never know, but H marveled at the very idea that a man like this should strafe people with a machine gun.

Confronted with a rifle pointed directly at him, the airman was shrinking in fear that he was about to be shot.

The sergeant too had looked scared at first, probably never having dreamed that he'd be thrust into a sudden confrontation with an enemy pilot. Once the latter had put his hands up, however, he suddenly recovered his spirits.

"Shove the bayonet a bit closer!" he ordered in a lordly voice. H's heart was pounding: he'd been trained in rifle drill to stab straw-bale "enemies" with his bayonet, but he'd never brought it up against a living human being.

The sergeant went around behind the American and, extending a timid hand, began a body search. This produced nothing from the top half of his clothing, but the airman's half-boots, the last place to be searched, yielded a handgun.

H wanted to know what kind of gun it was, but the sergeant put it away in the pocket of his own jacket before H could see it.

"Right! Let's take him away!" said the sergeant. With his bayonet still at the ready, H moved behind the man and said "Go away!" wishing at the same time that he'd studied English a bit harder.

He tried to feel heroic at having just captured an American pilot but, oddly, the appropriate feelings of enmity refused to come. He tried telling himself that this was one of the men who'd burned down his own home, but still the hatred refused to rise up in him. He was puzzled, almost saddened by his own inability, in his heart of hearts, to think of them as "American and British fiends."

It occurred to him suddenly that any hatred he felt was less toward the American they'd taken prisoner than toward the MP who was walking with him. The thought was unnerving.

"Is the gun's safety catch on all right?" he asked the sergeant as they walked along. "You don't want it to go off in your pocket. Mightn't it be better to get it out and train it on him?"

He'd expected that this would make the sergeant get the gun out—which would also give him a chance to see it. But the sergeant merely said in a threatening voice, "You won't catch me using a weapon confiscated from the enemy!" This convinced H that the man really was stupid. Most likely he didn't actually know how to check the safety catch or operate the gun, and wanted to keep the fact from H.

Under the watchful gaze of the factory hands, the sergeant marched proudly on behind the American pilot, who still had his hands raised.

H, who knew how the sergeant had been quivering with fear a few minutes earlier, was disgusted.

They had reached a point halfway from the wharf to the gates when a motorbike with a sidecar came up and stopped beside them. The driver was a private first class and the man in the sidecar an MP second lieutenant.

Getting out, the lieutenant immediately handcuffed the prisoner and put him in the sidecar.

He turned to H. "What school are you at?" he asked. When H told him, he said abruptly, "You are to forget everything you saw and did today."

"But …," H objected, startled. "But everybody else here saw it too."

"This is a matter of military secrecy," the man went on, "so you are forbidden to talk to people about it."

H was appalled. He might at least have been given a word of thanks for cooperating in the arrest, but to be told to forget it! He felt anger rising up from somewhere deep inside him.

"Military secret"—what a lot of crap! Why, the present exchange, even, was being witnessed by a whole crowd of factory workers. What "military secret" was there in it? "Forget everything," indeed! He felt a great loathing for the *kempei*.

The plainclothes detectives who'd hauled his father off to the police station, the MPs in uniform who put on such arrogant airs, the staff officers at Imperial Headquarters who were responsible for strategy—never once had any of them helped or supported H or any of his acquaintances in any way.

As he detached the bayonet from his rifle and put it back in its sheath, he felt like shouting at the top of his voice, "The enemy for me's not so much America or Britain—it's the Japanese army, the military police, and the special police!"

He went back to the factory and asked the guards if they had any message for him from manager Tokita.

"Wait a moment," one of them said, and went off on his bike toward the rear of the works. The one who was left said to H, "Seems they downed two Grummans today. Only a few came and they didn't drop any bombs or incendiaries either. I wonder what was up with them?"

After a while the guard with the bike came back with a message and a letter from Mr. Tokita. The message was to say that the Second Middle students who'd been given the bread rolls had left via the east gate some while ago, but that H would catch up with them if he ran.

Why had they gone off without their escort, H wondered, bewildered. What had he come for in the first place?

Feeling somehow let down, he gave up the idea of chasing after them. The senior students, who were now presumably walking back along the road to the school with their cartload of rolls, were probably unaware that H had been to the factory on a strange, secret mission to escort the rolls. H himself had absolutely no idea what was behind it, or what was in the letters.

Back at the school he handed Instructor Hisakado the letter from manager Tokita, and was about to give him an account of what had happened when the other interrupted him. "MP headquarters called a while ago and told me," he said. "Do as they say and don't tell anybody." H felt he couldn't believe anybody anymore, not even Instructor Hisakado, who seemed to say the same things as the military police.

The way everything became a "military secret" made him really mad. If there was anything to keep secret, surely it was the disgrace incurred by the military police in being unable to apprehend an enemy airman without enlisting the aid of a middle school student. The desire to keep that quiet was probably what had inspired the order to "forget everything he'd seen and done."

Rarely, he thought in disgust, had he had a day so filled with absurdities of every kind.

38

Germany Surrenders

Germany had finally announced its unconditional surrender.

There'd been signs of what was going to happen: headlines in the newspapers on May 4 had announced "Berlin Falls"; "Chancellor Hitler Killed in Action"; "Propaganda Minister Goebbels Kills Self."

Hot on their heels came the report on the front page of the May 9 issue: "At dawn on May 7, all German armed forces surrendered unconditionally. The European war is finally at an end."

His eyes on the words, H muttered to himself several times over, "So even Germany lost in the end...."

Five years earlier, when the Tripartite Alliance had first been formed, they'd said, if he remembered correctly, "Thus is completed an alliance with walls of impenetrable steel."

He'd been shocked enough when the first of the allies, Italy, had surrendered, but now the supposedly invincible German forces had also surrendered unconditionally....

From now on Japan, the only one left, would have to fight the combined forces of the allies. H wondered what would happen. The answer he came up with was that America, with the war in Europe over, would divert the forces thus freed to Japan, redoubling the strength of its attacks. There was no way, surely, for Japan to win.

Even the people who'd once declared that Japan, the "Land of the Gods," was indestructible and that the "Yamato spirit" would ensure victory in every case, must be gradually losing their conviction. How could they still go on asserting their faith in victory? To anyone living in a city that lay in ruins, the truth, however unpalatable, must be apparent.

Apparent—but not to be given voice to. Not only did people fear the military police and the special police; they were afraid, too, that to tell the truth would at the same time destroy them by removing the props that had so long supported them. For all their brave talk in the past, the grownups were weaklings who shut their eyes to reality.

He wondered what had happened to the Berlin he knew from photos he'd seen in the past.

The Japanese newspapers had dismissed even the March raids on Kobe in two or three lines: "A considerable number of fires were started within the city as a result of bombing by a force of approximately sixty B29s, but they were almost all brought under control by 10:00 A.M." So he hardly expected them to report in detail on Berlin.

But—surprise, surprise!—there it was, in the *Asahi Shimbun*: an eye-witness report by a foreigner, a dispatch from Stockholm by a Reuters correspondent called Harold King. Eagerly, H started to read: "The capital Berlin is no more. This reporter ..."

As H read, the images of destruction overlapped in his mind with those of burned-out Kobe. "*We* know what war's like," he remarked to himself, "without going all the way to Berlin."

Why couldn't Japanese newspapers report what the city was like in the same way, in concrete, easily understandable language? *A considerable number of fires were started within the city, but ...* To hell with their "buts," he thought angrily. They seemed to be trying, with the greatest thoroughness, to suppress anything that might be inconvenient for them. Yet the more they suppressed it, the more transparent it became.

To the left of the account by the Reuters correspondent, there was another piece: "Students applying for entry to the Army Officers' School need no longer submit photographs and reports on their families." Already, candidates for admission to the school needed only to be between twelve and fourteen, and now, it seemed, the army was trying to make it still easier to apply. Things like this clearly showed just how desperate the shortage of troops was.

At H's school more than a dozen third-grade students had already left to become naval cadets, and those who remained were engaged in work in the factories just like regular factory hands. The only times they could in any way feel like "students" was in the alternate weeks when the "work squads" and "study squads" changed places.

Running down the steps after finishing work at the machines, H met Hirobe coming the other way. Several days earlier his friend had been switched from the same motor-assembly squad as H to the coil-making squad, and H hadn't seen him for four or five days. H wondered whether he was dissatisfied with his new workplace, since he looked a little down.

"What, your squad's still got to work?" H asked. Hirobe shook his head. "No—Watanabe hurt his eye, and I've just been taking him to the hospital," he said.

There'd been an accident in the school factory that morning, according to Hirobe.

"They were just telling us how the coils are made. About five of us third-grade students and the fourth-grader in charge were standing around the bench. 'This is how you cut it, so watch carefully,' the senior said. He put a chisel against a bit of wire and hit it with a hammer. Just then someone gave a yell. It was Watanabe. For a moment nobody knew what had happened, but it seems a chip had flown off the blade of the chisel and lodged in Watanabe's right eye. The senior and the rest of us took him to the Mitsubishi Electric clinic, and tomorrow they're going to operate to remove the sliver. The doctor said he may lose the sight of that eye."

They were always being warned to be careful about accidents at work in the school factory, but already one student had lost a finger in a lathe, and another had had a thumb crushed by the hammer used in cutting copper plates.

The heads of Mitsubishi Electric and Mitsubishi Heavy Industries both visited the school and inspected its factory, then discussed operations policy with the school authorities before leaving.

Although teachers and students would still sometimes laugh and talk in a carefree way, they were actually exhausted, as such accidents showed. It wasn't just the stress of the air raids—having to take shelter, for example, every time the air raid warning sounded; the worst thing was that no one knew what was going to happen to Japan from then on. By that time nobody put any trust in the words "Japan, the Land of the Gods, is invincible."

H himself was rather tense and bad-tempered these days. That same afternoon he was on the verge of an argument with a senior student in the school corridor when Yokota came dashing up and said, "Instructor Hisakado's got his papers!"

H had had a feeling that Hisakado would be going to the front before long, but the actual news produced a sense of disappointment and helplessness that reaffirmed just what a source of strength this instructor had been for them.

"He got them after all," said Yokota. "I wonder why His Lechery didn't get *his*? I wish he had, instead...."

Being in charge of the rifle club, Hisakado naturally enjoyed the loyalty of the club's members; but he was popular among other students too, and several of them who'd got wind of the news had gone to see him. The reason for the affection he was held in was that, unlike most military officers, he didn't spout idealistic phrases such as "the warrior spirit," "the Yamato spirit," or "the indomitable will to fight."

As a military training instructor, he was of course strict in his methods. But the essence of what he taught was that the true warrior was not someone who didn't fear death, but someone who possessed the skills necessary to protect himself to the very end. Without that skill, he said, no one could be truly "brave." His ideas were of the kind that were applicable not just in doing battle but in living ordinary day-to-day life, and as such they rang true. The logic and clarity of his thinking might well have had something to do with the fact that he had been a clock- and watchmaker in peacetime.

Even now he would cheerfully mend, for free, the broken clocks and watches that his students brought him. "Just occasionally you should clean it and give it some oil," he would say. Then he'd add, possibly as a dig at the idealism that prevailed at the time, "Clocks don't work on strength of spirit, you know!"

Only two days later the physics and chemistry teacher, Mr. Nakata, got his papers too.

H had lots of memories associated with this teacher as well, but temperamentally he and Mr. Nakata—whose nickname was "Youngster"—were poles apart.

Naturally enough, the other man also disliked H and his defiant ways, and there'd been a number of incidents that made even H himself feel he could understand his feelings. One of them concerned an examination when he'd been in second grade....

Since H made a point of handing over his answer sheet with nothing on it with teachers who often hit their pupils, that day too he'd simply written his name at the top and made to leave the classroom.

"No one is to leave the room until the examination is over," announced Mr. Nakata at that point. Unwillingly, H returned to his place and occupied the time by drawing a picture of his own left hand on the back of the answer sheet. That was what did it.

Mr. Nakata apparently took this as a deliberate challenge to himself. H hadn't intended it as such, and felt that the sketch of his hand had gone rather well. But to Mr. Nakata it was like a red rag to a bull: he flew into a violent rage. Quivering with anger and apparently out of control, he punched H on the jaw.

The "Youngster" nickname suited him all too well.

On the other hand, H had also submitted a blank answer sheet with a picture on the back to another teacher—Mr. Sumitani, who taught math. "Valjean," as Sumitani was known, simply took the paper and said with a smile, "No marks for the front, one hundred for the back."

Either way, H was no good at subjects like math, physics and chemistry. It wasn't that he hated all teachers who taught subjects he disliked; it depended on the teacher's personality.

H and the other students all liked Mr. Sumitani. They enjoyed his classes, during which he'd sometimes take a piece of chalk in each hand and demonstrate his skill at writing with two hands at once. When he was in a particularly good mood he would even declaim to them, in his best voice, passages from *Les Misérables*, the story of the Jean Valjean from whom his nickname derived.

Mr. Nakata himself must have known he wasn't as popular as Mr. Sumitani, so when H heard that his call-up papers had come, he decided to give him a farewell present, something that would convey the message that there'd been nothing personal involved, just an inability to get on together.

The present was a piece of thick card about the size of a namecard on which he'd drawn a likeness of Nakata himself, thoughtfully making him a little better-looking than he really was. As an extra bonus he got the students who'd been hit most often to inscribe their names on the back.

When he took it to the teachers' room and handed it over, Mr. Nakata looked perplexed for a moment. For a while his gaze went to and fro between the sketch and H's face; then suddenly he said, "Thank you—I'll take this with me wherever I go," and gripped H's hand. Embarrassed at the unexpected warmth of the grip, H left in some confusion.

The two teachers were leaving to join up on different days, but one farewell party was held for both. Late in the afternoon two days after that, a group of members of the rifle club went to Kobe Station to see Instructor Hisakado off. H, though, wasn't able to join them.

That morning his stomach was upset, and in the afternoon he began to have violent diarrhea. Trotting to and from the toilet, he ended up by soiling his pants. He would willingly have put a plug in himself if it meant being able to see Instructor Hisakado off, but finally, to his great annoyance, he had to give up the idea.

Thinking at least to send the instructor a note, he wrote one saying, "I regret very much not being able to see you off on account of diarrhea. Please take great care of yourself," and entrusted it to Yokota, only to have second thoughts: it didn't seem appropriate to talk of diarrhea to someone just leaving for the front. With a hand clutching his backside, he rushed in search of his friend and got the note back just in time.

The cause of the diarrhea was soybeans. At a time when foodstuffs were in such short supply, soybeans ranked second only to rice, so he didn't like to blame the beans themselves; it must have been the way he'd eaten them.

The beans were a precious windfall. They'd been brought home by his father, who'd been given a considerable quantity that had survived a warehouse fire he'd helped put out; so he shared them with Uncle Hadano, in whose house in Myojin-cho H was now living.

Uncle Hadano declined the offer for himself. "No thank you," he said. "Soybeans always upset my stomach." But H went off to the kitchen and toasted the beans in an earthenware pot, eating them instead of breakfast. He knew that to eat too many toasted beans was asking for trouble, but he was so hungry most of the time that he steadily crunched his way through them all, resigning himself to a certain amount of discomfort.

He'd been foolish, missing the chance to see off Instructor Hisakado for the sake of some toasted beans.

Back home, he was lying down with his hands pressed to his stomach when Uncle Hadano returned from the city hall. "You'll have to learn the right way to eat soybeans," he said with a smile, handing H a newspaper.

What H read there, though, was enough to make his diarrhea worse still.

A call for a "Final Battle on Imperial Soil" had been issued to all Japanese forces. What it said in essence was this: "Officers and men of the Imperial forces must prepare to defend the main islands to the death, throwing themselves into the fray with no concern for themselves, standing in the vanguard of their one hundred million compatriots." It was a clear admission that the only thing left to fight with was "spiritual strength."

H wondered where the spiritual strength was going to come from without anything to eat.

Everybody—not just H—was half-starved; diarrhea was commonplace.

Day after day came calls for "increased production." The school factory had stopped having days off; they worked at night, too, in shifts, and on days when there was no electricity they did all the work that was possible by hand.

"I'll tell you something," George Fujita whispered in H's ear as they were working together one day. "There's going to be a big raid on Kobe on June 5."

"How do you know?" H asked.

"They said so on the American radio."

H couldn't help laughing out loud. "It's talking rubbish like that with such a straight face that makes people call you 'Big-Mouth George,'" he said. "In the first place, they're not going to broadcast American military secrets over the radio. And if you listened in to enemy broadcasts you'd be taken into custody by the military police on suspicion of spying."

Wagging a finger, George clucked his tongue at him. "The MPs haven't got time to keep a check on that kind of thing," he said with a smile, "nor do they have the manpower."

In point of fact, though, a large force of B29s did turn up on the morning of June 5, just as George had said.

Whether or not it was a simple coincidence, the attack seemed to be directed particularly at areas left standing after the March 17 raid. The air raid warning came at 6:07 A.M.

H had been woken by the alert at 5:30, but he was still between the quilts.

Uncle Hadano was in the kitchen filling his flask with water. As H was getting dressed, he said, "I think today's raid is going to be worse than the last one. I have to go to the city hall myself, but you're not to go anywhere. Just get into the cave shelter and stay put. Promise me, now!" With which he got on his bike and pedaled off.

H did as he'd been told and hurried to the shelter, which was only a hundred meters or so from the house.

Dug into the side of the hill, the shelter consisted of a huge artificial cave four meters wide, two and a half meters high, and a good twenty-five meters from front to back. You'd be safe from any bombs here.

H made his way to the very back of it, this being the spot where he'd buried the wooden box containing his books.

Other people from the neighborhood had been there ever since the alert, bringing with them straw mats to spread on the ground, together with bits of furniture, pots and pans, and even quilts—everything needed, probably, for a stay of many days if necessary.

Before long the drone of B29s was audible even inside the shelter, unnaturally loud and close at hand; they must be flying rather low. Though he knew he would be safe in the shelter, H just couldn't stay put. Donning a cotton-padded air raid hood and topping it with a steel helmet, he stood up.

"Where are you going?" asked Mrs. Tazaki. But H gave a non-committal grunt and, stepping over the legs of the people lying or sitting all around, made his way outside. The sky was a clear blue, dazzling to look up at after the gloom of the shelter.

He could see the formation of twenty or so B29s flying lower than any he'd seen before, and he could hear the engines of more following behind them. This was really going to be something.

The Myojin-cho district was a long, narrow strip, with the Myoji River flowing right before his eyes, and hemmed in both at the rear and in front by steep banks and low hills, so it was impossible to get a wide view of the sky. H decided to look for a spot where he could get a better view.

He hesitated as to whether to climb the hill behind the Zenshoji Temple opposite or the hill to the rear, but decided in the end on the latter.

Unlike the previous occasion he felt free to do as he pleased, having nothing to protect but his own person.

The hillside was steeper than he'd expected and several times he slipped back as he climbed, but after about thirty minutes he reached a high point with a broad outlook. Directly to the south was where his own home had stood; the Takatori marshaling yards in front of it seemed to be already in flames. Black smoke was rising, too, from places in the area between there and Suma, to the west.

To attack like this, not at night but in broad daylight and from a low altitude, showed a fine contempt for the Japanese defenses. However, the anti-aircraft gun emplacements on Karumo Island and Mount Okura were firing busily.

H saw a B29 get hit and fall, and shortly afterward watched a Japanese plane make a sudden turn and score a direct hit on an enemy plane's engine. At times like this, naturally enough, he was totally on Japan's side and watched excitedly. The great bomber formations, coming in wave after wave, dropped their loads accurately, explosives or incendiaries depending on the objectives. Damage was particularly bad in the east, and black smoke was still rising from fires in the built-up areas at three in the afternoon.

As he'd feared, Hirobe's home had suffered. Standing in Ninomiya 3-chome, to the north of Sannomiya, it was one of the districts entirely consumed by flames. Hirobe's father, a skilled carver of *ramma*, had naturally been unable to continue his original work, and was working instead in the woodwork section of a factory producing military accessories. His eldest brother was away at the front in Burma, so at the time of the raid there would have been five of them at home—Hirobe's mother and father, his brother who worked as a replacement teacher at a national school, his elder sister, and Hirobe himself.

"We were all ready to get out when the air raid warning sounded," he told H later. "Somebody told my mother apparently that if nothing else you should always take futons with you, otherwise you'd be in trouble right from the first day. She kept saying 'Futons! Futons!' so we grabbed a few, but we were in too much of a hurry to take anything else. They said it was dangerous to go north, so we went south. It was safer in that direction, apparently, because everywhere from Kotonoo-cho to the wharves had burned down in the March raids.

"I looked up at the sky as we were getting away and actually saw the bomb bays in the fuselage of a B29 open as it came over, they were at such a low altitude. The incendiaries it released came raining down with a loud hissing noise. One of them scored a direct hit on a girl student who was running in front of us. Killed outright. We thought *we* were done for, too, but in fact we all came through safely. That night we slept in a kind of shack we made using wood left on one of the firebreak sites and bits of scorched tin. Even so, we got drenched in the night when it rained. Black rain, you know—black with soot from the fires."

Having been burned out himself, H could understand exactly how Hirobe felt. But his friend simply said, "So we lost our home. But it can't be helped: just have to start all over again."

H heard that George's home, too, had been destroyed in the June 5 raid. When he came to school, H tried to offer his sympathy, but George just chuckled and said, "Actually, you know, I knew about Germany's surrender, too—on the same day," and said nothing at all about his house.

Well-disposed toward George though H was, there were times when his friend made him feel rather uneasy....

39

Hand-to-Hand Combat

It wasn't until three days later that H got hold of a paper carrying news of the June 5 raid on Kobe. There'd been none available till then, since the store in Itayado had burned down.

Wanting to know how the raid that day was being reported, he got Yuzawa to bring the June 6 paper to school for him.

The *Asahi Shimbun* headlines said: "350 B29s Raid Osaka-Kobe Area"; "Fires in Kobe, Nishinomiya, Ashiya; 200 Enemy Planes Downed."

H was astonished to learn that there'd been as many as 350 bombers, though they'd certainly come too thick and fast for him to count.

Another surprise was the statement that Japanese forces had shot down two hundred enemy aircraft. The anti-aircraft guns had certainly been busier than usual that day, and had probably shot down more planes than ever before, but still the figure of two hundred was almost unbelievable.

Concerning the most important thing of all—the damage done—the newspaper was equally brief: "Fires were started in the eastern part of Kobe, Nishinomiya and Ashiya, but are steadily being extinguished through the valiant efforts of our firefighting forces." That was all.

Taken at face value, the article suggested that only the three areas mentioned had been set ablaze in the raid. Some districts had, in fact, survived, but only a very small proportion of the whole; actually the city of Kobe had been virtually wiped off the map by the raid.

"I wonder why the papers can't write about things properly?" Hirobe said angrily. Having had personal experience that day of fleeing with his family through a hail of incendiaries and losing his own

399

home to the flames, it was no wonder that he should be dissatisfied at the newspapers' complete failure to tell the truth about the raids and damage.

"Perhaps they don't report details because that would give useful information to the enemy?" suggested Masuda.

"Do you really think so? Don't you think the American forces know more accurately than anyone else just what was destroyed and how? Their reconnaissance planes probably take aerial photos afterward, so they may actually know more than our people," said Yuzawa, and H agreed with him.

The practice of keeping anything and everything secret had been common since before the beginning of the war. H had been in fifth grade at primary school when he'd first felt surprised that it should be necessary to keep certain things secret. One example was the weather forecasts that disappeared from the newspapers on December 8, 1941, the day on which Japan had gone to war with America. The reason given was that information about the weather might be put to use by the enemy. But H had been astonished even so that such things should be treated as "military secrets."

Anyway, the newspapers published almost nothing that the public really wanted to know, while cramming their pages with messages from the government and military.

One thing H would have liked to know, for example, was the situation in Okinawa. The newspapers had said that American forces had landed and that fierce fighting was in progress, but gave absolutely no concrete details.

They had, though, published a statement by Prime Minister Kantaro Suzuki: "In any final battle on the main islands, our side will have the advantage. We must fight through resolutely to the end. A mightier effort than ever before is called for."

From this H surmised that Okinawa had been given up for lost, and that the only thing left was a last-ditch defense of the mainland. In spite of changes of government, however—the Koiso government had by now given way to a Suzuki government—there'd been no official change in the course of the war; on the contrary, it was moving in an ever more unrealistic direction.

The idea, briefly, was that Japan should lure the American forces onto the main islands and deal them a decisive blow there. This was the "master plan": a "final battle" that would smash the enemy and lead to ultimate victory.

In fact, though, the whole country—the very country that was supposed to be lying in wait to deal the enemy a knockout blow—was being blasted by air raids and steadily reduced to rubble. And this was the case not just in the major cities but in the smaller towns and communities in the provinces too. H refused to believe that it could be strategically advantageous for a country in such a position to allow itself to be invaded by American forces.

Until quite recently the rule had been that when an alert went off students were not to come to school, or were to be sent home immediately if already there. However, alerts had become such a daily occurrence that this was changed, and they were instructed to come to school unless there was an actual air raid warning.

One day, when H and his classmates were at work in the school factory, a warning sounded, the second since morning.

"To the farm!" said Yokota with a smile.

"Right! Off we go!" responded George and Okubo promptly, leaving their workbench.

When a warning sounded, the individual was free to use his own judgment in deciding where to take refuge until the all-clear came. "To the farm!" probably meant that they were going there to steal onions.

The onions were scheduled to be harvested in a week's time, when each student, H had heard, was due to receive a share, so the onions must be more or less ready to eat now.

"I only hope they don't get caught," Masuda said ominously. "They say that doing in people who steal crops is treated as legitimate self-defense nowadays."

"I don't believe it!"

"No, really—there was an actual case in Yokohama. A vigilante corps member beat to death someone he found stealing sweet potatoes from a field. He was arrested, but wasn't charged on the grounds that it was legitimate self-defense. It's true—it was in the *Mainichi Shimbun*."

H, who only saw the *Asahi*, hadn't known you were allowed to beat someone to death in "self-defense."

"Half the teachers haven't turned up today—the vice-principal was pretty angry about it—so there's not actually much chance of them getting caught. Even so, you can't be too careful these days."

They were all hungry, and one part of their brains was forever plotting ways and means of getting hold of food.

Since the previous week all students working in the school factory had been provided with their midday meal. This in itself was welcome, but checks on the number of set meals served were astonishingly rigorous. Only those who were working at the time when the lunches arrived at the school were to receive them, and there was not a single spare.

Sometimes the "staple food" would consist of bread rolls, sometimes "rice-balls" with an admixture of sorghum. It was rumored that the "bread" contained powdered straw, but even so it was more popular than the rice, to which the added sorghum gave a pinkish hue.

This sorghum rice didn't just taste unpleasant, it had a dreadful smell too, which combined with the smell of the bakelite container so that when you took the lid off you were overcome by a stale, warm odor. To go with these "staples" there would be, for example, a stew of dried herrings or a simple pickle of giant radish leaves rubbed in salt. When lunchtime came, though, they devoured the stuff ravenously even while they complained.

"Do you know they're going to reduce the ration of staple foods by about ten percent in July?" asked Masuda.

"2.1 *go* of rice instead of 2.3, isn't it? And even that's not real rice but a substitute."

Whenever talk turned to food, they all immediately and without exception became extremely animated.

"You should try chopping up an onion and frying it, flavoring it with a few drops of soy sauce on the way. It's real good if you put it on top of a bowl of rice—there's no meat in it, but it tastes as though there is," said Yuzawa, illustrating the delights of his dish with appreciative gestures. "Shall we go along to the farm too?" he suggested. "You never know whether we'll be alive tomorrow or not."

What with this talk of not being alive tomorrow—which he felt was quite a possibility—and a desire to try Yuzawa's recipe, H was easily persuaded to join the onion-thieves.

Leaving behind Hirobe and Masuda, who firmly refused to join them, H and Yuzawa set off for the farm on the north side of the school.

On the way they encountered Sumiyama and three of his friends from the judo club grappling with each other on the sports ground. They pretended not to have noticed them, but were hailed even so—though not, apparently, with any aggressive intent.

H could hardly ignore Sumiyama after accepting his recent gift of undershirts and pants. Going up to him reluctantly, he said "No judo for me just now."

"It's not about judo. You've seen this thing *A Citizen's Resistance Handbook* they're putting out, I suppose?" He thrust a newspaper cutting in H's face. "We're having a go at doing what the articles tell you. You have to have some practice if it's going to be of any use."

H himself had seen the *Resistance Handbook*, which was being published in instalments in the papers. The aim was to tell the public how it should fight in the event of a final battle on home soil, and he had read it with considerable skepticism.

Now, here were Sumiyama and his pals bent on trying out each exercise for themselves. His interest aroused, H decided he'd stop and have a look.

Sumiyama, who was tall and well built, was playing the part of an American soldier, while Tabuchi and the other two were Japanese.

The sticks the latter held in their hands were supposed to be kitchen knives.

"It says here, 'With a kitchen knife it is more effective not to slash cross-wise but to make a stab for the man's belly,'" said Sumiyama, quoting the article aloud. "Let's try it, then." And they proceeded to put it into action.

Tabuchi rushed at Sumiyama, but the latter sidestepped smartly, grabbed the other's arm and, with a twist of his hips, flung him to the ground.

"You've got to put more *impetus* into it, or he'll sidestep and get you," said Sumiyama; but either way they were obviously going to be no match for someone as big and agile as he was.

Next, two of them came on the attack together, but they also ended up on the ground. Even though a real American soldier wasn't likely to have Sumiyama's judo skills, it was quite clear that the enemy wasn't going to be felled all that easily.

H picked up the cutting with the article on "Close Combat and Hand-to-Hand Fighting" and read it through again.

Possibly the effect was heightened by the training actually in progress as he read, but he found the content rather overpowering.

> Not just rifles and bayonets but anything else—swords, spears, bamboo spears, even sickles, hatchets, sledgehammers, kitchen knives and fire hooks, can all be used as weapons in close combat.
>
> In using swords and spears, a vertical or horizontal slash is less effective with a tall adversary than a sharp jab toward the abdomen. When using instruments such as hatchets, sledge-hammers, kitchen knives, fire hooks and sickles, a surprise attack from the rear is most effective.
>
> In face-to-face confrontations, one should turn half sideways, sweep aside the enemy's bayonet as he thrusts, and at the same instant close with him and stab him to death in the chest. With sickles, a three-inch handle is the most convenient. In hand-to-hand fighting, hit him in the pit of the stomach or kick him in the testicles, or else use karate or judo techniques to throttle him. Either way, kill at least one enemy before you are killed yourself. You must use every method at your disposal to get him.
>
> As the situation is at present, it is no longer a question of "letting the enemy cut your flesh so as to break his bone," but of "breaking his bone as he breaks your own." What is absolutely certain is that victory in battle will go to the brave of heart.

H handed the article to Yuzawa for him to read.

"Do they really think we can win like that?" H muttered. "Do they really expect the public to do the things it says in the 'Hand-to-Hand Fighting' section of that handbook? They used to say you could put out incendi-aries with bucket relays; now it's 'kill the enemy with your bare hands'!"

"That's nothing," said Yuzawa. "In a copy of *Boys' Club* my kid brother was reading, there was an article, complete with illustrations, on 'How to Throw Hand Grenades.' You know what it said? 'On the Okinawa front,' it said, 'boys the same age as you flung themselves into the enemy positions with grenades in their hands. Now we too must train ourselves for the decisive battle on home soil. You can train perfectly well using stones. So let's start at once!' That means even kids are being counted on to take part in the big battle on home ground. The war won't end till the whole nation's been killed! I wonder what good they think *that*'ll do?"

"Keep your voice down a bit!" said H nervously. "Sumiyama'll hear you!"

They watched Sumiyama and the others wrestling with each other for a while longer, but then the all-clear sounded. They hadn't got their hands on any onions after all, but neither had they had to be thrown around by Sumiyama, which was something, at least.

They'd just got back to their workbenches in the school factory when Yokota and the rest of the boys who'd been to the farm returned equally empty-handed.

"Nothing doing?" asked H. Yokota winked and made a gesture signifying "We'll give you your share later." They must have hidden them somewhere.

H was a great admirer of Yokota's resourcefulness, but there was one thing that bothered him lately: Yokota was sometimes absent from school and, though normally cheerful and open about everything, on this one score gave no one any explanation. H suspected that he had something to hide.

Yokota's father had been killed in the fighting in the South Pacific, leaving the boy to look after his mother and younger sister in his stead. It seemed that he was doing something in this connection, but H and his other friends were always careful not to inquire what exactly it was.

A few days later the nature of the work he was doing became clear, thanks to the testimony of a younger student who said he'd seen Yokota walking through the ruins of Isonare-cho going toward Suma, hauling a cart loaded with someone's possessions. So a rumor that had gone around a while earlier that he was working as a carter or something similar had been true.

He'd been earning money by undertaking to transport the belongings of people moving out to the country, or things saved from the ruins of people's houses.

"I don't expect he earns very much," Okubo said. "They say it's getting more and more expensive to hire a cart, even."

This reminded them that Yokota himself had confided, unusually for him, that he'd gone to Akashi on foot recently and been caught, to his alarm, by an air raid warning on the way. Quite likely he was pulling a cart loaded with belongings at the time. He'd stayed the night in Akashi, he said. Even so, that was a good twenty-five kilometers or so away, which meant a round trip of fifty kilometers. Normally those listening would have asked what he went all the way to Akashi for, but they just shook their heads and made commiserating noises without inquiring any further, feeling sure he wanted neither sympathy nor support from anybody.

Once, Okubo said, when he'd tried to give Yokota some underwear, the other had refused with a "No offense meant, but no thank you." H reflected that he himself would have taken them like a shot—but Yokota was too proud.

H hadn't seen his father for some time, so he went to the church, only to be told that Morio wasn't back from the fire station yet. So he went there and found him, apparently just back from a fire, with his face all black with soot. Since the men at the station seemed to be busy washing down the engine and hanging hoses to dry from the lookout tower, H decided to wait outside. He'd heard that the photo they'd had taken of themselves side by side was ready. The studio had apparently been burned down in a raid on the Suma area only three days after his father had gone to get it.

While he was waiting, a fireman he knew by sight came by. H asked him where they'd been, thinking it was odd since there'd been no raid on Kobe that day, and was told they'd been to Nishinomiya, the city just midway between Kobe and Osaka.

"Kobe's almost all disappeared," the man explained, "so we're going to other places like Nishinomiya to help them out. Your father did terrific work today—went in and got two people out of the flames." H could hardly believe that his father, who'd never been remotely athletic, could have performed such a feat.

The fire engine was considerably grimier and less impressive than it used to be. Fire engines had stopped being red in 1943, when they'd all been painted in the "national defense color," a dirty ocher that looked particularly seedy when it got sooty or muddy. It was a camouflage color, replacing the old red which was too easy for enemy planes to spot.

"You saved two people?" he asked when his father finished work and came out.

"In a way, I suppose," Morio replied, offering no further information.

But another fireman who was with him put in, "He really deserves a medal, that's what!"

"Senoh," said one of the station staff, "why don't you have a bath and take your boy along too?"

"Yes, I'd like that," H said, sounding pleased; he wanted to see what the station bath was like.

The bathhouse at the back of the station was just about big enough to take ten people at a time, and looked like a public bathhouse with its tiled tub and row of showers. The firemen must all have been covered with soot from their firefighting, because when they got under the shower, the water that ran away over the tiles was black and soupy.

Seeing his father naked, H was reminded once again how small he was, and wondered how he ever managed to be a fireman.

"I've got some bread—do you want some?" Morio asked when they came out. H grunted as though he hadn't needed to be asked. The station bread was a bit darker than what they got in the school factory, but it didn't contain straw and tasted a lot better.

"Tomorrow's my day off, so shall I come to Hadano's tonight and we can have supper together?" his father offered.

"That's a good idea," said H, welcoming the unusual suggestion, even though he was bothered by the hint of another Last Supper.

Uncle Hadano, pleased to have both of them in the same place at the same time, killed one of the chickens he kept in the back garden. "I couldn't have kept it forever," he said when H looked sorry for the still-fluttering bird, "and I've been wanting to put it to rest decently when the right time came." This made H feel easier about it.

The outcome was a feast of sukiyaki made with chicken meat. The onion bubbling in the pan with it was a precious share-out from Yokota; the meat was tough, but tasted fine.

The three of them talked until late in the night, a black cloth pulled down low to shade the electric light. It was then that Uncle Hadano told them of the pain he sometimes had in his stomach. "I think it's probably stomach cancer," he said.

"I don't believe it," H exclaimed. "Look at how much sukiyaki you just ate!"

"Today was special," he said, adding with a smile, "*and* the chicken was good." So H assumed the talk of stomach cancer was a joke, and a joke in bad taste at that.

When he woke up the next morning Mr. Hadano was already up. "Apparently they dropped a new type of bomb on Hiroshima yesterday," he told H. "It was on the radio. They don't know yet what kind of bomb it was, but it seems the damage was terrible."

They were eating the remains of the previous night's sukiyaki for breakfast when an alert sounded.

Although Morio had said it was his off-duty day, he started getting ready for work. H wondered whether this might not be their last time together, and then reassured himself by remembering that he always had the same feeling.

H's route was the same as his father's as far as Itayado, where they separated, one going east, the other west, H himself heading for the school.

Yuzawa had brought a paper for him to see. The headlines were bigger than usual: "New Type of Enemy Bomb Hits Hiroshima; Sudden Raid by Small Number of B29s; Considerable Damage and Casualties, Details under Investigation." The article that followed said, among other things:

> Imperial Headquarters has announced (1530 hours, August 7, 1945) that at a few minutes past eight o'clock yesterday morning, August 6, a few B29s entered the skies over Hiroshima City and dropped a small number of bombs. As a result, a considerable number of houses in the city collapsed, and fires were started in various areas. It appears that the enemy used a new type of bomb for the attack, which was apparently dropped by parachute and exploded in midair. The power of the bomb is

at present under investigation, but it is believed to be not inconsiderable.

"No Imperial Headquarters communiqué has ever said 'considerable' damage and casualties before, so it must be pretty awful. What do you think 'a new type of bomb' means?" A group of them discussed it excitedly together, but no explanation of what had happened was forthcoming.

H went around looking for George. He found him lying in the sun, smoking, on top of the bank by the sports ground.

"Hey!" H hailed him. "Did they say anything about Hiroshima on the American radio?"

"It was an atom bomb." He used the English word "atom."

"What's 'atom'?" H asked.

"An atomic bomb," this time in Japanese. "It's not like the usual type using explosives; it's a terrible kind that uses the fission of the atomic nucleus. The buildings and people in Hiroshima were probably all wiped out in a flash. The Americans are saying that unless Japan surrenders, other towns will suffer the same fate."

"Do you think the bigwigs in the Japanese army and government know what the broadcast said?"

"I imagine so, seeing that even *I* heard it. They must surely have been listening in."

H thought of his cousin Tatsuo in Hiroshima, and wondered anxiously whether he too had perhaps been "wiped out" by the new bomb....

40

The Atom Bomb

"What's this new bomb that was dropped on Hiroshima?" someone asked.

"In all those raids on Kobe," said another, "it took tens of thousands of incendiaries and ordinary bombs to destroy the city, but in Hiroshima they're supposed to have caused terrific damage and casualties with just a single bomb. Why's that?"

In various parts of the school factory students were discussing the new weapon before starting work.

"George said it was an atomic bomb," said H. "According to him, they said so quite definitely on the American shortwave."

"So George's at it again. Are you sure it's not just one of his stories? What's this atomic bomb supposed to be, anyway?"

"I don't know exactly myself, either, but I think he's telling the truth. He said something even more shocking, too—that ten days ago they handed Japan what they call the 'Potsdam Declaration,' demanding that it should surrender. Apparently they dropped the atomic bomb because Japan didn't reply."

This produced various exclamations of surprise and disbelief.

"Where's George?" asked someone.

"He's in your squad, isn't he, Senoh?" said another. "Is he here today?" Even Fukushima, who normally didn't get on well with George, wanted to hear his information.

George was no longer in the same squad as H, in fact, a reorganization a week earlier having transferred him from the motor assembly team to the squad whose job was to fry insulators in oil.

His place of work had shifted to a room known as "the tempura shop" on the first floor of the old school building, which stood to the west. The nickname came from the fact that the operation performed here consisted in deep-frying compressed cardboard.

The close, stale smell rising from the pans of hot oil was enough to make anyone working there feel sick.

George disliked the monotony of the work, and he often disappeared, declaring defiantly that the school could expel him if it wanted to, so there was no guarantee he'd be found even if they went looking for him.

Even if they did get hold of him, it wasn't likely that an awkward character like George would pass on what he knew to the same bunch that were always calling him "Big-Mouth George" and poking fun at him.

"George may not tell you anything," H said a bit nervously, "so don't go hitting him or anything!"

Fukushima and Tabuchi ran off in the direction of the old school building.

"Shall we try asking Stonefish?" Masuda suggested to H. "Stonefish" was Mr. Nawata, the physics teacher.

"Don't be stupid! If it was simple enough for someone like Stonefish to understand, Japan would have made its own 'atomic bomb' or whatever ages ago!" It was frustrating to hear about a mysterious, unidentified weapon yet have no reliable information about it.

Fukushima and Tabuchi came back looking disgruntled.

"That bastard George! He wouldn't say a word, just went on whistling. Then, when I grabbed his collar and made as if to hit him, all he said was, 'It'll be in the papers sooner or later—you'll find out then.'"

Just as H had expected. Personally, he had every intention of keeping an eye on the papers himself—though not because of what George had said—to see how they would report the new bomb.

On the site of the old Itayado newspaper delivery center they'd set up a simple hut, made of galvanized iron and odd boards salvaged from the ruins, where you could pick up a newspaper. There weren't many available so they soon sold out, but H was always sure of one, having promised to drop in every day on his way to school. What you read in the papers shouldn't be swallowed whole, but there was no other source of information.

Taking his paper from the woman in the improvised store, H would devour it voraciously as he walked. Since there were no cars or people to bump into as he went along between the ruins reading, and since the newspaper itself was just a single sheet printed on both sides, he could glance through almost everything by the time he got to school. On the other hand, though, it took almost twice as long to walk and read at the same time, so he had to leave home thirty minutes earlier.

On the eleventh he got his paper as usual, and gave a shout of surprise. Coming so soon after the shock of the new bomb dropped on Hiroshima two days earlier, here was something that went beyond the merely startling: the Soviet Union had declared war on Japan.

The only information the newspaper article gave was that "Around midnight on August 8–9, Soviet forces crossed the border into Manchuria.... Japanese forces in the area, acting jointly with Manchurian forces, have engaged the illegal intruders and are fighting a valiant battle of self-defense."

Arriving at school, H immediately went in search of George. To his surprise he found him where he was supposed to be, virtuously engaged in cooking "tempura."

"What's happened to *you*?" H asked.

"If I took every day off they'd treat me as a persistent offender," said George, "but if it's only every other day or so I can say I'm staying home because I'm not well." H was impressed by his canniness. Second Middle, in fact, was full of clever people, whom H was always easily impressed by.

He asked George whether he knew about the Soviet declaration of war, and found to his surprise that he hadn't known anything until the Imperial Headquarters announcement. The American broadcasts had made no mention of it at all.

So far the Soviet Union had taken a neutral attitude toward Japan, but once the U.S. dropped the new type of bomb on Hiroshima it rode in on America's coattails and promptly declared war. In war, of course, there is no such thing as good faith, but this was particularly underhand, and H felt angry.

With the Soviet Union also in the fray, Japan was now being pressed from the rear too.

The same newspaper reported that Tokyo and Kita-Kyushu had

been bombed by flights of 100 and 260 B29 bombers respectively. "Damage on our side is being investigated," it said, "but it is believed to be light."

How long did they intend to go on declaring that "damage was light"?

H wanted to find out what exactly the "new-type bomb" really was. Every time he found some reference to it in the paper he read it over two or three times.

The Japanese government had apparently "made a stern protest to America, via the neutral Swiss government and the International Committee of the Red Cross, concerning the dropping of a new, inhuman type of bomb in defiance of international law."

Directly below this report there was a headline saying "U.S. President Truman Boasts of Power of Atomic Bomb in Radio Speech on War Against Japan." This was the first time H had seen the word "atomic bomb" used in print. What George had said was correct. The report was a cable from Zurich dated August 9, and it confirmed what George had told him: the Japanese people—the speech had said—had seen for themselves the power of this weapon; if Japan did not surrender, America would continue to drop similar bombs on Japanese cities.

Apart from this, there were various details regarding the decisions made at the Potsdam talks.

Then, shockingly, on August 12 the newspapers reported that another atomic bomb had been dropped, this time on Nagasaki. The talk of more bombs if Japan didn't surrender had been no idle threat.

Two things surprised H: the fact that the U.S. had dropped the bomb as promised, and the style of the article reporting it. The headline, given only two columns, said "New-Type Bomb on Nagasaki Also," and the article itself consisted of a mere seven lines. "An announcement by Western Japan Military District Headquarters (1445 hours, August 9, 1945): 1. Around 11:00 A.M. on August 9 two large enemy aircraft entered the skies over Nagasaki City and dropped what was apparently a new-type bomb. 2. Details are at present under investigation, but damage and casualties are believed to be relatively small."

Apparently a new-type bomb—what the hell were they thinking of, when it was perfectly clear that an atomic bomb with the same terrifying power as the Hiroshima bomb had been dropped? And to talk yet again of "relatively small damage"!...

Somehow, the whole deviousness of the military mind seemed to be summed up in this article, and to let off steam H tried counting the number of words it contained: ninety-three! The sufferings of the people of Nagasaki had been reduced to a mere ninety-three words.

The same page carried a still more dumbfounding piece too. The headline, in bigger print than that announcing the "New-Type Bomb on Nagasaki," said "Dealing with the New Bomb."

Underneath this, stretching across three columns, was the subheading: "Third Announcement from Air Defense Headquarters. Measures Against the New Bomb: Dress in White and Make for the Cave Shelters."

The piece was said to be based on surveys by specialists from the army, navy and ADH who had taken an on-the-spot look at Hiroshima:

1. If you see something like a parachute coming down, take shelter without fail.

2. Reinforced concrete buildings are relatively safe, so make full use of them. Any glass will shatter, however, so be careful to avoid injury due to flying fragments, and make full use also of walls, areas beneath windows, and parapets likely to afford shelter.

3. Fires sometimes start in damaged buildings, so prompt fire-fighting is important.

4. Injuries include those caused by the blast and by burns; the latter are more common, so you should have knowledge of their treatment. The simplest method of treatment is to apply oil or fat or saltwater compresses.

5. Air raid shelters dug into hillsides and banks are just as effective as other strongly constructed shelters.

6. White underwear and other garments are effective in preventing burns. The entrance to shelters should be blocked where possible. With "octopus pot" dugouts, a simple cover of boards or anything else handy is effective.

Taken alone, this seemed to suggest that the bomb was not really so horrendous; that the blast from the detonation of a conventional bomb was more violently destructive of things round about. Were they suggesting then that the threat of the atomic bomb lay in fact mostly in the burns it caused? That if one dressed in white and got into a dugout with a board for a lid one would be safe?

They claimed that bandages soaked in salt water were effective, but were there any medical grounds for this?

Another thing that bothered H was that although the day before they'd used the expression "atomic bomb," here they'd reverted to the meaningless "new-type bomb."

He was desperately worried that his cousin Tatsuo in Hiroshima might have been killed or injured.

His concern wasn't solely for Tatsuo, of course. He knew that an enormous number of other people had in fact suffered, though it occurred to him that worry about someone you knew was, after all, a good lead-up to a more wide-ranging concern for people in general. What was really happening in Hiroshima and Nagasaki? If possible, he'd have liked to get on the first train and go see the damage for himself....

To his surprise, though, the newspaper went on to give a graphic report.

He'd never before seen this kind of account concerning actual damage, in which a specially dispatched correspondent described things as he'd seen them on the spot.

> This correspondent is now standing, with feelings of irrepressible wrath, amidst the still-smoking ruins of the city.
>
> According to the inhabitants, it was almost all over in a moment. The noise of the B29's engines was extremely faint; it may in fact have cut off its engines at a high altitude before gliding in over Hiroshima. A keen light like a photographer's flash passed across their vision. The next moment, the scene in the city changed entirely. Ordinary dwellings, as distinct from ferroconcrete buildings, collapsed almost without exception, and citizens in the streets felt a searing heat on their skin and suffered injuries. Most of the injured had bleeding burns on the exposed portions of their bodies, especially their faces. Even in areas of the city that suffered least, the blast was enough to blow

off roofs, and in the worst areas great trees, many armspans around, were snapped off half way up the trunk.

It was a picture of utter inhumanity. Yet the thing that aggravated the suffering and damage was, essentially, a lack of readiness—though this is not surprising considering that the all-clear had already been given. And, in spite of everything, it is quite impossible that this on its own could ever be enough to bring the Japanese people to its knees.

As your correspondent sees it, the lessons to be learned from this are, as has already been pointed out: One should never ignore even a single aircraft. One should always take refuge in a shelter. Shelters themselves should be reinforced. One should never go out without taking basic medical necessities such as mercurochrome and a triangular bandage. One should keep exposed portions of one's body to a minimum.

Once again, though, the most important thing is the will to fight—ultimately, the determination to overcome fear and to die rather than submit to the enemy.

H could accept the first part of this, but the second part—from around where it said "As your correspondent sees it"—sounded suspicious. Probably without this part the article would never have passed the censors and been published at all. Even allowing for that, though, were they really expected to believe that mercurochrome would help to treat burns caused by an atomic bomb?…

H would have liked to see photographs showing the actual state of Hiroshima. The only photos the paper carried were one of the Crown Prince with a caption reading "His Highness deeply concerned about war situation," and another showing "Crack fighter pilots awaiting the order to go into action"—in neither of which H was the least bit interested.

Never once since hostilities began, he thought, had he seen a photo showing what war was really like. This gave him the idea of going directly to a newspaper office and asking the reason. There was a reporter with the *Kobe Shimbun*, Odagiri by name, for whom his father used to make suits. Whether he'd remember H or not wasn't certain, but if H went to see him he might perhaps show him some photographs.

The building housing the *Kobe Shimbun*, he remembered, had been in the Higashi-Kawasaki district, on the side of Kobe Station nearer the sea. Suspecting that it had been burned down, he went there to find his fears justified: the area, being close to the Kawasaki Shipbuilding yards, had been subjected to particularly concentrated bombing.

The newspaper's temporary address in Kaigan-dori 8-chome was posted on the wall of the entrance to the gutted building, so he set off to look for it. This area had suffered too, but it consisted largely of modern-style office buildings whose scorched and blackened ruins still stood here and there, giving it a very different aspect from that of the razed residential areas.

When he finally found the building he wanted and gave Odagiri's name at the reception desk, he was told to wait: Mr. Odagiri was out on a story at the moment, but should be back soon.

H had been waiting for a while when a man went past and the receptionist called out to him, "This boy here's come to see Mr. Odagiri." The man, who said his name was Miyata and who turned out to know the Senoh tailoring shop, worked with Odagiri on the city desk, and offered to let H have a look at the office while he was waiting.

"Where are the rotary presses?" H wanted to know, hoping to see the newspaper actually being printed.

"The printing's done in a different place. Since the raids we've had to spread things around a bit."

Mr. Miyata led H through a room full of cluttered desks, pointing out the editorial and city desks as they went, to the room that housed the photographic section.

As soon as he got there H put his question: "Why doesn't the newspaper carry photos of the ruins?"

"We have done, actually: 'Young citizens clearing burned-out areas' and so on…. But, I mean, we couldn't publish pictures showing just how much of the city has gone, could we? It would be giving information to enemy agents for one thing, and besides it would damage public morale."

They couldn't show photos of the damage in Hiroshima either, he said. It seemed the rumors had been true: the flash and blast when the bomb burst in the sky had just dissolved everything, buildings and people alike, in a moment. The ban on publication of photos of Hiroshima was particularly strict, he said.

"So you can carry descriptions but not photos?" H asked.

"That's about it," said the other, confirming H's suspicion.

One thing that particularly interested him in the photographic section was the work of the man in charge of touching up photos.

"Newspaper photos are done with halftone plates, so they come out fuzzy unless you touch them up to emphasize the contrasts." The clouds in the background of a photo of "Young eagles going off to battle" that lay, stamped "OK," on his desk were not in fact real clouds but clouds added by hand later.

"Did you do these clouds?" asked H.

"Yes—they turned out rather well, don't you think?" said the man proudly.

"You mean, you put in things that aren't in the original photo?"

"It emphasizes the feeling of 'going into action' if you have a few clouds, doesn't it? It's a kind of lie, but not a serious one. And the number on the hull of this submarine here, for instance, naturally has to be painted out."

So even photos, H realized, were sometimes added to or subtracted from. Another surprising fact he learned was that the colors wouldn't take properly on the glossy surface of a photo, so it was necessary first to wipe it with a piece of cotton dipped in egg white. They let him try it for himself.

"What do you do with the yolk of the egg after you've used the white?" H asked, concerned.

"It's all part of the retoucher's work, so he gets to eat the yolk," he was told with a smile.

I wouldn't mind doing this kind of work myself, thought H. You got to eat eggs every day, and the business of touching up photographs looked interesting in itself....

The man in the photographic section showed him all kinds of pictures they'd taken of the ruins in Kobe. H asked if he couldn't have one for himself, but was curtly refused.

Mr. Odagiri still hadn't come back to the office, so in the end H reluctantly gave up the idea of asking him about Hiroshima and left. As he was passing the Shuraku-kan movie theater in Shinkaichi, an alert sounded.

He told himself they weren't likely to drop an atomic bomb on a city already as devastated as Kobe, but decided to call in at the school just the same, since he'd heard it was safer inside a concrete building.

Under the blazing sun the heat was shimmering over streets unshaded now by any buildings. On the way a full air raid warning started up, so H broke into a run. By the time he reached the school he was soaked in sweat. Panting up the steps, he bumped into George coming out. H was pleased, because there was something he very much wanted to ask him.

"We've been told to come to school tomorrow as there's going to be an important announcement—do you know what it is?"

"Yes, I do. They're going to announce that Japan's lost the war."

This statement, in such an ordinary tone of voice, was so shocking that H asked him to repeat it.

"I mean, an announcement saying that Japan's surrendering unconditionally," George went on. "The 'important announcement' to be made at noon tomorrow can only be that—surrendering unconditionally, in acceptance of the Potsdam Declaration. The American shortwave broadcasts were reporting it, so I'm sure it's right. But mind you don't tell anybody yet! They won't take you seriously, and you might well get yourself killed by some bloodthirsty maniac into the bargain."

H felt burdened by the idea that he'd got to know a vital state secret before anyone else.

When he got home he found Uncle Hadano already back from the city office. H had been worried about him lately: he seemed to be suffering badly with his stomach pains, though he didn't say anything about it. Today, though, he must be feeling all right, for he was sitting in a rattan chair, naked except for a loincloth, fanning himself with a round paper fan. Watching him, H remembered seeing the movie *Muhomatsu no Issho*, and was seized with an urge to ask him straight out the reason for the goodwill he'd always shown H's family.

"Uncle, you've been good to me ever since I was a baby. Were you a kind of Muhomatsu, perhaps?"

"That's right—Muhomatsu," the other said, so straightforwardly that H was taken aback.

419

The answer was both expected and unexpected—unexpected, because he just couldn't understand how his mother could be attractive in *that* way. His expression was so quizzical that Uncle Hadano was moved to explain further.

"Your mother, you know, is a really genuine person. In the early days I used to be amazed that someone like her could exist. In a way, I suppose, I was in love with her, though there was never anything between us. I mean, your father's a good, gentle soul too.... That was before you were born, so it's a good eighteen years by now. I've been happy all that while to have such people as friends, and I've always felt I'd do anything I could to help them."

H sat in silence, deeply moved, as though he'd just heard something terribly important.

"Just as I told you some time ago, I'm really not very well," Uncle Hadano went on. "For the sake of my health I'm thinking of going back to Seki in Gifu prefecture, where the family were evacuated to. I stayed on in Kobe because I needed the salary, but I've had enough. It's been tough on the wife and Buichiro—he's two years younger than you so he'll be thirteen by now, and Kiyoji's eleven. The girl's only a baby still, but I feel I should go back now if I'm going to have any time with them."

H wept as he listened, his sadness reinforced by the awareness that the long-awaited end of the war might be just around the corner....

41

The Potsdam Declaration Accepted

On the way to school on the morning of August 15, H met Takimura. Like Sumiyama, Takimura was an aspiring naval cadet and as such no great friend of H's. Today, however, he seemed to be in high spirits.

"In today's broadcast we're going to hear His Majesty's own voice, I'm sure!" he said. "He's going to tell us personally that however tough things look we should fight on to the bitter end!"

"Really?" said H, feeling awkward. "How do you know?"

"Don't *you* know?" Takimura demanded, looking at H with an expression of surprise. "Everybody else does!"

This worried H. What would Takimura do if he found that today's broadcast was just the opposite of what he'd been expecting? The rest of the way to school he struggled hard to find topics that wouldn't involve speculation about today's broadcast.

They were approaching Nagata when they met Takeshi Akiyama. Akiyama was son of the owner of the well-known Akimai Rubber company. The factory had burned down on the same day as H's home, but the family residence had been spared.

H welcomed the encounter with relief; he got on well with Akiyama, and conversation with him was easy. Discussing the books Akiyama had lent him recently, for example, would nicely fill the time until they got to school.

To his dismay, though, before he could get in a word to Akiyama, Takimura had launched into the same subject again.

"In today's broadcast," he declared, "His Imperial Majesty is personally going to give us gracious words of encouragement. Senoh didn't know, but I expect *you* do, don't you?"

Akiyama looked uncomfortable. "Are you really sure that's what the Emperor's going to say?" he asked.

With a start, H sensed from Akiyama's voice that he knew the truth. Just how Akiyama had learned that the war was about to end he'd no idea, but something told him it was so.

When they got to the school, H looked around for George, but he hadn't put in an appearance. If Sumiyama—that embodiment of militaristic youth—was there, thought H, all hell would be let loose, but for some reason he too was nowhere to be seen.

It was a long time since the whole school had gathered in the schoolyard, and it was a lively scene. Naturally enough, speculation about the broadcast predominated. The overwhelming majority were of the view that there would be "gracious words of encouragement." Since those who held the opposite view kept their silence, any simple opinion poll would in fact have suggested that the students of Second Middle were without exception advocates of the do-or-die attitude.

Noon approached, and the whole school drew up in orderly ranks on the sports ground.

On the dais normally occupied by the principal at morning assembly, a speaker had been installed, a sign that today's protagonist was to be a radio broadcast.

H's heart was beating hard. He still didn't know the real truth. Would the broadcast confirm what George had said? Or could it conceivably be just the opposite—an exhortation to further efforts?

If an end to the war were to be proclaimed, would the nation as a whole immediately go along with it?

You could slam the brakes on a locomotive traveling at top speed, but it wouldn't stop at once. In this case, moreover, it wouldn't be just a question of the brakes: the tracks themselves would vanish; ploughing ahead, the train, deprived of its guidelines, would inevitably overturn. Utter chaos would ensue.

Only the day before there'd been nothing in the newspaper suggesting an end to hostilities. If anything, the emphasis had been on resistance to the bitter end. For instance, of the atomic bombs dropped on Hiroshima and Nagasaki the paper had said:

> So far as has been ascertained at present, the new-type bombs dropped by the American and British fiends are not as powerful as was at first rumored, and need not be feared so long as proper precautions are taken. A stoutly built shelter is safe, even directly below the bomb blast. The Land of the Gods will never be brought low by a mere bomb!

Supposing today's important broadcast were to announce the end of the war, what would happen? The thought scared H rather. At the same time, life wouldn't afford him many chances to witness something as momentous as this, and he resolved to keep a careful eye on what happened, what course Japan would follow, and who would do what.

The noontime signal came from the speaker. A male announcer said, "An important broadcast is about to begin. Will all listeners throughout the nation please rise to their feet." The national anthem was played.

As the music ended, another man's voice said, "His Imperial Majesty the Emperor has graciously consented to deliver personally an Imperial edict to the nation. We now bring to you, with a deep sense of awe, the Imperial voice in person."

The whole school stood erect and motionless, heads slightly bowed, as they awaited the Imperial words.

"After pondering deeply the general trends of the world and the actual conditions obtaining in Our Empire today, We have decided … " The voice that issued from the speakers was so high-pitched and uninflected that H was taken aback. It dismayed him too to find that however hard he listened, it was impossible to catch completely either individual words or meanings. One sentence, though—"We have ordered Our government to communicate to the governments of the United States, Great Britain, China and the Soviet Union that Our Empire accepts the provisions of their Joint Declaration"—was clear enough to give him the general idea. Japan had agreed to the Potsdam Declaration.

The broadcast went on at length, but there was so much static that it was impossible to catch and make sense of everything.

It didn't matter, thought H; the full text of the edict would certainly be carried in the next day's paper....

Either way, the war was over.

At last! Relief welled up from the bottom of his heart. But he gritted his teeth and looked tragic, sensing that too happy an expression could land him in trouble.

"With that, we bring to an end this broadcast of His Imperial Majesty's personal message to the nation."

A babble of voices immediately arose.

It had been difficult to grasp what the Emperor had said. Those who'd understood that it meant the end of the war stood in silence, biting their lips like H; others were ruefully rubbing tears from their eyes with their fists. None of them seemed in his heart of hearts to have the slightest idea how to respond to what had happened.

H noted with surprise that the teachers showed unexpectedly little emotion, though a few had tears in their eyes; but they all seemed to appreciate that the broadcast had been a ceremony whereby the Emperor informed the nation, in his own words, of the end of the war.

Suddenly someone started shouting: "It's ridiculous—it's just not possible!" The voice was Takimura's. It seemed he'd been checking the significance of the broadcast with Mr. Kameoka, who'd probably told him that Japan had, regrettably, surrendered. "It can't be true!" he was yelling. "And even if it is, I'm going to kill at least one or two of the enemy as they come ashore before they kill me! I'm not afraid of dying!"

H could hear five or six other students who were gathered around Takimura saying similar things. No, they were insisting, there was no doubt about it: the Emperor had been telling his subjects to unite in a continued struggle. They were quite sure they'd heard him say at the end of the speech, "We trust that the nation will commit itself to demonstrating the glory of the national polity so as not to be left behind by the rest of the world."

H was impressed that they'd caught that part properly, at least. He was sure they'd got the meaning wrong, but it was better not to enlighten them in their present bloodthirsty frame of mind, since they almost certainly wouldn't accept the truth.

Those who'd already realized that Japan had lost the war had quietly moved away from the "all-out resistance" group and were dispersing. H was startled to see how many of them, in fact, there were.

Takimura and his group went off toward the gymnasium as though they were going somewhere else to discuss things. He'd heard some of them muttering something about the Byakkotai. The latter was a band of youths who died in a last effort to save the Shogunate in 1868, so it seemed Takimura and the rest were thinking of fighting on alone if necessary.

Although H's own views—being "un-Japanese"—were just the opposite of theirs, he could understand in a way how they felt.

From early childhood on, from primary school right up to the present, in middle school, they'd been taught that they were born to die for the Emperor, so they could hardly be expected to think any other way. Only recently, with the publication of *A Citizen's Resistance Handbook*, they'd been urged to even greater efforts: "Every member of the nation must defend the national polity to the end, even at the cost of giving his own life in exchange for that of an enemy." They'd believed this intensely and unquestioningly throughout lives lived solely to be given up for the sake of His Majesty. It was no wonder that they were unable to make mature judgments based on cool, flexible appraisal of a particular situation at a particular moment. They were too simple-hearted....

By now the students were splitting up into groups and standing around talking in different parts of the school grounds.

Spotting some third-grade students gathered beneath the big eucalyptus tree, H went over and found them seated in a circle around Mr. Hata, the mathematics teacher.

He didn't know what course the conversation had taken before he got there, but Mr. Hata was saying, "You don't have to worry—America's not such a savage country as they say. The talk of 'American and British fiends' was a lot of lies aimed at fostering hatred and promoting the fighting spirit. It's not true, either, that if the Americans land they'll slaughter all the men. You shouldn't be deceived by such talk. America has a culture of its own; in fact, its troops may well behave in a more civilized way than our own forces. You don't have to worry unnecessarily. His Majesty the Emperor wouldn't have accepted the Potsdam Declaration if he'd thought the Americans and British were going to treat the Japanese people savagely, okay? Do you understand? The best thing you can do is to keep calm and go on studying...."

Though H himself was hopeless at math, he'd always been favorably disposed toward Mr. Hata, partly because he'd never been slapped around by him in class. This speech, though, made him admire the math teacher for a different reason: he was a man to be relied on.

As H stood listening, Yukawa-san came with a message from Sugita-san telling him to come to the armory. H called to mind the large quantity of rifles and live ammunition stored there. Surely, he wondered anxiously, they weren't thinking of using them against the Americans when they came in?

When they arrived at the armory the door was locked. Yukawa-san gave it a loud rap and called out, "I've brought Senoh. There's nobody else with us." At this, the door, which had apparently been locked from the inside, was opened. H went in, a bit nervous, to find Sugita and Matsukawa installed there.

"Senoh," Sugita began, "what did you think of the Emperor's announcement today?"

H was momentarily at a loss for an answer. He didn't know how Sugita himself felt about things, and the wrong reply could put him on the spot.

"I felt," he said carefully, "that His Majesty, out of concern for his subjects, had made a decision not to prolong their sufferings any longer. I personally felt that, though this was a most regrettable matter, it would be disloyal not to comply with His Majesty's wishes."

He looked anxiously at Sugita, wondering whether he'd said the right thing.

Sugita grunted, then was silent for a while.

"Quite right," he said eventually. "And one other thing: what do you think should be done with the rifles here?"

So this is what he's really getting at, thought H, and wondered uneasily whether Sugita was suggesting that the rifles and ammunition should be distributed to the "last-ditchers" for a fight to the death.

But he decided that he'd have to communicate what he really felt even at the risk of being beaten up; otherwise he might be given a rifle himself and shoved into a squad for a last fling at the Americans as they came ashore. The only way out was to throw in the Imperial name itself.

"His Majesty," he declared, "has decided that we should stop fighting. The rifles we have here are being held on his behalf, and I don't think it would be right to use them to shoot American troops against the Imperial will. However regrettable it may be, I feel that the only course is to comply with the order to lay down arms and hand the rifles over to the Americans."

"Quite correct," said Sugita-san. "I was thinking so myself, in fact. If these rifles got into the hands of people planning resistance and they used them to put up a fight, it could become a major national problem with irreparable consequences. It was to prevent just such a thing that we locked the door on the inside, stopping anybody from coming in."

H almost sagged at the knees in relief. Maybe it was because they were so intimately acquainted with weapons that Sugita-san and the other people in the rifle club—who one might have expected to be particularly jingoistic—could make such an objective judgment.

"We'll put two more locks on the armory to make it triple-safe; then three of us will take one key each so that it can't be opened unless all three get together. I'll have one and Yukawa another, and you, Senoh, can take the third."

"Don't you think Matsukawa-san might be better?" asked H hastily. "He's senior to me."

"It's okay," said Sugita-san. "We need one from each grade. We trust you, so *you* look after it."

The two extra locks would take time to procure, so it was decided that Yukawa and Matsukawa should stop over in the armory that night. This measure was to be kept strictly secret both from the school authorities and from other members of the club.

Sugita-san, who wanted to go home to pick up something for the two to eat as well as the padlocks, left the armory with H.

The air outside was sweltering after the chill of the armory. "Hot!" grumbled Sugita as they walked. "Are your family all right? Your mother and sister were evacuated, weren't they? When do you expect them back?"

When Sugita talked as a senior member of the club he used more formal language and something approaching a standard accent, but away from the club he spoke rapidly and in the Kobe dialect. H always found the difference amusing.

Together they walked in the direction of Hyogo Station. Looking up, H saw white summer clouds rearing up in a dazzlingly blue sky. No more B29s, no more air raid sirens: the thought filled him with a sudden happiness.

"It's over at last, isn't it?" he said to Sugita. "I'm *glad*!"

Stopping in his tracks, Sugita gave H a terrifying scowl. The next instant he punched him on the chin.

The unexpectedness of the attack sent H flying. Utterly taken aback, his befuddled mind struggled to account for it, but in vain. His mouth, which felt warm and wet, must be cut inside.

Sugita was weeping. Gazing up at him from where he lay, H could see great tears running down his face. It was the first time he'd seen him cry.

Then understanding dawned. Sugita's father was at the front and there was no word as to whether he was alive or dead; his home had burned down and his mother was in serious condition with burns all over her body. H's own joy and relief at the war's end had contrasted too sharply with Sugita's personal feelings.

Putting out a hand, Sugita pulled H to his feet. "I shouldn't have done that," he said. "I'm sorry. Don't take it badly."

Suddenly the tears spilled from H's eyes too—not from regret at the defeat, but out of sheer, frustrated puzzlement as to what the war had been all about.

There in the middle of the road, not speaking, they both wept aloud.

After a while Sugita said with an embarrassed expression, "You're not to tell anyone I cried."

"I won't tell anyone you hit me, either," said H, smiling, and was rewarded with a playful slap at his head.

When they arrived at the ticket barrier of Hyogo Station, Sugita assumed a serious expression. "Tomorrow's a school holiday," he said. "Come to the armory the next day after class and I'll give you your key."

They went off to board trains going in opposite directions, H for Suma in the west, Sugita for Mikage in the east.

H was headed for the beach at Suma. Somehow he wanted to lie on the sand by the sea. He'd played on the beach at Suma ever since he was small; today he felt it was the only place where he could relax.

Walking down the steps from the platform and onto the sand, he took off his shoes intending to walk barefoot, but the sand was so hot that he danced in pain. Reluctantly putting his shoes on again, he ran to the water's edge.

He'd been going to sprawl out on the beach, but again the sand was so scorching that he had to give up the idea.

Thinking vaguely as he stood looking at the sea stretching to the horizon in front of him, he felt frustrated at his inability as yet to feel the end of the war as a reality. The end had come with too little fuss for such a momentous event....

If it could be put an end to so easily, he wished they'd done it earlier. If the Emperor had only made a decision sooner, the atomic bomb probably wouldn't have been dropped. And if it had been just five months earlier, H's own home would have been spared.

How many houses all over the country, he wondered, had been destroyed in the same way? How many people had been killed or hurt in the war?

The Emperor, he reflected, bore the brunt of the responsibility. In everything the slogan had been "for His Majesty the Emperor." They'd fought "for His Majesty the Emperor," and soldiers had died shouting "Long Live His Majesty!"

The Greater East Asian War, launched in the first place against America and Britain, had started with an Imperial edict to the nation. Without the name of the Emperor, in fact, the war would have had neither beginning nor end.

Suddenly, an odd thought struck him: if the Emperor hadn't broadcast a personal message to the people today, would the nation have taken the end of the war so quietly?

H himself had made use of the Emperor's name earlier that day, and Sugita-san's resolve not to let the rifles pass into other hands had likewise been taken because he'd learned that an Imperial decision was ending the war.

It was odd that hardly anybody seemed to resent things having come to this pass because of the Emperor, or demanded to know what he was going to do about it. Japanese though H himself was, he still didn't understand.

What had they been fighting to defend, then? The only answer forth-coming was that from beginnning to end they had been protecting the "national polity."

As for the real nature of the "national polity," H hadn't the faintest idea. He'd asked his father about it once, and been told, "the nation's basic integrity, I suppose. To put it another way, the form of the state as created by His Majesty the Emperor." Which left him as much in the dark as ever.

Perhaps it was too much to ask a middle school student to under-stand such things. Even so, they'd been told to defend this "national polity" even if it meant the whole country being reduced to ashes and the whole population destroying itself in a last-ditch battle. Was it all *that* worth defending?

The possibility occurred to him that the Emperor had been kept unaware of the true state of affairs, but that didn't seem likely. Even assuming that he'd had the wrong people around him, in the form of Hideki Tojo and the other wartime leaders and his own immediate advisors, then surely that was part of his responsibility too? If it wasn't the responsibility of the Emperor, then whose was it?

H lay on the beach lost in thought until dusk began to set in.

The sun, descending toward the west, had begun to tint the clouds red. H got up, brushing the sand off the seat of his pants.

More than anything, he wanted to go back to the house and see Uncle Hadano, but before that, he decided, he'd call in at the fire sta-tion to see his father. Boarding a streetcar, he got off at Takatori-cho 2-chome, in front of the station, to find that his father wasn't there. It seemed he'd gone back to the church.

H wavered for a moment between calling in at the church and going straight home, but decided to go straight back to Myojin-cho. That evening, he felt sure, there would be a "Meeting of Thanksgiving" at the church to give thanks for the end of the war, and he didn't feel like singing hymns.

As the streetcar was passing by the ruins of the Takatori marshaling yards, there was a bright red sunset in the sky to the west.

Gazing at the clouds he felt that the only things that had remained completely unchanged both before and during the war were the sea he'd been watching a while back and the sky before him now.

At the house he found Uncle Hadano already home. "I'm back," H called out as he entered.

"Hello, there!" came the familiar response, but not a word about that day's broadcast.

Indoors, the house was startlingly bright. The black cloths dictated by air raid controls had been removed from the electric lights.

So, thought H, at last with some conviction, the war *is* over. I suppose this is the light of peace!

42

Buried Rifles

As soon as he awoke the next morning, H raced out to buy a news-paper.

"There were people banging away at my door this morning even before the papers arrived," grumbled the woman at the stall as she gave it to him.

At the top of the front page there was a headline, printed horizon-tally, reading "Imperial Edict Announces End of War." The characters were bigger than H had ever seen in a headline before. Below it, two vertical subheadings said, "Imperial Concern at Horrors of New Bomb" and "Empire Accepts Four-Power Declaration."

The complete text of the edict was also given, this too in larger print than that used for ordinary articles, but the characters themselves were so difficult that it took repeated readings before he finally got the gist of it. No one could have been expected to get the sense of the written word just from listening to the broadcast—besides which, the Imperial voice was so unfamiliar, and the pronunciation so different from that of ordi-nary people, that no one could have caught all that was said straight off.

From the printed text H was finally able to understand everything that had been said, but search as he might he could find no mention either of "losing the war" or "surrendering to America and Britain."

Nor, either in the Imperial edict or in the ordinary articles, did the word "defeat" appear. H found this peculiar, too.

Back home, H showed the newspaper to Uncle Hadano and asked him: "How come everybody seemed to realize that the war was over just from listening to that broadcast yesterday?" he said. "I don't see how they could have understood all that difficult language the Emperor used."

"I suppose people got the general drift without knowing how. That's how it was with me. They said there was going to be an important broadcast, so I half expected it. I mean, given that His Majesty was going to talk to the nation personally, there wasn't much else it *could* be, was there?"

H was impressed: being an adult did have its advantages, he had to admit.

H was interested in hearing lots of different people say what they really felt at last. There were five things he wanted to ask them. Did you immediately realize from the broadcast that Japan had been defeated? Had you thought we'd win the war or that we'd lose? If you thought we'd lose, when did you start thinking that way? Do you think the Emperor was responsible for the war, or not? Did you believe all along that the Emperor was a god?

He'd already asked Uncle Hadano the first of these questions, so he decided to ask him what he thought of the Emperor. Hadano looked rather embarrassed.

"Are you going to ask other people the same thing?" he queried. "I don't think you'd better ask about the Emperor; nobody wants to be asked about that. Not that they really thought he was a god, but as the center of the 'national polity' he was, after all, a *kind* of god. And I think you'd better not go around putting such questions before people have had time to sort out how they really do feel." This said, he went off for an appointment at the hospital.

Since this was in fact the thing H had most wanted to ask, the reply rather disappointed him.

On the eighth of every month without fail the newspapers had reprinted the Imperial edict announcing the beginning of the Greater East Asian War, and at schools too there'd been a ceremony at which it was read, so people could hardly ignore the relationship between the Emperor and the war.

Having been reprinted in the newspapers every month since the out-break of hostilities, the edict had become, like the Emperor Meiji's Imperial Rescript on Education, a point of reference for the nation as a whole, a source of strength encouraging them to put up with all the hardships of the war.

What about the fact that this same edict declaring war on America and Britain had been carried in the papers on August 8, just a week before the Emperor announced the end of the war over the radio? H would like have liked to hear more about that.

He calculated how many eighths of the month there'd been since the day the war began: forty-five, thanks to which, he—and presumably other people as well—could have recited the edict almost entirely by heart:

> We by grace of heaven, Emperor of Japan, seated on the Throne of a line unbroken for ages eternal, enjoin upon ye, Our loyal and brave subjects:
>
> We hereby declare war on the United States of America and the British Empire. The men and officers of Our army and navy shall do their utmost in prosecuting the war, Our public servants of various departments shall perform faithfully and diligently their appointed tasks, and all other subjects of Ours shall pursue their respective duties; the entire nation with a united will shall mobilize their total strength so that nothing will miscarry in the attainment of Our war aims.

The text went on and on, to some four times this length in all, but the gist of it, spelled out in words attributed to the Emperor personally, was that this was a holy war for the sake of lasting peace in East Asia, and that all obstacles to its aims were to be resolutely broken down.

So it was apparent even to H that the war couldn't have ended without a personal message from the Emperor himself, a fact that made him all the more keen to know how people felt about the connection between the war and the Emperor.

Even so, he could appreciate what Uncle Hadano had said. For the moment there was a gaping hole left in people's minds that made it impossible for them to view things objectively, and he could understand that they wouldn't want anyone poking around in the wound.

The school had been directed to reassemble on the seventeenth, which left them one more day's holiday. This probably meant that in the interval a meeting of teachers had been hastily summoned to discuss what was to be done.

With no school that day and no fear of air raid warnings, H caught up on his laundry and was hanging it out to dry in the yard when the gate in the back fence opened and Mrs. Tazaki came in. He spotted at once the single steamed sweet potato sitting in the bamboo basket she clutched to her chest.

The Tazakis, who lived on the other side of the alleyway at the back of Uncle Hadano's place, were almost like relatives. They were in and out nearly every day, and H knew immediately what she'd brought the sweet potato for: to be traded for figs. A large fig tree grew outside the toilet of the Hadano house, and there was plenty of ripe fruit on the branches that stretched out over the roof.

"I don't mind picking the figs for you, but I wish you'd come earlier in the morning," H grumbled. "The roof gets so hot in the afternoon, it's a real chore."

But he tucked the basket under his arm just the same and climbed up onto the roof. As he'd expected, it was hot enough to burn the soles of his feet. Hurriedly he pulled off ten or so of the ripest fruits, put them in the basket, then climbed down again. After doing this he put his question:

"Did you get the meaning of yesterday's broadcast right away?"

"I didn't understand what he was saying, but what I did get was that we were stopping the war."

H wondered how on earth she'd managed that.

"To be honest, my old man said things began to go wrong from the time Admiral Yamamoto was killed in action. You couldn't say things like that outside the house, so I kept quiet, but besides that I'd read the leaflet the B29s dropped, so when they said there was going to be an important broadcast, I thought 'Aha!—the Potsdam Declaration!'"

H was astonished that she'd already known about the Potsdam Declaration.

"Do you still have the leaflet?" he asked. "I've never seen it, so I'd like to have a look." He'd heard that leaflets had been dropped, but he hadn't actually seen one himself.

"Yes, I've got it hidden in a drawer at home. I'll get it and show you," she said, going off.

It struck H forcibly just how little even close neighbors had been aware of what others knew or were thinking.

Anyone who picked up a leaflet dropped by an enemy plane was supposed, on pain of punishment, to go and hand it over immediately to the military or ordinary police. But Mrs. Tazaki had kept one hidden, even though she must have known there'd be trouble if she was found out.

She reappeared and produced the piece of paper, folded small, from the pocket of her baggy cotton breeches. H was amused to see the way she took a quick glance around her as she handed it over. There was no longer any danger of being arrested by the military or civil police, but the habit of caution was too deeply ingrained to disappear overnight.

The propaganda leaflet was filled with Chinese characters written, originally, with a writing brush. Quite likely it had been translated and written by a second-generation Japanese in the U.S. forces. It was headed "To the Japanese People": "Today we have come, not to drop bombs, but to inform you of the reply that the U.S. government, representing the United States, Britain, China and the Soviet Union, has made to the terms of surrender proposed by the Japanese government." It went on to describe the terms of the "Potsdam Declaration" as sent by the U.S. secretary of state to the Japanese government.

So Mrs. Tazaki had already known about what George had heard on American shortwave radio.

"I'm sure the Emperor never thought Japan would be defeated like this when the war started," she said. "But it must have been hard on him all the same to have to stop the war."

"I *see*," said H, still pondering what she'd just said. "Do you think other people thought the same way too?"

"I don't know—I mean, we never talked to each other about things like that. But I don't suppose I was the only one who knew. You got pulled in for the smallest bit of loose talk, so you kept what you knew to yourself."

H's skin tingled at the realization of the enormous gap between grownups like this—if they really had looked at things in such a detached way—and the "student soldiers" who'd gone to the front, or other boys at school.

He began to feel alarmed, remembering how the day before, after

436

the broadcast, Takimura and the others had been talking of the Byakko-tai and of "getting a couple of enemy soldiers before being killed oneself." What if there were rallies to protest the surrender at places all over the country, too—at military barracks, for example?

He began to understand more clearly why Sugita-san had decided to have extra keys made, and had talked about "not letting anybody get hold of the weapons under any circumstances."

The following day, when school was to reconvene, H left the house thirty minutes earlier than usual in order to get there before Sugita-san. The older boy also arrived early, well before the other students.

"Here's the key. Don't let anyone else have it whatever you do. Oh yes—and come to the rear of the armory at nine this evening. Put on something that you don't mind getting muddy, and workman's rubber-soled socks, if possible, not shoes. Do you have any?"

"I expect my uncle's got some he'll lend me," said H.

"No," said Sugita quickly, "don't go borrowing them. The shoes you've got on now will do. This is an absolute secret, you're not to tell anyone."

This repeated insistence on secrecy alarmed H rather. He'd trusted that Sugita-san wasn't set on Byakkotai-type do-or-die resistance, but this talk of action to be undertaken apparently under cover of darkness made him uneasy. He put the key in his pocket, but it was so small that he started worrying again in case it should get lost.

He went to the classroom and helped himself to some of the hemp string holding together the attendance register. Asked what he wanted it for, he said it was to repair the broom used for cleaning the room, which was a lie. He passed the string through the hole in the key and hung it around his neck; that finally stopped him worrying, though the hairy string made his chest itch.

When the time came for morning assembly, the whole school formed up on the sports ground, but the message was brief. "You are to take in the spirit of the Imperial edict," the principal declared from the dais, "and strictly avoid any rash or foolhardy behavior. Your next attendance at school will be at 8:00 A.M. on Monday the twentieth. I believe there will be important matters to impart, so all students are required to be present." With that, the students dispersed again.

437

It looked as though the school authorities had not yet made up their minds what to do about the situation.

H was concerned about how Takimura and his cronies would behave. For some reason or other, they didn't seem to be thirsting for blood as they had been immediately afer the Imperial broadcast, but he wondered if they were perhaps plotting something in secret.

He put his five questions to a number of his friends, but they were all taking things surprisingly calmly.

"I first began to think we might lose around the time the air raid sirens started sounding every day. Then, when Kobe got flattened and the papers started talking about a final battle on home soil, I realized we'd never win back the lost ground. Even so, to be honest, I was shocked when I heard that broadcast. What do I think about the Emperor? I'm not sure. But I wonder if the real people responsible aren't the military and politicians who used the Emperor's name to press ahead with the war...."

Such, more or less, was the general drift of what people said. They felt the Emperor was somehow apart from everything else, and seemed to feel it was almost sacrilegious even to use phrases such as "responsibility for the war" in reference to him.

Hunting out Ogura, H asked him the same questions.

"I often heard my father assessing the war situation with his friends," he said, "and I had a vague hunch as to what was going to happen, so I wasn't all that surprised. As to whether His Majesty should be held responsible for the war or not, I don't know, but I admire him for putting an end to it."

Ogura agreed with the view that without the Emperor's broadcast such an end to the war would have been impossible.

It was from Ogura that H learned how Mr. Hata had called together Takimura and his friends and spent two hours dissuading them from action. What had finally won the day, it seemed, was the plea that "to fight on on their own responsibility, without understanding what His Majesty had really meant, would be tantamount to turning their weapons against the Emperor himself—the ultimate act of treachery."

They were persuaded, but they must have felt pretty sick about it, thought H. Since the government and military had gone on instilling into the nation's youth, until the very day before the end of the war, the message that the highest purpose of all Japanese men was "to give up their lives in exchange for the lives of American and British fiends in a final battle on home soil," they must have felt that they'd been left out on a limb.

Relieved though he was that the war was over, H still retained his mistrust and sense of frustration toward "the state," that monstrous entity that had so consistently deceived the ordinary people.

That evening his father came calling for the first time in a while, but made no mention of the end of the war. What he did do, though, was hold out a bag containing two liters or so of rice and say, "Here's some rice we had in stock at the station."

The rice had apparently been part of an emergency stock of food kept for times when the firemen were too busy fighting fires caused by the raids to go home. Now that there were no more raids, they'd rationed it out to the men at the station as a kind of gratuity for all the work they'd done.

In some way it seemed as if giving the rice to H to eat constituted Morio's war-end message to his son.

H enjoyed the white rice, the first he'd had for months. They ate it boiled and plain, with nothing but a light sprinkling of salt. He'd never before realized how good plain white rice could be. On the last of it— his third bowl—he trickled just a little soy sauce; it was every bit as good as the *oyako-don* he'd once eaten on the way home from the moxibustion sessions, and he all but shed tears at the taste.

Uncle Hadano smiled at the pleasure he saw on H's face, but himself ate barely a few mouthfuls. His illness seemed to have taken a turn for the worse recently, and H felt anxious.

After supper H went out with his father as he left to go back to the church. To Uncle Hadano he simply said, "I'm going to a friend's place. I might stay overnight."

He wondered if he was too early, but found Sugita-san and Yukawa-san already there behind the armory. They were sitting on the bare earth with picks and shovels in their arms. There was no need for dugouts anymore, so H wondered what they were going to dig holes for.

439

Now that all three were present, they each inserted a key in one of the dangling padlocks and opened the door of the armory.

"Here's what we're going to do tonight," began Sugita-san. "We're going to take the twelve rifles capable of firing live ammunition that the rifle club has been using, carry them to Mount Ege, dig a hole and bury them. Since we borrowed these rifles from the army, they're still officially in service. The Imperial chrysanthemum crest hasn't been erased, and they were originally recorded in the army's files. However, on May 23 this year the army transferred them to the rifle club and they disappeared from its books.

"Instructor Hisakado was away at the front at the time, so I myself was given the job of seeing to them. But then the war ended before they could be entered in the school's inventory. In other words, these twelve rifles don't officially exist. Sooner or later, rifles, other weapons and ammunition will all have to be surrendered to the American occupation forces. When that happens, the one thing I don't want to hand over is these twelve guns that the rifle club has been using for so long—that symbolize the club, if you like. If there's nothing else for it, then at least I'd like us to bury them ourselves. But if people got wind of what had happened to them, we might be brought to court by the occupation forces and charged with concealing weapons with subversive intent. So keep it absolutely to yourselves, okay?—we're all three to guard the secret to the grave."

H felt himself trembling a little, but he didn't actually oppose what Sugita had said. He too would have resented the idea of tamely handing over these Type 38 infantry rifles to the American forces.

The three of them shouldered four rifles each, emerged from the armory and locked the door behind them. They left all the ammunition where it was, since if any cartridges should ever be dug up along with the rifles, people might assume they'd been hidden with an eye to future resistance activities. To bury the rifles alone would minimize that danger.

Mount Ege was only a kilometer from the school, but each rifle weighed four kilos, and to carry four at a time was quite a load. Moreover, to avoid attracting attention they had to cross roads one at a time cautiously and as quickly as possible. H was tense, remembering the night maneuvers of the past.

Sugita-san, who'd apparently reconnoitered the ground in advance, led them around to the north side of Mount Ege. They stopped to rest a number of times on the way, but even so all three were soaked in sweat by the time they arrived. Stripping to the waist, they hung their shirts on the branch of a tree and wiped themselves with the cotton towels they carried at their waists.

"Right—we'll dig a trench here," said Sugita-san, marking out lines on the ground. "Length, one meter forty; width, fifty centimeters; depth, seventy centimeters. There's not much room, so let's be careful not to injure each other as we work."

Yukawa-san started the work by turning up the soil with his pick, and H took over from him after a while.

The ground was hard at first, but got softer after the first thirty centimeters. As the trench gradually got deeper, H began to feel almost as if they were digging a grave.

"Perhaps we'd better go a bit deeper—another thirty centimeters," said Sugita-san, so in the end they ended up going down a full meter.

"Senoh, get down there ready to take the rifles."

H jumped down into the trench. One by one, he took the rifles as they were held out to him and lined them up at the bottom of the pit, taking care to do it as neatly as possible. When Sugita-san, who was peering in from above, finally gave the okay and told him to come out, Yukawa-san gave him a hand up. Then they shoveled the earth down onto the rifles, and the Mark IV that H had taken such care of disappeared beneath the dirt flung down on it along with the rest.

They went on shoveling in silence, and H was suddenly reminded of how he'd buried the blackened fork in the ruins of his home.

Refilling the trench with the earth they'd excavated produced a slight mound, partly because of the increase in volume caused by digging and partly because of the space occupied by the rifles. This would have given away the fact that something was buried there, so they decided to pare it down carefully to make it flat. A little at a time, they took the surplus dirt and dumped it at a distance, traveling to and fro again and again.

Stamping vigorously on the rectangle to make sure it was really flat, they brought grass and weeds with earth still clinging to their roots and painstakingly planted them on the site.

Their work done, they collapsed on their backs on the grass and gazed up at the sky. Watching the stars twinkling, H wondered to himself how, years from now, he would recall the events of this night.

All his life, he felt sure, he would remember how in trepidation they had buried the rifles late that night, the night of August 18, 1945, three days after the end of the war. For him, probably, the day they'd buried the rifles would always be the day on which the war had really ended.

Sugita-san sat up, crossed his legs, and took a packet of cigarettes out of his pocket, offering one to Yukawa-san at the same time. One of them struck a match, then lit the cigarettes, and both simultaneously inhaled deeply. Suddenly H wanted to smoke too.

Watching the tips of the cigarettes glow and fade like fireflies as the two seniors smoked, H felt a kind of peace. He'd never yet smoked, not just because to be caught would mean expulsion from school, but because it hadn't appealed to him. Tonight, though, he wanted to try it.

"May I have one?" he asked.

Sugita-san looked surprised, but gave him a cigarette. Watching H putting the cigarette clumsily between his lips, he laughed and said, "Don't blame me!" and then lit it for him.

At the first puff, H was seized with a furious fit of coughing.

43

The Army of Occupation

"I met His Lechery this morning—in a suit, not a uniform, so I didn't recognize the old Instructor Tamori. All smiles he was, too. I wondered at first who this nice middle-aged gentleman was!"

"Me too," said Hirobe. "Asked me politely how I was doing—it gave me the creeps."

"He's what they mean when they talk about a '180-degree flipflop.' It's disgusting," declared Okubo. "When you remember all the things he said up to now, he really ought to slit his belly. But no—now he's suddenly greasing up to the students. It makes you sick."

Conversation in the classroom focused on the remarkable transformation of the "demon instructor" into a perfectly ordinary middle-aged gentleman.

A number of teachers besides Instructor Tamori were wondering anxiously how they should behave from now on.

There were others, though, who blithely went on hitting students or shouting "collective responsibility!" and having the whole class sit on their heels in a line on the hard corridor floor, still wearing their gaiters. After thirty minutes of this favorite punishment, they would lose all feeling in their legs and fall flat when they tried to stand up again at the end of it. The students themselves were angered by such slyly sadistic methods, but the teachers using them were probably just trying to demonstrate that their approach to education was unaffected by the end of the war.

In short the teachers, like everyone else, seemed unsettled, probably worried as to what the occupation forces would do when they landed, and undecided as to what they themselves should be doing in the meantime.

As for the school board as a whole, frequent meetings of the teaching staff were apparently being held but, perhaps because there'd been no detailed directives from the education ministry, the only real decision reached was to warn students "not to do anything rash or foolhardy."

Meeting Mr. Hata in the corridor, H took the opportunity to ask, "Why do they keep postponing the address they said the principal was going to give?"

"One thing," Mr. Hata said, "is that when we asked the prefectural authorities what we should do with the photographs of Their Majesties, they just said they'd 'be in contact later.' If the principal's going to talk to the students it would be best to wait for clear instructions, but it seems that's going to take some time."

"Then why don't you say something on those lines? Like telling them to wait a while, for example?..."

At this, Mr. Hata stared at H for a moment, then walked off without saying anything more. It looked very much as though he was upset. H, who hadn't meant to criticize, regretted having talked out of place. Far from being critical of Mr. Hata himself, he held him in respect. Nor was H the only one: even as the system had become steadily more militaristic, a lot of students had sensed in his classes that Mr. Hata had always had the students' interests at heart.

Mr. Matsumoto, the English teacher, was another who was popular among them. In H's first class on entering Second Middle, Mr. Matsumoto had told them, "I'd rather see you become bighearted fools than clever and mean-spirited."

The sudden encouragement to become fools had startled the new students, but impressed them all the same.

Although some teachers like Mr. Hata and Mr. Matsumoto continued to behave toward their students in exactly the same way as before, however external circumstances changed, others were flustered and panicky at having to tell their pupils things totally at variance with what they'd been saying up to now.

Rather like the litmus paper they used in physics experiments, the acceptance of the Potsdam Declaration served to draw the line more clearly between the teachers they could trust and those they couldn't.

Mr. Murobushi, generally resented for his harsh treatment of students doing farm work, had suddenly turned gentle. Not that the end of the war spelled an end to such work—the food shortage was far too general for that.

The Central Japan Unit 4126, which had been stationed at the school, was disbanded and withdrew.

The school factory was closed down. The machines that had been installed in the assembly hall and classrooms were loaded onto trucks, the students helping the factory workers carry them. For three days after that, all classes were suspended so that the student body as a whole could join in cleaning and setting to rights the newly vacated assembly hall.

Finally it began to look something like a school assembly hall again. Even so, machine oil must have impregnated the floor fairly thoroughly, for the smell, not so bothersome while the machines had been there, suddenly asserted itself unpleasantly.

The "octopus pot" dugouts that had pockmarked the grounds were likewise to be filled in before the occupation forces arrived, and students were going busily to and fro wheeling barrows full of earth. Nor was this the only manual work: for four full days the students were out among the city's ruins clearing bomb sites. Classes were out of the question.

The reason why students were sent out to clear ruins may have been that to make them do community work seemed the safest course for the prefectural and school authorities to take, since at this stage it wasn't yet clear what the occupation policy would be.

The mayor of Kobe City paid a visit to the school. What he'd discussed with the principal wasn't clear, but there was a new burst of activity in the teachers' room.

The newspaper for August 31 carried an item, with a photograph, announcing: "At 2:05 P.M. yesterday General MacArthur, Supreme Commander of the Allied Forces, arrived at Atsugi airfield in Kanagawa." Here we go, thought H; from now on, Japan's going to be ruled by occupation forces. He wondered how they'd set about it.

There was morning assembly that day, the first for a long time.

"From now on," the principal told them from the dais, "I'm sure you'll often come into contact with the American flag and the American national anthem. You must be careful to show them respect. You must not look on America as the enemy anymore, and avoid doing anything that might be seen as insulting or defiant. You must also be careful not to go on using things designed to foster the fighting spirit, or the history and geography textbooks in use until now. The gliding, rifle, bayonet, fencing and judo clubs will be disbanded forthwith so as to avoid the suspicion that we are still carrying on military training. The equipment involved will be scrapped or handed over in accordance with occupation instructions."

Listening to all this, H wondered what he should do about the key he still had to the armory.

On his way to the classroom, he made a quick detour via the armory to take a look. The three padlocks still dangled from the door so nothing untoward seemed to have happened. He was heading back when he encountered Yukawa-san.

"Sugita-san was looking for you," the older boy said. "You've just missed him. Be behind the armory at lunch break, and make sure no one else sees you. I'll be coming with him."

When lunchtime came and he went around to the back of the armory, he was startled to find that a change in the surroundings had made it almost impossible to obey the warning not to be seen by other people. The judo training hut recently vacated by Unit 4126 had been taken over by Mr. Kameoka's and other teachers' families who'd lost their homes in the raids. The back of the armory was visible from the windows of the judo building. Disturbed by this, H concealed himself behind the shed where agricultural implements were kept, about fifty meters from the armory, to await the two seniors.

He felt a certain reluctance in doing all this. With the burial of the rifles he'd felt he personally was finished with the war, but it seemed he'd been wrong. He wanted to be free from this kind of thing just as soon as possible.

He caught sight of Sugita-san and Yukawa-san coming up the steps from the sports ground below. Sticking his head out from behind the shed, he waved to signal his presence and also to warn the two seniors

446

to beware of the judo building window. As he waved, it occurred to him that the hand signals he'd learned in the rifle club were proving useful.

They immediately got his meaning, casually parted company, and walked slowly and separately to the back of the tool shed. They were seen by Mr. Kameoka's wife, who was hanging out the washing, but didn't seem to arouse her suspicions in any way.

H opened the front of his shirt, took off the key dangling from his neck, and held it out silently to Sugita-san.

"Okay," said the other as he took it, "now I can hand all three of them over to the school authorities and leave responsibility for supervising the armory to them. On the day of the Emperor's broadcast my one concern was to guard the keys, but I needn't have worried so much. Even so, who'd have thought the whole country would take the end of the war as calmly as this? Oh yes—and there's a piece of good news too: Instructor Hisakado's been demobilized and is coming home. The word came from his family yesterday."

It was the first cheerful piece of news H had heard in ages. Hisakado's call-up papers had been late in arriving, so he'd come through safely without ever being sent to fight overseas. However, since he'd been a military instructor it didn't seem likely he'd get his job back at Second Middle.

"No need to worry what he'll do now," said Yukawa-san with a smile, as though reading H's concern. "I expect he'll go back to being a clockmaker again."

Now that H had returned the key and heard that Instructor Hisakado was coming home, he felt much easier. It was over at last. The question now was what the occupation forces were going to do. He was interested and rather anxious at the same time to see how they went about clearing up after the war.

It had been announced that the occupation forces would be coming into Kobe over a period of three days from September 24. To avoid confusion during that period, traffic was to be restricted in various parts of the city, and classes were to be suspended for three days at schools.

H wanted to know what kinds of weapons the American troops had been using to fight the Japanese. To find out for himself, he decided to watch them come in on one of the roads where traffic was restricted.

He went to the office of the *Kobe Shimbun* to ask Mr. Odagiri which places in Kobe were being set aside for use by occupation forces. A fairly large site near Kobe Station was to be devoted to the construction of living quarters, he was told; in addition, a number of office buildings in the vicinity of the Daimaru department store in Sannomiya were also to be taken over. If he waited on one of the roads leading to either of these places, he should be able to see the occupation troops as they came in.

On the morning of September 24, he thought he'd invite Yokota to go and watch with him, partly because his friend hadn't shown up at school for some time and he was eager to see him, and also because he thought he'd be interested in the American equipment in the same way as himself.

Yokota wasn't at home, though. His younger sister, who answered the door, told H that he wouldn't be back until evening. She didn't know where he'd gone, she said, but he went out every day hauling his hand-cart around.

H wrote a note for him, then set off for Shinkaichi. Both sides of the broad street where the streetcars ran were already lined with spectators.

He took up a position in front of a burned-out office building on the west side, where he'd have the sun behind him and not be dazzled and could also be sure of some shade. The route was closely guarded, with police stationed along it at regular intervals keeping a strict lookout. They were obviously on edge, since there'd be hell to pay if anyone rushed out into the road in a gesture of opposition to the occupying troops.

He had to wait an hour and a half at least, but it was worth it. What he saw—mainly the small arms carried by the soldiers on their jeeps—settled the issue once and for all.

The box-shaped magazines were on the outside, so they must hold a large number of rounds. No bolt-type reloading mechanism was visible either, which meant that—unlike the Type 38 infantry rifle that H was used to—you didn't have to work the bolt after every shot in order to put another cartridge in the breech, but could fire continuously just by pulling the trigger.

No wonder the Japanese had lost, thought H, gazing at the guns. And it wasn't just the guns either: the American vehicles, too—the ultra-mobile jeeps—left him open-mouthed. Japanese infantry units had had no such vehicles; in the intervals between battles, they'd slogged around on foot....

Relying partly on memory, H sketched the Americans' weapons in the sketchbook Ogura had given him. If he wanted to do anything more accurate, the only way would be to infiltrate a U.S. army camp and draw a rifle from life. He'd have to think of ways of doing it.

Watching the steady procession of covered trucks and jeeps as it passed, H marveled at the difference between them and the former Japanese army, and at the cheerfulness of the American troops. Perhaps the citizens lining the streets felt the same way; they actually waved at the men whom only a while earlier they'd been calling "fiends."

Possibly the shock of seeing the occupation forces with his own eyes had been greater than H had thought, for suddenly that night he had a violent attack of diarrhea. It reminded him of how he'd had diarrhea on December 8, 1941, when he'd heard of the outbreak of the Pacific War.

He went to the toilet, hands pressed to his belly, so many times that Uncle Hadano got worried.

"You're young, with a lot of years ahead," he said. "You should look after yourself. I'm going back to Gifu at the beginning of next month. I'll pay the rent for this place up to the end of November, so you can live here alone or with your father. I don't know how I'll be next year, but I'm ready for whatever comes, so it's okay."

Perhaps this had something to do with it, but H woke up that night crying from a terrifying nightmare.

He'd been intending to go and watch the occupation forces every day during the three days off school, but to his great regret the diarrhea kept him in bed. In all he had to take four days off school before the giddiness and the weakness in his limbs got better.

Sleeping in the same room as Uncle Hadano during those days, H noticed that from time to time he had quite severe attacks of pain and was struggling not to let it show.

When he went back to school he found several mimeographed sheets bearing notices from the occupation forces and directives from

449

the ministry of education posted on the notice board in the corridor outside the teachers' room. For the school authorities to make communications from the occupation forces available to the students showed a remarkable determination to ensure that they were carried out.

The instructions from the occupation forces covered, among other things, the removal of the small shrine in the school grounds containing the Imperial photographs; the abolition of the martial arts and military training; the prohibition of group worship at Shinto shrines; a ban on the enforcement of belief in any particular religion at school; and a ban on anything restricting the individual's freedom of thought and belief.

A message came from Mr. Ichihashi telling students to assemble for work in the judo training hall. On doing so, they were told that the school had decided to take up the tatami mats covering the floor of the *dojo* as proof that it had purged Second Middle of the martial arts.

Whether or not the school had in fact been instructed to go as far as that, the tatami were to be loaded onto a truck and taken elsewhere, leaving six each for the families of Mr. Kameoka and other teachers who'd lost their homes.

The bulk of them were to go for use in temporary dwellings for the homeless, which was fair enough, but the extreme haste with which they were disposed of looked to H like oversensitivity to the occupation forces.

Hearing that Instructor Hisakado had come to the school, H went to see him. "Welcome home, sir!" he started in a loud voice, saluting.

But the other held up a hand to check him. "Not so loud," he said, "and stop saluting."

Having been an army officer, Mr. Hisakado wouldn't be getting his job as a teacher back, and H wanted to take this opportunity to ask him two things: "Was that training undertaken on special instructions from the army?" he inquired. "And secondly, that time when you told me to go to Mitsubishi Electric in full military gear with a rifle, I was told to keep it secret. I've always wondered what was secret about it—can you tell me now, please?"

But Mr. Hisakado refused. "It's all over now," he said. "Just forget you ever asked me, too."

"When you start your watch and clock shop," said H, to change the subject, "I'll paint the letters on the glass of the show window for you." He'd never done painted letters before, but he was confident that he could.

"The shop was burned down in the raids, so I'm going to set up a stall in the main street at Shinkaichi and start by doing repairs. I hope sometimes you'll drop in on your way back from school and look after the stall for a while."

At school, all kinds of things had changed during the past month or so.

The first major change was the abolition of saluting and other formalized greetings.

In the past, whenever a student went to the teachers' room he had first to announce in a loud voice his grade, class, name and the nature of his business; then, when granted permission to enter, to say "I am coming in" before actually doing so. Then again, as he left, he had to repeat his name and announce "I am leaving." Now, though, all you needed to do was bow briefly and state your business as you opened the door.

It was no longer necessary, either, to make formal acknowledgment every single time you met a teacher on the school premises. Until now you'd had to snap to attention and exclaim in a loud voice "Sir!" if you encountered a teacher on a streetcar or train, but this was abolished too.

It was Mr. Sumiya who seemed most pleased by the scrapping of this practice; the students, though, were rather disappointed. Up to now, whenever a group of them had encountered him on a streetcar they would chorus loudly "Saluting Mr. Sumiya!" and smartly salute together, thus alarming him by perfectly legitimate means. With an embarrassed "Making a fellow jump...!" he would worm his way through the crowd until he was out of reach. Students would aim to take the same Sanyo line train just for the pleasure of seeing him do it. But they'd only done it because they were fond of him; with teachers they disliked they tried to avoid getting on the same train, and took care as far as possible not to meet them on the street, even.

Besides the abolition of formal greetings, measures to "democratize education" as a whole were being introduced at a rapid pace.

One measure for which students were thankful was the prohibition of "corrective punching," in which teachers used their fists on students suspected of some offense. There were some teachers, though, who interpreted this as applying solely to fists, and even after the ban H was still subjected to slaps across the face. It seemed he was rather prone to giving the teachers cause for anger.

The general impression given by occupation directives sent to the school was that they were concentrating on completely eradicating Shintoism, the view apparently being that Japanese militarism was a product of Shintoism, with its focus on Emperor-worship, as a state religion. To ensure that neither was being practiced any longer, an occupation inspector, together with an interpreter, paid repeated visits to the school.

The focus of these checks included whether the Shinto-style miniature shrine in the *dojo* had been removed; whether the building enshrining the Imperial portraits had been demolished; whether there were any lingering signs of Shinto rites; whether all other things that might suggest or symbolize Shintoism had been done away with.

There were specific rules laid down for worship at Shinto shrines too. Until this time a visit to the nearby Nagata Shrine had been an almost daily ritual at the school, but now group visits were to be prohibited.

The ban extended not just to the Nagata Shrine, but also to worship at the Minatogawa Shrine, a favorite with the people of Kobe.

The Ise Shrines and the Meiji Shrine in Tokyo were singled out by name as subjects of the ban on group worship. What was surprising, though, was that obeisance in front of, or in the direction of, the Imperial Palace in Tokyo was specifically excluded from the ban.

To H this seemed incredibly odd. The separation of Emperor and State Shintoism was presumably a primary object of occupation policy, yet here it was, in seeming contradiction, according the Emperor special treatment! After much thought, H finally worked out a theory. America had known that the only way to occupy Japan without bloodshed was to get the Emperor himself to proclaim an end to hostilities. So it probably felt now that, in order to carry through without resistance policies involving a fundamental reform of the country, it would be better not to deny the existence of the Emperor.

Another thing the occupation forces were particularly careful about was snuffing out any latent militarism.

Soon after the beginning of October an officer from the Nagata police station and an American army inspector came to impound the rifles in the armory. The 200–250 rifles that had been used in military training were taken down from their racks, loaded onto a truck, and driven away.

To H's relief, nobody noticed that twelve rifles had disappeared. The very thought of what would have happened if the fact that they'd buried them had come to light was horrifying, since the earlier discovery of a few dummy rifles used in bayonet fencing in a corner of the *dojo* had caused a great fuss. These, being made of wood, could never have been used as weapons, but in the eyes of the American inspector they seemed to smack of latent militarism.

It was natural enough for an occupying army to confiscate rifles and ammunition, but even the gliding club had been ordered to dismantle its gliders into unrecognizable pieces.

"They won't even allow us gliders," grumbled an older student from the club, "because, quote, 'It wouldn't do to disband the forces and leave them the capacity to make planes'...."

H found this so stupid that he had an urge to smoke. He knew that cigarettes were all bitter taste and smoke, but he somehow had a powerful urge to inhale one deeply and blow the smoke out again—hard.

44

The M1 Carbine

By the traditional calendar autumn was already well under way, but the sun's rays were still strong.

The third-grade students who'd been rounded up for what was called "clearing bomb sites" had had no classes at school for nearly a week.

This time, they'd been told, it was "work on the water supply," but all it consisted in was hunting out leaks in the water mains among the ruins and cutting off the supply.

H and his classmates, supervised by a few teachers, assembled in the grounds of the Nakamichi National School, where an employee of the water board explained how to go about the work. What it came down to was finding the box containing the main tap for each house and turning it off tightly to prevent wastage from leaks.

The students were disgruntled to find that the end of the war hadn't meant an end to being mobilized for war work. But the sight of their home district stretching before them, a burned-out wasteland, was enough to stifle complaints. Nothing could be done about it without work.

Armed with picks and shovels, they went about the ruins in groups of three, digging through tiles and plaster from walls that had collapsed in the fires, looking on each site for the main tap. It was quite hard work, and they got hungry. The man from the water board directed the work with a lordly expression. He kept them hard at it, and watched so closely that it was nearly impossible for them to take it easy, and H and his companions worked off their feelings by talking deliberate nonsense among themselves as they scrabbled at the dirt.

They were rewarded for their work with one bread roll each, much to their indignation. "Do they expect us to be grateful for a single roll like this?" they grumbled, the sense of insult all the stronger for the knowledge that they were privately counting on it.

Work was to be suspended if it rained, so they kept a watchful eye on the sky.

"I wonder if those clouds couldn't be made to come this way," said Fukushima to H one day. "Why don't you pray to that God of yours for some rain?" H wasn't a believer, and even if he had been the idea of praying to the Christian God for rain seemed ludicrous, but he said "Right, here goes," and with a suitably pious expression and his own idea of a rainmaker's gestures, muttered something unintelligible, rounding it off with an "Amen."

Before an hour had passed it did in fact start to rain, a coincidence that startled H himself more than anybody. "Christian rainmaking really *works*," teased Okubo, with a laugh.

Threatened with a downpour, the three of them quickly shouldered their picks and shovels and made a dash for it. Running a hundred meters or so through the ruins in drenching rain, they finally found a place that offered some shelter. A lean-to clinging like a garbage bin to the wall of a gutted building, it had a roof of scorched galvanized iron that promised at least a little protection from the deluge.

Tumbling over each other in their haste to get inside, they found the interior too dark to make anything out at first. Soon, however, they noticed two pairs of eyes staring at them in the gloom. These belonged to an elderly man and a boy who looked like his grandson, both crouching in a corner of the room with frightened expressions. It must certainly have been terrifying to have three figures armed with picks suddenly come bursting in.

The three boys, who'd assumed the hut was uninhabited, were also surprised. Looking around the leaky shelter, all they could see in the way of living necessities were a single straw mat, futons, a pot, a washbasin and a few blackened pieces of crockery.

They had been looking for a sheltered place to eat their bread rolls, but they could hardly keep them all to themselves in front of the old man and the boy.

Thrusting a hand into his backpack, Fukushima winked as though to say to the others, "Let's share them out."

Rather reluctantly H got out his own. The rolls were a bit damp from the rain, but each of them pulled off a quarter and handed it to the boy and the old man. As they took the bread, the old man bowed and thanked them with almost embarrassing effusiveness, and H felt a bit ashamed of his own meanness.

Everyone sat chewing in such stony silence that H finally told a story about His Lechery that he'd heard from one of the seniors.

"This senior took a watch to the Tamori pawnshop and got a better offer for it there than anywhere else, so he asked H.L. if he should recommend people to bring their stuff there. He was only being sarcastic, of course, but H.L. said quite seriously, 'Oh yes, please!'"

"He's a nasty type!" said Okubo indignantly. "The way he carried on till then, he was as good as a war criminal—ought to have slit his belly on the day the war ended—but here he is now, carrying on living with no sense of decency. He's got no more guts than that fellow Hideki Tojo."

At this point the old man suddenly interrupted.

"Tojo's a disgrace to the Japanese military! Who was it talked about 'never suffering the shame of being captured alive'? Hideki Tojo himself, of course. In that way, General Anami was much more true to his beliefs. Both my own sons were called up and got killed in action. This boy's mother, too—she was burned to death in a raid. I'm an army man myself, so I know anything can happen in a war; you have to resign yourself to it. But if you ask me, the man who directed the war—Tojo —should have killed himself immediately the day it ended."

His voice had been getting louder and louder, and the tirade left H and his friends feeling overwhelmed and confused.

There was certainly something in what the old man said. For a whole month after the end of the war, Tojo had done absolutely nothing to suggest he accepted any responsibility, but had skulked, alive and well as ever, in his own home.

GHQ had embarked on a campaign to arrest "suspected war criminals." When they arrived at Tojo's home, he called to them through the window to "wait a while," then went to his room and shot himself in the left abdomen with a pistol in an apparent suicide attempt. Kicking in the door and rushing inside, the American MPs took him to a hospital, where his life was saved. The facts were reported in the press, and everybody knew about the episode.

"Any normal person who wanted to commit suicide would shoot himself in the head," resumed the old man. "Shooting himself in the belly probably meant he didn't mean to die in the first place. If he wanted to live on because he had something he absolutely must testify to, there'd have been no reason to panic and try to kill himself when he looked like being arrested. It was a fake suicide! General Anami, now, *he* did it like a man—slit his belly, then cut the artery in his own neck."

General Anami, who'd held the post of Minister of War when peace was declared, was one of the government ministers who signed the Imperial proclamation of the end of hostilities. When his brother-in-law, Major Takeshita, who'd planned a coup d'etat for the eve of the war's end, came to call on him, he had already written his parting poem and his final message. They drank together, and then around dawn killed themselves. Anami's final message—a note saying "With a small life I seek to atone for a great transgression: August 14, evening"—was found, stained with blood, on his desk.

Many other military men besides Anami committed ritual suicide, among them Vice-Admiral Takijiro Onishi. Said to be the originator of the suicide squadrons that terrorized the American navy by flying their planes head-on into its warships, Onishi killed himself at his official residence. His final message, as reported in the press, was as follows:

> To the heroic spirits of the suicide squadrons:
>   You fought well, and I thank you from the depths of my heart. Transforming yourselves into living bombs, you went to your deaths with faith in final victory. Yet your convictions were, in the end, not to be fulfilled. I apologize to you, my subordinates who died in battle, and to the families you left behind, with my own death.

"I don't mean that just killing yourself is enough to settle everything," the old man went on, "but people should clearly accept responsibility for what they themselves have done. It was through bastards like Tojo that I lost my sons and my daughter-in-law." He was practically shouting by now, and H became curious as to his real feelings.

"Do you mean it was all right to die if it was for the Emperor?" he ventured. "What about the Emperor's own responsibility?..."

"And what might you mean by that?" the man burst in in a startlingly loud voice. "His Majesty was the victim! All this happened because the people around him never told him the facts!"

His face became so red as he yelled this that H panicked, fearing that any more excitement might cause him to collapse on the spot.

"I'm sorry.... It's stopped raining," he said hastily, "we have to get back to work," and rushed out of the shack.

"I was scared," said Okubo, running by his side. "You always ask so many things! You ought to be more careful—if that guy had been younger, you'd have got pasted."

"You certainly would!" Fukushima concurred, nodding vigorously.

Although the rain had stopped, they found nobody around when they got back to the bomb site, not even the man from the water board, so they took the opportunity to knock off for the day.

There was somewhere H wanted to drop in at on the way home, so he asked Okubo to return his pick for him.

"I'm going to Yokota's place to see what's happening," he said. "I've been worried about him for some time."

"He's hardly likely to be home around this time," said Okubo. "They say he's making money on the black market. He's a lot better off than *we* are."

"What's that?" H exclaimed, not taking it in immediately.

Yokota, Okubo explained, had gone into business on his own account, and was hauling his cart out to the farms in Kakogawa, buying up food and selling it to black market dealers.

"I just found out the other day. I bumped into him near Daikai-dori, and he grinned and looked a bit embarrassed. He'd got his cart to look as though it was loaded with household goods being brought back to Kobe from the country, but actually he'd got black market rice and vegetables hidden in a dresser. He was boasting that he'd never once got caught in a police check. I suppose when the police see a boy pulling a cart they just think, 'Nice to see a kid who's looking after his parents.' "

H felt a renewed admiration for Yokota. Instead of worrying about who'd been responsible for the war, he was shrewdly getting on with the business of living.

But instead of going to Yokota's place the three of them went off to Shinkaichi, where Instructor Hisakado was supposed to have his stall.

The picks and shovels they carried on their shoulders attracted repeated bids from street sellers offering to buy them for good prices. It seemed there was a premium on such tools at the moment. "Why don't we just sell them and get something decent to eat?" they joked as they walked along the main street of Shinkaichi.

This had been the main entertainment district, and though the buildings on both sides were charred ruins, the street was already bustling with life. People were selling furniture and crockery by the roadside, and one stall even offered both secondhand shoes and repairs.

Hearing the clanging of metal being hammered and seeing a small crowd gathered, they took a look and found a man with a cotton towel bound, workman-style, around his forehead, hammering metal helmets on an anvil to refashion them into cooking pots.

Only a short while before, when the raids had been at their height, helmets had been essential for personal protection, but now they typified everything that was useless. The three boys stopped to watch the process of transforming them into cooking pots. First the cloth and leather were removed from the inside and the holes filled with rivets, then the rounded top of the helmet was hammered out to make a flat base for the pot. They asked the man how much he charged for the work: "Ten yen a helmet," was the answer.

The number of stalls lining the street on both sides seemed to have increased since H had last been there.

Besides the stalls selling *zosui*, broth with dumplings and fried foods, there were others selling secondhand undershirts and even black market cigarettes.

There, amongst the hustle and bustle, they found Hisakado's watch and clock stall. He was repairing a clock, with a magnifying glass screwed into one eye, so the three of them lined up in front of the stall to surprise him.

"What, you lot?" he exclaimed, noticing them and laughing. "Customers are welcome, but how can I make a living from people who don't even own watches?"

They asked him how business was. His best customers were the newly arrived American troops, he told them. There was a U.S. army base close by, so his choice of a site for the stall had been a good one.

"They bring their watches along and ask me to mend them—some because the glass got cracked in the fighting, others because water got in and they stopped. It brings it home to you that they're soldiers who've actually seen action."

H asked about the model of gun the occupying troops had been carrying, thinking that Hisakado would be the man most likely to know.

"That gun?—it's an M1 carbine. I heard about it from a soldier who came to get his watch repaired. It can fire thirty rounds automatically. You say you want to have a look at one, but I hope you're not thinking of going to the camp and asking them to show you. You'll get shot if you don't look out!"

As he listened, though, H already had a good idea of how he might get a look at the gun. He'd do sketches of the American troops for free; then, once he was friendly with them, persuade them to show him one.

Hisakado agreed that it might be a good idea. "Show me if you get to sketch the gun," he said.

The next Sunday H set out for a building near the Daimaru department store that had survived the fires and was being used as an occupation forces hospital. It looked like a promising place to begin.

A black American was standing guard at the entrance, holding a rifle. It took some courage to approach him, but H resolutely went up and informed him—or more accurately, showed him a prepared text that he'd got George Fujita to write in English on the cover of his sketchbook—that he would do portraits of the sick soldiers for free to cheer them up.

H was rather nervous about his reaction, but the guard showed a surprising interest and, although he was on duty, said, "You do *my* portrait to begin with." Gesturing to him to keep still, H began drawing. He'd never examined another person's face at such close quarters before, and found it fascinating.

About ten minutes later, when the outlines were done, the sitter began to get impatient to see the result. When H let him see it, he showed an almost exaggerated delight and kept repeating "Well! It's just like me!"

"I'll make it a bit blacker, then it'll be still more like you," H suggested.

"No!" said the man, putting a hand on the sketch to indicate that he didn't want it any darker. So H tore out the page and gave it to him, to be thanked effusively.

From this incident H learned that some black people preferred to be shown paler than they actually were.

The guard showed the picture to an officer who happened to be passing and pointed to H. "This kid did it," he said.

The officer looked from H to the picture and back again, and then said "Would you do me too?"

H, inwardly rejoicing, made a counterproposal: "If you'll let me sketch an M1 carbine." To his astonishment, the officer said quite simply "Okay."

Well, thought H in amazement, what a difference from the Japanese forces! In order to track down an M1 carbine, he'd been prepared to come here for any number of Sundays on end, never dreaming that he'd achieve the cherished goal in less than an hour.

H was taken into the lobby of the hospital and told he could do his pictures there. Several other soldiers gathered around, all of them tall and well built. He didn't know whether they were male nursing orderlies or ordinary soldiers being treated there, but being surrounded by them made him feel a little uneasy.

The officer he'd started sketching was also an Afro-American, so H took care not to make him too dark.

As he worked he asked the other about the Empire State Building.

"I've never been to New York," he was told. The officer's home was in a town not far from Arizona, which H knew of from Western movies.

H had known from the map that America was a big country, but to hear that there were people who didn't know anything about New York made him feel it was bigger even than he'd imagined.

He'd have liked to ask all kinds of other things, but unfortunately his English didn't extend beyond a few phrases. Next time he came, he thought, he'd bring George along as interpreter.

When he handed over the finished sketch, the officer was delighted.

"Hold on a moment," he said, and had someone fetch the carbine as he'd promised.

The M1 that was placed on a table before him was far shorter than the Type 38 infantry rifle that H had fired.

"May I measure it?" he asked with the aid of gestures.

"Okay."

H promptly produced a tape measure from his pocket and measured the distance from the muzzle to the stock: a mere ninety centimeters. The Type 38 measured one meter twenty-seven—a full thirty-seven centimeters' difference.

He took the gun in his hand: it was astonishingly light. He asked a soldier standing nearby how much it weighed. He didn't know, so the officer told a subordinate to go and weigh it.

"How many rounds does it hold?" he asked.

"Normally fifteen, but thirty if you change the magazine."

The soldier who'd gone to weigh the gun came back. "Five and a half pounds," he reported.

At 450 grams to the pound, that worked out at slightly under 2.5 kilos.

H almost groaned aloud: the Type 38 infantry rifle weighed a good four kilos!

No wonder Japan had lost, he told himself yet again. Those tall, tough American troops, with their jeeps that could manage even mountain tracks, had been armed with carbines that were short, light, and could fire thirty rounds automatically. The Japanese forces facing them, hiding in jungles and caves without hope of supplies or reinforcements, constantly battling hunger, had had to shoulder manually operated guns that were long and heavy and could fire only five rounds at a time.

Just comparing the two infantry rifles would make it clear even to a primary school kid which side would have the advantage in battle. Nor had the disparity only developed after the beginning of the war. The Type 38 rifle had been designated the official army rifle in the thirty-eighth year of the Meiji era—1905. Japan had fought until 1945 with a gun that had basically not been improved for a full forty years.

It was true that in the middle of the war, in 1940, a new rifle, the Mark 99, had been produced, but even that was only fifteen centimeters shorter than the Type 38 and had only a slightly larger caliber. This new gun, which had been used on some fronts, was hand-operated like its predecessor, and the magazine still held only five bullets.

As he sketched the M1 carbine, H could almost have cried. Everything, right down to the smallest firearms, had been on a totally different scale; yet not even the Japanese troops, let alone the general public, had been told the truth. The top brass must have known the facts since prewar days, but their motto had been, "Don't waste a single bullet; fight with faith in victory! The Yamato spirit is on our side!"

Unlike the Russo-Japanese war of the Meiji era, though, the Pacific War had been a war of material resources and logistics.

H was so intent on drawing the carbine and asking questions about it that the officer, intrigued, asked him half-jokingly, "Were you a soldier yourself, then?"

"Of course!" said H with a smile.

"My, my!" he exclaimed, spreading his hands and roaring with laughter.

H left the building after shaking hands with five or six American soldiers and pursued by the officer's voice saying behind him, "Come and see us again, and do some sketches for the other boys too."

On the way back he dropped in at Mr. Hisakado's watch and clock stall. Examining the sketch of the M1 carbine with interest, the instructor plied H with questions, greeting the answers with repeated exclamations of surprise and admiration.

"No wonder we couldn't win, even on the ground," he said. Even he himself, a military instructor teaching in a school, hadn't known what kind of infantry rifles enemy troops had been armed with.

Returning to the house, H found his father there. Uncle Hadano was to return to Gifu two days later, and Morio was helping him pack his futons and clothing. His physical condition was deteriorating visibly, and Morio had apparently decided to accompany him on the train. Long-distance trains were so crowded that the only way to get on and off was through the windows, which was a strain even for someone with the necessary physical strength.

There was another piece of news too: his mother and Yoshiko were returning to Kobe. The family had at last got lucky in the lottery for a "home for air raid victims," so all four of its members, till now spread under three separate roofs, would at last be able to live under the same roof again together.

45

Homes for Air Raid Victims

A long, long letter came from H's mother, eight pages packed with fine handwriting.

It said, among other things, that Yoshiko was excited to be coming back to Kobe in the near future, and that H's cousin Tatsuo, who'd been in Hiroshima City when the atomic bomb was dropped, had had a miraculous escape and was back home again now.

H was overjoyed to hear that "Tatchan," who he'd feared might be dead, was safe after all.

On the day the bomb fell Tatsuo had been in class inside the school building; that had saved his life. His desk had been on the corridor side, the side farthest from the windows, so it seemed he'd got away with only slight injuries. The students nearer the windows had suffered burns, and were covered with blood from being pierced all over by fragments of glass. Other students of another class in the same grade, who'd been doing gymnastics stripped to the waist on the sports ground, had been annihilated by the flash and blast.

H, who'd only learned about the full horror of Hiroshima and Nagasaki since the end of the war, realized that the power of the atomic bomb was of a very different dimension from what the newspapers at the time had suggested, with their talk of white underwear being effective in preventing burns, and putting wooden boards over an "octopus pot" for protection.

Even a middle school student like H knew that the military's censor-ship was very strict, and that any paper that described the actual damage and wrote the truth would immediately have had publication suspended. Even so, he felt that their cooperation with the military in publishing false information over a long period had gone too far.

Once the war ended they should have admitted it and apologized to their readers. In practice, not a single piece had appeared that recognized their fault in continuously publishing misinformation. What was more, they seemed reluctant even to use the word "defeat." The expression "surrender" too was nowhere to be found in their pages until the September 2 edition, when there appeared an article headed "Surrender Ceremony Today on Board the *Missouri*."

In other ways, too, H was annoyed by what he felt was the duplicity of the press.

Again and again, it seemed to him, the newspapers would urge something that seemed perfectly reasonable, then fail to carry it out themselves. One case in point concerned the new method of spelling Japanese and writing it horizontally.

It had been in 1942, the year before H entered middle school, that it was decided that whenever Japanese was spelled out in the phonetic syllabary, the spelling should be changed to represent the pronunciation more accurately, and that when it was written horizontally it should read from left to right, not from right to left as hitherto.

The newspapers of the day, if he remembered rightly, had all declared that these reforms were necessary "to help spread the Japanese language throughout Asia"—so they themselves ought to have set an example. But what had actually happened was peculiar, with left-to-right and right-to-left headings to be found on one and the same page. Then before long the papers had reverted to printing all horizontal headlines from right to left again, as though they'd forgotten ever having supported the "reform of the Japanese language."

If they were going back to the old style they should have stated the reason clearly. There was no real problem for grownups, for whom it simply meant going back to the familiar; but for children in the midst of learning to write, it was confusing to have things written from the left at school and from the right in the newspapers.

H had expected that with the arrival of the occupation forces, horizontally written Japanese would go from left to right as in English, but it was not to be.

On the other hand, one thing they'd been forbidden to publish during the war had now made a comeback in their pages—the weather forecast. Banished from the day the war had begun, December 8, 1941, as information potentially helpful to the enemy, it had been restored with the edition of August 23, 1945, when "Today's Weather" made its appearance in a small box at the very bottom of the back page.

H was happy when he saw it. It wasn't so much that he was looking forward to checking out the accuracy of the forecasts again; it was the fact that a ban had been lifted, and that you could look up at a sky free from the threat of B29s and think about the next day's weather—a sure indication of peace.

H assumed that because the newspapers had been freed from the ban on certain subjects they'd be able from now on to carry anything they liked, but it wasn't as simple as that. A new censorship—GHQ censorship—had begun, replacing that of the military. He first realized this when the *Asahi Shimbun*'s Tokyo edition had to suspend publication for two days by order of Supreme Commander MacArthur. The Kansai edition of the paper, which H read, went on publishing without being punished, so he wasn't aware at first of what had happened. He only learned of it when the papers for September 19 and 20 carried detailed accounts of why the article had fallen foul of the GHQ censors in Tokyo.

The piece didn't occupy much space, but the headline spread over two columns and there were 111 lines of closely packed print. What had angered MacArthur, it seemed, was basically as follows:

> We would like to have the Americans inspect the carnage caused by the atomic bombs and cooperate positively in the rebuilding of Japan by way of compensating for their own actions.
>
> The American forces have published details of atrocities by the Japanese army in the Philippines, but the accuracy of such reports is questionable. What is their real intention in suddenly making public at this point accounts of atrocities by Japanese forces? It has been suggested in some quarters that there is some connection between such accounts and newspaper reports of

violence by U.S. troops in Japan against Japanese citizens. There is a difference between atrocities committed under the influence of abnormal psychology in the heat of battle and violence committed in the course of a peaceful occupation, a distinction that is sometimes relevant in the case of the allied forces in Japan. In making a fresh start toward a new and peaceful Japan we would like to ask the allied forces themselves, too, to behave correctly on a consistently humanitarian basis.

This report and the accompanying headline in the Tokyo *Asahi* had annoyed the occupation censors who deemed it a distortion of the facts.

General MacArthur was reported to have been unable to conceal his irritation. "Japan is unrealistic about its own position at the moment," he had said. "It is not the equal of the allies."

"MacArthur," it was said, "loves the freedom of the press as much as any man. But he will not allow it to carry unconstructive criticism of the allies or false reports likely to stir up people's feelings. It is a mistake to think that Japan is on an equal level with the allies. Japan lost the war; yet the impression gained from the news provided by the press is that Japan is negotiating with the Supreme Commander. 'Negotiations' are carried out between equals; there can be no negotiations with the Japanese government."

Reading this, H was struck by the difference between this censorship and censorship by the Japanese military. He remembered the photos and articles stamped with "Not OK" that he'd seen when he'd been shown around the *Kobe Shimbun* office. When he'd asked why they weren't okay, the newspaperman had said, "There's no *why* about it. If we're told 'no go,' that's it—we're just left to figure it out as best we can."

The GHQ censors had at least said what they didn't like about the article; they were tough but straightforward.

Awed perhaps by MacArthur's firm stance, the notices concerning the occupation forces sent to the school by the education ministry and prefectural authorities were said to contain warnings "to follow all allied directives without objecting," and "to be circumspect in dealing with them."

Within just a short time, the occupation forces had replaced the military as an authority figure never to be disobeyed.

As if to make the Japanese public thoroughly aware of this, the newspapers on September 29 carried a large photograph showing General MacArthur and the Emperor standing side by side. The accompanying explanation stated that it had been taken when the Emperor had gone to call on MacArthur at the American embassy.

Whereas the Emperor, in formal morning dress, stood stiffly upright, General MacArthur stood relaxed, hands behind his back, informally dressed, his uniform with buttons undone at the chest and open at the neck.

The release of this single photograph had huge repercussions. For older people in particular, the effect was equivalent to a sharp blow to the head, since it showed quite clearly that the highest authority was no longer His Majesty the Emperor but General MacArthur.

The twin pillars of the occupation policies that MacArthur was aiming to carry through were the eradication of militarism focused on the Emperor, and the elimination of ideas of "the whole world under one roof" with Japan at its center. Yet at the same time MacArthur seemed to be saying that he didn't reject the existence of the Emperor as such; and what he was trying to instill in the Japanese to replace the spirit of "the whole world under one roof" was the spirit of democracy. Of that H approved heartily. But he felt less happy about kowtowing to everything the occupation forces said without question. Perhaps for that reason he'd recently been in a particularly unsettled and irritable frame of mind. He was aware of it himself.

A thing he found particularly irritating was the large number of irresponsible timeservers among older people.

There were quite a few phonies among the teachers at school, for example. It made him feel sick to see a man who'd been militarism incarnate until the day the war ended behaving as though he'd always been a champion of democracy, all the while preserving his customary magisterial air.

H was disgusted by this hypocritical display of hastily borrowed democracy. He decided that when one of these teachers he disliked came into the classroom he would bow as required and then just walk out of the room.

468

When H did this to someone called Mr. Kobayashi, the teacher rushed out into the corridor after H and shouted, bright red in the face, "You may be at school, but you'll go down in the register as absent!"

Mr. Kawano, too, seemed to harbor a particular grudge against H. Himself an alumnus of Second Middle, from which he'd graduated eleven years before, he was passionately devoted to the place, and his sense of mission as a teacher at his old school made him particularly intolerant of any student who stepped out of line.

When exam time came and H tried to submit a blank sheet with nothing but his name on it, he exploded.

"Nobody leaves this classroom until the examination is over!" he bellowed, quivering with rage.

Since there was no help for it, H spent the time, in the same way as with Mr. Nakata, drawing a picture of his left hand on the back of the answer sheet.

When the time was up, his friend Hirobe, who was working his way from the back row toward the front collecting the answer sheets as he came, grinned as he took the paper from H's desk and saw the picture of his hand on the back.

Following that, H submitted a sketch of his hand in place of answers in several teachers' classes besides Mr. Kawano's.

A classmate, Yasuhiro Nomura, came to warn him. "Senoh," he said, "if you don't call it off soon you'll go too far. I hear the teachers whose backs you've put up are getting together to discuss what to do about you." Nomura, who rivaled H in his passion for movies and was also something of a rebel, lived in Itayado, which was on H's way to school, and the two often walked together.

H made up his mind that he didn't care how they punished him, or what grades he was given.

Even the friends who'd been tickled at first by H's gestures of resistance had gradually started to get worried.

"Look here," said Fukushima, "it's all very well to insist on what you think is right, but *everybody* was militarist during the war. You were different—I knew you had your doubts—but people like you weren't the norm. Now the occupation forces have come along and are saying that militarism's out and democracy's in, so everybody's kind of caught on the hop at the moment. Can't you see? They feel ashamed about it, I guess, which must make it all the more difficult for them to apologize. If the teachers didn't put up a front they wouldn't have a leg to stand on. You should show them a bit more understanding."

As he listened, H realized that he'd been overrreacting, but even so he didn't feel he could change his way of thinking. He still didn't fancy being preached to about democracy by people who'd done a two- or three-month cram course. Their preaching should be prefaced with at least a brief acknowledgment of the speakers' change of heart. He still felt that anyone who couldn't do that was a failure as a teacher.

He felt it all the more strongly because there was one at least of the teachers at Second Middle who had admitted his mistake in front of his students and apologized.

This was Mr. Watanabe, the man generally feared for inflicting the dreaded "ear-twist" treatment. Some students claimed it was an empty apology and warned against being taken in by it, but H felt it was something at least to have admitted in front of everyone to having been wrong.

Parting from Fukushima and the rest of his friends as they emerged from the school, H decided he'd make a detour in order to take a look at the "homes for air raid victims," one of which his family had been allotted. He was eager to see what kind of places they were, having heard that the apartments had been made by remodeling the Waka-matsu National School, which had been gutted in the raids. The basic concrete structure of the building had been left standing, and they'd taken advantage of this to convert it into temporary dwellings. H was familiar with the former school, since it was in Wakamatsu-cho 7-chome, not far from where his own home had been.

Entering the school gates he saw the smoke-blackened concrete building standing before him. The place H and his family were due to move into was Room 6 on the first floor. He found the inside of the building more severely damaged than the exterior had suggested; it was only too easy to imagine it enveloped in flames during the raid. The walls were scorched black, and on the corridor side of the classrooms' what should have been windows were boarded over. The door at the entrance was a crude affair of planks, with the figure "6" painted on it in black ink. Opening the door and going in, he found the interior dim although it was broad daylight, with sunlight filtering in through cracks in the boards and making a pattern of fine horizontal stripes on the wall.

In size, it was roughly the equivalent of a twelve-tatami room, with six tatami laid out on the wooden floor to make a "Japanese-style" space. He realized that one single classroom twice the size had been divided in two with a board partition in order to make two homes. The boards used for the partition were offcuts left over from preparing timber, with the bark left on at both edges. There were gaps between the boards—inevitably, since there were no straight edges—through which it was possible to peer into the next room.

The cracks are bad enough, but it's awfully dark without windows, thought H. Just then, though, he discovered that the board covering what had been the window on the other side of the corridor had a hinge at the top, which suggested that it could be opened and shut. He tried pushing it up and found it was made so that it could be propped open with a rod to form a window. He remembered with amusement that he'd seen just such a window in a picture of a Heian-period dwelling.

Even so, the "window" couldn't be left open on days when there might be a wind, since there wasn't a single pane of glass. On the other hand, if you shut it the room was pitch dark. For light you had to rely on a solitary bulb suspended from the ceiling. H was still pleased that the four of them could at last live together again, but looking at their future home he felt rather uneasy.

He headed for the fire station to report to his father on what he'd seen, but Morio wasn't there.

"Oh—do you mean nobody's told you? Your father's quit the fire department."

"*What*? When?"

"A couple of days ago. A young fireman who was in the army was demobilized and came back to his old post."

H was shocked, wondering unhappily why his father hadn't let him know right away.

He hurried to the church. As he rushed panting into the entrance he was greeted by Pastor Kawaguchi, who'd returned safely from his spell of service in the navy. After being conscripted he'd been stationed with a naval air unit near Takarazuka, not far from Kobe, so he'd been able to get home almost immediately after the end of the war.

"Your father's gone to the place where you're living in Myojin-cho," the minister informed him.

H raced off again, considering his route carefully in case he should miss his father on the way.

Arriving back at Uncle Hadano's he found his father sitting alone in the best room.

"Did they make you quit the fire brigade?" H demanded immediately.

"The war's over, so I'm going back to tailoring. Sewing clothes, that's my real job."

H told him in detail about the "homes for air raid victims" as he'd seen them.

"I just can't imagine what life'll be like in a smoke-blackened concrete box where you can't get any light," H said. "Why don't we give up the idea of going there and come and live here in Myojin-cho?"

His father remained silent for a few moments, then said, "This would be too good for us. We should be grateful so long as we get a roof to keep the rain off. There are lots of people still living in shelters among the ruins. Besides, if we gave up the chance to get into a temporary place we'd disqualify ourselves for a municipal apartment when they start building them, so we *have* to live there."

Morio felt they should leave the church just as soon as possible: "The Reverend Kawaguchi's back now, so we can't go on putting up in the three-mat room upstairs."

In the end they decided that Morio and H should move into the temporary housing first, to get it ready for when Yoshiko and her mother came back in the New Year.

The first thing the two of them did in their new home was to paper over the gaps between the boards. The stuff they used was some left-over pulp paper that H had brought from school, which they cut into strips five centimeters wide and stuck on with paste. The gaps stretched from floor to ceiling, so a ladder was needed and the job took time. The ladder, which they borrowed from an acquaintance whose house had survived the raids, was a firefighting one.

"It must be surprised at being used for this," joked H, but his father just handed him a strip of pasted paper in silence and without so much as a smile.

It was near midnight on the second day when they finally finished papering over the cracks. There were no more drafts, at least, but the former classroom, with its high ceiling, was cold. When H put out his futon and went to bed, he took with him his flask, filled with hot water, as a hot-water bottle; but it was too small to be effective and soon got cold.

Sleeping beside his father again after such a long interval, H talked to him almost every night about future plans; but Morio simply made noises of assent, with none of his old incisiveness. H felt frustrated and depressed by this unaccustomed faintheartedness he sensed in him.

"I thought you prided yourself on being a tailor," he urged. "Pull yourself together, Dad!"

"I used to," muttered Morio, "but do you think people are going to come to a tailor's in a place like this? You can't see it from the street, and nobody's going to imagine there's a tailor's in a burned-out school, are they?"

"But they would if you put up notices in Taisho-suji and around here, wouldn't they? You could say 'Senoh Tailors, Room 6, Homes for Air Raid Victims, former Wakamatsu National School. Cheap repairs and alterations.' That would tell them where you are, and I'd make the posters for you!"

"Mmm. That might be an idea...."

"*Might* be? It's the only thing we *can* do!" shouted H, losing his temper.

The next day H started making great numbers of signs, writing them in black ink on the rough paper left over from covering the cracks in the partition.

"How would it be," his father suddenly put in as he watched, "if we said 'Overcoats made from old blankets, etc.'?"

"Yes, that's a great idea! And I can do a picture of an overcoat on the notice!" said H with a happy vision of "Senoh Gentlemen's Tailors" resurrected. Now it was up to his father to get going and let his old customers know about his new premises....

The New Year, 1946, arrived.

The front page of the newspaper on New Year's Day carried an Imperial edict and an article proclaiming "Emperor Not a Living God."

H's first reaction was to feel that this was a bit late in the day, but on

473

second thoughts he agreed that it was necessary to let people know once and for all that the Emperor had only been a human being all along.

He wondered how the older people were taking it. He tried asking, but nobody seemed particularly surprised.

The cobbler who had a stall in front of Itayado Station voiced the general view: "I knew *that* already. What was more of a shock was that photo of His Majesty and MacArthur standing side by side."

Two days later, the newspaper reported MacArthur as expressing "satisfaction that the Emperor had taken the lead in democratization." A related article was headed: "The 'Land of the Gods' View of Japanese History—Reappraisal Necessary."

For ordinary households, though, the pressing question was not a reappraisal of history but how to get hold of enough food.

The impatience with which H awaited the return of his mother and Yoshiko combined eagerness to see them again with—if the truth were told—the expectation that they'd bring some real rice with them.

On the day of their return his father went alone to the station to meet them, since H himself was in school at that time.

When he arrived home and opened the door of Room 6, Yoshiko flew into his arms with a cry of "Hajime!" and burst into tears.

The train had been so packed, they said, that they'd had to get on and off through the windows. Probably the overcrowding was due to the shortage of rolling stock, together with a rumor that fares were shortly to be raised to two and a half times their present level.

The question that preoccupied H, though, was whether his mother had brought back rice from the country.

"What about the rice?" he asked impatiently.

"I've brought some," she said, and he breathed freely at last.

46

Eyes in the Wall

A week after they'd moved to the temporary dwellings, a lively, noisy family came into the next apartment. They could tell this from the sounds of belongings being carried in and wooden clogs clattering on floorboards that reached them through the partition.

Suddenly there came a boy's voice: "Hey—there's a good smell! They must be cooking real rice next door. I wouldn't mind some real rice."

It was followed immediately by what sounded like the mother's voice, shrill and mingled with the sound of a child crying: "And where do you think the money's coming from to buy rice? If you don't like what you've got you can leave it!"

H was horrified: he'd never thought that conversations and other sounds would be so clearly audible through the wall.

"I wonder how many of them there are?" his mother said.

H knew at once what she was thinking. Judging from their voices, there was a girl of eleven or twelve, then the next oldest, a boy, and, youngest of all, a girl of five or six. The only adult they could hear was the mother, with no indication of any male presence.

"Four of them," said Toshiko. "I think I'll take some rice-balls around to them, just to say hello."

"I suppose that's what you call 'love,'" said H irritably, "but can you keep it up? They might expect it every day, you know. You shouldn't start something you can't go on with."

Without replying, Toshiko began to spoon some just-cooked rice from the pot and shape it into balls, dipping her hands in cold water to avoid getting burned. The voices next door, H noticed, had ceased. They must have realized what was happening and be waiting for the food to arrive.

To his astonishment he saw that holes had been made in the paper with which he'd covered the gaps in the wall, and two pairs of eyes were peering through, one above the other. In a fit of anger, he flung a cushion at the partition. The eyes disappeared from the holes for a moment, but took up their positions again almost immediately. The higher of the two pairs of eyes was probably the mother.

Toshiko went off to the next apartment bearing the finished rice-balls.

"These are for you. They're the only thing I've got as a present for our new neighbors."

"Oh, you *shouldn't*! It's so nice of you—we haven't had any real rice for *ages*!"

"Wow! Can I have one?"

"One at a time, now! You don't have to grab with both hands—nobody's going to take them away!"

He could hear, almost as though they were in the same room, the children's excited, delighted voices and even the sound of them eating.

"The neighbors were very pleased," his mother said happily when she came back.

" 'It is more blessed to give than to receive,' " H quoted sarcastically.

"That's right," replied Toshiko, apparently taking this for approval: "Acts 20:35."

H all but exploded. "What on earth do you think you're up to?" he demanded. "The rice they gave you in the country's almost all gone!"

The sound of his voice frightened Yoshiko. "I had rice all the time I was in the country," she put in, looking up at their faces, "so please give plenty to Hajime."

"I don't want *your* share!" he shouted at her. "That's not what I'm getting at!"

Part of his irritation was due to his father's just sitting there in silence.

"What do *you* think, Dad?" H wanted to know.

"Well, now ...," said Morio, looking flustered.

"And what does 'Well, now' mean?" he demanded furiously. His father looked troubled and averted his eyes.

H flung open the door and rushed outside. As he went he heard Yoshiko calling, "Hajime, wait! Don't go! There'll be some more rice ready in a moment—*wait!*"

Leaving the grounds by the east gate, he ran in the direction of the street with the streetcars.

He was hungry, but he hated the idea of just waiting for the rice to cook.

"Mother may be right when she talks about love," he told himself, heading for the Shirakawa drugstore on Taisho-dori, "but I'm too self-ish for that. If I forced myself to behave in the same way, it'd just be phoney."

He'd remembered the woman at the drugstore saying, "There are some old posters for medicines you can have if you like. Why don't you do a notice on the back of one, and I'll put it up in the shop?"

The couple at the drugstore were friendly with H's parents, probably because they'd originally come to Kobe from the same part of Hiroshima prefecture. They'd always been helpful to the family, and the first cus-tomer when "Senoh Tailors" reopened in the temporary dwellings had come at their introduction.

Their second son, Akio, had originally been one year ahead of H at school; it was he who'd once given him advice about likely questions in the spoken exam for Second Middle. He'd subsequently been away from school for a year for health reasons and was now in the same grade as H.

Akio wasn't home yet. His mother said he'd soon be back and urged H to wait, but H declined and dashed off again with the poster, since it seemed they hadn't had supper yet. Normally, if they'd asked him to stay for a meal he might have jumped at the chance, but today he firmly rejected the idea.

On the way back he stopped in front of the movie theaters for a look at the posters and photos on display. A movie called *Zephyr* was being shown at the Shochiku-kan. "*Zephyr*," proclaimed the placards, "brings a breath of cheerfulness and romance to the Japanese movie world." The film's theme song, "Song of the Apple," was all the rage among the grownups in those days:

> Lips to the rosy-red apple,
> With the blue sky watching from above!

Even people who hadn't seen the movie went around singing it in loud voices. A song from a movie was about the best they could do for good cheer at that time.

Although H hadn't yet seen the movie himself he knew the plot, which was about a plucky girl, a lighting assistant on a movie set, who unexpectedly comes into the spotlight and becomes a star. Along with the familiar faces of Ken Uehara, Shuji Sano and Mitsuko Miura, the photos showed a new face, that of the Micho Namiki who sang the theme song.

But it didn't look very interesting to H, and he decided not to bother with it.

Arriving home, he found they'd had supper already, but his own share was waiting for him. Along with the rice and soup there were a few broiled, salted sardines.

His mother was complaining in the background that mackerel had been three yen for one fish—far too dear for them.

As he sat eating in silence, he reflected on how good plain, boiled white rice tasted. It was far better when cooked in an iron pot than in an aluminum saucepan. The pot they'd had in the kitchen at home was all pitted and rough where it was burned in the fire bombing, and the one they were using for their rice now had been given them by Uncle Hadano when he went back to the country. It was a real, old-style pot with a thick lid, which must be why the grains of rice turned out so plump and firm.

He was still brooding about this when he suddenly realized what his parents were talking about; they were discussing whether they hadn't better give up taking a newspaper.

"Give up the paper?" he demanded, putting down his chopsticks the better to glare at them. "Don't you dare. I want to see a newspaper every day."

Startled perhaps by this vehemence, his parents said nothing for a while. Then his mother said apologetically, "We don't *want* to give it up, actually, but with your father leaving the fire brigade we've lost about five hundred yen in income every month. If only he had orders for suits, he could get about one thousand five hundred for each one, but it's nothing but alterations and repairs these days, so we have to cut down even on the five yen for the paper."

She spoke directly to H, and his father again remained silent. H watched him, hoping he might say something. Morio stayed silent a few moments longer, then slowly started speaking.

"A sewing machine would cost five thousand yen to buy," he said. "Ours got burned, but it's running nicely again now. That's thanks to you, because you brought it out in the raid. So we'll look on the paper as payment for the machine and carry on taking it."

Listening, H felt happy: for the first time in ages this sounded like the father he knew.

He'd been vaguely aware that they were hard up, but hadn't thought they were in such bad straits as this. He'd gradually come to realize, too, that they didn't have much in the way of savings.

He made up his mind to start working to help them out. One way he could earn some money, he knew, was to go to the American army hospital and do portraits—but strictly for a fee this time.

The next day he called in at the army hospital on his way home from school. The officer he'd met the first time was no longer there, but he got in as he'd done before by showing the English text that George Fujita had written for him.

He decided to select only black soldiers, since he felt they'd be more interested in seeing themselves sketched than the white ones, and he'd take care this time not to do them too black.

He sketched three black soldiers in an hour, receiving one pack of cigarettes per sketch instead of money. That pleased them a lot, since for them it worked out cheaper. As he was leaving, one soldier actually grabbed his arm to stop him: "Do me too," he urged. "I'll give you two packs."

But H said, "Next time—see you again," and left the hospital.

In fact he'd been tempted by the idea of two packs for one sketch, but decided it would be better in the long term to keep the price uniformly low. He was afraid, too, of attracting attention if he earned too much, and of being refused entry.

On the way back he exchanged the cigarettes for rice on the black market in a back street behind Shinkaichi. The transaction itself had to be conducted furtively, but the transformation of three packs of cigarettes into one *sho* two *go* of rice represented a major profit. The cigarettes he'd received were two packs of Lucky Strikes and one of Camels, but he was told that Lucky Strikes, with the red circle on the box, were the more popular.

It was dark by the time he got home. There was bread today with supper, not rice. The "bread" was a fifty-fifty mix of corn and wheat flour kneaded with water and a little baking soda, then baked in an electric oven.

The electric "bread oven," a home made affair that H had constructed himself from pieces of scrap wood, was a rectangular box 20 cm. by 10 cm. by 12 cm. high. The baking was done by placing iron plates that served as electrodes inside the box, one on either side, then putting the dough in the box and passing an electric current through it. When you switched it on there was a crackling noise and small blue sparks were visible. The bread, which came out as a rectangular loaf, could hardly be called good, but it served at least to fill the belly.

It was silent next door, so H thought they must be out until he noticed pairs of eyes watching them through the partition. It seemed that the children were alone in the apartment that day. H had fixed the holes they'd made the day before, only to have new holes—and more of them, too—made today. Angrily, he flung down the piece of bread that was halfway to his mouth and rushed to the partition. The eyes promptly disappeared.

"If you make holes and peep through again, I'll come in there and smack you one!" he shouted menacingly. Cutting a piece of paper with scissors and plastering it with paste, he covered up the holes.

Almost immediately, though, there came the sound of fingers poking at the newly pasted paper, and a number of fresh holes appeared. There were dismal cries of "I'm hungry—*hungry*!" then sudden silence again. They were watching H's every move. Along with his irritation, H began to have the eerie feeling of struggling against some hidden creature he could never get the better of.

"Don't be hard on them," said Toshiko, who was watching. "Somebody told me at the temporary kitchen today that their father was killed in action, leaving the mother to bring them up alone. She's got a stall selling dumplings by the roadside in Rokken-michi, but she doesn't do much business, they say, and she can barely give them enough to keep them alive. It's no wonder they're hungry—so be patient with them."

The children must have been listening to what she was saying, because they punctuated her speech with murmurs of approval.

H had thought that by moving into these temporary quarters the family would at last be able to lead a relaxed life together, but his expectations had been sadly disappointed. Nor was it just the annoying family that lived next door: relations with his mother too were becoming strained.

Toshiko's religiousness had become even more intense than before they'd been bombed, and nowadays she gave the impression of being preoccupied with one single question: what she could do to help people in trouble.

Between his mother, whose answer to everything was to preach about love, and H himself, who was skeptical of this approach, the gap was becoming almost too wide to cross.

He couldn't begin either to understand or to agree with his mother's attitude.

If anything he found it easier, to some extent at least, to understand his father's new found apathy. Morio's way of thinking during the war had been irreproachable. Unlike the great majority of people, who had swung over to out-and-out "democracy" only after the war had ended, he'd always been a democrat in his own way. Now, though, watching as all the people who'd gone along unquestioningly with the war suddenly began preaching democracy, he must find it impossible simply to agree weakly with them. Quite likely he had little faith in a sudden wave of "democracy" spawned by reaction to what had gone before. Possibly he preferred in the circumstances to stay silent about everything.

Unlike his father, H couldn't stay silent but got angry about anything and everything.

Seeing the state that H sometimes got into, Okubo said to him, "You know, I can't help feeling you shouldn't get so worked up about things. If your thinking's too rigid, something's going to snap suddenly. I don't exactly mean that you should play along with your opponent, but like in judo you'll break a bone if you don't keep yourself flexible. I can't help being worried about you these days."

Deep down H thought he might well be right.

During the war he'd felt he was like a stick standing up in the middle of a stream. At first the river flowed gently, but once the war started the water went faster and faster, and it was all the stick could do to stay standing without being carried away. But then, on the day of the Imperial declaration ending the war, the flow had suddenly stopped—just like that—and started going in the opposite direction.

H had watched to see what people would do now, but they'd gone with the flow with awesome conformity. They were like the seaweed he'd seen when diving in the sea: waving, never going against the current. And yet, the roots of the seaweed were attached to rocks. Perhaps it was more natural to live like that?...

No. There may be something wrong with me, but I can't be happy as seaweed, he thought. So I've ended up again like a stick standing in a stream, resisting it.

"You see, your family was different," Nomura had told him on the way to school. "During the war ordinary people just fought without knowing anything. There were lots of things they didn't find out until the war was over, so then they thought they'd better change their way of thinking. That's so, isn't it? The trouble with you is you're too philosophical about it!"

H was startled to hear that this was "philosophy."

"I don't know much about philosophy, but I don't feel I'm philosophizing," he said. "As for democracy, it's something I've always wanted myself, but now everybody's started talking about it I begin to have doubts about what they're saying, and my mind's kind of in a muddle."

His feeling was heightened by the fact that the city was busily preparing for the first general election since the end of the war.

A man called Sanzo Nosaka, of the Communist Party, was one of those who'd come to Kobe to make election campaign speeches. He was referred to as a "Kobe man," but H had heard that he'd actually been born in Yamaguchi prefecture. He apparently based his "Kobe origins" on the fact that he was a graduate of Kobe Commercial College.

Nosaka, who'd fled to China to take refuge from political persecution, had come back to Japan after an absence of sixteen years. Hearing that he was to make a speech in Minato Park, in Shinkaichi, H decided to go along. The friends he asked to come with him seemed reluctant, so he went alone.

On the way he met up with a young man in a flying suit, with a white muffler around his neck, who said that he too was on his way to hear Nosaka. He was a former naval cadet, just demobilized, and H would have liked to ask him all kinds of things but kept quiet, not wanting to get punched for saying something that offended the other person. Instead, he resolved to hold his peace and listen to what the other had to say as they walked along.

"The war ended just the day before I was due to fly on a suicide mission," said the former cadet. "Having it end just when I'd prepared myself to die made me feel I wasn't sure any longer what I'd been doing up till then. During the war I used to look on the Communist Party as an enemy, but now they say that America, the big enemy, was right all along, so it set me wondering whether I oughtn't to listen to what the communists have to say, too. What are *you* going to hear a Communist Party lecture for?" He turned to look at H, who was flustered by the sudden question.

"I just wanted to hear what this man Nosaka has to say," he replied hastily. That was, in fact, the whole truth. He was particularly interested to hear what the first words of the speech would be.

Climbing the steps into the park, they found a tremendous number of people already there. H hadn't seen so many people gathered in one spot since the National Foundation Day celebrations. That day, though, they'd all been drawn up in an orderly fashion.

H tried to push his way to the front, but found it so difficult that he gave up.

Going around to the back of the crowd, he got up onto the fence. If he stood in the middle, other people's heads would block his view. A fall from the fence into the road far below where the streetcars were running would have meant serious injury or even death, so he climbed with special care, then seated himself firmly on top. It was high enough here to look down on everything, so even seated he had a clear view of the platform and the whole crowd packed into the open space.

Surveying the scene he could see large red flags flying at various points, and wondered if the young man at the noodle shop who'd got arrested for being "red" had returned safely from the front. If so, he might just possibly be here among the crowd....

They were all waiting for the appearance of the man called Sanzo Nosaka. Then the master of ceremonies said something, and Nosaka himself appeared on the platform. This alone was enough to prompt a great roar from the crowd, a storm of approval that left no doubt about Nosaka's popularity.

Nosaka raised both arms in a gesture to quieten them; then in slow, measured tones he said, "Look … at this devastated … city. Who … is reponsible … for this? *You know who*—the *military* … and the *zaibatsu* … with their ringleader … the *Emperor!*"

People went wild; it seemed the great roar of voices and applause would never end.

H himself hadn't immediately taken in what Nosaka had said, since he spoke with such an odd, unfamiliar accent. Waiting until the uproar had subsided, Nosaka began to speak again. But H wasn't listening, being busy trying to digest and make sense of what he'd just heard.

Yes, I suppose you're right, he thought when he'd finally worked it out. But even as he formulated these thoughts, he began to feel rather scared. The wild scene before his eyes had suddenly reminded him of the people who'd shouted "Long live Japan, the Land of the Gods!" at the 2,600th anniversary celebrations.

That night, H's sleep was disrupted by a nightmare. He couldn't tell whether it was dream or reality, and woke up shouting and struggling.

The wall was covered with tightly packed eyes, round eyeballs like the stoppers on old-fashioned lemonade bottles, all of them staring at him. When he tried to flee, they promptly moved en masse with him. They were the eyes not of children but of adults, a crowd of eyes terrifying in number that went on steadily reproducing and increasing.

Suddenly the eyes detached themselves from the wall and came flying in H's direction. First one, then another would approach until it seemed it would crash into his face, then suddenly vanished. The persistent attacks were so frightening that he willed himself to wake up—if in fact he was *not* already awake—as soon as possible.

But he couldn't move; it was as though someone was holding him down. Finally he managed to sit up, but when he looked around to see whether the swarm of eyes had been a dream or not, he saw them still flying about the room. He yelled at the top of his voice—and with that they disappeared, sucked into the partition between their room and the next.

His cry seemed to have woken not only his own family but the children next door as well.

"What's the matter?" asked Yoshiko. "Were you dreaming?"

"Think of the neighbors!" said his mother.

Looking over at the partition, he saw eyeballs moving—*real* eyeballs, watching him.

Again he yelled at the top of his voice, and thumped with his clenched fist on the partition.

He had a splitting headache.

47

Hold on, There!

H entered fourth grade. Once again, though, they were hauled out before classes began to do a week's "water mains repair work." The previous time it had been called "water supply work," so this suggested something diffferent, but all it meant was stopping leaks in the mains among the ruins in exactly the same way as before. The single bread roll they were given was the same as before, too. By now he was used to working on bomb sites, but it was wearying work even so. If anything, though, he was grateful for it, as his tension appeared to dissipate while he was on the job.

He seemed to be getting more and more unstable emotionally, and it worried him. If it got any worse, he felt, he'd run amok and do somebody harm.

He did his best not to let his classmates realize what was happening, but Fukushima and Okubo must have been aware of it, judging from their unusual gentleness toward him and the way they tried to cheer him up.

"I heard it was an occupation order that puttees mustn't be worn except while working on sites," said Okubo, "but without them I feel awfully chilly around the legs, as though I'm going to catch cold."

"They banned gaiters because they're afraid of a revival of militarism," said Fukushima, "just like they banned drawing the whole school up in the yard or marching in formation. I don't really think they need to worry so much—you'd think they were haunted by the Japanese army even in their dreams!" He said this with a laugh.

The mention of dreams reminded H of the vision he'd had of being attacked by eyeballs. It was obvious that the original source of the nightmare had been the eyes of the children peering through the partition, and he felt he'd go mad unless he did something about them. But quite apart from the eyes, more and more things were upsetting him and making him lose his temper.

Only three or four days earlier he'd taken his feelings out on a utility pole near his home, tearing to shreds a Japan Progressive Party poster pasted on the pole and shouting abuse at the party. The elections were over, so actually it didn't matter, but the way he'd torn down the poster had, he realized, been abnormally vicious, and it scared him.

The intensity with which he'd set on the poster had been at least partly because the Japan Progressive Party had stuck it over a notice saying "Senoh Tailors: for speedy, cheap tailoring and repairs."

For H, the whole fate of the family had seemed to depend on that one sign. Just as his father had feared, it was difficult to make a go of a tailoring business in a smoke-blackened former school building. They'd been resigned to that, but the shop, invisible from the road and without any windows, was just too inconspicuous.

One day, arriving back from school, he'd encountered a woman coming out of the gates. She held something wrapped in a cloth in her arms, and he knew at once who she'd come to visit.

"Did you want the tailor's?" he asked. "If so, it's the second door on the right."

"Yes, I found the door," she answered hesistantly, "but somehow it didn't look like a proper tailor's…." His fears confirmed, he led her back to the apartment. It was no wonder the party poster stuck over the "Senoh Tailors" sign had so outraged him….

Quite apart from the posters, he was annoyed too by the results of what had been the first postwar general election.

So overwhelming had been the sight of the crowd wildly cheering Sanzo Nosaka's speech that he'd been almost scared, wondering what would happen if everybody in Japan reacted in the same way—only to be disgusted in turn when he found that the Communist Party had won so few seats: five, out of a total of 143 candidates it had put up. The trouble, it seemed, had been its criticism of the Emperor.

The Liberal and Progressive parties, on the other hand, who'd made much of "preservation of the national polity," had won 141 and 94 seats respectively. The Socialist Party, many of whose members had been subjected to repression during the war, had won 93 seats.

H asked his father who he'd voted for. "Kaneto Matsuzawa of the Socialist Party," he'd replied. A professor at Kansei Gakuin University, Matsuzawa was one of the first-time candidates in the election.

His mother, who'd been excited by the idea that women were voting for the first time, said she'd voted for Tama Nakayama, an independent.

"Mrs. Nakayama's a doctor, director of the Suzurandai Hospital," she announced proudly. "It's her first election."

H was pleased that both the candidates his parents had voted for, first-timers though they were, had got in, but he felt that the communists, as a party explicitly opposed to the conservatives, ought to have done better. The Liberal and Progressive Party candidates included a lot of Diet members who as members of the Imperial Rule Assistance Association had been active in promoting the war.

Reading the paper, H began to get angry again: he was totally at a loss to understand what the older people were thinking.

He couldn't go on like this. Considering ways of dealing with his frustration, he decided that the most effective thing might be to go to the occupation hospital and do some more sketches for the soldiers, with their infectious cheerfulness. The process whereby a sketch was transformed into cigarettes, and cigarettes into white rice, would probably help too....

George Fujita had asked to be taken along next time H went there, so he invited him to come on Sunday morning. George's English was pretty good, so he was hoping to use him as an interpreter.

Meeting up at Motomachi Station, they set off along the road by the Koikawa River toward Motomachi itself. As they walked, H complained about the fickleness of politics with such bitterness that George was led to say: "You know, you're wasting your time getting so fired up about elections and politics. Either way, things will be manipulated to suit GHQ."

Again, H wondered whether George knew something that nobody else did, but all he would do was smile and say, "You'll see before long."

Arriving at the hospital they encountered a setback: they were not to be allowed inside anymore.

"No!" they were told firmly by the guard at the entrance. George managed an exchange in English, but still they didn't get any further than the checkpoint.

The reason why security had been beefed up was that Japanese black-marketeers and American army patients in the hospital had started trading goods.

"We're not black-marketeers—we cheer up the patients by doing sketches of them," George protested.

"If you go inside you'll get arrested by the MPs," yelled the guard, "so fuck off!"

To be scowled at and told to fuck off by one of the normally happy-go-lucky U.S. soldiers was disheartening.

No rice anymore, thought H gloomily. No more rice would mean going back to dumpling broth with pumpkin and sweet potato tubers. He was fed up with pumpkin—and particularly fed up with steamed pumpkin used as a substitute for rice.

Arriving home and opening the door, he was relieved to smell the fragrance of rice being cooked. His mother was already back from Sunday morning service at church and was preparing the meal.

His father was busy treadling the sewing machine, mending what H felt sure was the garment the woman had brought in the other day. Yoshiko must be out playing, for she was nowhere in sight.

H went over to the rice pot and, flaring his nostrils, inhaled the gushing steam: there couldn't be all that much rice left, so even the smell mustn't be wasted.

At that moment he sensed the presence of someone behind him. Whipping around, he saw, as he'd expected, the eyes of the neighbor's children peering in his direction. In a rage, he rushed around to the next room. He'd had enough—he'd get rid of the eyes once and for all! He banged at the door, but however much he banged there was no response, so he tried the door and it opened at once.

The light that preceded him picked out the children in a corner of the gloomy room. The three of them were sitting in a huddle on some folded futons, staring fixedly at him.

The mother must have been out tending her stall. There was nothing in the room worth calling furniture. On an apple crate that seemed to serve as a table there was a plate with a few dumplings—obviously the same kind as the mother sold on the street—two each for the children's midday meal. H wished he hadn't seen them.

The eleven-year-old girl drew her young brother and sister close to her, as though scared of H as he stood there glaring about the room. The eyes that watched him so uneasily were the eyes of small children; it was hard to believe they were the same eyes that had been peering through the holes. H felt his resolve wilting, but said in a loud voice, "Next time you make holes and peep through, you'll really be in for it—all right?"

"Mm, mm," said the children, with repeated nods.

Just then there was the sound of someone knocking at a door and calling "Telegram! Telegram!" It hardly sounded far enough away to be next door, at H's place. Scarcely realizing what he was doing, H peered through a hole in the partition and saw his mother walking toward the door calling "Just coming!" and his father, too, looking around from the sewing machine at which he was working. Peering through the hole wasn't like looking at them in the same old room, it was like watching something in the theater.

Taking his eyes away from the partition, he found that the children were beside him, watching too. They looked at H and laughed.

He, who'd been going to get rid of the peepers once and for all, had ended up peeping himself! And he was disgusted to find himself feeling that, though it wasn't exactly a puppet peepshow like the one he'd seen at the shrine so many years before, the desire to look through the holes seemed quite natural.

Hurrying back next door, he looked at the telegram. It was to announce the death of Uncle Hadano: "Kinshiro Hadano dead stop no need come funeral stop letter following stop Kichiyo." H had forgotten that Uncle Hadano's name was Kinshiro and his wife's Kichiyo. He would have been just sixty.

H's father went on with his sewing in silence, only his shaking shoulders showing that he was weeping.

His mother cried aloud.

Just then Yoshiko came home and wanted to know what was wrong with everybody. H didn't want her to see him crying, so he went up onto the roof and wept alone.

His eyes and nose ran till his face was all wet and slippery. He'd

490

known they couldn't save Uncle Hadano, and had been resigned to the fact, but his carefully prepared acceptance of it was no use in face of the actual news of his death.

Going back some thirty minutes later he found Yoshiko and his mother setting the rice bowls on the table.

They sat in silence, but it was clear they were all remembering Uncle Hadano.

Toshiko was just putting the freshly cooked rice into their bowls when there was a loud thump.

It sounded as though someone had collided with the door of their room. Toshiko got up and opened the door to reveal a man lying collapsed on the floor. He was in uniform, so he might be just back from the army, but he was so sunken-eyed and emaciated that he looked like an old man. In reality, he was probably around the same age as H's father. Toshiko said something inaudible to the man, then picked up the bowls of rice on the table, scooped a little off each in turn, and put it together in another bowl.

"There you go again!" said H, grabbing his own bowl back.

"He's hungrier than you are," said his mother. "Let's give him just a little bit each."

"You just can't help *everybody* who's hungry," said H, looking at his father as he spoke, "so stop trying to!"

He wanted his father to say something for once, but Morio was silent.

"Why don't you stop her?" he shouted at his father. "Don't you *care* at all?"

His father still said nothing but went on looking at H in silence. Surprisingly, he showed no sign of being troubled; if anything, his gaze seemed to be pitying his son in his frustration.

"Why don't you *say* something?" yelled H with increasing fury. "You're a *father*, aren't you?"

Yoshiko started crying and his mother stood poised hesitantly, the rice bowl in her hand.

Grabbing the lid of the rice pot, H raised it high above his head and flung it full at his father. The thick, heavy lid flew straight toward Morio's face. To H's alarm, he made no attempt to avoid it but went on staring at H without changing his expression. The lid hit his face, rebounded, and fell on the floorboards with a loud clang.

Seeing the blood trickling from his father's forehead, H panicked. Why hadn't he moved out of the way? He could have if he'd wanted to, but he hadn't—that was the greatest shock.

"Oh, you're bleeding!" cried his mother, pressing a hand towel to the cut on Morio's forehead.

"Hajime, I wish you were *dead*!" Yoshiko wailed, pummeling him fiercely on the back.

The children next door, who must have been watching through the holes, were thumping at the partition.

That's right—I'd be better off dead, thought H. There's no telling what I mightn't do if I go on like this. The world was all wrong, and it was too much trouble to go on living. He'd nothing to regret.

It wasn't, in fact, the first time he'd thought about suicide: sometimes he'd thought he'd rather finish it all, and he'd even picked a spot where it could easily be done.

The place in question was a little railroad bridge over a narrow road slightly to the west of Suma Station. A simple affair of short iron girders with four ties resting across them, it was so low that when you passed under it you could touch them if you stretched up your hand. Standing on the highway side and looking through this small gap, you could see white sand and blue sea like a landscape painting set in a vertically rectangular frame.

For a while in primary school H and his friends had often played there. The game they'd played was "blowing up trains." They would wait beneath the tracks for a train to come along; then, just when it was overhead, cry "Boom!" in loud voices. The voices were lost in the roar of the wheels, but for kids it was exciting all the same.

Among themselves they referred to the game as a "secret military operation," and swore to say nothing about it, under any circumstances, to the grownups.

They called the bridge itself—which, being only two meters or so long, had no official name—the "Hold-on Bridge." This was a reference to the white-painted post that stood beside the tracks with the words, "Hold on, there!—God is Love. *Suma Church*" inscribed on it in fat black letters.

The Suma Church was another small church to the west of the one that H's family attended. It wasn't clear just how many would-be suicides the white post had actually succeeded in deterring, but it was famous anyway.

The reason why suicides were common near the bridge was that the tracks here curved along the beach, so that visibility at this point was poor.

Like others before him, H favored the idea of a death in which you were scattered in fragments in an instant. He didn't fancy dying by hanging like Girly Boy.

Getting off the streetcar at the Suma terminal, H set off in the direction of the "Hold-on Bridge."

He borrowed a pencil from a woman at a tobacco store on the way and wrote a last message on the back of a small piece of paper that he ripped off a film poster. He got as far as "I can't go on living—forgive me," then hesitated as to how to continue. In the end he just added his name and address and left it at that.

Approaching the bridge he saw the post standing there, and on it, just as it always had, the legend "Hold on, there!—God is Love."

"I *can't* hold on anymore," he said as he put the piece of paper down by the post and picked up a stone to place on it.

He was oddly unafraid of death. Was it, perhaps, because he'd been living so close to it recently? Or was it that to die of one's own free will was different from being killed by someone else?

As a way of dying, he calculated, throwing yourself under the train was less certain than dangling between the ties, then hauling yourself up just as the train arrived so your head was above the tracks.

Several times as he waited for the up-train to arrive, he practiced pulling himself up between the ties.

After a while he felt the faintest of vibrations in the rails. This is it, he thought.

The vibration got steadily stronger, so that he could feel the approach of the train with his whole body. The locomotive came into view, rushing toward him around the curve. Only a little while now, he thought—and the next moment the shaking was so violent that it was all he could do to cling to the ties.

Just like in a movie, the train bore down, huge, upon him.

The ties jumped up and down so violently that he was almost shaken off. This was something he hadn't bargained for.

The next moment he felt a shock as though he'd been struck from directly above, a fearful roaring enveloped him, and simultaneously everything went dark. He no longer knew where he was or what was happening.

When he came to his senses it was light again and the train had already passed. Feeling the vibration gradually receding into the distance, he knew that he hadn't been killed. To his astonishment he was still clinging grimly to the wooden ties.

His first thought was not so much that he was safe, but that he had failed to kill himself.

Relaxing his hold, he jumped down onto the sand below the bridge. He needn't have hung on to the ties like that: he could just have let go and dropped to the ground. But he'd been in no state to consider such things. He staggered down to the beach and collapsed on his back on the sand.

His mind was vacant, unable as yet to grasp what had happened to him.

There were layers of crimson-tinged clouds in the sky above.

"Why couldn't I do it?" he murmured repeatedly. As he vaguely pondered the question, it slowly dawned on him that he'd made a huge miscalculation.

Mentally he'd had every intention of killing himself, but when the moment came the cells of his body, alarmed by the unexpectedly intense vibrations, had rejected his conscious will and concentrated all their strength on staying alive.

When he'd played here as a child it had always been on the sand beneath the bridge, so the fierceness of the shaking had come as something entirely unexpected.

He'd been saved, he realized, by a second self, a self strong enough to brush aside his puny "will." The idea left him stunned. Briefly he wondered if it had been the power of God's love saying to him "Hold on, there!" But he wasn't naive enough to believe *that*.

What he was gradually beginning to understand was that he'd been seriously mistaken in believing he could direct his own body as his mind imagined it could. He'd been horribly presumptuous. Anyone who heard about the episode would probably say, plausibly enough, that his subconscious hadn't wanted to die in the first place, and that the fear of death had stopped him from killing himself. But what H realized still more clearly—all such theorizing and talk of the subconscious aside—was that the flesh had proved more straightforward and robust than the spirit.

And it came home to him just how arrogant and stupid his "will" had been.

He realized, lying there on the beach, that strangely enough the fog that had clouded his mind had cleared.

He'd heard that they sometimes used electric shocks in the treatment of mental illness. Maybe the train passing by so close over his head had had a similar effect?

Some people, H thought as he looked up at the red clouds of the sunset, would call it being reborn, but that would be a lie. The important thing is that I didn't die. I didn't die, and my existence so far and my existence from now on are parts of a continuous whole—that's what I've got to remember, always.

Getting up, he slapped himself down to get rid of the sand, then went under the little bridge again, back to the post with its "Hold on, there!—God is Love."

His farewell message was still there, with the stone on top of it. Picking up the scrap of paper, he tore it into shreds and flung it to the breeze.

The pieces caught in the draft of a passing down-train, rose up into the air, and scattered.

48

The Classroom Dweller

For a long while after his failed attempt at suicide at the "Hold-on Bridge," H lay low in a room in the Second Middle School building. Having used it as a hideout in the past he was reasonably at home there, but he'd never dreamed the time would come when he'd actually live in the school.

The room in question, an annex to the art classroom behind the assembly hall on the third floor, was a virtual ruin.

The reason for its deserted, neglected state was that there were no longer any art classes. There'd been a time when Kobe Second Middle had produced a large number of artists, among them such well-known men as Ryohei Koiso and Kaii Higashiyama, but the war had put paid to the teaching of fine arts at the school.

The pretexts for doing away with it were symbolized by a remark of Instructor Tamori's: "This is an emergency! Nancy stuff like art and music is no use in a war." So art and music had been sacrificed to the pursuit of martial activities.

Although the fine arts had disappeared from the curriculum, the survival of the art room as such was one small compensation for H, since it meant he could go there from time to time to sketch from plaster models.

The annex in which he was to live now had once been used by the teacher in charge. About the size of six tatami mats, it contained stacks of pictures done by students long-since graduated and, thick with dust, an iron folding bed and futons that must have been used by the teacher when he stayed overnight.

During the period when the third-floor assembly hall had been a school factory, the same room, lying as it did directly behind the hall, had been a place of rest and refuge. Even after the war had ended, he'd creep in there and sketch to avoid the classes of teachers he disliked. That he had a key giving him free access to the room was a piece of good luck.

When he was in third grade, on a day when the machinery in the school factory was idle on account of one of the scheduled power cuts, he'd obtained official permission to use the key so that he could sketch there. He took it from the teachers' room with a promise to return it by four that afternoon—a promise he'd duly observed. Before returning the key, however, he'd had a copy made. This was simple enough: in the school factory there were thin steel plates and files of all sizes, ample material for making a key. Fortunately, too, the key was a simple affair with only three notches, so that a copy was made in next to no time.

Without more ado he tested the counterfeit key; then, having made sure that it worked perfectly, performed one further operation: using a file, he removed a vital projection on the original.

When he returned it, he worried rather because the place he'd filed was shinier than the rest of the key. But Mr. Fukuda, the teacher on duty that day, took it without any sign of suspicion and hung it back in its place on the key board.

Although the key had a wooden tag saying "Art Room Annex," it no longer fitted the lock, so the copy in H's possession became the only means of opening or closing the annex. Thanks to this, he was able to take up residence in the room from the very day of the "Hold on!" episode.

On the first night, though, he tossed and turned miserably, unable to sleep at all. It wasn't fear of being holed up in the silent school night, but preoccupation with all the things that had dawned on him following his failed suicide.

He was horrified in spite of himself to realize that, as he'd hung from the ties on the bridge, he'd been focused solely on obliterating himself: no thought for his family or friends, or for the trouble he'd cause the school, let alone the people who'd have the job of clearing up a mangled body or the disruption caused to train services....

Admittedly, he'd been in no state really to consider such things, but he'd been excessively narrow-minded even so.

No doubt about it, he'd been spiritually sick. To remember the things that had happened was acutely painful.

He'd left the beach that day and gone back home after dark. But as he approached the room, something made him hesitate to go inside, and he took two turns around the outside of the temporary lodgings.

Seen again from below in the dark, with light from each household leaking through chinks in the boards where windows had been, the scorched school building that now sheltered air raid victims looked even blacker and more sinister.

He was standing irresolutely by the east gate when a woman who lived nearby said "Good evening," finally prompting him to go in and open the door of their room.

His father was at work, pedaling the sewing machine. He turned around. Seeing his face, H was shocked, and the carefully prepared words wouldn't come. Although it was shaded from the light, the bandage around his father's head looked unnaturally white.

"I'm sorry," H said. "I wasn't in my right mind."

The reply was prompt, instantaneous: "I understand. You don't have to worry," said his father gently, "it's nothing serious."

His mother and Yoshiko were out. They had gone to evening service at the church. His father would normally have gone with them, but hadn't apparently because of the bandage.

"I'm thinking of going to Ogura's place and asking him to put me up," H said.

"It may be a nuisance for them, but it would be good if they would. You'd do better to get away from here for a while. If you go on living here you might go a bit crazy again. I'll talk to your mother so she doesn't worry." As usual, H thought to himself, his father understood him well.

He was dreadfully hungry and remembered that he'd rushed out of the house without having his midday meal.

"I haven't had anything to eat—I'm starving," he said in a purposely cheerful tone. "Is there anything in the house I can have?"

"We left yours for you, it's still there," said his father, smiling beneath the white bandage, and pointed to the table where they always ate.

H removed the cloth covering it and saw the white rice in his bowl just as he'd left it at lunchtime. He felt the tears coming and, changing his place, ate with his back turned so his father wouldn't notice.

When he'd finished eating he stuffed a few basics and the things he needed for school into a canvas shoulder bag, and made a bundle of his underwear and a few other items in a wrapping cloth. As he was doing this, his father said, "Here—take this," and gave him some spending money. It was only the second time he'd ever given H money apart from his school fees. Taking it, H felt emotion welling up again.

"I'll be staying with Ogura for the time being," he said as he left, "so don't worry if I don't come back."

Not wanting his father to worry unnecessarily, he couldn't bring himself to say outright that he was going to put up in the Second Middle School building.

Getting off the streetcar at Goban-cho 2-chome and climbing the slope up to the school, he looked up and saw a light in the night watchman's room on the second floor. After stealthily climbing the stairs, he crouched down and crept along the corridor past the watchman's window, then went up the stairs on the north side to the third floor.

Passing through the art room, he stuck the key in the door of the annex. It turned easily, but the great creak the door gave as it opened made his blood run cold.

Inside the room, the first thing he did was cover all the windows so that no light should escape, putting to good use the stacks of pictures painted by his predecessors. The idea of a new blackout even though the war was over rather tickled him. Going outside the room to check on his work, he found that the three layers of pictures he'd used had effectively shut off the light; even if the watchman came around, he'd never realize someone was living in the room.

This first task completed, he gave himself a wash. He'd have to go out to get to a toilet, but fortunately there was running water in the room itself.

Setting up the iron bed, he lay down. It had been a long day. The futons were so dusty, though, that he had a violent fit of coughing. What with this and the thoughts preoccupying him, that first night was a sleepless one.

In the morning a lively babble of voices from below made him open the window a fraction and peer down. He could see a steady stream of students arriving at the school. Watching them, he suddenly felt his energy coming back.

He determined to stop worrying about what other people thought and what was wrong with society forthwith. The important thing was to be true to what he himself wanted to do. From now on, he was going to live for himself.

He saw Haruko Kameoka, the daughter of the vice-principal, pass beneath the window and go out through the north gate. She was living with her family in the school's *dojo*. She attended the school popularly known as "Pre-2," and H was quite attracted to her.

Once the students were all in their classrooms, H slipped out of the annex and went downstairs to the first floor.

Class 5, fourth grade, was on the first floor next to the staff room, facing the schoolyard. Grabbing Ogura at the entrance to the classroom, H arranged to meet him behind the assembly hall during the lunch break. He wanted to let Ogura, at least, know his present circumstances.

Ogura's round eyes became still rounder when H told him the situation.

"Of course I'll keep it secret, absolutely," he said. "But what'll you do for food?"

"I know where one of the teachers keeps some of the sweet potatoes grown at the farm, so I can go and swipe a few when it gets dark. You know that three-cornered closet on the first floor under the stairs?—they're in there. Anybody could open the lock. I've an idea who hid them there, but I'm not accusing him. It's going to be my food store. I'm sure there's enough for the time being—but I wish I had some white rice...."

"I'll get some for you somehow," said Ogura.

His friend was keen to see the room, so H unlocked it and let him in.

"So you've got a canteen," he said, looking around him. "I think you need a pan, too. I'll bring one for you. Did you bring this electric heater from home?"

"No, it was in the room."

Ogura unearthed a phonograph from a corner of the room. "I wonder if it works?" he said, brushing off a layer of dust and vigorously turning the handle. To their delight the turntable started revolving. There were three records in the lid, but all three were military songs.

"I'll bring you some records."

"Well then, make it Debussy if possible," said H, who'd heard some once at Ogura's home. "You don't have any Yoshie Fujiwara, I suppose?"

"No, my father's all symphonic and chamber music. But won't you be lonely, living here all by yourself?"

"I like it. It's nice and quiet. I mean, it was living in the air raid victims' housing that made me go a bit strange."

"I see," said Ogura, nodding. Having been to H's place once, he appreciated the situation. But H didn't tell even him about the incident at the bridge.

The next day Ogura brought him a bag of rice. After school they cooked it in the canteen and ate it together with some sweet potato cooked in soy sauce. H's first real meal in what seemed like ages tasted good.

After it got dark they listened to Debussy's "Clair de Lune," Rossini's *William Tell* Overture, and some other records that Ogura had brought. He felt he'd never before been so settled and happy.

"What's good about this place," said Ogura with a smile, "is that it takes exactly zero minutes to get to school."

"Why not come and stay sometimes?" said H, returning the smile.

They decided on a signal of raps on the annex door and practiced it: *dot, dot-dot, dash-dash*.

After a week H paid a brief visit to his parents. He'd heard that his mother had been going around his friends' houses looking for him, Ogura's place included.

"I told her you came to school every day but I didn't know where you were living," Ogura had said.

When H opened the door, his father said, "Hello, how are you doing?" but his mother started back, apparently afraid H might get violent again.

He looked at the partition between their room and the next, and saw peering eyes suddenly whipped away: the children next door were still at it. Pasted on the walls of the room were biblical texts transcribed by his mother:

> And now abideth faith, hope, charity, these three; but the greatest of these is charity. (I Corinthians 13:3)

> Blessed are the pure in heart; for they shall see God. (Matthew 5:8)

> Be thou faithful unto death. (Revelation 2:10)

> In lowliness of mind let each esteem others better than themselves. (Philippians 2:3)

Looking at them all plastered on the walls, H felt anew the impossibility of living there.

"If I live here," he said in as calm a voice as possible, "I might *really* go crazy next time. I think it'll be better for all of us if I stay away for a while. I don't want to worry you, but I can't tell you exactly where I'm living. Don't come looking for me, whatever you do. I'm not causing anybody any trouble."

"Right!" said his father. "We'll be glad to have you back any time you care to come. You see, we trust you."

"Are you eating properly?" asked his mother, dabbing at her tears. "If you *have* to go, at least take your ration of rice and some vegetables...."

"It's all right, I'm eating better than when I'm here," he replied, though he could appreciate only too well his mother's concern.

"I can't believe it," she said and started crying again.

H made haste to leave. If Yoshiko came back while he was there she'd probably cry even more than his mother.

Back at the school he stayed up till dawn sketching a bust of Voltaire in charcoal.

In future, he felt, he wanted to be an artist like his uncle Masao in Onomichi. But he knew that as things were his family could never afford to send him to art school.

More immediately, he didn't even know whether he'd be able to graduate from Second Middle. Since he frequently took against a particular teacher's methods and disappeared from the classroom, he was put down in the register as absent on a large number of days. Not only was he short on attendance, but since he'd often hand in a blank answer sheet in exams for some subjects, he didn't have enough total credits and was more or less certain to fail.

He was less concerned about whether he could graduate or not, though, than about how soon he could start studying art.

He'd had an idea: he'd go and call on Ryohei Koiso, the well-known artist who was a graduate of the same school, and show him some of his sketches.

The artist's house, he'd heard, had been destroyed in the raids, and he was now living in temporary quarters in Shioya. He didn't know the exact address, but decided at any rate to start by going to Shioya, which was the next station to the west of Suma.

He got off the train and asked at the police station, only to get an abrupt "Koiso, you say? No idea." However, at a bookstore in front of the station they said they knew the sensei's place because they delivered books to him.

With the map they'd drawn for him in his hand, H ran panting up the hill on top of which the single-storied house stood.

He opened the sliding door of the entrance hall and called out, "Good morning! I've come to ask the sensei to teach me to draw." Emerging from the rear of the house, the artist looked startled to see this boy who'd suddenly turned up with sweat running down his face and no letter of introduction.

"Hajime Senoh, in fourth grade at Kobe Second Middle School," he announced in a loud voice. As he spoke, he wondered if perhaps he was wrong to introduce himself in the kind of voice they'd used during military training.

"I don't take any pupils as such," Mr. Koiso said, "but I don't mind having a look at your stuff, if you'll show me."

Relieved, H spread out on the raised floor of the entrance hall the sketches he'd been carrying rolled up under his arm. The sensei looked down at them in silence for a while, and then said, "I'm too cramped here to have a proper studio, but you can come anyway if it's all right with you. I teach at a school in Kyoto, so I'm out quite a bit of the time, plus I have meetings and so on, but you can come and sketch while I'm out."

For H it was like a dream. After he'd closed the front door behind him, having arranged when he should come next, he gave a whoop of glee and ran flat out all the way to the station.

The waves were glittering on the sea as he came down the hill. Awaji Island, lying on the other side of the straits, seemed to loom directly before his eyes.

As he ran, H was *glad* he'd stayed alive. He'd never been so pleased about anything in his life before….

He didn't go straight back to the school but called in at Ogura's house in Yumeno, wanting to report to his friend who was also interested in art.

Ogura was as pleased as if it had been himself. H wanted to show Ogura's pictures to the sensei too, but his friend rejected the idea; he'd done nothing worth showing people, he said.

Before long H was going to Mr. Koiso's place three times a week. The artist's method of teaching was to say over and over again, "Now take a *really* good look …," without ever touching the picture directly.

A few weeks later he suddenly said, "Why don't you try doing a nude? Tsuguro Ito's studio in Ashiya survived the raids, and artists get together there to sketch. It's a good thing to work alongside a lot of other people." H was pleased, but felt worried about the fee. Mr. Koiso must have realized this, because he added, "You won't have to bother about paying the model." The impression H got was that he himself would take care of it.

At Tsuguro Ito's studio, on the hillside above Ashiya Station, he found, besides Ryohei Koiso himself, other well-known painters such as Konosuke Tamura, Jiro Fujii and Yukio Kodama. There wasn't a single middle school boy there apart from himself, and he felt rather tense working amongst such people. And quite apart from that, his heart thumped at the prospect of seeing a naked woman from the front.

When he told Ogura about it, his friend looked envious.

As they talked, H had an idea: how would it be if art-loving middle school students and girl students from all over Kobe got together to form a "Kobe Students' Art League"?

"Boys and girls together?" murmured Ogura. "I wonder if the schools would give permission?" His doubts were natural enough; until then it had been unthinkable for boys and girls to study or work together in the same room.

"But they're thinking of making schools coeducational from now on to get in line with America, aren't they? Times are changing. Of course, we'll have to meet the principal of each school and explain what we're trying to do. Make a list: cheap group tickets to exhibitions, arranging exhibitions ourselves, art study groups, inviting Ryohei Koiso to give lectures, and so on. And we'd have to emphasize that, from now on, to get too worried or nervous about boys and girls studying together would be behind the times, 'undemocratic.' Once we've formed the league, it'd be up to you. I'm no good at running organizations, so you'd be in charge."

Ogura gave a diffident smile. "I see," he said. "Doing pictures with girl students … not so bad, that. I'll try and rope Nishi and Uchida in too."

H decided to start by calling on the head teacher of "Pre-2," as Kobe's Hyogo Prefectural Second Girls High School was popularly known. The school, which stood on a hill to the north of Second Middle, was a focus of keen interest for the boys of the latter, and Ogura agreed with alacrity to accompany H.

Meeting the principal and the teacher in charge of art classes, H explained why it was necessary at that point to form a "Kobe Students' Art League." The principal gave his consent with surprisingly little resistance. "I see no harm in it," he said. "After all, that's the way education's going to go from now on…." It looked as though it had been a smart move to tie in the idea of forming the league with democracy. Quite possibly, even, the school *had* been afraid that to miss this opportunity might be to have itself labeled undemocratic and stick-in-the-mud.

Next they went to "First Junior," which agreed to participate without so much as a murmur. They then set their sights on "Pre-1." This girls' school was known for its cautious correctness, but when the principal heard that "Pre-2" was joining, they were promptly given his personal blessing. After that, almost all the middle schools and girls' schools in Kobe followed suit in a kind of chain reaction.

The first undertaking of the newly launched league was a lecture meeting at Second Middle at which Koiso-sensei was invited to speak. On the day of the meeting, individuals and small groups from the different girls' schools converged on the school grounds, creating a very different atmosphere from usual. A large number of Second Middle students were to be seen loitering restlessly in the neighborhood of the venue.

The *Kobe Shimbun* carried an article headed "Kobe Students' Art League Born: Japan's First Venture in Coeducation."

Their next project was a visit to an exhibition of Western art being held at the Hankyu department store in Osaka. Assuming that it would be next to impossible to get everybody together at a specified time, they arranged for the store to let in anyone who showed his or her membership card at the entrance. They also succeeded in negotiating a cut in the admission fee over and above the reduction for groups. Thus everybody was able to go on any day they chose with the companions of their choice.

H and Ogura arranged to go in a group of four with Haruko Kameoka and another girl from "Pre-2" called Junko Nakai. When they met up at the station, though, H was disconcerted to find a bunch of Second Middle boys on the same platform.

The rugby final between First Middle and Second Middle was being held at Nishinomiya on the same day. It was customary for the whole school to turn out to support their own side in the match, and any defaulter automatically became the equivalent of a wartime "non-Japanese." H would be seen as guilty of treachery—behavior unbecoming in a Second Middle student.

One of the senior students approached H, his eyes blazing with anger. H braced himself and was duly punched. Ogura's instant intervention saved him from a second blow, but his nose had already spurted blood. Startled by the suddenness of this attack, the two girl students wailed in distress. Hearing them, H decided that the assault had been inevitable. His bruised face became a symbol of the jealous rage of all the Second Middle students on the platform.

49

Candidate for Failure

The rugby club at Second Middle had a powerful team. In matches with First Middle in particular, it was grimly determined never to be beaten. "Of course—" someone told H, "we've been rivals ever since 1908." He was surprised but it was a special kind of sibling rivalry, apparently, dating from the time when Second Middle had come into existence by splitting away from First Middle.

Discord between brothers is often said to be worse than that between strangers, and the clash of temperaments between the two schools— the gentlemanly elder brother and the rougher younger brother—was particularly apparent in their rugby matches.

There was another reason now why these matches aroused such passion in the students. Because of the ban on martial arts such as Japanese fencing and judo, they provided an outlet for explosively pent-up energies.

The strength of which Second Middle's rugby club traditionally boasted extended not just to defeating its opposite number from First Middle, but to an astonishing run of victories over other schools in the national championships that had restarted following the end of the war. At the first of these events it had won through to the finals, defeating Shuyukan Middle School from Fukuoka 11–6 to become West Japan representative. Then, in the finals it had beaten Akita Industrial Middle School 16–8 to become the national champion.

H disliked rugby, though, because the weight of obligation on the whole school to be uniformly passionate about the game brought back unpleasant wartime memories. Unfortunately, he let the dislike show instead of keeping it firmly buttoned up inside himself.

More than once he was set on and beaten up by members of the cheerleaders' group and senior students: "Don't you have any loyalty to your school, you scum?" they demanded.

Nowadays, it was strictly forbidden for teachers or senior students to use violence in correcting juniors in schools, but in fact a blind eye was turned to such practices where rugby was concerned. This frustrated H. Would real democracy, with respect for the individual, ever be established?

When he went up into fourth grade, however, someone had appeared who promised to help in fulfilling that dream, in the shape of a teacher called Yoshiharu Naito.

H took to Mr. Naito directly, in his first class, much like a puppy that wags its tail on sniffing out a likable human being.

Emerging from the annex to the geography room and stepping up onto the dais, Mr. Naito launched straight into a self-introduction: "My name's Yoshiharu Naito," he said. "I used to teach at this school, but I was called up before you lot came in, and was at the front in China for some time. I'm happy to be safely back home, to return to Second Middle, and to be standing here on the teaching platform again. I teach what's called 'human geography.' It's called 'human' because it sets out to examine the relationship between human beings and nature. To take rivers as an example: all rivers are different depending on the area they're located in, and the ways of life and methods of, say, fishing of people living in the neighborhood differ correspondingly. 'Human geography' aims to find out, and learn from, these differences in ways of life and culture."

Up to this point he'd been talking in the "standard" language, but now he suddenly dropped into the familiar Kobe dialect.

"It's like this: the word 'river' just by itself won't mean much to you, but if you take an interest in *particular* rivers, you'll find they all have characters of their own. What I want to do in these classes is to get you interested in that way of studying. And not just in class, either—I want to get to know each of you individually, too, so you can come to my room for a chat whenever you feel like it. I'll be glad to see you."

Then he drew the curtains to darken the room and used a magic lantern to show them a series of photos on the screen: the Yangtse River flowing acros the vast spaces of China, the Ishikari River meandering across a plain in Hokkaido, the Sumida River in Tokyo, the Yodo River running through the built-up areas of Osaka, and finally the meager flow of the Shin-Minato River in Kobe. Each time a new picture appeared he talked to them about the differences between the rivers and their individual relationship with the areas they passed through.

With a feeling of excitement, H told himself that he'd never had such a fascinating class before. When Mr. Naito said, "Rivers are all different, and it's precisely in those differences that their individual worth lies," the words fell on his mind like water on parched earth.

Mr. Naito, who was a bachelor and lived in Takatsuki, far from the school, hardly ever went home at night but stayed in the annex to the geography room. After a while H, having himself also taken up residence in the school, began to look in on him frequently.

Before long H began calling him not "sensei" but "Shiisan." Hearing from Mr. Naito that in Chinese they pronounced the characters for sensei as *shiisan*, he decided to use the nickname to distinguish him from the other senseis.

Mr. Naito himself seemed if anything to like being called Shiisan by his students. It wasn't only H who'd taken a liking to him, and several boys were always to be found in the geography annex after class.

Often H would visit his room in the early evening, when there was no longer enough light for sketching. Occasionally Mr. Naito would cook rice in a canteen and share it with H while he talked to him about wartime China. Unlike most adults, though, he never used the word *Shina* when referring to that country.

It was some while after that that the vice-principal, in an address informing the school of an official occupation directive, told them not to use the word *Shina* either in speech or writing. "*Shina* has insulting connotations, and is disliked by the people of the country concerned. From now on, you should refer to it as *Chuka minkoku* or *Chugoku*, and the people as *Chugokujin* or *Kajin*."

Shiisan had been way ahead of the directive.

There was one thing H had found unusual about Shiisan ever since he had first met him. Although he was interested in each of his pupils individually, he never, from his side, probed into their family affairs. This suited H well enough, and made him feel at ease with the older man.

Mr. Matsumoto, H's homeroom teacher, would visit Shiisan's room from time to time. The two men seemed to be on such good terms that H asked Shiisan if they were old friends. "Yes indeed. He was always a good friend to me before I went into the army; I used to go climbing with him. We're well matched."

This fitted with H's own view of things: Mr. Matsumoto was one of the few teachers whose attitude to his pupils had remained consistent both during the war and after it, so it seemed natural that he should be a close friend of Shiisan's.

There were all kinds of teachers at Second Middle, but a few stood out for their almost pitiful oddity. Chief among them was a man called Shinyashiki, who'd been dismissed from the school in disgrace.

He'd had a habit of declaring boastfully, "I was at the University of Tokyo—no other teacher here can say that." Privately, the students had little respect for him. "Tokyo University?" they'd say. "What's the good of being a Todai graduate if no one can understand your classes?" When they finally heard that he'd made false claims about his academic career, the whole class burst into laughter.

He'd been given away by a form he'd submitted to the "Commission on the Suitability of Teaching Staff," in which teachers had been required to give a detailed account of their careers. In the course of this investigation, carried out on instructions from GHQ to identify people who'd had an active hand in militaristic education, it had transpired that Shinyashiki had never been to Tokyo University at all.

He must have slipped in during the war, when teachers were in short supply, by faking his academic record. He had, in fact, long been somewhat suspect on account of his extreme dislike of being asked questions by his students.

Another member of the staff who, surprisingly, fell foul of the commission was the new principal, Hisashi Katayama. A few months after he'd taken up the post in April, notice had been given, apparently, that there were "doubts about the way he pursued the duties of principal."

They'd had a short period without any principal; then finally, ten months later, he'd been proclaimed "unsuitable." It seemed something suspicious had come to light in his wartime record.

Democratization within the school too, which seemed to be proceeding smoothly, was in fact subject to various detours and delays.

One episode in this process of trial and error occurred when fifth-grade students summoned the younger students to the assembly hall and proclaimed the formation of a "Students' Self-Governing Body."

The demands of this "self-governing body" were that the students themselves should participate in determining the school's educational policy, and should be allowed to question teachers about whose wartime behavior and teaching methods they felt any doubts.

In an overbearing tone, a fifth-grade student read aloud the resolution embodying these demands, and then demanded to know if there were any questions. But the atmosphere was hardly encouraging, so that most of those present were too intimidated to speak up.

The teachers themselves, flustered by the sudden emergence of a "self-governing body," wavered indecisively. Finally, after many conferences, they concluded that "henceforth student meetings would not be permitted without prior notification," and that "the time was not ripe for a self-governing body run solely by students."

The reason for the unexpected ease with which the students were squashed may well have been that awareness of their own partial responsibility for supporting the war blunted the edge of their challenge. The majority view among students was that, for better or worse, times had changed and values been upset, and that it was better to consider what should be done next rather than spend all the time digging into each other's past.

This view was all the more acceptable in that there were some boys who'd just returned from a spell at an army college. H asked a few of them why they'd chosen to go there.

"Well, everybody thought the British and Americans were 'fiends' in those days, didn't they?" said one of them. "So you kind of assumed you'd go into the military. What with the school urging you as well, you hardly needed to make up your own mind at all. But to be honest, some of it was due to family circumstances too. You didn't have to pay fees at military schools, and your future was guaranteed—that's the real reason why *I* went. I couldn't say it before, but I can now...."

H digested this information and felt his understanding of his fellow-men deepen.

But then he heard a rumor that even Iwao Sumiyama—who'd sworn that if the Americans landed he'd make sure he got two or three of them before being killed himself—had recently given up his hawkish outlook, taken up the ukelele, and was now obsessed with Hawaian music.

"You used to be the embodiment of the Yamato spirit," teased H when he met him. "Do you mean to say you've taken up 'enemy music' now?"

"The times have changed," the other said sheepishly. "Let me play something for you next time we meet—I'm pretty good!"

H got a similar shock when he met Iwao Hayashi, who was already in fifth grade when he came back from a military college.

"Were you 'grand champion' there too?" he asked.

"Sumo's old hat," Hayashi said, waving a dismissive hand. "Going around bare-assed in just a loincloth! I'm into volleyball now—thought there'd be more chance to meet the girls that way."

H laughed. The students were all eagerly trying to find some way or other of making contact with "the girls."

On one occasion there was very nearly a brawl behind the gymnasium because Fukushima, who'd at last managed to get a girlfriend, claimed she'd been stolen by Saigo Yoshida, who'd recently transferred back from his military school. It was averted by Yoshida himself, who, to the disgust of Fukushima and the others present, said in his clearcut Tokyo accent, "There's no need to fight about it! Coeducation'll be starting before long now, and then you'll be able to take your pick. The one you happen to be with at the moment isn't the only girl in the world!"

The matter was settled when Yoshida agreed he'd have no more to do with the girl. And the talk of coeducation proved to be correct: in April 1948 the education system, apparently at American instigation, was to be changed. The hitherto exclusively male middle schools were to be merged with the girls' schools, and the five years of middle school were to be replaced by three years each at middle and high school.

H and his classmates, who were in fifth grade of middle school at the time, found themselves on the dividing line, and were given the choice of graduating at once from middle school or staying on another year and entering third grade of high school under the new system.

H himself wanted to graduate from Second Middle without going on to a new high school. Unfortunately, it didn't look as though he'd be able to graduate at all, since to do so he needed an average mark of at least fifty-seven. Even if he couldn't graduate, though, he intended to stay on till the end of fifth grade and quit school altogether at the end of the year.

One reason why he made no attempt to improve his grades was that he saw no way he could go on to art school in his family's present economic circumstances. He was sure that if he asked his father he'd say they could manage it somehow; but he himself knew it was impossible, and preferred to put the blame for not being able to take the art school exam on himself and his poor grades rather than on family circumstances. There was no ethic of noble self-sacrifice behind this: if anything, he had a feeling that the future might be more interesting that way.

Something Mr. Koiso had said, too, might well have encouraged him in this: "Going to art school isn't the only way to become an artist."

Besides, there was another thing that was on his mind. Morio had told him that he'd been only fifteen when he first came alone to Kobe from the Hiroshima countryside to work as an apprentice. H himself wouldn't be self-supporting until he was seventeen, two years later than his father, so he wanted, at the very least, to make sure that he didn't take a single sen from his family after that.

On becoming a fifth-grader, he began to put even more time and energy into his drawing, though not out of any spirit of self-justification. Besides this increased preoccupation with art, the fascination movies held for him grew steadily keener. The reason for this rather inconvenient development was that one of his closest friends, a boy called Nomura, was an avid movie fan.

Not having any spare money of his own, it was only by letting Nomura pay for him that H was able to see the occasional film. Nomura himself took responsibility for raising the necessary funds by helping himself to flour from the noodle shop that his family fortunately happened to run.

H's role as henchman was to engage Nomura's elder sister in conversation while Nomura hastily put some of the flour into a bag. H was always on edge while this operation was in process in case the sister should suddenly turn around, but in the event they never once got caught.

With the money they got from selling the flour on the black market, they were able to see Western films such as *Casablanca*, with Humphrey Bogart and Ingrid Bergman, and Dietrich's *Blue Angel*, for which admission was more expensive than usual.

The school itself gave permission for students to see films such as the French *Poil de Carotte* and *Boys Town*, but they were not enough to satisfy the more ardent movie fans among them, who managed to see quite a number of others as well. In time they formed a Second Middle Film Study Club and published their own magazine, for which, naturally, H did the cover design.

Even so, H kept the fact that he'd been living all the while in the art room annex a secret from these friends.

One day, however, he heard a knock at the door and Ogura's voice saying "It's me." The knock he'd given, three equal raps, was suspiciously different from what they'd agreed on.

H waited, without replying and with bated breath, to see what would happen next. There were signs that someone else besides Ogura was on the other side of the door.

The knock was followed by a low murmur and the sound of someone putting a key in the lock and trying to turn it.

H still felt tense, although he knew the key wouldn't work. Three times the key rattled in unsuccessful attempts to turn it; then he heard a voice say, "Ogura, just what is going on?" It was Mr. Kawano, the math teacher. As H had suspected it had been an ambush.

"You there, open up and come out! I know you're in there!" called the teacher, growing angry and beating and kicking furiously at the door, until finally he turned his wrath impotently on Ogura. H felt guilty toward his classmate, but still he kept quiet and didn't open up.

For the past two weeks, in fact, someone had been coming and trying the door from time to time. Ogura had been warning him for a while that people seemed to have discovered that he was living there, and that he'd better be careful. Now the day had come.

The door went on rattling for a few more minutes, then Mr. Kawano must have given up, and he and Ogura went away. Even after their footsteps had died away down the corridor, H kept an ear to the door for some time, listening for sounds of movement outside. About an hour later Ogura turned up alone. This time he gave the correct knock, so H opened up at once.

"That was a close shave!"

"Lucky we fixed on a signal!" They clapped each other on the shoulder in mutual congratulation.

Mr. Kawano had come, apparently, because someone had told him that H was holed up in the art annex. A serious sort and dead keen about education, he'd been very angry. "Senoh's holding the school in contempt!" he'd declared. "If he doesn't mend his ways and study properly, I'll see he fails!"

"He said he knew you were there," Ogura told H, "and told me to come with him. You wouldn't come out for *him*, he said, but I was your friend so you'd open up if I called. So I *had* to come." It was just as H had imagined.

Besides Mr. Kawano, Mr. Matsumoto, the homeroom teacher, had also summoned Ogura and asked his opinion.

"If Senoh goes on skipping classes and handing in blank answer sheets he's going to fail," he'd been told. "The trouble is, he can do it if he really wants to. What do *you* think about him?"

"And what did you tell him?" asked H, curious to know.

Ogura smiled. "I told him you were fixed in your ways, and that I didn't think you'd come to class whatever he said. It would have been funny if I'd made excuses for you, wouldn't it?"

"Quite right," said H, smiling back.

But though H had resigned himself to failing, he was, to his great surprise, permitted to graduate.

At the conference held at 2:00 P.M. on February 24, there'd been a dispute as to whether he should be allowed to or not. There'd been five students in H's grade who'd failed to get the required average mark. Two of them who'd been away for a long time sick were virtually out of the running; that left three to be discussed, Hajime Senoh among them. Senoh not only had a below-par mark, he'd been "absent" on sixty-eight days without being ill. One of the things that upset teachers was that although he'd turned up every day, he hadn't attended some of the classes and had been put down in the register as absent.

Although the general atmosphere of the conference favored failing him in line with regulations, two teachers, Mr. Matsumoto and Mr. Naito, stubbornly objected. It was wrong, they argued, to stifle the abilities of a student with an individuality that couldn't be measured in terms of marks and school attendance by forcing him into some abstract educational mold. For the sake of his future he should be allowed to graduate.

This eventually became possible when Mr. Kawano, who'd insisted at first that H should be failed, finally switched to his side.

H, who in theory hadn't been bothered by the idea of failing, felt an uncomplicated pleasure when they told him the result of the conference.

On top of this came another piece of news that made him particularly happy: his family had been lucky in the draw for new municipal housing.

Hearing the news via the Shirakawa drugstore, H went off immediately to #2 Nozaki-dori 4, Fukiai-ku, which was the address of the new house. It stood on a slope overlooking the built-up area below. His mother and Yoshiko were already there, busily wiping the tatami.

There was glass in the windows of the house—naturally enough perhaps, but he was pleased just the same. The air raid victims' housing had only had boarded windows, and his room in the school had been dark too, with all its windows blacked out, so to see the outside world through plain, transparent glass was a moving experience.

"Don't you think real glass windows are nice, Yoshiko?" he asked. "Look—you can see all the way to the harbor!"

"Yes, I like this house—it's nice and light," she said. "Are you coming back now we're here, Hajime?"

"Yes, I'll be with you from now on—now there won't be any more spying from next door."

"I'm glad," said Yoshiko, and started crying.

The new house was single-storied and had a small yard. There was a small entrance hall, a four-and-a-half mat room, a six-mat room, and a kitchen, with a toilet inside the house, next to the hall. A bathroom would have been asking too much, but there was a public bath nearby, so the lack didn't bother them.

There was a gas ring in the kitchen, too. For H, a new wooden building with real glass windows, gas, and floors fitted with tatami was a veritable dream house.

In the late afternoon his father turned up with curtains that he'd sewn himself and light bulbs. Delighted, H went around turning on the lights in each of the rooms; it was dazzlingly bright compared with the temporary accommodation with its solitary bulb. They hadn't brought any futons or furniture yet, so that night they were to go back to their apartment. Toshiko wanted them all to go together, but H refused, saying that he wanted to make a fresh start with them in the new house, and went back to the school. Oddly enough, neither of his parents showed any curiosity as to where he was staying. It seemed they'd had a vague idea for some time.

On his last night staying at the school, H went to Mr. Naito's room to thank him for helping him to graduate, and to inform him that he was going back to his parents' place after four months' absence.

Mr. Naito gave him a look of mock disgust and laughed. "I did hear vague rumors," he said. "So you really were living at the school, were you? I didn't quite believe it. You're a terror!"

50

The Phoenix Studio

H was to start work at a sign-painter's called the Phoenix Studio. He'd been found the job by Ryohei Koiso, who took a personal interest in him in all kinds of ways.

"It's run by an artist called Hayato Okumura," the sensei had said. "It's a sign-painting business by day, but at night it's an art studio. It would be ideal for you, I feel, because you could do pictures and work at the same time. Why not try it? A lot of artists living in Kobe hang out there, so it should be good for you."

H felt that anywhere recommended by Koiso-sensei was likely to be good enough for him, and it sounded an interesting kind of place, so he didn't waste much time in making up his mind. He was attracted, too, by the fact that the boss of the place was Hayato Okumura.

Mr. Okumura, along with Konosuke Tamura and Yukio Kodama, was a member of the Niki group of artists and well known in Kobe. The biggest attraction for H, though, was the talk of its being a sign-painter's by day and a studio by night. Almost as exciting was the information that it was situated centrally, between Sannomiya and Motomachi, and was in a newly constructed building.

He went to have a private look at it after the graduation ceremony on March 3—"private" because the postcard, complete with map, that had come from Mr. Okumura had invited him to come at 2:00 P.M. on Saturday, March 6. He'd been too impatient to wait.

The Phoenix Studio stood at the end of a narrow street running westward from the lower end of Tore-dori, but he wandered around for a while, unable to find it immediately. The first time, he went right past it. Checking again with the map, he retraced his steps and finally found it, with a sense of letdown at its depressingly makeshift, jerry-built appearance. It didn't even have a sign outside.

This wasn't so surprising, perhaps. The district had been razed completely in the fires, and every building now standing was new with, in most cases, a temporary air to it. Even so, this one was a single-story structure of exceptional meanness, and H was rather disappointed.

He was about to go away when the door opened and a man wearing a beret came out and, seeing him, hailed him by name. It was Masuki Komatsu, whom H knew well, having met him many times at Tsuguro Ito's place in Ashiya. Thus discovered, there was nothing for it but to bow and say good afternoon.

"I heard you're coming to join us," said the other in a loud voice. "Mr. Koiso told me about it. Okumura was talking about it too, only a while ago. That's perfect: I'll introduce you to him myself."

H hesitated. "Actually, though, I was told to come on the sixth, so I'd better come back again then."

"Don't worry, don't worry! The sooner the better," he roared, opening the door and leading the way inside.

The wooden floor of the room was littered with cans of paint, in the midst of which a man badly in need of a shave was painting a picture of fruit on a signboard. H knew at once that this was Mr. Okumura. He greeted them with a broad grin.

"Let me introduce you—this is young Senoh," said Komatsu.

"I knew that even before you came in," said Mr. Okumura, looking amused. "You talk in such a loud voice!" He turned to H. "So you're the unusual lad I've heard about, then? I'm told you can paint in any style."

H was nonplussed. That must have come from Mr. Komatsu, he thought. People who talked too much were a nuisance. He scowled at the suspect, who hastily said, "Not me, not me! Okumura got it from Mr. Koiso."

Everything that had happened at Ashiya, then, must be common knowledge here too—reported, H realized in dismay, by Koiso-sensei personally.

What bothered him was that he'd played a trick there which, on reflection, he was thoroughly ashamed about.

Each of the established artists who gathered at Ashiya had, of course, his own style. This interested H, and he got the idea of trying to imitate each of them in turn. First he did an imitation of Jiro Fujii, who did colorful pictures reminiscent of Bonnard.

"You could make money doing fakes!" Mr. Kodama had said, watching him work.

This had encouraged H to declare smugly, "I'll do a fake Ito next, then."

"It won't be easy," Ito himself had put in: "my technique's a secret!"

"Give me two weeks," H had said.

Ito did unusual pictures in a pointillistic style suggesting Segantini. He used a very fine-tipped brush to apply the paint in layers; then, while the surface still wasn't quite dry, applied transparent oil pigments in a method known as glazing, later shaving the surface with a razor to reveal complex layers of color.

Apparently he did this secretly in the studio at night when no one else was around. When H discovered paint shavings wrapped in newspaper and discarded in a corner of the studio, he thought he could probably copy the secret technique.

Getting a general idea of the method, he tried it out with surprising success. When the picture was completed he put his own name on it, imitating even the style of the signature, and stood it next to a picture by Ito.

The others all laughed, but Ito himself, a mild man, might well have been offended. Probably he'd only restrained his anger because the offender was a middle school student—a boy, moreover, brought along by Mr. Koiso. H himself, though, remained determined to study by imitating these distinguished older artists while he could.

Koiso-sensei, however, while approving of H's enthusiasm, must have found it something of an embarrassment. One day, as they left the studio and were walking to Ashiya Station on the way home, he said, "You know, if you're interested in painting in all kinds of styles you might be better suited to commercial art. You can vary the style as you like with every piece of work, and it's a field that's going to offer more and more opportunities from now on. There's more to being an artist than just oil painting."

Perhaps that was why he'd introduced H to Mr. Okumura of the Phoenix Studio.

H himself still wasn't sure what kind of a painter he wanted to be; he only knew that he wanted to go on doing pictures.

The Phoenix Studio had only two rooms: the six-tatami room at the back was where Mr. Okumura and his wife slept, and the studio proper was a much bigger room of about fourteen mats. The work space had a wooden floor on which nothing stood but cans of paint and a coal stove. The walls were of thin, unpainted board, so the general effect was similar to the temporary housing elsewhere.

The first thing that disconcerted H a little on starting work there was that he found himself among a bunch of unconventional adults quite different from his teachers and friends at school.

To begin with Mr. Okumura, the boss, smelled of alcohol even in the daytime. Sometimes he was unsteady on his feet even while he was painting, but the pictures themselves were so good that H respected him even though he found him "odd." The worst thing was that on the way home from collecting a payment, he'd sometimes spend the money on drink.

Koji Mitani, who did patterns and designs, also painted, though he was reluctant to show his work to other people. One of them that H got a surreptitious glimpse of was a gloomy affair of thickly layered paint out of which, if you looked carefully, a human face loomed faintly.

Six months earlier Mr. Mitani had been repatriated from Siberia, where he'd been a prisoner. Normally his conversation made them laugh, but when he got drunk he would mutter to himself in Russian. The word that cropped up most frequently, *damoi*, meant "to go home," he told H. In Siberia, apparently, his one concern had been when he'd be able to get back to Japan. Perhaps it was memories of those days that made his pictures so dark.

Masaru Sayama, who had a reputation as a calligrapher, had formerly worked for Nitten, a large advertising company, but had been fired and come to Phoenix. The reason he'd lost his job, Sayama himself told H, was his obsession with mahjongg. Even after coming to the Phoenix Studio he spent most of his time in mahjongg parlors, seemingly with no inclination to do any work. H would often be sent in a hurry to a mahjongg parlor in Koigawa-suji with a message for him to come back immediately, because the deadline for filling an order for a signboard was close at hand. Finding him shuffling the tiles in the dimly lit second-floor room, H would urge him to come as soon as possible.

"I'll be back after another half-round," he'd say, but he never was.

On one occasion he didn't return for three days after saying he'd be "back soon." When he finally did get back, his eyes were all bloodshot and he stank. Once he started, though, he did good work at an astonishing speed, so he still retained his reputation as a first-rate calligrapher.

Seiji Takagi, who described himself as a novelist, was also a heavy drinker. He'd apparently first joined the studio on the strength of his alleged skill in doing script, but his letters were as bad as his pictures. "That's because I'm really a novelist," he'd boast. "I'll soon be having something published in a magazine, so I'll stand you a drink when it comes out." But no one had ever been given any of his stories to read.

He too had been in the forces and had been demobilized recently. Why Okumura had taken on someone who was no good at either calligraphy or pictures wasn't clear, though it may have been that he was physically strong and that somebody was needed to carry and install the signboards.

They all drank like fish. Since H's father never touched alcohol at all for religious reasons, he was horrified at the quantity they consumed.

Occasionally he'd been more or less forced to drink himself, but he couldn't get to like the stuff. On one occasion he'd felt so sick he thought he was going to die, and on another he found himself lying on the sidewalk, looking up at people as they stepped over him on their way to work. On the latter occasion he was scared to find that try as he might he couldn't remember how he came to be lying in the street. Seventeen was too young to start drinking, he decided.

At the Phoenix Studio it wasn't only the people that surprised him; in the early days he was in a constant state of amazement at the way the work itself was done.

First of all there was the fact that they mixed the paint themselves. Until now H had always thought of paint as something that came in cans or tubes. You certainly *could* buy it, but it was expensive, so at the studio they made their own.

White was made by buying a powder called "flowers of zinc" and blending it with linseed oil and turpentine on a tin tray. Sometimes H was kept at work with a spatula from dawn to dusk.

To make red paint, powdered red lead or carmine was mixed in a similar way, while for blue and green the basic ingredients were powdered pigments known as *gunjo* and *rokusho* respectively.

After the first month or so he was given a thorough training in applying the undercoat to signboards. The important thing here was to apply a small quantity of paint evenly over a large surface, the total quantity of paint used being determined by the price for which the job had been undertaken. If Mr. Okumura said, "This bookstore sign is *pin-nuri*," it meant, "The proprietor was mean and knocked down the price, so a single coat is enough." The finished job looked the same, and no non-specialist could have distinguished whether there was one coat or three, but the lifespan of the signboard varied accordingly. With only one coat, rust would eventually come through and the paint would flake off. You didn't tell the customer that, though. Business is a tough world, thought H.

The toughness affected H himself, too: he was short of money even though he'd got a job now. Because of steadily rising inflation, the fifteen hundred yen he'd been promised wasn't actually such a large sum. Nor, in reality, did he get a full salary every month, only five hundred yen or so—mere pocket money—which Mr. Okumura would give him casually from time to time. So things were tight, and the U.S. army-surplus laceup boots he'd been hoping to buy cost a full twelve hundred yen, so they remained forever out of reach.

All artists were poor, not just the people in the Phoenix Studio. Shops and houses were beginning to spring up on the bomb sites, but nobody could afford to buy pictures. You could never make a living by painting, which was why Mr. Okumura ran a sign shop. Unfortunately, since he was as unprofessional as the proverbial "samurai in business" in the way he managed it, there frequently wasn't even money enough to buy the ingredients for paint. At such times his wife would emerge from the back entrance bearing a kimono done up in a wrapping cloth and pay a visit to the pawnshop just over the way.

Despite their poverty, they never let it get them down but joked cheerfully together, so H didn't mind too much and actually enjoyed life there.

The thing that pleased him most about working at the Phoenix was that two nights a week, on Mondays and Thursdays, the workplace was transformed into a real artist's studio.

As night fell the paint cans were gathered together in one spot and the signboards in progress put outside to make space. These tasks were all left to H, but he was cheerful as he cleared things away since he was allowed in return to place his own easel and stool in the best spot, not too far from the model and not too close, with a good, unhindered view of her.

As it got dark a whole crowd of artists would gather and the place would become lively. The regulars were Masuki Komatsu, Yukio Kodama, Kanichi Matsuoka and Waichi Tsudaka, together with the people working in the studio.

Mr. Komatsu was good at doing paintings of buildings such as the exotic-looking Western-style residences of foreigners up in the Yamate district, but bad at human figures, so he never did oil paintings of the model but concentrated on a series of rapid sketches done in pencil.

Perhaps because he was less an artist than a poet, Mr. Tsudaka's basic design was always wrong. H, watching at his side, would tease him: "Don't you think a poet should stick to abstract patterns? There are so many people who can do proper pictures; it's too late to try and catch up at this stage." The other would playfully make as though to box H's ears, but the fact remained that his nudes didn't bear looking at.

The nude model was a woman from the local office of a newspaper. H had heard that it was Koiso-sensei who had arranged for her to come. She was very pretty; undressing in the back room, she came out into the studio wrapped in a blanket which she took off to dazzling effect when she posed.

She kept the fact that she was modeling secret from the people in her office, so here they never used her real name but called her "Miss Koga."

Apparently she'd once wanted to be an artist herself, "but I realized I'd no talent," she said, "so I thought I'd be of some use to real artists." She didn't have a Kobe accent, and for some reason she never talked about where she came from, or her family, so they refrained from asking her.

H was warned by Mr. Matsuoka not to get too friendly with her. "It's a rule here," he said. Probably they're all interested in her, thought H, so they have to keep a tight rein on themselves.

Two hours or so of sketching and painting with the model in their midst was invariably followed by a drinking party. The saké would be paid for by someone who'd come into some money recently. The one-liter bottle of *shochu* that Mr. Komatsu planted on the table, for example, came courtesy of a bank that had put up a new building and had bought a picture to hang in the lobby.

They all proclaimed loudly that pictures were going to sell well from now on, and there certainly seemed to be grounds for hope: new buildings were beginning to go up along the streets, so the demand for paintings would probably increase proportionately, and orders for signboards seemed likely to go up too.

The people who gathered there reminded H of garret-dwelling bohemians in some French movie—a cheerful lot, content if they could buy paints, canvas, and enough food and drink to stay alive. As the youngest among this group of artists, he was liable to be treated as an errand boy and ordered peremptorily to "go and buy a bottle of saké," but where painting was concerned they treated him as an equal, so all in all he was happy.

Once he was able to do the undercoat for signs, Mr. Okumura suddenly told him to study lettering.

"Why?" asked H in surprise. "You've got Mr. Sayama already, haven't you?"

"We'll need you to help out when there's too much for him to do," he replied. "Besides, it'll be useful for you in the future if you can do script. Then you can make a living doing either pictures or lettering, can't you?"

H saw the sense of this and determined to study lettering, too.

Since there was no one to instruct him he used the newspapers as his teacher. He knew that from January 1, 1947, they'd finally started writing horizontal headlines from left to right, but hadn't realized that there was a subtle difference between the *Asahi* and the *Yomiuri* in the shape of their typefaces. He cut out the biggest letters from their headlines and stuck them in a notebook to serve as his "textbook." At first he'd expected that the Gothic typeface, which was of a uniform thickness, would be easier to do, but in practice the reverse was true, and he preferred the Ming typeface.

"Your lettering's beginning to look quite professional," Mr. Okumura told H one day, to his delight. "Right, then—you can do the cutout sign for a tailor's in Tore-dori. Will you try it?"

The shop was the Suang Hong Tailors, run by a Chinese, and the sign was to be H's first professional work.

Looking at it after they'd put it up on the wall, with its cutout Chinese characters gleaming gold in the sun, H felt a wave of pride.

What followed, though, was a much tougher proposition—painting the lampposts topped with snowdrop-shaped lamps that lined the main Motomachi shopping street. As plans for rebuilding progressed, it was decided that the main buildings of the whole street should be covered with Duralumin sheets, which had originally been intended for making planes and had been left over at the end of the war.

To match this, they decided to paint the newly designed street lamps with silver paint, too.

One-quarter of this work was to be undertaken by the Phoenix Studio—a major undertaking that would bring in more money than anything it had done previously. H was delighted, but the actual work proved to be extremely hard going.

First he had to set a tall ladder against the lamppost, climb to the top and put his arms around the post, then get someone to take away the ladder. Next he would stick a brush in the can of paint suspended from his waist and, with his right hand, begin painting the pole. Loosening the grip of his left arm around the pole would mean slipping down, so he couldn't let his attention wander for a moment. On top of that, the drops of silver paint spraying from the brush covered his hair and face with silver spots, giving him a disturbingly ghostly look.

He was busy at work when, happening to glance down, he saw a girl student he knew by sight walking past. With a feeling of utter humiliation, he turned his face the other way so it shouldn't be seen. They say all occupations are equally honorable, he thought, but it's not true. He was so overcome with shame that when his painting brought him to the bottom of the pole and he wanted to move on to the next one, he ran with bowed head.

The idea that they had to do all the poles extending for three blocks made him want to escape. Nor was it only H: on the fifth day Mr. Takagi, who was also going up the poles, suddenly quit his job and never reappeared. He said he'd made up his mind to "go back home to Kakogawa and write novels," but H doubted whether this was true.

Mr. Okumura and the rest of them had other work to do, so the task of painting the snowdrop lamps was left to the two of them—the elderly day laborer who was in charge of the ladder, and H himself.

"If I go on feeling so ashamed of this work," he told himself as he worked at the top of a pole, "it'll be bad for me. So ... I'll just make myself go on painting them right to the end without worrying what people think!"

His resolution paid off. Little by little he relaxed. Despite himself, he found the change interesting.

In the end he stopped being ashamed of the work altogether. He had objective confirmation of this when one day he happened to see Yokota passing below and was able to hail his old friend.

"Hey, Yokota!"

Yokota gazed about him to see where the voice had come from. Finally he realized H was directly above him.

"What are you up to?" he asked in surprise.

"You can see, can't you? What about *you*, though?"

Yokota was dressed in a neat suit, the model of a man-about-town. He smiled. "Me?—I made a pile on the black market."

He looked astonished at H's silver face, but the two of them, one aloft, one below, chatted for a while as old friends.

George Fujita too, he told H, seemed to be doing well, working as an interpreter for the occupation forces.

As H and his assistant were carrying the ladder back to the studio,

527